THE ZAMBEZI RIVER BASIN

The Zambezi River is the fourth longest river in Africa, crossing or bordering Zambia, Angola, Namibia, Botswana, Zimbabwe and Mozambique. The river basin is widely recognised as one of the most important basins in southern Africa and is the focus of contested development, including water for hydropower and for agriculture and the environment. This book provides a thorough review of water and sustainable development in the Zambezi, in order to identify critical issues and propose constructive ways forward.

The book first reviews the availability and use of water resources in the basin, outlines the basin's economic potential and highlights key concerns related to climate vulnerability and risk. Focus is then devoted to hydropower and the water-energy-food (WEF) nexus, sustainable agricultural water management, and threats and opportunities related to provision of ecosystem services. The impact of urbanisation and water quality is also examined, as well as ways to enhance transboundary water cooperation. Last, the book assesses the level of water security in the basin, and provides suggestions for achieving Sustainable Development Goal (SDG) 6. Throughout, emphasis is placed on entry points for basin-level management to foster improved paths forward.

Jonathan Lautze is Senior Researcher at the International Water Management Institute (IWMI), based in Pretoria, South Africa.

Zebediah Phiri is Executive Secretary of the Zambezi Watercourse Commission, based in Harare, Zimbabwe.

Vladimir Smakhtin is Director of the United Nations University, Institute for Water, Environment and Health, in Hamilton, Ontario, Canada.

Davison Saruchera is a PhD candidate at the Wits School of Governance, University of Witwatersrand, Johannesburg, South Africa.

EARTHSCAN SERIES ON MAJOR RIVER BASINS OF THE WORLD

Series Editor: Vladimir Smakhtin

Large river basins are dynamic and complex entities. Defined by hydrological boundaries, they are nearly always shared by more than one country. Encompassing a diverse range of landscapes with often-huge temporal and spatial variability of resources, they are put to different and often conflicting uses, and managed by a range of institutions and organisations. While an intrinsic part of nature, many have been extensively engineered and used by people, often with adverse consequences. Each major river basin has its own development trajectory and often fascinating history. Bringing together multidisciplinary teams of experts, this series explores these complex issues, identifies knowledge gaps and examines potential development pathways towards greater sustainability.

The Nile River Basin
Water, Agriculture, Governance and Livelihoods
Edited by Seleshi Bekele Awulachew, Vladimir Smakhtin, David Molden, Don Peden

The Volta River Basin
Water for Food, Economic Growth and Environment
Edited by Timothy O. Williams, Marloes Mul, Charles Biney and Vladimir Smakhtin

The Ganges River Basin
Status and Challenges in Water, Environment and Livelihoods
Edited by Luna Bharati, Bharat R. Sharma and Vladimir Smakhtin

The Zambezi River Basin
Water and Sustainable Development
Edited by Jonathan Lautze, Zebediah Phiri, Vladimir Smakhtin and Davison Saruchera

https://www.routledge.com/series/ECMRBW

THE ZAMBEZI RIVER BASIN

Water and Sustainable Development

Edited by
Jonathan Lautze, Zebediah Phiri,
Vladimir Smakhtin and Davison Saruchera

LONDON AND NEW YORK

First published 2017
by Routledge
2 Park Square, Milton Park, Abingdon, Oxon OX14 4RN

and by Routledge
605 Third Avenue, New York, NY 10017

First issued in paperback 2020

Routledge is an imprint of the Taylor & Francis Group, an informa business

© 2017 International Water Management Institute

The right of the editors to be identified as the authors of the editorial material, and of the authors for their individual chapters, has been asserted in accordance with sections 77 and 78 of the Copyright, Designs and Patents Act 1988.

All rights reserved. No part of this book may be reprinted or reproduced or utilised in any form or by any electronic, mechanical, or other means, now known or hereafter invented, including photocopying and recording, or in any information storage or retrieval system, without permission in writing from the publishers.

Trademark notice: Product or corporate names may be trademarks or registered trademarks, and are used only for identification and explanation without intent to infringe.

British Library Cataloguing-in-Publication Data
A catalogue record for this book is available from the British Library

Library of Congress Cataloging-in-Publication Data
Names: Lautze, Jonathan, editor, contributor, writer of introduction. |
Cai, Xueliang, editor, contributor. | Mapedza, E., editor. | Wishart, Marcus J.,
editor. | Phiri, Zebediah, editor, writer of introduction.
Title: The Zambezi River Basin : pathways for sustainable development /
[edited by] Jonathan Lautze, Xueliang Cai, Everisto Mapedza, Marcus Wishart
and Zebediah Phiri.
Other titles: Earthscan series on major river basins of the world.
Description: New York, NY : Routledge, 2017. |
Series: Earthscan/IWMI series on major river basins of the world |
Includes bibliographical references and index.
Identifiers: LCCN 2017005879| ISBN 9781138240902 (hardback) |
ISBN 1138240907 (hardback) | ISBN 9781315282053 (ebook) |
ISBN 1315282054 (ebook)
Subjects: LCSH: Water resources development—Zambezi River Watershed. |
Water–supply—ZambeziRiver Watershed—Management. | Sustainable
development—Zambezi River Watershed.
Classification: LCC HD1699.Z32 Z36 2017 | DDC 333.7309689—dc23
LC record available at https://lccn.loc.gov/2017005879

ISBN 13: 978–0–367–73604–0 (pbk)
ISBN 13: 978–1–138–24090–2 (hbk)

Typeset in Bembo
by Florence Production Ltd, Stoodleigh, Devon, UK

CONTENTS

CHAPTER PHOTOS

NOTES ON AUTHORS

Yvan Altchenko is a hydrogeologist (senior researcher) at the International Water Management Institute (IWMI), based in the southern Africa office in Pretoria. He is a French secondment from the French Ministry of Agriculture. After more than 10 years of experience as an engineer on sewage and drinking water in France, he is currently active in his primary field: hydrogeology and groundwater management. Throughout his career his focus has been developing solutions for sustainable water use. Present areas of interest include groundwater, transboundary groundwater management, conjunctive use of surface water and groundwater, food security with a special focus on the development of sustainable groundwater use in Africa and climate change adaption. Yvan has published several peer-reviewed articles and presented his work at many international conferences. Yvan has previously worked for the Environmental Agency in the UK. He holds an MSc in hydrogeology from the University of East Anglia (UK) and he is busy finishing his PhD at the University of Pierre et Marie Curie in Paris.

Richard D. Beilfuss is the President and CEO of the International Crane Foundation (ICF), an NGO working worldwide to conserve cranes and the ecosystems, watersheds and flyways on which they depend. Beilfuss provides oversight, direction and prioritisation to ICF programmes across Asia, Africa and North America. Beilfuss is a professional hydrologist and has engaged in the science and management of river and wetland systems for more than 25 years. He spearheads long-term efforts to implement environmental flows in the water-stressed Zambezi River Basin in Africa, and has engaged in water research and wetland management in Texas and Wisconsin in the US, in China, Iraq, Nepal and Vietnam in Asia, and in Ethiopia, Kenya, Mozambique, Rwanda, Uganda and Zambia in Africa. He has authored more than 100 scientific papers, technical reports, proceedings and lay-audience publications on water issues, and presented his research and conservation findings to governments, communities and peer-scientists worldwide. Beilfuss is an Adjunct Professor for the University of Wisconsin-Madison College of Engineering, where he teaches graduate courses on water management. He serves on the Wisconsin State Examining Board of Professional Geologists, Hydrologists and Soil Scientists.

Xueliang Cai is a Senior Lecturer at UNESCO-IHE, formerly a researcher at IWMI. He has over 10 years' international working experience in Asia, Africa and the Netherlands. Cai's key research interests are in land and water resources management for sustainable agriculture development. He started as a postdoctoral fellow at the IWMI in Colombo, Sri Lanka, where he was involved in global irrigated area mapping and water productivity assessment in South Asia, Central Asia and southern Africa. In 2010 Cai became an international researcher and moved to the IWMI regional office in Pretoria, South Africa, where he worked on a number of topics including: integrated modeling of rural water resources for irrigation and fisheries; participatory irrigation management; hydrological function of ecosystems; and floodplain management. He was leader of several research projects including the ecological footprint of food security, which mapped irrigated, rain-fed and water-managed agricultural areas across Asia and Africa. Cai obtained his PhD degree in irrigation management from Wuhan University, China. He authored about 50 papers including 25+ in peer-reviewed journals.

Geoffrey Chavula is an Associate Professor in Water Engineering and former Director of the Center for Water, Sanitation, Health and Technology Development (WASHTED) at the University of Malawi – The Polytechnic. He teaches undergraduate courses in engineering hydrology, hydraulics and water resources management in the Department of Civil Engineering. He has a BSc in Physics and Earth Sciences from the University of Malawi, an MSc in Water Engineering from the University of Newcastle, England and a PhD in Water Resources Science from the University of Minnesota, USA.

Claudious Chikozho is the Research Director at the Africa Institute of South Africa, a department within the Human Sciences Research Council (HSRC) in Pretoria, South Africa. He has been active in a number of applied research and development projects and networks, with special focus on thematic areas such as: local and transboundary water governance; food security; environmental sustainability; community-based natural resources management; adaptation to climate change; and technology transfer processes. Claudious has published more than 20 peer-reviewed articles as journal papers and book chapters. He routinely serves as a reviewer for the journal *Physics and Chemistry of the Earth*. His previous positions in the sector include: working as a Research Director at the Gauteng City-Region Observatory, Wits University in South Africa; Biodiversity Programme Director at the Centre for Responsible Leadership, University of Pretoria; Science Uptake Coordinator for Africa at the IWMI in Accra, Ghana; Senior Researcher at the Council for Scientific and Industrial Research (CSIR) in Pretoria, South Africa; and Research Fellow in Water Resources Management at the University of Zimbabwe. Claudious holds a BSc (Hons) in Political Science, an MSc in Public Administration and a PhD in Social Studies from the University of Zimbabwe.

Charlotte de Bruyne is an academic scholar and a practised professional in the field of transboundary water governance and institutional development. She conducted interdisciplinary doctoral research in global water governance at the Hebrew University of Jerusalem, focusing on institutional design under conditions of uncertainty. The results of her research were published in the journal *Global Environmental Change* and resulted in an EU-funded policy booklet for international water management practitioners. Previously, Charlotte was a consultant to IWMI on ways to strategise and initiate transboundary water cooperation in the Shire Basin between Malawi and Mozambique. For the Centre of Transboundary Water Management of the Israeli Arava Institute she conducted a study on renewed institutional approaches to cross-boundary wastewater management in Israel and the Palestinian territories. Charlotte lived and worked in the Democratic Republic of Congo, Egypt, Germany, Israel, the Palestinian Territories, South Africa and Sri Lanka. Since August 2015, she has been working at the Office of the Quartet in Jerusalem as an advisor in the field of water and infrastructure.

Pay Drechsel holds a PhD in Environmental Sciences and is a principal researcher and research division leader at IWMI, based in Colombo, Sri Lanka. Pay has 25 years of working experience in the rural-urban interface of developing countries, coordinating projects addressing the safe recovery of irrigation water, nutrients and organic matter from domestic waste streams for agriculture, with a special interest in business models. Pay has authored about 300 publications, half in peer-reviewed books and journals. He has worked extensively in West and East Africa, and South and South-East Asia. In 2015, Pay received the IWA Water and Development Award for Research.

Lisa Guppy has extensive experience in international development and humanitarian response, both as a researcher and practitioner. Her research has focused on water, sanitation and hygiene (WASH) and water management, and she has experience in humanitarian coordination, capacity development and information management. Before joining United Nations University Institute for Water, Environment and Health (UNU-INWEH) in Canada, Lisa worked most recently as an early recovery advisor for the United Nations Development Programme (UNDP), and as a senior research advisor for Save the Children, UK. She has also worked for the federal government in Australia and international organisations including UNICEF and UNOCHA. She has lived and worked in several countries including Sri Lanka, Kenya, Switzerland and the UK. Currently, Lisa is managing international projects centred on water and the Sustainable Development Goals and science for policy support. She is also directing the 'Water Without Borders' graduate programme, in partnership with McMaster University in Canada.

Munir A. Hanjra was an economist at IWMI, Pretoria, South Africa. Before that he worked as Senior Research Fellow (Poverty and Water Policy Specialist) at the Charles Sturt University (CSU), Institute for Land, Water and Society (ILWS), and CSIRO Land and Water, Australia. He is a development economist with over 20 years of professional experience on issues related to sustainable water management such as global and regional water scarcity, water quality, food security and poverty reduction. Dr Hanjra has been involved in research and development programmes on water, food, agriculture and the environment in Australia, China, Canada, South and South-East Asia, and eastern, western and southern Africa. He has co-authored more than 100 peer-reviewed publications, and has made numerous other professional contributions. Current research interests include water and food security, water management solutions for poverty reduction, the water-energy-food nexus, urban agriculture, and resource recovery and reuse (RRR) solution series including an IWMI catalogue on business models for promoting wastewater reuse, nutrient capture, energy recovery, and ecosystem resilience and water sector adaptations to climate change.

Bunyod Holmatov is a consultant at the IWMI's office in Uzbekistan. He has an inter-disciplinary academic background and was involved in a number of research projects focused on transboundary water management, water security, water governance, water quality and climate change. Holmatov has authored and contributed to a number of peer-reviewed articles and serves as a reviewer for water-sector journals. He is fluent in English, Russian and Uzbek languages and has lived and travelled extensively in Asia, Africa, Europe and North America. Prior to joining IWMI he worked as a Research Fellow at Yale University and has conducted internships at UNDP, the Latvian NGO 'homo ecos' and at the Alliance for Global Water Adaptation. His leadership appointments include serving as a Latvian civil society representative at the UNFCCC COP 18, a member of the Uzbekistan delegation at the 67th session of the UN's

General Assembly, and a US delegate at the XIIIth Biennial Symposium for Peace and Justice. Holmatov holds a Master of Environmental Management from the Yale School of Forestry and Environmental Studies and is about to start a PhD programme at the University of Twente in the Netherlands. He is originally from Kokand, Uzbekistan.

Jusipbek Kazbekov is a water management specialist at the Regional Environmental Centre for Central Asia, formerly regional researcher at the IWMI-Central Asia Office in Tashkent, Uzbekistan. He has more than 15 years of academic, research and development experience. He taught academic courses on hydraulics, integrated water resources management (IWRM), rural water supply, and ecology and environmental protection. He has developed and conducted various training programmes for basin, canal, extension and farmer organisations on IWRM. He has designed and implemented capacity-building courses for the Water User Associations (WUAs) on crop water requirements, water planning for WUA, irrigation scheduling and distribution, water measuring and accounting, performance indicators and evaluation, social mobilisation and institutional development for establishing and strengthening WUAs. He has more than 30 peer-reviewed publications. His international experience covers Malawi, Mozambique and southern Africa and attendance at various events and training in Bangladesh, Belgium, France, Germany, India, Israel, the Netherlands, the Philippines, Sri Lanka and the USA. He holds an MSc from Colorado State University (USA) and a PhD from the Tashkent Institute of Irrigation and Melioration (Uzbekistan). His research interests involve an analysis of various aspects of water governance in Central Asia and beyond, including transboundary water cooperation, irrigation sector reforms and socio-technical features of water management.

Jonathan Lautze is a senior researcher at the IWMI southern Africa office in Pretoria. He has led or contributed to a range of applied, interdisciplinary research and development projects focused on topics such as water governance, water security, transboundary water management, climate change and water, and water and health. Lautze has published more than 40 peer-reviewed articles and edited a bestselling book on key concepts in water resources management. His research has been featured on global media outlets such as the British Broadcasting Corporation (BBC), Radio France International (RFI) and Voice of America (VOA). He routinely serves as a reviewer for water-sector journals and is currently an associate editor of *Water International*. He mentors young professionals in the regions he has worked, and plays other roles in the water sector by, for example, contributing to steering committees or sessions at international conferences. Lautze's development experience includes time living and working in East, West and southern Africa, as well as in South Asia, and short-term assignments in Central Asia and the Middle East and North Africa (MENA). Lautze has previously worked for USAID and the World Bank. He holds a Master of Arts in Law and Diplomacy from the Fletcher School, Tufts University and a PhD from Tufts Department of Civil and Environmental Engineering. He is originally from northern California.

Emmanuel Manzungu is a Professor of Agricultural Landscapes, Waterscapes and Environmental Management in the Department of Soil Science and Agricultural Engineering in the Faculty of Agriculture at the University of Zimbabwe, where he is also the Deputy Dean. He holds a PhD in irrigation/water management from Wageningen University in the Netherlands. He has researched and written extensively on water resources/irrigation management in southern Africa, focusing on technical, policy, legal and institutional aspects of smallholder irrigation management, catchment management, climate and water-smart agriculture, environmental management and food security. He has published over 80 articles that encompass peer-reviewed journal articles and book chapters. He has also edited five books and authored two monographs.

Hillary M. Masundire is a Professor in Ecology in the Department of Biological Sciences at the University of Botswana. He studied the ecology of Lake Kariba (Zimbabwe, Zambia) for his PhD, and has published on water, wetlands and waste management in the Zambezi since the 1980s. He participated in EIAs of major dam developments in the Zambezi Basin including the Batoka Hydro-Scheme and the Gwaai-Shangani Dam. Hillary is currently working on a State of the Basin report about Lake Malawi/Niassa/Nyasa as part of the Building River Dialogue and Governance (BRIDGE) Project of the International Union for Conservation of Nature (IUCN). He is also spearheading plans for an international symposium to commemorate the 60th year of Lake Kariba scheduled to be held in 2018. Hillary is an advocate of environmental flows and, in this regard, has been training policy and technical staff within the SADC region on the concept of environmental flows. He is former global chair and currently regional chair of the IUCN Commission on Ecosystem Management.

Matthew McCartney is a principal researcher at the IWMI, specialising in water resources and wetland and hydroecological studies. He is currently IWMI's theme leader on ecosystem services and simultaneously acting theme leader for water availability, risks and resilience. His experience stems from participation in a wide range of research and applied projects, often as part of a multidisciplinary team, frequently as project leader. He is experienced in data collection, extension of data records, application of hydrological methods and the calibration and use of computer models, as well as planning, designing, managing and coordinating research studies. Matthew was a steering committee member on the UNEP Dams Development Project (2002–2004) and a member of the Ramsar Science and Technical Review Panel (2007–2015). Matthew's career has given him substantial international experience including time living and working in both Africa and Asia.

Justin Mutiro is a project engineer (irrigation) at Illovo Sugar Ltd (Ubombo Sugar Limited) in Big Bend, Swaziland, responsible for planning, designing and implementing European Union-funded sugarcane irrigation projects in Swaziland. Justin holds a BSc (Hons) in Agriculture (Soil Science) (1999) from the University of Zimbabwe, an MSc in Water Resources Engineering and Management (2005), and is currently pursuing a PhD (part-time) at UKZN. He has worked in the irrigation sector as an irrigation engineer for the past 17 years, which has seen him working in Mozambique, South Africa, Swaziland, Tanzania and Zimbabwe. Justin has made extensive contributions to irrigation and water research projects. He has published several peer-reviewed articles on irrigation and water resources management, and has worked as a Lecturer in Irrigation Water Management at the Lowveld College of Agriculture (now called University of Mpumalanga, South Africa). Justin has also worked as an irrigation consultant under the supervision of Dr Jonathan Lautze at the IWMI southern Africa office in Pretoria, where he produced a prominent paper on irrigation performance in southern Africa.

Juliet Mwale is an IWRM knowledge management and monitoring and evaluation (M&E) specialist, with more than 10 years' experience in the southern Africa water sector. Her key experience in the water and sanitation sector includes: M&E; knowledge management, advocacy and communications; IWRM planning; and social research. She has worked in South Africa and Zambia, and has undertaken some research work in Zambia and Zimbabwe. She has mostly worked with donor-funded programmes, including the Department for International Development (DfID)-funded Climate Resilient Infrastructure Development Facility (CRIDF) in South Africa, the Canadian International Development Agency (CIDA)-funded Partnership Africa's Water Development (PAWD) Project in Zambia, and the Water Information Network-South Africa (WIN-SA) programme, which was partly funded by the European Union through the South African Department of Water and Sanitation. She holds a Postgraduate Diploma in Monitoring and Evaluation Methods, a Master's degree in IWRM and an Honours degree in Public Administration. She is currently engaged as M&E Manager for CRIDF, a flagship DFID water infrastructure programme for southern Africa working to deliver sustainable small-scale infrastructure across 11 SADC countries.

Regassa Namara is senior water resources economist at the World Bank. He is especially known for his expertise in investment operations and research/analytical tasks in water/agriculture sectors. His areas of operational experience include: flood risk protection; water supply and sanitation; agricultural water management; hydropower development; water resources management; and resilience to climate change. His current research areas include economic analysis of transboundary water cooperation and evaluation of the economy-wide, poverty and distributional impacts of water development and policy. Prior to joining the World Bank, he was head of the West Africa office of IWMI in Accra, Ghana. He started his career as a research officer with the Ethiopian Institute of Agricultural Research in 1987, where he contributed to the understanding of the reasons why Ethiopian smallholder agriculture has been trapped in a state of low-input low-output production system incapable of supporting farm households year-round. Regassa holds a PhD in Agricultural Economics and Rural Development from Gottingen University (Germany) and an MSc in Agricultural Economics from the University of London (England).

Luxon Nhamo is a researcher at IWMI based at its southern Africa office in Pretoria, South Africa. A holder of a PhD with the University of Santiago de Compostela in Spain, Luxon has participated in a number of research projects at the University of Santiago de Compostela, the Scientific and Industrial Research and Development Centre (SIRDC) in Zimbabwe and at IWMI where he was a fellow and researcher, respectively. At the University of Santiago de Compostela he was a fellow of the Spanish Agency for International Cooperation. His areas of interest are the application of Geographic Information Systems (GIS) and remote sensing (RS) in hydrological modelling, spatial analysis, watershed management, climate change mitigation, water resources management and soil-water dynamics. Luxon also acts as an external supervisor for Masters and Doctoral students at the University of South Africa (UNISA). Besides being a reviewer for water and GIS/RS journals, Luxon has also published research findings in peer-reviewed ISI journals.

Charles Nhemachena is a regional researcher at the IWMI southern Africa (IWMI-SA). Before joining IWMI, Charles worked with the Economic Performance and Development Research Programme of the HSRC, focusing on problem-oriented research, analytical studies and policy analysis in a wide range of natural resources and developmental challenges facing South Africa and other African countries. Prior to joining the HSRC, Charles worked at the CSIR with both the Built Environment and Natural Resources and Environment Units. His technical areas of expertise include: climate change (impacts, adaptation, mitigation and vulnerability); sustainable development; monitoring and evaluation; project management, food security, applied agricultural and environmental economics; and R&D within multidisciplinary and multinational teams. Furthermore, Charles has experience in designing, managing and conducting fieldwork, data collection, data cleaning and analysis. He has vast experience using several statistical packages including STATA, SAS, Eviews, SPSS and Limdep. He obtained a PhD in Environmental Economics from the University of Pretoria in 2009, an Advanced Project Management postgraduate certificate from UNISA School of Business Leadership and MSc and BSc (Hons) degrees in Agricultural Economics from the University of Zimbabwe.

Imasiku Anayawa Nyambe is a Professor of Geology and Director of the Directorate of Research and Graduate Studies (DRGS), responsible for research and postgraduate studies at the University of Zambia (UNZA). He is also the coordinator of the UNZA IWRM Centre, a centre that he established. He obtained a PhD in Earth Sciences (Sedimentology) in 1993, an MSc in Geology (Hydrogeology/Sedimentology) from Canada in 1989, and a B. of Min. Sciences (Geology) from the University of Zambia in 1982. Professor Nyambe has worked in the copper mining industry in Zambia (1982–1986) before joining the University of Zambia (UNZA) where he has over 25 years' experience as a geoscientist undertaking research in the areas of geology, hydrogeology, environment and mining, in IWRM and basic remote sensing and GIS. Professor Nyambe has published over 100 papers as book chapters, journals articles, technical reports and presentation papers. He has presented at many conferences, fora, symposia, workshops and meetings all over the world, and has travelled extensively. His involvement in research on mining and the environment earned him an award from the Zambia Environmental Management Agency in 2012. On public service, he is the coordinator of Zambia Water Partnership – the Zambian Chapter of the Global Water Partnership and the chairperson for Zambia Water Forum and Exhibition. Professor Nyambe has been the Secretary General of the Geological Society of Africa (2004–2008) and President of the Geological Society of Zambia (GSZ) (2000–2010). During his tenure as President of GSZ, Professor Nyambe was instrumental in popularising geosciences in high schools, which increased female enrolment in the geoscience career, as well as obtaining scholarships for students in the School of Mines from the mining companies.

Zebediah Phiri is the Executive Secretary of the Zambezi Watercourse Commission (ZAMCOM) – a transboundary river basin organisation whose mission is to promote the equitable and reasonable utilisation of the water resources of the Zambezi watercourse, as well as the efficient management and sustainable development thereof. Professor Phiri has over 28 years' experience in management, consultancy, research and teaching, with a focus on transboundary water resources management and development, civil engineering, and environmental engineering and management. He has, over the years, served as project manager of SADC's Zambezi Action Plan Project (ZACPRO) and Zambia's Water Resources Action Program (WRAP). He has also served as Dean of the School of Engineering at the University of Zambia. Professor Phiri has served on the boards of many organisations including the International Water Resources Association (IWRA), the International Water Association (IWA), Global Water Partnership Southern Africa (GWPSA), Lusaka Water and Sewerage Company (LWSC), Kafue Gorge Regional Training Centre (KGRTC), Engineers' Registration Board (Zambia) and the Water and Sanitation Association of Zambia (WASAZA). His educational background is in management, civil engineering, environmental engineering and management, and water resources engineering. He is the holder of BEng, MSc (Eng), PhD and MBA degrees. He has published extensively in journals and conference proceedings, and has contributed chapters to books.

Manzoor Qadir is an environmental scientist with a focus on policy, institutional and biophysical aspects of water recycling and safe reuse, water quality and environmental health, water and food security, and sustainable natural resources management under changing climate. He has implemented multidisciplinary projects and directed research teams in different regions, particularly Central Asia, the Middle East and North Africa. He led teams of eminent professionals to contribute to international initiatives such as the Comprehensive Global Assessment of Water Management in Agriculture, and the International Assessment of Agricultural Science and Technology for Development. In addition to supervising postdoctoral fellows, postgraduate students and interns, he has undertaken several international and regional capacity development initiatives such as organising knowledge-bridging workshops and training courses for young researchers. Before joining UNU-INWEH in Canada, Manzoor previously held professional positions as senior scientist jointly appointed by the International Center for Agricultural Research in the Dry Areas (ICARDA) and the IWMI, Visiting Professor at Justus-Liebig University, Giessen, Germany, and Associate Professor at the University of Agriculture, Faisalabad, Pakistan. He has authored over 120 peer-reviewed publications. He is a fellow of the Alexander-von-Humboldt Foundation and serves on the editorial boards of three international journals.

Davison Saruchera is a researcher in the field of water governance, with a special focus on water institutions and transboundary water management. He has about 10 years of experience working on issues surrounding water policy, livelihoods and irrigation water management in national and international basins of southern Africa. He has been consultant to a number of national and international organisations, including the IWMI, the Food and Agricultural Organization of the United Nations, the Development Bank of Southern Africa, the World Bank and the Water Research Commission. Davison holds a BSc in Tourism Management from the University of Zimbabwe, an MPhil in Integrated Water Resources Management from the University of the Western Cape and an MSc in Environmental Studies from the University of Pretoria. He has also completed a Postgraduate Diploma in Water and Sanitation Development from the Institute of Water and Sanitation Development (Harare) and is currently reading for an inter-disciplinary PhD in Development Management with the School of Governance at the University of the Witwatersrand in South Africa.

Aidan Senzanje holds a PhD in Agricultural Engineering from Colorado State University and is currently with the Bioresources Engineering Program at the University of KwaZulu-Natal, South Africa, where he is responsible for lecturing in irrigation engineering and soil and water conservation systems. His research interests are in the areas of agricultural water management, irrigation engineering and rural water infrastructure, with a particular focus on small-scale or smallholder systems. He has participated in diverse research activities as part of both local and international interdisciplinary research teams. He has co-edited two books, and authored and co-authored 10 book chapters and over 30 journal articles, numerous peer-reviewed papers and many conference papers. He has supervised postgraduate students at both the MSc and PhD level. He was previously a guest editor responsible for the water and land section for the journal *Physics and Chemistry of the Earth*. He was a visiting scientist at IWMI (Pretoria) in 2002/03. He was previously a Head of Department and also Deputy Dean at the University of Zimbabwe. He has wide-ranging experience in technical consulting, for local and multinational organisations, in the areas of irrigation and water management in countries as diverse as China, Egypt, Ethiopia, Malawi, Saudi Arabia, Tanzania, Thailand and Zimbabwe.

Osborne N. Shela is a graduate from Colorado State University, USA with an MSc in Civil Engineering, specialising in hydrology and water resources management. He has more than 38 years' experience in the water sector in the specific disciplines of irrigation, water supply, hydropower, disaster risk management, environment and climate change management. He is the former Director of Water Resources in the Ministry of Irrigation and Water Development, Malawi, from 1995 to 2000, chairman of GWPSA for 2001 to 2004 and SADC Liaison Officer for Water Resources at SADC ELMS in Lesotho from 1993 to 1995. He has also been World Bank Technical Assistant as Water Resources Manager for International Rivers in Mozambique from 2002 to 2005 and World Bank Regional Disaster Risk Consultant for Disaster Reduction and Recovery in Malawi and Mozambique (2007). Shela has been involved in the development of institutional and capacity building for the joint integrated water resources management for the entire Zambezi River Basin and also the Pungwe River between Mozambique and Zimbabwe. He is currently the managing director of Majiatua Engineering Services International based in Malawi, which provides consulting services in the SADC region.

Vladimir Smakhtin is the director of the UNU-INWEH, based in Canada. Prior to UNU-INWEH he led the Water Availability, Risk and Resilience Research Department at the IWMI, based in Colombo, Sri Lanka. He co-led the research flagship on Managing Variability and Competing Uses of the CGIAR Research Mega-programme on Water, Land and Ecosystems (WLE). Vladimir holds a PhD in hydrology and water resources from the Russian Academy of Science. His research and management experience spreads across agricultural and environmental water management, low-flow and drought analyses, assessment of basin development and climate change impacts on water availability and access, provision of hydrological information for data-poor regions, water-related disaster risk management, water storage infrastructure planning and management, and global water availability and scarcity. He initiated, managed and contributed to numerous research initiatives in over 20 countries worldwide, authored and co-authored over 200 publications, and was consultant to a number of national and international organisations, including the Department of Water Affairs of South Africa, IUCN, Ontario Ministry of Natural Resources, UNEP, World Bank and World Commission on Dams. He has been an active promoter of environmentally sustainable water resources management globally through science and policy gatherings in over 50 countries. He was involved in the state programme for mitigating the consequences of the Chernobyl accident, actively contributed to the development of ecological reserve methods in South Africa and pioneered a groundbreaking analysis of ecosystem water requirements at the global scale.

Amaury Tilmant is a Professor in the Department of Civil and Water Engineering at Laval University, Quebec, Canada. Professor Tilmant's expertise is in water resources systems analysis. His work focuses on the integration of engineering, economic, political and environmental considerations in regional water and energy systems. To achieve this, Professor Tilmant applies principles in hydrology, economics and other relevant sciences to solve various water resources planning and management problems such as reservoir operations, irrigation scheduling, water allocation, watershed management, water pricing, and so on. He also contributes to operations research (OR) by developing sophisticated models and algorithms to analyse water and energy systems and to support optimal system design and policy development. Over the past 20 years, Professor Tilmant has acquired significant experience in large-scale, international, water resources systems, primarily in the Middle East (Euphrates-Tigris and Jordan River Basins), in Africa (Nile, Senegal and Zambezi River Basins) and in South America (Parana River Basin). Much of his work was carried out in partnership with local engineering companies, academic institutions, NGOs, development banks and utilities. Professor Tilmant has served two terms as an associate editor of *Water Resources Research*, one of the leading scientific journals in the field of water. He co-authored more than 80 publications and recently won the Quentin Martin Award from the American Society of Civil Engineers.

FOREWORD

The Zambezi is one of the largest river basins in Africa, shared by eight countries. The basin possesses exceptional economic opportunity but also faces critical risks. Economic opportunity is manifested through the basin's untapped hydropower, the harnessing of which is key to both providing electricity to many more households, and supporting much-needed industrial growth – in the basin and broader region. Risks relate to potential costs imposed on the environment not just for its own sake, but for the services derived therefrom – on which population, rural in particular, depends. With multilateral development banks re-engaging in water infrastructure and the presence of China increasingly felt, opportunities will soon be exploited and risks taken. The stakes are high to get this right, as the hydrological landscape of the Zambezi Basin could look irreversibly different within the next couple of decades.

High stakes call for informed decisions. The Zambezi's impending water resources development indeed underscores the need for decision-making that is informed by evidence and aware of consequences. In this context, it is with great joy and pleasure that I present to you the well-researched and very timely book *The Zambezi River Basin: Water and Sustainable Development*. The book adds to the knowledge base on the Zambezi Basin and lays an improved foundation to support the basin's development as the path forward is charted. Published immediately after the adoption of the Sustainable Development Goals (SDGs) by the United Nations, the book provides practical directions on the Zambezi River Basin development for the benefit of citizens, political leaders, decision-makers, technicians, researchers and young professionals in the water and sanitation sector in the basin and beyond.

There is no analogue to this book to date in how comprehensively the basin's water resources issues are examined. And for the first time ever, the book explores ways to achieve Sustainable Development Goal (SDG) 6 at a basin-level, rather than doing this by individual country. Overall, the book examines a set of very pertinent topics for policy and development in the basin, including: availability and use of water resources; economic potential of the basin; impacts of climate change; hydropower; sustainable agriculture; and ecosystems. It also analyses trends, opportunities and threats related to urbanisation, water quality and water reuse, transboundary cooperation and water security at large.

This book directly contributes to the attainment of the *Africa Water Vision 2025* of 'An Africa where there is an equitable and sustainable use and management of water resources for poverty alleviation, socioeconomic development, regional cooperation, and the environment'. The book also contributes to a better understanding of the importance of the basin not only for its eight riparian countries, but for the Southern Africa Development Community (SADC) region and the entire African continent. At a continental level, the African Ministers' Council on Water (AMCOW) family appreciates the efforts of the contributors to this book. The team of editors and authors apply their collective expertise and comprehensive research to generate judiciously distilled messages that inform basin stakeholders on the cooperative development opportunities that the Zambezi River Basin presents.

In short, I very much welcome this first comprehensive, multidisciplinary account of knowledge that we have about the basin that helps riparian countries to attain the *Africa Water Vision 2025*, supports the achievement of Sustainable Development Goals at the basin scale and contributes to the foundation of the *African Union Agenda 2063*.

Dr Canisius Kanangire
Executive Secretary, African Ministers' Council on Water (AMCOW)

ACKNOWLEDGEMENTS

The editors wish to extend their gratitude to all the contributors to this book, who kindly volunteered to share their knowledge, and we hope that the messages delivered by the book will inform the growing development and cooperation in the Zambezi River Basin. We would also like to acknowledge support from Marcus Wishart (World Bank), who provided key input into the book's conceptualisation, as well as financial support provided by the International Water Management Institute (IWMI). We are thankful to the following people for supplying photos used in the book: Leonard John Abrams (private consultant), Richard Beilfuss (International Crane Foundation), Geoffrey Chavula (University of Malawi), Egline Tauya (Southern Africa Regional Documentation Centre), Elizabeth Karonga (Zambezi River Authority), Everisto Mapedza (IWMI-West Africa), Imasiku A. Nyambe (University of Zambia), Sanjiv de Silva (IWMI-Headquarters), Jusipbek Kazbekov (Central Asia Regional Economic Cooperation Program) and Charles Nhemachena (IWMI-Southern Africa). Finally, we wish to gratefully acknowledge the dedicated administration and graphic support from Upamali Surangika and Sumith Fernando, respectively, from IWMI-Headquarters, chapter reviews provided by John Metzger (ZAMCOM) and support from Kingsley Kurukulasuriya in copyediting the contents of the book.

ACRONYMS AND ABBREVIATIONS

ADB	Asian Development Bank
AfDB	African Development Bank
AMCOW	The African Ministers' Council on Water
ARA-ZAMBEZE	Administração Regional de Águas do Zambeze
AWM	Agricultural Water Management
BBC	British Broadcasting Corporation
BCU	Basin Country Unit
BRIDGE	Building River Dialogue and Governance
CA	Conservation Agriculture
CAM	Congo Air Mass
CAPCO	Central Power Corporation
CCAFS	Climate Change, Agriculture and Food Security
CGIAR	Consultative Group for International Agricultural Research
CIDA	Canadian International Development Agency
CMIP	Coupled Model Inter-comparison Project
COMESA	Common Market for East and Southern Africa
CRIDF	Climate Resilient Infrastructure Development Facility
CSIRO	Commonwealth Scientific and Industrial Research Organisation
CSU	Charles Sturt University
DANIDA	Government of Denmark, Ministry of Foreign Affairs
DfID	Department for International Development
DFID	UK Department for International Development
DRGS	Directorate of Research and Postgraduate Studies
DSS	Decision Support System
EF	Environmental Flows
ERWH	Ex-field Rainwater Harvesting
ESCOM	Electricity Supply Commission (South African electricity public utility)
ET	Evapotranspiration
FAO	Food and Agriculture Organization
FRIEND	Flow Regimes In Experimental Network Data
GAEZ	Global Agro-Ecological Zones

GCM	General Circulation Model
GDP	Gross Domestic Product
GHCN	Global Historical Climatology Network
GIZ	Deutsche Gesellschaft für Internationale Zusammenarbeit
GRDC	Global Runoff Data Centre
GSZ	Geological Society of Zambia
GTZ	German Organization for Technical Cooperation
GWP	Global Water Partnership
GWPSA	Global Water Partnership Southern Africa
HBS	Heinrich Böll Stiftung
HCB	Hidroeléctrica de Cahora Bassa
HDI	Human Development Index
HFR	High Flow Requirements
ICARDA	International Center for Agricultural Research in the Dry Areas
ICF	International Crane Foundation
ICT	Information and Communications Technologies
IFC	International Finance Corporation
IGO	Inter Governmental Organisation
IGRAC	International Groundwater Resources Assessment Centre
IIDA	Icelandic International Development Agency
IIP	Fisheries Research Institute of Mozambique
ILWS	Institute for Land, Water and Society
IMERCSA	India Musokotwane Environmental Resource Centre for Southern Africa
IPCC	Intergovernmental Panel on Climate Change
IRWH	In-field Rain Water Harvesting
ITCZ	Inter-Tropical Convergence Zones
IUCN	International Union for the Conservation of Nature
IWA	International Water Association
IWMI	International Water Management Institute
IWRA	International Water Resources Association
IWRM	Integrated Water Resources Management
JMP	WHO/UNICEF
KGRTC	Kafue Gorge Regional Training Centre
LCBC	Lake Chad Basin Commission
LFR	Low Flow Requirements
LIMCOM	Limpopo Watercourse Commission
LMIC	Low and Middle Income Countries
LWSC	Lusaka Water and Sewerage Company
M&E	Monitoring and Evaluation
MDGs	Millennium Development Goals
MEA	Millennium Ecosystem Assessment
MENA	Middle East and North Africa
MSIOA	Multi-Sectoral Investment Opportunities Analysis
MW	MegaWatt
MWh	Mega Watt Hour
NBA	Niger Basin Authority
NBI	Nile Basin Initiative

NGO	Non-Governmental Organisation
OKACOM	Okavango River Basin Water Commission
OMVS	Organisation pour la Mise en Valeur du fleuve Sénégal
OR	Operations Research
PAWD	Partnership Africa's Water Development
PIDA	Program for Infrastructure Development in Africa
RBO	River Basin Organisation
RCP	Representative Concentration Pathways
RFI	Radio France International
ROR	Run-of-River Power Plant
RRR	Resource Recovery and Reuse
SADC	Southern Africa Development Community
SAPP	Southern African Power Pool
SARDC	Southern African Research and Documentation Centre
SDG	Sustainable Development Goal
SRBDP	Shire River Basin Development Programme
SRES	Special Report on Emissions Scenarios
SWC	Soil and Water Conservation
TFDD	Transboundary Freshwater Dispute Database
UN	United Nations
UNDP	United Nations Development Programme
UNEP	United Nations Environmental Programme
UNGC	United Nations Global Compact
UNICEF	United Nations Children's Emergency Fund
UNISA	University of South Africa
UNU	United Nations University
UNU-INWEH	United Nations University Institute for Water, Environment and Health
UNZA	University of Zambia
USAID	United States Agency for International Development
USGS	United States Geological Survey
VBA	Volta Basin Authority
VOA	Voice of America
WASAZA	Water and Sanitation Association of Zambia
WASHTED	Center for Water, Sanitation, Health and Technology Development
WCD	World Commission on Dams
WEF	Water-Energy-Food
WHO	World Health Organization
WIN-SA	Water Information Network-South Africa
WLE	Water, Land and Ecosystems
WRAP	Water Resources Action Program
WUA	Water User Association
WWTP	Waste Water Treatment Plants
ZACPLAN	The Zambezi River Basin Action Plan
ZACPRO	Zambezi Action Plan Project
ZAMCOM	Zambezi Watercourse Commission
ZAMWIS	Zambezi Water Resources Information System
ZESCO	Zambia Electricity Supply Corporation
ZRA	Zambezi River Authority

1

Introduction

Zebediah Phiri, Jonathan Lautze, Vladimir Smakhtin
and Davison Saruchera

The Zambezi River Basin is one of the most diverse and valuable natural resources in Africa. Its waters are critical to sustainable economic growth and poverty reduction in the region. In addition to meeting the basic needs of a population of some 40 million and sustaining a rich and diverse natural environment, the basin plays a central role in the economies of the eight riparian countries – Angola, Botswana, Malawi, Mozambique, Namibia, Tanzania, Zambia and

Zimbabwe. It provides important environmental goods and services to the region, and is essential to regional food security and hydropower production. Characterised by strong climatic variability, the river and its tributaries are subject to increasing seasonal variation in the hydrological regime, with a cycle of floods and droughts that have devastating effects on the people and economies of the region.

The basin has always been central to visions of economic growth and prosperity in the southern African region and there is a long history of sustained efforts to foster cooperative development. These efforts have acknowledged the need for a combination of growth-based investments and strategic analytical work in support of a sustainable vision and framework that can inform and guide integrated, resilient regional development to unblock the significant potential for economic growth. However, despite the strong analytical foundations, cooperation has remained elusive. This reflects the complex interaction of social, technical and political considerations.

Sustained economic growth above 5 per cent in recent years in many of the riparian states is providing new opportunities and increasing development pressure on the resources of the basin. More than USD16 billion worth of investments have been identified at the prefeasibility or feasibility stages of preparation and the combined GDP among the riparian states is estimated at over USD250 billion today. Despite this increasing prosperity, poverty is persistent across the basin and coefficients of inequality for some of the riparian states are among the highest in the world. Reflecting the dual nature of the regional economy, new investments in large infrastructure coexist alongside a parallel, subsistence economy that is reliant upon environmental services provided by the river.

The benefits of cooperation in the Zambezi River Basin have been well demonstrated. There is an extensive body of literature supporting the notion that cooperation over shared waters promises substantial benefits. These typically include: peace dividends; preventing the escalation of disputes into conflicts by opening dialogue and increasing potential for problem-solving; improving access to external markets; increasing economies of scale (e.g., lower marginal cost of unit power production in the case of hydropower); improved management and coordinated operation of water infrastructure to accommodate multipurpose uses of water; the possibility of jointly facing common external threats (e.g., climate risks, malaria); and optimising the location of infrastructure to increase benefits and reduce costs.

Results of a multisectoral investment analysis (World Bank 2010) have shown that cooperative water development in the Zambezi River Basin could result in substantial benefits. For example, the development of hydropower generation plans could facilitate several billion dollars in investment alone, improving regional energy security by increasing electricity generation capacity by some 13,000 megawatts (Euroconsult and Mott McDonald 2008). More than 200,000 ha of increased irrigation could enhance regional food security and expand the total irrigated area beyond 500,000 ha, creating more than several hundred thousand jobs in the agriculture sector. The Zambezi River Basin also represents one of the few options for securing water supplies for the dryland areas south of the river in Botswana, Namibia and Zimbabwe, as well as further afield across the region. Socioeconomic benefits derived from investments in river crossings, bridges and transport networks would have substantial benefits, improving trade efficiencies and linkages. Similar cooperation around strategic interventions relating to disaster management could increase resilience within the basin and reduce the exposure to floods and droughts. These interventions could increase economic resilience through avoiding estimated losses of as much as USD1 billion a year due to these 'water shocks'.

The evolution of basin-wide cooperation on the Zambezi has developed over more than three decades, building on the earlier foundations initiated during the 1940s with the efforts to establish bilateral mechanisms to advance development of the Kariba and Cahora Bassa hydropower schemes. In the 1980s new initiatives were launched in an effort to reach 'Agreement on the Establishment of the Zambezi Watercourse Commission' (the ZAMCOM Agreement). However, these negotiations were suspended in the early 1990s to allow for discussions on the 1995 SADC Protocol on Shared Watercourses. The Protocol was revised in 2000 and ratified in 2003 with fresh negotiations on the ZAMCOM Agreement resuming in 2002.

The principal objective of the ZAMCOM Agreement is 'to promote the equitable and reasonable utilization of the water resources of the Zambezi watercourse as well as the efficient management and sustainable development thereof'. The Agreement was signed on 13 July 2004 in Kasane, Botswana, by ministers responsible for water from seven of the eight riparian states – Angola, Botswana, Malawi, Mozambique, Namibia, the United Republic of Tanzania and Zimbabwe. Zambia did not sign but reportedly pledged to do so before the August SADC Summit in that same year after further consultation at the national level. The ZAMCOM Agreement subsequently came into force on 19 June 2011 after six of the eight riparian countries completed their ratification processes and deposited their ratification instruments with the SADC Secretariat. Zambia subsequently acceded to the agreement in 2013 and Malawi, which signed on 13 July 2004, has not yet finalised its accession.

After more than 30 years with little investment in the Zambezi River Basin, the entry into force of the ZAMCOM Agreement reflects increasing recognition of the need among the riparian states to find cooperative solutions to the challenges of development within the basin. To create a framework of visions, activities and projects, an Integrated Water Resources Management (IWRM) Strategy for the Zambezi River Basin was developed in 2008. The potential outcomes envisaged over the next 15 years under the IWRM Strategy through cooperation include:

i   *Poverty reduced* throughout the basin as a result of expanded development, improved coordinated and sustainable water resources management.
ii   *Energy security* through hydropower investments (USD several billion) resulting in substantial additional firm and average energy.
iii *Agricultural production* increased, enhancing regional food security through more than an additional 200,000 ha, thus increasing irrigation to more than 500,000 ha.
iv   *Increased employment*, particularly in the agriculture sector, with substantial job creation.
v   *Economic resilience* increased and growth benefits sustained through reduced exposure to floods (>USD1 billion losses avoided, on average, per year) and adaptive measures to climate change.
vi   *Regional transport* costs and travel times reduced through bridge investments and navigation.
vii *Water supplies* secured for urban and industrial demands (>1,000 million cubic metres/year to Botswana, Malawi, Zambia and Zimbabwe).
viii *Environmental restoration* of the Zambezi Delta improved fisheries production through systematic introduction of basin-wide environmental flows.
ix   Contributions of *tourism and mining* to GDP increased through integrated, sustainable development.
x   *Fisheries production* enhanced through improved management of water resources.

This book is the first of its kind in the Zambezi River Basin to examine and link in a single volume hydrology, water resources management, transboundary water governance, hydropower generation, climate risks, environmental conservation and strategies to improve the use of water and other natural resources in the basin to enhance food security, livelihoods and economic growth. A common limitation of previous books is their focus on only some particular areas among those just highlighted. Chenje (2000) assessed the basin's then-current ecological, social and economic sustainability status. The World Bank's *Multi-Sector Investment Opportunities Analysis* (2010) focused on the potential for investment in the basin – mainly in hydropower and irrigation. Tumbare (2010) evaluated the implementation of IWRM in the basin, with limited reference to infrastructure development and climate change. *The Basin Atlas* by SADC *et al.* (2012) also attempted to cover various basin issues, including ecology, conservation, climate change and institutions. However, the atlas is a popularly oriented illustration of changes in the basin, but thin on analytical content. Finally, ZAMCOM *et al.* (2015) assessed the state of the environment with particular focus on trends over the preceding 15 years.

The aim of this book is to provide a thorough assessment of the development context in the Zambezi River Basin. This is a comprehensive one-volume book that critically interrogates the historical framework and current context for the development and management of water resources in the Zambezi River Basin and explores potential future scenarios within the changing regional contexts. This is presented through an analysis that links biophysical, socioeconomic, policy, institutional and governance issues in a solutions-oriented manner, and identifies pathways for future management of the Zambezi River Basin that foster economic, social and ecological sustainability, along with the role of research in achieving these pathways.

The book provides a frame of reference that will appeal to Zambezi riparians as well as river basin organisations and water agencies across Africa and further abroad. It is aimed at a wide and diverse audience including government decision-makers, private-sector investors, universities, development partners, intermediary organisations that work directly with farmers, researchers, practitioners and students, along with a host of others working in the Zambezi River Basin and more generally around issues of transboundary river basin management. It provides important insights into the development of hydropower generation and the integration of commercial sectors, such as agriculture and mining, while also comprising a reference point for the academic community, civil society and other interested stakeholders working on development challenges related to water, food and energy in the Zambezi River Basin.

The description and analysis in the following chapters yield, among many others, the following key messages:

- Currently, Zambezi waters are underutilised, with only about 20 per cent of the resource exploited. Surface water storage is 245km^3. Groundwater use is increasing, especially for domestic water supplies. The management of both groundwater and surface water needs to be strengthened to realise maximum benefits.
- The basin has vast potential economic benefits that can be derived from hydropower, irrigation and other water uses. The current economic value that can be placed on irrigation and hydropower from these large storage infrastructures is around USD1.27 billion per year, whereas the additional potential benefits that can be harnessed from hydropower and irrigation in the Zambezi system is at least USD2.6 billion per year. Tapped benefits are likely to also fall well below potential in other sectors.
- By 2050, the Zambezi River Basin is expected to become hotter and drier, with a 0.3–0.6°C increase in temperatures per decade, a 10–15 per cent reduction in rainfall, and a 26–40 per cent decrease in runoff relative to a 1961–1990 baseline. A shift in the timing (a delayed onset) of the rainy season is expected, as are more amplified seasonal variations (increasing high flows and reducing low flows). These changes are likely to compromise firm and total hydropower generation in the Zambezi Basin, and result in substantial reductions in agricultural production in Zambezi countries. Such impacts are likely to be felt most acutely in cultivation of rain-fed agriculture, particularly for maize. To reduce

climate risks, it is imperative to incorporate climate change impacts and uncertainties into dam design, promote crop and power diversification, and strive to implement environmental flows.

- In the near future, the irrigated area in the Zambezi Basin is expected to double and exceed 500,000 ha. In terms of power, ongoing and planned projects will add 2,700 MW to the electrical grid. Projects in both sectors – agriculture and energy – are all located in the Middle and Lower Zambezi. The ultimate goal of a nexus approach in the Zambezi is to manage the trade-offs between new irrigation projects, flood recession agriculture and hydropower generation. Because ZAMCOM is the only institution overlooking the entire situation in the basin, its mandate could be expanded to explicitly include the promotion of a nexus approach. ZAMCOM is particularly well placed to manage trade-offs and maximise co-benefits through intersectoral water allocation in the Zambezi Basin. Through enhanced cooperation with the Southern Africa Power Pool, ZAMCOM could assist countries in reforming their energy and water policies to ensure coherence.

- More than 60 per cent of the basin's population are active in agriculture. While the vast majority of agriculture is rain-fed, most of the water used in the basin is for irrigation. Ambitious plans exist to scale up irrigation in the basin, which will have serious implications on water use. The recent emergence of ZAMCOM may enhance opportunities to improve water management through: i) improvements in rain-fed agriculture as a means to mitigate potential future disruptions to water withdrawal; ii) exploration of groundwater sources as an alternative to surface water on which there will likely be more future demand; and iii) improvements to water productivity where appropriate.

- The basin's ecosystem services may not be fully appreciated, but are valued at over USD1.3 billion annually. The ecosystem services supply currently exceeds demand. However, pressure on the ecosystem is constantly growing, driven especially by economic development, climate change and a rapidly growing population. Environmental degradation is increasing and water quality decreasing, severely threatening ecosystem services, with potentially serious implications for the livelihoods of the rural poor. The large rural population, which has a considerable dependency on natural resources, means that safeguarding ecosystem services must be central to strategies for poverty reduction, food security and economic development in the basin.

- Water quality and quantity are heavily threatened by urbanisation, population increase and activities like mining, coupled with a limited capacity for wastewater treatment and reuse. The consumption of domestic water and production of wastewater is expected to double by 2050, further exacerbating the problem. Strategies to develop wastewater reuse and improve local government capacity to deal with waste are urgently required, especially to support Sustainable Development Goal (SD6) 6.3, which seeks to reduce wastewater and pollution.

- More than 10 transboundary water agreements – increasingly multilateral and increasingly water-centred – have been concluded on the Zambezi over the last 130 years. Despite critical progress culminating in the entry-into-force of the ZAMCOM Agreement in 2011, risks related to equity and access, and sovereignty and autonomy may constrain cooperation – particularly for Zambia, Malawi and Angola. While such risks are partially mitigated through transboundary water laws, uncertainty related to the interpretations of equitable use principles, as well as a lack of clarity on potential impacts on national development plans, may deter cooperative engagement.

- When appropriate, subbasin-level cooperation may be effective and practical. The Zambezi's geography presents opportunities for subbasin-level cooperation that can be coordinated with the broader river basin organisation framework. In the Shire subbasin, for example, cooperation could focus on flood control, navigation and water hyacinth. ZAMCOM can play a facilitative role in promoting this kind of cooperation.

- The basin faces water security challenges. Vulnerability is high and agricultural water security is low across the basin, while the provision of basic water supply and sanitation is also a major challenge in several countries, most notably in Angola, Tanzania and Mozambique. Substantial investment will be required to mitigate water security challenges through, for example, the erection of infrastructure to increase water storage and reduce vulnerability, and improved agricultural water management.
- ZAMCOM can play an active role in fostering cooperation, leading engagement with development partners and guiding the development of 'green' infrastructure. As the basin strives to strengthen cooperation and improve benefit-sharing, the role of ZAMCOM becomes more critical in facilitating such processes. The realisation of some SDG goals in the basin, notably health, access to water, safety from risk and food security, can be facilitated with the effective and efficient use of water resources, led by ZAMCOM.

Box 1.1: Illustration of a disputed boundary

The editors wish to point out that the boundary between Malawi and Tanzania over Lake Nyasa/Malawi is disputed. In the chapters of the book, the boundary is typically portrayed one way due largely to borders embedded in the data layers of ArcGIS shapefiles. However, we wish to make clear that this in no way implies this is the final legal boundary – which is still in dispute and subject to continued negotiation.

References

Chenje, M. (ed.). 2000. *State of the environment in the Zambezi Basin.* Harare: Southern African Research and Documentation Centre.

Euroconsult and Mott McDonald. 2008. *Integrated water resources management strategy and implementation plan for the Zambezi River Basin.* Gaborone: Southern Africa Development Community-Water Division.

Southern Africa Development Community, Southern Africa Research and Documentation Centre, Zambezi Watercourse Commission, GRID and United Nations Environmental Programme. 2012. *Zambezi River Basin atlas of the changing environment.* Gaborone, Harare: Southern Africa Development Community.

Southern Africa Research and Documentation Centre. 2015. *The status report on integrated flood and drought mapping.* Harare: Zambezi Watercourse Commission-Southern Africa Development Community-Southern Africa Research and Documentation Centre.

Tumbare, M.J. 2010. *The management of the Zambezi River Basin and Kariba Dam.* Oxford: African Books Collective.

World Bank. 2010. *The Zambezi River Basin: A multi-sector investment opportunities analysis.* Volumes 1–4. Washington, DC: World Bank.

ZAMCOM (Zambezi Watercourse Commission), SADC (Southern African Development Community) and SARDC (Southern African Research Documentation Centre). 2015. *Zambezi environment outlook 2015.* Harare, Gaborone.

2

Availability and use of water resources

Xueliang Cai, Yvan Altchenko and Geoffrey Chavula

Key messages

- The Zambezi Basin has significant potential for water resources development. It is the largest and the most shared basin in southern Africa. Currently, only 20 per cent of its surface water resources are exploited. The Zambezi River has a total length of 2,700 km, with an average surface runoff of 103 km^3 and mean annual groundwater recharge of 130 km^3.

- The development of infrastructure to enhance water resources management in the Zambezi River Basin is critical in buffering adverse effects of climate change and variability and unlocking the growth of key economic sectors. The combined storage of the two main dams on the Zambezi River, namely Kariba and Cahora Bassa, adds up to 243 km^3, which is almost 100 per cent of the total existing reservoir storage of 245 km^3 in the entire basin. In light of the above, there is need to promote the construction of small- and medium-scale dams in order to satisfy the growing demand for water in the basin arising from irrigated agriculture and domestic water supply requirements, particularly for cities.
- The adoption of smart investments in the Zambezi River Basin may help build links among the energy sector, water resources and irrigation development and flood protection in the riparian countries. There is a need to streamline government funding as well as that of smallholders' own initiatives, and to make optimal use of existing natural ecosystems in the Zambezi River Basin.
- The development of groundwater resources has the potential to revolutionise the way water resources are being managed in the basin. Currently, groundwater is the main source of water supply for rural households and a few cities. But how surface water and groundwater resources in the basin are currently managed requires substantial revision if maximum benefits accruing from these resources are going to be realised.
- Hydrological and water use data in the basin are still scarce, especially on groundwater resources. Various data and information systems initiatives have not been very successful in the past. In order to redress the situation, there is need to explore innovative data monitoring and acquisition approaches, for example, using information and communications technology (ICT) and remote sensing, complemented with strong commitment from riparian governments.

Introduction

The Zambezi River, with a total length of 2,700 km, is the most shared basin in southern Africa. It traverses some of the world's least developed countries, covering an area of about 1.34 million km^2 spanning over eight riparian states, namely: Angola, Botswana, Namibia, Malawi, Mozambique, Tanzania, Zambia and Zimbabwe. It arises from Kahene Hills in Zambia at an altitude of 1,500 m before it enters Angola. It then re-enters Zambia at Chavuma Falls and flows southward to its confluence with the Lungue Bungo and Kabompo Rivers. Downstream of this confluence, the Zambezi enters the Barotse subbasin and thereafter flows into the Barotse wetland. After exiting the wetland, it confluences again with rivers originating from the Cuando-Chobe subbasin before entering the Kariba subbasin, where it flows through the famous Victoria Falls. After Lake Kariba, the Zambezi is joined by the Kafue and Luangwa Rivers before it flows into Cahora Bassa Reservoir in the Tete subbasin. From Cahora Bassa, the Zambezi is joined by the Shire River (which drains the Lake Nyasa/Malawi subbasin), before emptying its waters into the Indian Ocean through the Zambezi Delta subbasin (Figure 2.1 and Figure 2.5). The long-term mean annual discharge at the basin outlet is 4,134 m^3/s (World Bank 2010). The total basin area is 1.3 million km^2 and is inhabited by approximately 40 million people, representing about one-third of the total population of the basin's eight riparian countries.

The rich water resources in the Zambezi River Basin have long been a focus for poverty alleviation and economic development endeavours by the riparian governments given the region's long-standing need for sustainable development. The basin's water is mainly used for hydropower generation, agricultural development and domestic water supply and industrial use in cities, with just over 20 per cent of the potential being exploited (Zambezi River Authority 2008).

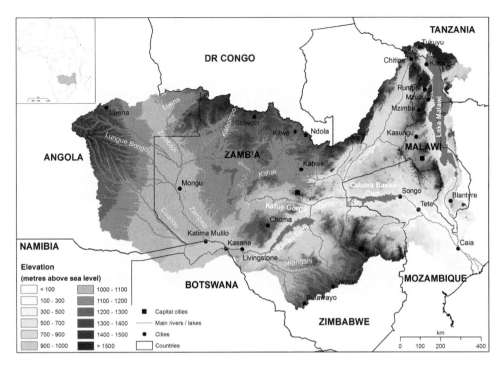

Figure 2.1 The geography and topography of the Zambezi River Basin
Source: Authors

Extensive research has been undertaken pertaining to the development of water resources in the basin, notably by the Southern African Development Community (SADC), the Zambezi Watercourse Commission (ZAMCOM), the Zambezi River Authority (ZRA), the World Bank and other donors (e.g., GIZ, DANIDA, DFID). Perhaps more importantly, work has also been conducted in individual riparian countries, which have been used as a basis for the development of the respective national water policies and master plans. Reports by SADC, Southern African Research and Documentation Centre (SARDC) and ZRA contain a wealth of information on basin geography, hydrology, water use, socioeconomic factors driving changes in water use, and the governance, policy and management practices regarding water resources in the Zambezi River Basin (for example: SADC and ZRA 2008; Euroconsult Mott MacDonald 2007; SADC *et al.* 2012). The fourth edition of the SADC *Regional Strategic Action Plan on Integrated Water Resources Development and Management* was recently completed. Its production involved extensive consultation processes with member countries, the research and development community, and international donors. The plan contains comprehensive approaches for investments on infrastructure, capacity building, governance and technological innovations (SADC 2016). The newly established ZAMCOM has identified a number of priority areas of development, of which infrastructure for improved access to water is central to the management of water resources for economic growth and development (ZAMCOM *et al.* 2015).

This chapter provides a general overview of the available information on water resources in the Zambezi Basin. It highlights key gaps and challenges for sustainable development in the basin, and provides an insight into the status of surface water and groundwater resources, current water infrastructure gaps in satisfying demand and water allocations among competing sectors, in particular the environment, irrigated agriculture, domestic water supply for cities and industrial use and mining. Key recommendations on water resources management practices among riparian countries in respect of water resources development and conservation are highlighted at the end of the discussion.

Climate, physiography and vegetation

The Zambezi River Basin experiences an intercontinental tropical climate, mainly controlled by the movement of the Inter-Tropical Convergence Zone (ITCZ). The ITCZ oscillates randomly across the basin during the rainy season and produces widespread rainfall. The subtropical ridge controls the weather over the basin during the dry season, spanning over the period May to September. The associated southeast trade winds are generally stable and hence very little precipitation takes place in the basin. However, from October to April, the weather is controlled by the Equatorial Trough, which moves from the Equator to latitude 20° and back again, and brings in unstable air that causes convectional rainfall. The basin receives an average rainfall of 990 mm annually, varying from over 1,200 mm in the northern part to 700 mm in the south and southwest (Figure 2.2). Less than 10 per cent of the precipitation is expected to flow through the river and reach the Indian Ocean; the rest evaporates and returns directly to the earth's atmosphere or infiltrates and recharges groundwater. Zambezi tributaries peak rapidly after rainfall events, reaching their maximum discharge between January and March, and decreasing to minimum flows in October to November during the dry season. The rainy season is unimodal and longer in the north and northeastern compared to the south and

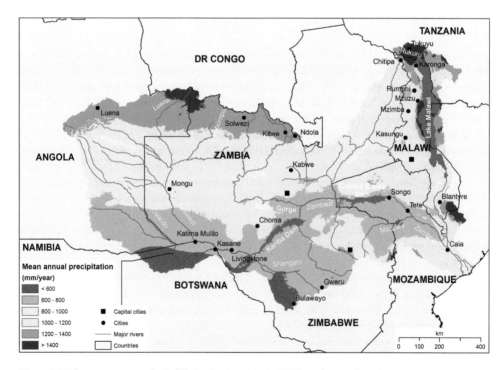

Figure 2.2 The average annual rainfall distribution (1950–2000) in the Zambezi River Basin
Source: Adapted from Hijmans *et al.* (2005)

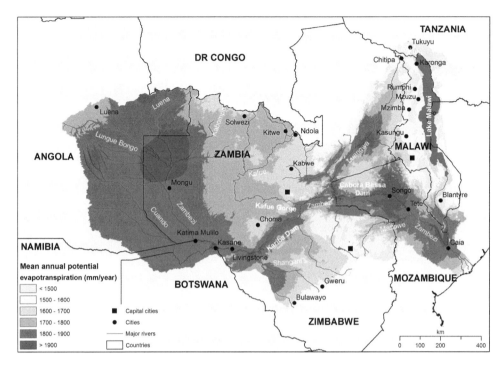

Figure 2.3 The average potential evapotranspiration distribution (1950–2000) in the Zambezi River Basin
Source: Adapted from the CGIAR-CSI Global PET database (Zomer *et al.* 2008)

southwestern parts of the basin. Apart from the ITCZ, additional synoptic systems that bring rainfall to the basin are the Zaire Air Boundary (ZAB) or Congo Air Mass, and tropical cyclones as they veer away from the Mozambique Channel.

The average temperature in the Zambezi River Basin is 21°C with a summer high reaching 32°C and a winter low of 8°C. The basin has an annual average sunshine of 7.8 hours/day, and an annual potential evapotranspiration of 1,754 mm (Figure 2.3).

Most of the Zambezi Basin is situated on the high plateau of the ancient Gondwana, with elevations ranging from 800 to 1,450 m above sea level (Figure 2.1). The nature of the topography exhibited by the Zambezi contributes significantly to the high hydropower potential present in the basin. The basin lies on basement rocks (pre-Cambrian crystalline and metamorphic rocks), which are part of the African and Post-African tertiary planation surfaces (Acres *et al.* 1985). The topsoil is generally shallow and prone to erosion by water and winds in some parts of the basin. The main soil types are arenosols, greysols and ferralsols that dominate the Upper Zambezi. Other dominant soils are the luvisols that mainly cover the Luangwa and Zambezi Delta subbasin. The upper catchment of the Zambezi is an extension of the Kalahari Desert and covered with windblown Kalahari sand. Depressed areas, including several major wetland systems and the delta area, are covered by sedimentary layers of varying thickness.

The basin is mainly covered by the Zambezian biome, which comprises mixed open woodland, savannah vegetation, swamps and lakes. The basin has extensive conservation sites of national and international significance, most of which are water-dependent ecosystems. These include three UNESCO World Natural Heritage Sites (Victoria Falls, Mana Pools National

Park and Lake Malawi National Park), 14 Ramsar conservation sites based on the Convention on Wetlands of International Importance, which came into force in 1975, the Okavango-Zambezi Transfrontier Conservation Park and many national parks. The abundance of conservation areas forms a fundamental part of the development and management of the water resources in the basin. Natural ecosystems, such as wetlands and forests, have strong regulating functions in reducing the frequency and magnitude of floods, and increasing baseflow in the dry season (McCartney *et al.* 2013).

Availability of water resources in the Zambezi River Basin

The Zambezi River Basin is generally endowed with rich water resources comprising both surface water and groundwater. An average annual runoff of about 103 km^3 is generated by the basin, with spatiotemporal variations across subbasins. The Zambezi River Basin can be divided into 13 subbasins based on distribution of surface water. Groundwater is, however, more complex and there is limited information regarding its occurrence and distribution in the basin. Current assessments show the existence of at least 10 transboundary aquifers in and across the basin (Figure 2.4).

The 10 transboundary aquifers, identified by the International Groundwater Resources Assessment Centre (IGRAC), can be further divided into two categories, namely: (I) four transboundary aquifers, which are located totally inside the Zambezi River Basin; and (II) six transboundary aquifers, which are located partly inside the Zambezi River Basin.

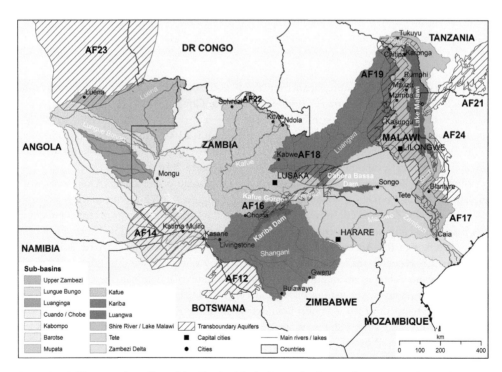

Figure 2.4 Subbasins and aquifers of the Zambezi Basin (AF codes for aquifers correspond to codes in Table 2.3)

Source: ZAMWIS and IGRAC

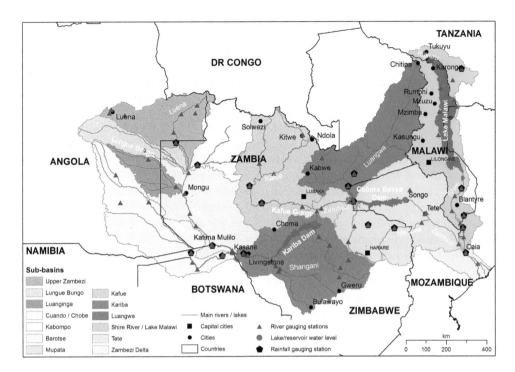

Figure 2.5 Distribution of the river gauging stations, lake/reservoir water level stations and rainfall
      station in the Zambezi River Basin

Source: ZAMWIS

Data on the basin's hydrometeorology and hydrology are scarce. New hydrometric stations
are rare and existing ones are often in various degrees of deterioration due to different external
factors, including age. A report published in 2007 identified more than 430 flow stations and
657 Global Historical Climatology Network (GHCN) Version 2 stations existing in the basin
(Euroconsult Mott MacDonald 2007). The GHCN dataset, currently in version 3, is compiled
with daily records from over 90,000 land-based stations worldwide. There were, however, only
about 160 flow stations included in the Zambezi Water Resources Information System
(ZAMWIS). Part of the reason for this observation was that out of 305 stations in Zambia, only
half (153) were operational with a declining trend. The same report also pointed out the sparse
or nonexistent water-quality monitoring networks in the basin. In other separate initiatives, the
Global Runoff Data Centre (GRDC) reported 120 stations for the entire basin, with Flow
Regimes In Experimental Network Data (FRIEND) of 101 stations. These two databases
combined contains daily flow of 184 hydrometric stations, of which only 104 have longer than
25 years of record, which is normally considered the minimum length of data required for long-
time hydrological analysis. The FRIEND dataset records end in 1994 and the most recent records
with GRDC are for 2006. Figure 2.5 shows the distribution of the 84 river gauging stations,
the seven water levels of the lakes and reservoir stations and the 19 rainfall stations recorded into
the ZAMWIS website[1] of the Zambezi Watercourse Commission. As a result of the paucity of
data, many previous water resources assessments were conducted with data with coarse resolution.
However, the advent of ICT and remote sensing technologies may prove valuable in enhancing
existing hydrometric data for the Zambezi River Basin. It is worth noting that the inadequacy
of hydrometric data hampers efforts to better manage water resources in the basin.

Surface water resources

Surface water resources in the Zambezi River Basin comprise the Zambezi itself and its tributaries, Lake Kariba, and the reservoir at Cahora Bassa Dam. The basin comprises the following key subbasins: the Upper Zambezi Region, the Manyame Catchment (which forms part of the Tete subbasin), the Shire subbasin, and the Songwe and Ruhuhu Catchments, which empty their waters into Lake Nyasa/Malawi (Figure 2.2).

Rainfall gradients in the basin show a decreasing trend from the north to the south, resulting in most river flows generated from a few selected subbasins in the north. The runoff from the Upper Zambezi, Luangwa, Shire/Lake Nyasa/Malawi and Tete subbasins (600,985 ha, or 43% of total basin area) accounts for about 66 per cent of total runoff in the basin (Figure 2.7). The Shire River and its tributaries are more of an independent system covering the entire Malawi, the most densely populated country of all the riparian nations. The biggest contributor to river flow from Upper Zambezi, together with five other subbasins, produces the flows to Victoria Falls with the world's largest single sheet of falling water, and Lake Kariba further downstream, the world's largest man-made lake and reservoir by volume.

Groundwater resources

While extraction of groundwater by volume is much lower than that of surface water, groundwater is a vital resource for social, economic and environmental sustainability across the

Figure 2.6 Surface water flow below Sioma Falls, Zambia
Photo: Richard Beilfuss

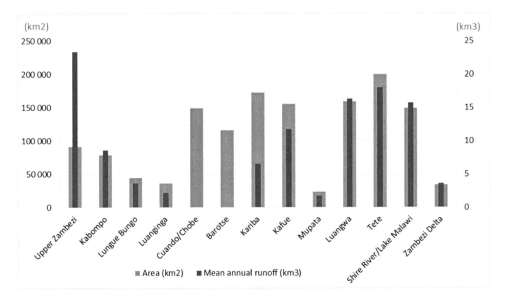

Figure 2.7 Subbasin areas and mean annual runoff values
Source: Adapted from SADC and ZRA (2008)

eight riparian states of the basin. Human welfare, livelihoods, food security, ecosystems, industries and growing urban areas are directly reliant on groundwater. However, information on groundwater in the basin is usually limited and disseminated inside countries, and can only support an overview of the resource potential (Euroconsult Mott MacDonald 2007).

The occurrence of groundwater is determined by the lithology of geological material, regional geological structure, geomorphology of landforms and the availability of recharge sources. There are four major types of aquifers in the Zambezi Basin shown in Figure 2.8, listed below and summarised in Table 2.1:

i   the Kalahari Sand,
ii   the basement granites and gneiss,
iii   the consolidated sedimentary (limestone, dolomites, quartzite, shales and sandstone) and,
iv   the alluvial sediments.

The Kalahari Sand corresponds to loosely consolidated sandstones and unconsolidated sands and silts. In Angola, groundwater goes deeper in the south where the Kalahari Group is typically dry. The thickness of the aquifer is generally about 40 to 50 m but over 100 m in South Angola. The basement granites and gneiss cover most of the Zambezi Basin outcropping in the eastern part of the basin. Groundwater can be found in the fractured and weathered area of the basement. Productivity is generally low to moderate in the second porosity areas. The consolidated sedimentary rocks (limestone, dolomites, quartzite, shales and sandstone) are located in the central part of the basin. These, especially the dolomites, are the most productive aquifers, which are the water sources of main cities such as Lusaka. The alluvial sediments are present in the valley and lakeshore. Productivity is variable and depends on the composition of the sediment layer. In addition, other aquifers exist in the metasediments, igneous complexes and volcanic material found along the northeastern boundaries of the basin in Zambia in the Luangwa subbasin and southeastern sections of the basin in Zimbabwe along the Kariba subbasin.

While the quality of groundwater resources is generally acceptable for domestic consumption, water quality problems exist and are mainly associated with high salinities, especially where the hydraulic gradients are very low. Other groundwater quality problems associated with drinking water supply within the basin include the presence of iron, sulphate and fluoride concentrations above acceptable limits.

Table 2.1 Summary of the hydrogeology of the Zambezi Basin adapted from Bee Pee (Pty) Ltd. and SRK Consulting (Pty) Ltd. (2002), Euroconsult Mott MacDonald (2007) and Earthwise-BGS[2]

Main aquifer type	Main geological formations (geological period)	Description	Location	Productivity	Water quality
Kalahari Sand	Kalahari group (tertiary to quaternary)	Unconsolidated to semi-consolidated and intergranular sand, gravel and silts with local duricrusts	Western part of the Zambezi Basin	Good productivity 0.2 to 5 l/s; sometimes, 10 l/s	Low level of mineralisation; sometimes, brackish
Basement granites and gneiss	Basement complex rocks (Precambrian)	Metasedimentary rocks and crystalline igneous and metamorphic rocks largely granites, gneiss and gabbros with some quartz veins	Central and eastern part of the Zambezi Basin (Shire Luangwa, Tete, Kariba *et al.* Mupata subbasin)	Generally low productivity except in fractured and/ or weathered areas and in zones of quartz vein and basic rocks 0.2 to 2 l/s	Generally, good quality; sometimes acid
Consolidated sedimentary	Katanga supergroup Karoo supergroup (neoproterozoic to Jurassic)	Limestone, dolomite, quartzite, shale and sandstone	Kafue subbasin Part of Kabompo subbasin	Generally good productivity ranging from 2 l/s in Shale for up to 80 l/s in dolomite	Generally good quality. Sometimes hard water because of dissolved calcium
Alluvial sedimentary	Alluvial unconsolidated sediments (quaternary)	Unconsolidated alluvial elements infilling valley	Main river channel, old river channels and lake shores plains	Variable potential depending on lithology whether dominated by permeable sands and gravels or low permeability fine grain deposit. Up to 15 l/s	Generally, more mineralized than the basement aquifers. Some salinity issue in the Shire Valley

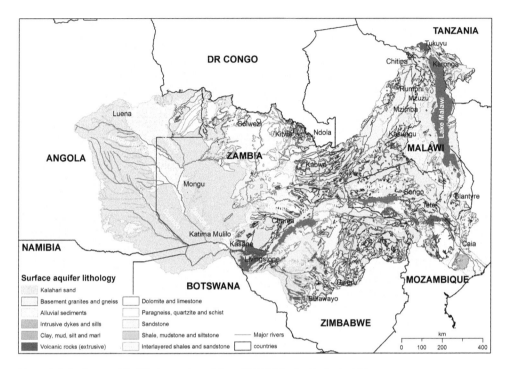

Figure 2.8 Surface aquifer lithology adapted from SADC HydroGeological Map
Source: SADC (2009)

The sustainable groundwater extraction rate potential depends on recharge. Recharge is the portion of water from rainfall (or river or surface water bodies) which infiltrates until reaching the aquifer. Average yearly recharge of the Zambezi Basin over the period 1960–2000 was estimated at 94 mm using the PCR-GLOBWB (Van Beek *et al.* 2011), which is about 130 km^3 – this is more than annual average surface runoff. The yearly recharge ranges from less than 30 mm in the southwest of the basin to more than 100 mm in the delta and in the north and northeast of the basin. Table 2.2 summarises country-wise recharge data.

The 10 transboundary aquifers of the Zambezi Basin are described in Table 2.3. The AF14 is the 'most shared' aquifer – shared by five countries, while Zambia shares five aquifers with

Table 2.2 Recharge estimation over the period 1960–2000; adapted from Van Beek *et al.* (2011)

	Recharge range (mm)	Mean recharge (mm)	Recharge (km^3)
Angola	3–318	96	25.1
Botswana	1–10	6	0.1
Malawi	67–410	172	18.7
Mozambique	6–345	115	17.8
Namibia	0–20	14	0.2
Tanzania	137–232	185	5.1
Zambia	0–231	97	55.8
Zimbabwe	1–138	34	7.5
Total mean annual recharge volume in the basin			130.3

Table 2.3 Transboundary aquifers in the Zambezi Basin, adapted from Altchenko and Villholth (2013) and IGRAC (2015)

Label (category)	Aquifer name	Sharing country	Total area (km²)³	Population estimation (inhabitant)	Aquifer type	Average rainfall range (mm/year)	Annual recharge (WHYMAP)
AF12 (II)	Eastern Kalahari Karoo Basin	Botswana Zimbabwe	34,333	54,300	Upper Karoo Sandstone	400–600	Very low to medium
AF14 (II)	Nata Karoo Subbasin/ Caprivi Deep-seated Aquifer	Angola Botswana Namibia Zambia Zimbabwe	79,490	195,000	Ecca sequence	500–750	Very low to medium
AF16 (I)	Medium Zambezi Aquifer	Zambia Zimbabwe	9,401	50,800	Quaternary and consolidated sedimentary rock	720–780	Very low to medium
AF17 (I)	Shire Valley Alluvial Aquifer	Mozambique Malawi	5,454	527,000	Tertiary/Quaternary	780–900	Medium to very high
AF18 (I)	Arangua Alluvial	Mozambique Zambia	18,718	12,500	Alluvial	700–1,100	Very low to medium
AF19 (I)	Sand and Gravel Aquifer	Malawi Zambia	18,718	12,500	Alluvial intergranular aquifer and weathered basement complex	800–1,200	Very low to very high
AF21 (II)	Karoo Sandstone Aquifer	Mozambique Tanzania	35,689	214,500	Consolidated sedimentary rocks	900–1,700	Medium to very high
AF22 (II)	Kalahari/Katangian Basin/Lualaba	Zambia DRC	7,010	803,000	Katangian and Kalahari sequence	1,200–1,300	High to very high
AF23 (II)	Coango	Angola DRC	328,887	3,000,000	Consolidated sedimentary rocks and alluvial	1,200–1,650	High
AF24 (II)	Weathered Basement	Tanzania Zambia Malawi	112,299	852,000	Weathered basement complex	900–2,000	Medium to very high

its neighbours. Together, these 10 aquifers have a surface area of 654,000 km², 252,000 km² being inside of the Zambezi River Basin, corresponding to about 20 per cent of the total basin area.

Water demand and infrastructure development

Water uses

Water demand in the Zambezi is currently low given the basin's relatively low level of development. About three quarters of the total basin population live in rural areas (ZRA 2008). As per the assessment of water use by Euroconsult Mott MacDonald (2007), the main water demand comes from hydropower through evaporation from the existing dams (mainly Lake Kariba and Cahora Bassa Dam), at about 17 km³. This is followed by irrigation at around 1.5 km³, and environmental requirement and flood releases at 1.2 km³ each (Table 2.4). The overall water use therefore stands at about 20 per cent of the total runoff (of 103 km³). This percentage is nonetheless projected to increase by 2025, reaching 36 per cent of the total runoff based on the following assumptions:

i   Irrigation and hydropower development achieves maximum development.
ii Total runoff remains unchanged.
iii Other consumptions remain at a similar level or with negligible changes compared with overall water resources.

Low and somewhat outdated water infrastructure development is the main constraint for access to water. The basin has significant hydropower potential. The 5,000 megawatts (MW) currently developed reflects less than one-third of the basin's overall potential (see Chapter 3). More than half of the remaining potential is in Mozambique, followed by Zambia and Zimbabwe (Figure 2.9). Water losses through the hydropower dams are already much bigger than all human withdrawals combined. Their impacts on flow regime, sediment, carbon and nutrients are significant. For example, Kunz (2011) concluded that the Itezhi-tezhi Dam alone receives sediment of 330,000 tons/year, and removes up to 50 per cent and 60 per cent of N and P in the river flow. The commissioning of large dams such as Kariba, Cahora Bassa, Itezhi-tezhi and Kafue Gorge have been associated with changes to the ecology (floodplains in particular) and utilisation

Table 2.4 Current and future water use of the basin (adapted from Euroconsult Mott MacDonald 2007)

	Current (2007)		Future (2025)	
	Mm³	%	Mm³	%
Available runoff	103.22	100		
Rural domestic consumption	0.02	0.02	0.04	0.04
Urban domestic consumption	0.18	0.17	0.68	0.65
Industrial consumption	0.03	0.02	0.09	0.08
Mining	0.12	0.12	0.41	0.4
Environmental/flood releases	1.20	1.16	6.45	6.24
Irrigated agriculture	1.48	1.43	6.11	4.49
Livestock	0.11	0.11	0.17	0.16
Hydropower (evaporation)	16.99	16.46	16.99	23.8
Total water use	20.13	19.50	30.93	35.86

of the river system. For example, the population of Kafue lechwe (Kobus kafuensis), a rare semiaquatic antelope, has reduced from 350,000 before 2000 to 30,000 by 2005 (Moore *et al.* 2007). And the construction of Lake Kariba has led to the displacement of 50,000 tribe people.

Other forms of surface water infrastructure are small and scarce. Regional development bodies and countries actively promote a participatory approach to water resources development by investing in different forms of water infrastructure including small storages (SADC *et al.* 2012; 2016). It is estimated that in Zimbabwe there are about 11,000 small dams, of which 5,820 are located in the Zambezi River Basin. This corresponds to a storage capacity estimated at about 4.6 million m^3 (Mm^3) (Sugunan 1997). In Zambia, the estimated storage capacity[4] amounts to about 12 billion m^3 (Bm^3). These small storages are often used for aquaculture, irrigation, livestock and domestic purposes.

Small storages are often constructed, owned and managed by farmers themselves with great flexibility in uses. The Malawi Government actively promoted and developed small dams as alternatives to large dams for irrigation development. Cai *et al.* (2014) examined a small catchment in Zomba District in Malawi (northeast of Blantyre). Using satellite survey, they identified 751 small storages over a stretch of about 50 km^2, reaching a density of 15 storages/km^2. These small storages lose a lot of water to evaporation. Reviewing water balances of a selected pond reveals that they lost some 2,590 mm of water in one year (March 2011–February 2012), of which 2,079 mm are lost as evaporation, and the rest as seepage and deep percolation. However, these small storages are highly flexible in supporting aquaculture and irrigation, which provide nutrient and cash income for some of the poorest farmers in the world. Small storages in the Runde Catchment, central to southeastern parts of Zimbabwe, also

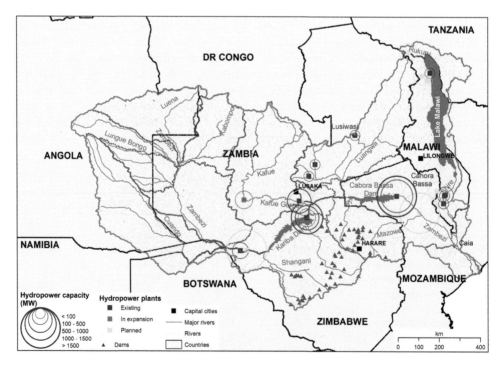

Figure 2.9 Existing and planned hydropower dams in the Zambezi River Basin
Source: SADC *et al.* (2012)

helped small-scale famers cope with competitive demand and inadequate infrastructure, and services provided by Zimbabwe Water Authority (Ruwona 2016). The role of small storages has seen some extensive debates about whether 'small is beautiful' (Nkhoma 2011).

Groundwater use is rapidly increasing in the region. In some areas, water use is already heavily dependent on groundwater, which involves less-complicated legal issues, requires lower initial investment and is relatively accessible in many places. The main users in the Zambezi Basin are cities, agriculture (i.e., irrigation, livestock watering and fisheries), rural households and industries (i.e., mining). Some major city centres, including Lusaka in Zambia and Tete in Mozambique, use groundwater as their main source of water supply. Groundwater, particularly from the basement granites and gneiss, is also suggested to be the main source of rural water supply providing potable water to the rural poor through boreholes fitted with hand pumps (Euroconsult Mott MacDonald 2007). In the northern part of the basin in Tanzania, irrigation is mainly dependent on groundwater because of the good yields in the weathered/fractured basement or the unconsolidated sand and gravel formation.

Groundwater also contributes significantly to the complex and interdependent hydrological processes in the Zambezi Basin. Natural ecosystems, especially those of various types of wetlands, have strong flow-regulating functions, which change the flow regime in the river and act as some types of *natural infrastructure* (McCartney *et al.* 2013). Groundwater plays a critical role in maintaining baseflow, which sustains the healthy functions of ecosystems, including wetlands, in the dry season.

There are various technologies for utilising groundwater such as solar-powered pumping, treadle pumps, along with large electric pump houses. Groundwater use is also frequently linked to dambos (shallow wetlands), which consist of varying degrees of groundwater discharge (Bullock 1992). Natural irrigation by capillarity from dambos is estimated to contribute a significant part of irrigation potential (up to 100,000 ha) in the Zambezi Basin (FAO 1997). The various approaches represent not only opportunities in groundwater development but also challenges in regulations, energy supply and sustainable management of water resources.

A demand–supply gap

At country level, four out of the eight riparian countries in the Zambezi are already below the Falkenmark stress line of 1,700 m^3/capita. Tanzania and Botswana have 1,621 and 1,081 m^3/person/year, respectively, while Malawi and Zimbabwe each has only 967 and 804 m^3/person/year, respectively (FAO AQUASTAT, accessed on 12 May 2016). Malawi, with a relatively small geographic area, has the highest population density in the region (Figure 2.10), which explains why it is the most water-stressed country in spite of large portions of Lake Nyasa/Malawi and the biggest tributary, the Shire River, in its territory.

Strong seasonality in the rainfall distribution and erratic changes, exacerbated by the lack of infrastructure, often cause a severe shortage of water in the riparian countries. The worst of such cases is recurring droughts, which cause widespread famine (Masih *et al.* 2014). Chronic shortage of water has major impacts on food security, economic development and livelihoods for rural population, and health and sanitation problems for city dwellers.

The riparian countries have set up ambitious goals to transform national agriculture, and convert more land into irrigated areas. The World Bank (2010) assessed the present irrigation area at approximately 259,000 ha/year. They estimated that under a high-level development scenario, the basin's irrigated area could vastly expand, particularly in the Kariba, Shire/Lake Malawi and Tete subbasins. This potential additional irrigation could require more than 15 km^3 of water delivered to the field. In a separate and previous approach, FAO (1997) estimated the

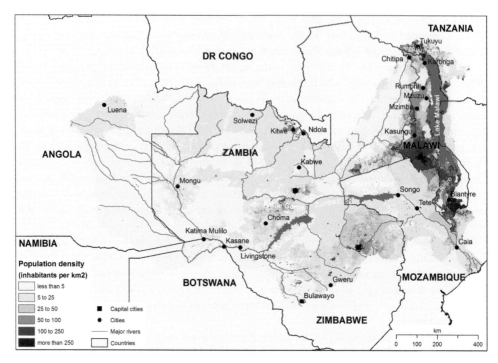

Figure 2.10 Basin population density in 2010
Source: Adapted from WorldPop (2015)[5]

irrigation potential to be 3.2 million ha, with a gross potential irrigation water requirement of 37 km³/year. The FAO estimate does not include groundwater potential, while the World Bank estimate was not specific. Achieving such development requires continued investments in water infrastructure to store, divert and apply water to crops.

Altchenko and Villholth (2015) estimated that there was 38.5 km³ of groundwater available for irrigation across the basin, which is calculated considering other groundwater uses (i.e., domestic, livestock and industrial) and that 70 per cent of the groundwater recharge returns to the environment. The irrigation potential using groundwater alone is estimated to be 2.55 million ha (Figure 2.11). Table 2.5 presents the current groundwater irrigation use at national scale and the calculated groundwater irrigation potential inside the Zambezi Basin. There is need not only for further investigation to understand the potential of groundwater for irrigation but also for other water uses, particularly the role of conjunctive use of surface water and underground water.

Floods and droughts under climate change

The basin is often affected by storms carried by tropical cyclones from the Indian Ocean, which have shown increasing frequency and magnitude over the past decade and, as a consequence, increase in the frequency of floods and droughts in the basin (SARDC and HBS 2010). This may be explained by a shift in trajectories and landfall locations of cyclones, which are becoming more intense, and causing exponentially increasing damage. Areas subject to frequent flooding include Lower Shire in Malawi, Caprivi in Namibia (eastern part of Namibia at the border

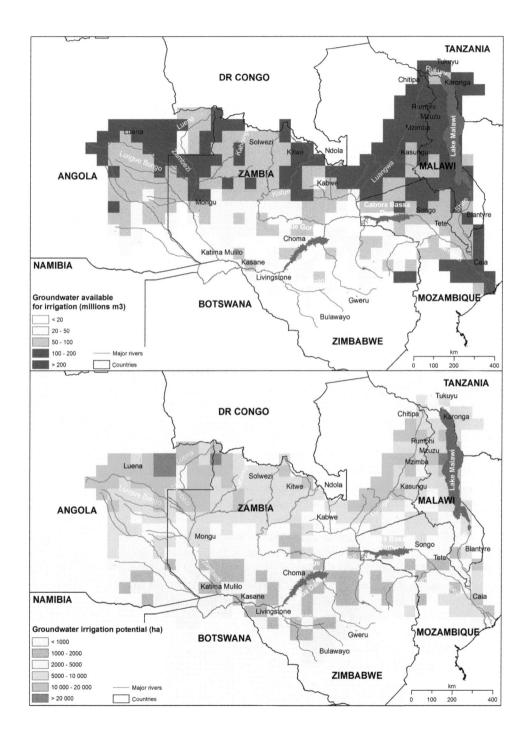

Figure 2.11 Groundwater available for irrigation and groundwater irrigation potential

Source: Adapted from Altchenko and Villholth (2015)

Table 2.5 Current and potential groundwater irrigation in the Zambezi riparian countries

	Country-level data from Aquastat database, (FAO)[6]			Data inside the Zambezi Basin adapted from Altchenko and Villholth (2015)	
	Percentage of the cultivated area equipped for irrigation (%)	Total area equipped for irrigation by groundwater (thousand ha)	Percentage of area equipped for irrigation by groundwater to total area equipped for irrigation (%)	Water available for irrigation (km³)	Potential area irrigable with groundwater (thousand ha)
Angola	2.3	17.1	19.99	7.5	729.3
Botswana	0.6	0.6	44.32	0.03	1.6
Malawi	2.3	0.015	0.05	5.4	248.5
Mozambique	2.5	0.6	0.54	5.3	247.3
Namibia	0.9	1.6	21.5	0.1	3.1
Tanzania	1.8	0.4	0.21	1.5	66.2
Zambia	6.0	6.8	4.3	16.5	1152.2
Zimbabwe	4.3	20	11.5	2.1	114.8
Sum	–	47.115	–	38.43	2563

with Zimbabwe), the Zambezi Delta in Mozambique, the Muzarabani District in the northeast of Zimbabwe and the Kazungula District in the south of Zambia. Major floods in the Zambezi Basin were reported in 1981–1982, 1986–1987, 1991–1992, 1994–1995 and 2001–2002, while floods ravaged parts of the basin in 1999–2000, 2005–2006 and 2007 (SARDC and HBS 2010).

A detailed assessment of floods in the Barotse floodplain reveals a worrying trend. Using satellite images with field-observed/-surveyed data, Cai *et al.* (2014) found that in the period 1982 to 2014, the flooding patterns of the large conservation area changed in terms of timing, duration, frequency and magnitude, all of which cause increasing damage to food production, assets and livelihoods of the local population.

The region also suffers from recurring droughts leading to crop failure, shortage in city supply, loss of livestock and consequently famine. Droughts in southern Africa occur mostly during the warm phase of El Niño Southern Oscillation, although it cannot be predicted based on El Niño alone. The most recent drought in year 2015–2016, affecting the entire of southern and eastern Africa, caused major food insecurity (World Food Program 2016), while the region's preparedness for such events is low.

Compounding matters, droughts are often not properly documented in Zambezi riparian countries. Masih *et al.* (2014), for example, reviewed 291 historic droughts across the African continent and found no evidence of droughts in the Zambezi and its riparian countries. Localised small droughts caused by dry spells often go unnoticed but pose major threats to household food security, and income generation for the rural population.

The fifth report of the IPCC (Intergovernmental Panel on Climate Change) (2014) projected increasing frequencies and magnitude of floods and droughts in the region. The rainfall total is projected to decrease but with increasing variability, which is characterised with more extreme rainfall events and longer dry spells. Such changes require an increase in flood protection levels, and a shift in cropping practices with more irrigated agriculture, and/or changes in crop types and calendar to be able to adapt to the rainfall changes.

Water resources management

Rapid economic development in most parts of the basin calls for greater attention to the use of natural resources including water. Integrated water resources management (IWRM) strategies have long been promoted as the basis of all planning (SADC and ZRA 2008). Countries have also been regularly producing water resources master plans. There are, however, rarely assessments into actual progress against the proposed plans. Expectations are that many of them are not adequately implemented due to a variety of factors such as lack of investment and technical and capacity constraints. At basin level this may also be attributed to lack of effective institutional mechanisms to enable cooperative decision-making in transboundary investments.

The high standards required as conditions by international financing institutions may also become obstacles for the limited projects that are funded. Bank loans are often accompanied by a rigorous checklist of conditions. While these may provide many benefits on social and environmental safeguards, there may be need to strike a balance between checklists and development. Blind application of checklists – well-intentioned though they may be – may indeed hinder development progress and create conditions that encourage developers to by-pass such standards, leading to unsustainable regional development. Investment projects, big or small, tend to be short-lived due to various reasons, but lack of contextualisation in local settings is certainly an important factor.

In 2007, the African Ministers' Council on Water (AMCOW) recommended that transboundary groundwater should be managed by the river basin organisations (RBOs), which have an important role as custodians of shared waters, with the added advantage and options for further integration of the management of all hydrological resources in the same entity (Altchenko and Villholth 2013). However, most of the RBOs in Africa do not have the financial and technical capacity, let alone authority, to take the responsibility of transboundary groundwater management. Their spatial mandate, defined by surface hydrology, does not align with most of the geographical sphere of the transboundary aquifers. This is certainly true for ZAMCOM, which has yet to incorporate significant actionable items on groundwater in its monitoring, basin planning and management.

Recent development on the nexus approaches highlights challenges and opportunities. Countries have the opportunity to link water-sector investments with other broad development needs including food production, energy and environmental conservations. Such integrated developments, much broader than IWRM, are complex in nature and successful experience is rare. They also tend to be associated with increasing difficulty on funding large-scale cross-sector infrastructure. The benefits of doing so are clear, however. Such approaches facilitate smart investments that reduce duplications across sectors, and improve efficiency and effectiveness with increasing returns to limited financial resources.

Successful, technically focused cooperation is observed at scales within the basin. ZRA is such an example that oversees operations of the Kariba Dam and contributes to knowledge generation on many topics related to the Zambezi River Basin. While conflicts on competing demands for water are still low in the basin, information and data-sharing (upstream and downstream) will certainly help predict and cope with devastating floods, and improve overall planning and coordination.

Conclusions

The Zambezi is a shared river basin with largely unused water resources at present. The water resources estimates are more than double when groundwater is included, increasing the total water availability doubles from 103 km^3 to 233 km^3. Food security and economic development of the basin population increases pressure on water management to boost agriculture, fisheries, livestock and energy production. In line with the general trend in SSA, the SADC region aims to double its irrigation while the Sustainable Development Goals, still in their development stage, set a suite of global targets to make the best use of water for development, health and nutrition, and ecosystems.

Infrastructure development is a key strategy in managing Zambezi's water resources for economic development and mitigating impacts of extreme events associated with water. Smart investment in infrastructure is required for truly integrated cross-sector development, so that the limited investment capacity can most effectively benefit the wider economy. There are usually many strategies and investment plans existing with different departments. There is a great need and opportunity to bring together strategies and plans on food security, water security and energy security. Further, consideration of ecosystem services represents new opportunities and identifies areas of joint investment. Smart investment indeed includes *natural infrastructure*, which is abundant in the basin in the form of wetlands, forests, and savannah biome and other natural vegetation, which, if appropriately incorporated into planning and operation, could greatly reduce the scale and costs of built infrastructure and contribute to the management of floods and droughts. Ultimately, the potentially complex planning processes around such integration, however, also require careful consideration that draws on innovative data solutions. Smart investment also needs to mobilise the public and private sector for pursuit of options at all scales – from large dams to basin transfer, to small communal and private ponds/small storages. Small storages, often invested in by local communities with marginal capacity compared to large dams, have huge potential to jump-start effective water resources development and build up community resilience.

Conjunctive use of surface water and groundwater will change the way we manage water. Institutions and know-how for groundwater use are still largely absent in the Zambezi Basin. Groundwater development may increasingly add opportunities that, in some cases, renders basin and catchment delineation obsolete as aquifers often do not match with the boundaries of a catchment. Specifically, actions are needed to

i   increase the capacity, knowledge base and monitoring of groundwater resources; data and knowledge on groundwater in the Zambezi Basin are very limited, much more so than the limited knowledge on surface water;

ii   incorporate groundwater in the planning of investment and management at all levels, from communities, to countries, to ZAMCOM;

iii encourage private-sector participation as opposed to the often-centralised approach to surface water management.

Acknowledgements

The authors acknowledge the financial support of the CGIAR research programmes on Water, Land and Ecosystems (WLE), and Climate Change, Agriculture and Food Security (CCAFS). Thanks are also due to Nienke Ansems from IGRAC for contributing to the transboundary aquifer map.

Notes

1 http://zamwis.zambezicommission.org/
2 www.earthwise.bgs.ac.uk
3 Sinusoidal World Projection
4 www.hcb.co.mz/eng/The-Zambezi-Basin/Dams
5 www.worldpop.org.uk/data/summary/?contselect=Africa&countselect=Whole+Continent&typeselect =Population+2010
6 www.fao.org/nr/water/aquastat/data/query/results.html

References

Acres, B.D., Rains, A.B., King, R.B., Lawton, R.M., Mitchell, A.J.B. and Rackham, L.J. 1985. African dambos: Their distribution characteristics and use. *Zeitschrift für Geomorphologie* 52: 63–86.

Altchenko, Y. and Villholth, K.G. 2013. Transboundary aquifer mapping and management in Africa: A harmonised approach. *Hydrogeology Journal* 21(7): 1497–1517.

Altchenko, Y. and Villholth, K.G. 2015. Mapping irrigation potential from renewable GW in Africa – a quantitative hydrological approach. *Hydrology Earth Systems Science* 19: 1055–1067. Doi:10.5194/hess-19-1055-2015.

Bee Pee (Pty) Ltd. and SRK Consulting (Pty) Ltd. 2002. *Compilation of the hydrogeological map atlas in SADC, Situation Analysis Report.* Gaborone, Botswana.

Bullock, A. 1992. Dambo hydrology in southern Africa—review and reassessment. *Journal of Hydrology* 134(1): 373–396.

Cai, X., Kam, S.P., Yen, B.T., Sood, A. and Chu Thai, H. 2014. *CaWAT – A catchment water allocation tool for integrated irrigation and aquaculture development in small watersheds.* New York: CUNY Academic Works.

Cai, X., Haile, A.T., Magidi, J., Mapedza, E. and Nhamo, L. 2016. Living with floods – Household perception and satellite observations in the Barotse floodplain, Zambia. *Physics and Chemistry of the Earth, Parts A/B/C* (in press).

Euroconsult Mott MacDonald. 2007. *Rapid assessment-final report: Integrated water resources management strategy for the Zambezi River Basin.* Lusaka, Zambia: SADC-WD/Zambezi River Authority.

FAO (Food and Agricultural Organization of the United Nations). 1997. *Irrigation potential in Africa: A basin approach.* Rome: FAO Land and Water Development Division.

Hijmans, R.J., Cameron, S.E., Parra, J.L., Jones, P.G. and Jarvis, A. 2005. Very high resolution interpolated climate surfaces for global land areas. *International Journal of Climatology* 25: 1965–1978.

IGRAC (International Groundwater Resources Assessment Centre). 2015. Transboundary aquifers of the world – Special edition for the 7th World Water Forum 2015. Available at www.un-igrac.org/download/file/fid/179 (accessed on 10 November 2015).

IPCC (Intergovernmental Panel on Climate Change). 2014. Climate change 2014: Impacts, adaptation, and vulnerability. In: *Contribution of Working Group II to the Fifth Assessment Report of the Intergovernmental Panel on Climate Change,* (eds.), Field, C.B., Barros, V.R., Dokken, D.J., Mach, K.J., Mastrandrea, M.D., Bilir, T.E., Chatterjee, M., Ebi, K.L., Estrada, Y.O., Genova, R.C., Girma, B., Kissel, E.S., Levy, A.N., MacCracken, S., Mastrandrea, P.R. and White, L.L. Cambridge, United Kingdom and New York, NY, USA: Cambridge University Press.

IWMI (International Water Management Institute). 2015. *Flood risks analysis of the Barotse floodplain.* Project report submitted to CGIAR Research Programme Aquatic Agricultural Systems. Pretoria, South Africa.

Kunz, Manuel, J. 2011. Effect of large dams in the Zambezi River Basin: Changes in sediment, carbon and nutrient fluxes. PhD thesis. Zurich, Switzerland: ETH.

Masih, I., Maskey, S., Mussá, F.E.F. and Trambauer, P. 2014. A review of droughts on the African continent: A geospatial and long-term perspective. *Hydrology Earth Systems Science* 18: 3635–3649.

McCartney, M., Cai, X. and Smakhtin, V. 2013. *Evaluating the flow regulating functions of natural ecosystems in the Zambezi Basin.* IWMI Research Report 148. Colombo, Sri Lanka: IWMI.

Moore, A.E., Cotterill, F.P.D., Main, M.P.L. and Williams, H.B. 2007. The Zambezi River. In: *Large rivers: Geomorphology and management,* (ed.), Gupta, A. Chichester, UK: John Wiley & Sons, Ltd.

Nkhoma, B.G. 2011. The politics, development and problems of small irrigation dams in Malawi: Experiences from Mzuzu ADD. *Water Alternatives* 4(3): 383–398.

Ruwona, P. 2016. Competing for water: The role of small storages for irrigation development in southern Africa. Case of Runde Catchment in Zimbabwe. Master's thesis. Delft, Netherlands: UNESCO-IHE.

SADC (South African Development Community). 2009. *Explanatory brochure for the South African Development Community (SADC) Hydrogeological Map & Atlas*, p. 61. Gaborone, Botswana.

SADC. 2016. *Regional Strategic Action Plan (RSAP) IV on Integrated Water Resources Development and Management (2016–2020)*. Gaborone, Botswana.

SADC, SARDC (Southern African Research and Documentation Centre), ZAMCOM (Zambezi River Commission), GRID-Arenda (Global Resource Information Database in Arendal, Norway) and UNEP (United Nations Environment Programme). 2012. *Zambezi River Basin Atlas of the Changing Environment*, p. 131. Gaborone, Harare and Arendal.

SADC and ZRA (Zambesi River Authority). 2008. *Integrated water resources management strategy and implementation plan for the Zambezi Basin*. Lusaka, Zambia.

SARDC and Heinrich Böll Stiftung (HBS) 2010. *Responding to climate change impacts: Adaptation and mitigation strategies as practised in the Zambezi River Basin*. Harare and Cape Town: SARDC and HBS.

Sugunan, V.V. 1997. *Fisheries management of small water bodies in seven countries in Africa, Asia and Latin America*. Rome, Italy: FAO Fisheries Circular No. 933 FIRI/C933.

Tumbare, M.J. 2004. *The Zambezi River, its threats and opportunities*. Harare, Zimbabwe: Zambezi River Authority.

Van Beek, L.P.H., Wada, Y. and Bierkens, M.F.P. 2011. Global monthly water stress: 1. Water balance and water availability. *Water Resources Research* 47, W07517.

World Bank. 2010. *The Zambezi River Basin: A multi-sector investment opportunities analysis*. Washington, DC, USA.

World Food Program. 2016. El Niño set to have a devastating impact on southern Africa's harvests and food security. Available at www.wfp.org/news/news-release/el-nino-set-have-devastating-impact-southern-africas-harvests-and-food-security. (accessed on 18 March 2016).

ZAMCOM (Zambezi Watercourse Commission), SADC (Southern African Development Community) and SARDC (Southern African Research Documentation Centre). 2015. *Zambezi environmental outlook 2015*. Harare, Gaborone.

Zomer, R.J., Trabucco, A., Bossio, D.A., van Straaten, O. and Verchot, L.V. 2008. Climate change mitigation: A spatial analysis of global land suitability for clean development mechanism afforestation and reforestation. *Agric. Ecosystems and Envir.* 126: 67–80.

ZRA (Zambesi River Authority). 2008. Transboundary issues on sustainable hydropower development in the Zambezi River Basin in the eyes of the Zambezi River Authority, A ZRA presentation at the Ministry of Energy and Water Development, Zambia, Hydropower Sustainability Assessment Forum Meeting: 4 September 2008, Kafue Gorge Regional Training Center.

3

The economic potential of the basin

Amaury Tilmant and Regassa Namara

Key messages

- The total GDP of the Zambezi Basin was estimated to be USD22 billion in 2005 and is projected to be about USD66 billion in 2025, which is equivalent to USD1,500 per capita. This per capita income level falls in the lower-middle income category according to the

World Bank's income classification categories. Major economic benefits are enabled by the Kariba and Cahora Bassa Reservoirs, as well as the Itezhi-tezhi and Kafue Gorge Reservoirs on the Kafue Tributary. The economic value that can be placed on irrigation and hydropower derived from these large storage infrastructures is around USD1.27 billion per year.

• On average, the potential benefits that can be harnessed from hydropower and irrigation in the Zambezi System are worth at least USD2.6 billion per year. The value of these benefits is twice as large as the value currently tapped.

• In order to make informed decisions about the basin's optimal future, it is critical to expand knowledge on the current and potential value of such water-related activities as navigation, fisheries, tourism and productive use of wetlands.

• Basin-wide management efforts may seek to foster research that measures economic value of different water uses; promote minimum flow thresholds that preserve economic activities until their value is better understood and quantified; and propose integrated approaches that counterbalance the conventional heavy economic emphasis on hydropower.

Introduction

The Zambezi Basin is widely viewed to hold vast and lucrative economic potential. Tumbare and the Zambezi River Authority (2004) highlighted the Zambezi's tremendous opportunities for sustainable growth and investment in hydropower development, interbasin water transfer schemes, regional power interconnectors and energy trading, and tourism and wetlands utilisation. The World Bank *Multi-Sector Investment Opportunities Analysis* (World Bank 2010) noted how the basin's rich resources provide ample opportunity for development of irrigation and hydropower. Beck and Bernauer (2011) point to the existence of many development possibilities in the basin.

While it is clear that the Zambezi's resources can bring numerous benefits, the reality is that such benefits have hardly been tapped at present. Economic potential refers to the amount of economically viable renewable generation that is available in an area (Brown *et al.* 2016). Typically, it implies that available resources have not been fully developed or exploited as yet. Harnessing the economic potential of water resources is usually achieved through investment in infrastructure, though other considerations such as coordinated management are also relevant.

The aim of this chapter is to quantify the economic benefits that can be harnessed from the use of the Zambezi's water resources. This chapter therefore reviews the current and anticipated economic benefits derived from water use in the Zambezi River Basin, and considers ways to enhance progress toward realising this potential. The chapter adds value to previous work on economic development in the Zambezi by exploring the role of basin-level management, and ZAMCOM in particular, in unlocking the basin's economic potential. The next section describes the historical background and current drivers of water use in the basin. The potential benefits to large water uses (hydropower, irrigation and the environment) associated with integrated development are then identified, followed by exploration of economic potential in individual sectors. A discussion section considers how basin-level management may contribute toward achieving the basin's economic potential. The chapter concludes with recommendations on how ZAMCOM may engage to promote progress toward realisation of the basin's economic potential.

History and drivers of water use in the Zambezi

Before focusing on the basin's economic potential that has not been tapped, it should be acknowledged that important development has taken place in the twentieth century – primarily driven by the energy sector. It started with a run-of-river power station commissioned at Victoria Falls in 1938. In the 1950s, the intensification of copper mining activities in Northern Rhodesia (Zambia) helped to drive the Kariba Project, a hydropower dam located a few hundred kilometres downstream of Victoria Falls, at the border between Northern Rhodesia (Zambia) and Southern Rhodesia (Zimbabwe). In the 1960s, the Zambian government began planning the Kafue Power Plant, a high-head power station located downstream of the Kafue Flats, a huge cover of wetlands of approximately 6,500 km². At the same time, in Mozambique, the Portuguese government initiated a massive hydroelectric project: the 2,075 megawatts (MW) Cahora Bassa Scheme. During that period, irrigation activities were burgeoning in the Zambian and Zimbabwean portions of the basin. These projects and activities have, no doubt, resulted in important benefits to the countries and the region: Kariba and Cahora Bassa, for example, remain two of the region's largest and most critical sources of energy. And irrigation remains critical to the livelihoods and economies of several basin countries.

Past efforts to translate the Zambezi's waters into economic benefits were not without costs. Because hydroelectric projects were planned and then operated without much consideration for their environmental and social impacts, flood recession agriculture and other human uses of ecosystems were seriously affected by the alteration of the flow regime. This issue was compounded by the lack of coordination between the riparian countries and the resulting cumulative impacts, which contributed to the decline of some of the major wetlands in the region (Turpie *et al*. 1999; Mumba and Thompson 2005; Chansa and Kampamba 2010; Beilfuss and Brown 2010). Fifty years of developments driven by the power sector in the Zambezi have now given rise to a temporal trade-off: there is enough water to produce energy and to sustain the ecosystems but the timing of the respective demands does not coincide. Ecosystems need a flood pulse during the high-flow season, and the dam managers may seek to minimise reservoir outflows in order to refill for the next dry season. As explained in Chapter 5, alterations to the reservoir-operating schedules could, in principle, mitigate adverse ecological impacts but at a cost of reduced power output.

The major drivers of water use in the Zambezi River Basin no doubt extend beyond objectives of tapping the basin's economic potential for energy and agricultural production. Looking forward, drivers can be divided into three broad groupings. These are: (i) economic development, (ii) population growth and urbanisation, and (iv) environmental flow requirements.

Economic development: The total gross domestic product (GDP) of the Zambezi Basin was estimated to be USD22 billion in 2005 and is projected to be about USD66 billion in the year 2025, which is equivalent to USD1,500 per capita.[1] This per capita income level falls in the lower-middle income category according to the World Bank's income classification criteria. To lift the basin population out of poverty and put it on a higher and sustainable income ladder, the basin's water resources are expected to be employed in the production of water-related goods and services. The major economic sectors with water implications include agriculture, mining, tourism, manufacturing, fisheries, navigation and flood protection. Energy is, in turn, an important input into the mining and manufacturing sectors, and is critical to increasing access to electricity among the region's population.

Population growth and urbanisation: The basin countries are characterised by rapid population growth of about 3 per cent per year. The basin's human population is projected to reach 51 million by 2025, about 82 per cent of which will be in just three basin countries, namely Malawi,

Table 3.1 The Zambezi Basin areas and human population by country (SADC/SARDC and others 2012)

Country	Area of the country within the basin (km²)	As % of total area of the basin	As % of total area of the country	Population in the basin in 2010	% of basin population	Population in the basin in 2025	% of basin population
Angola	256,500	18.5	20.5	651,480	1.71	950,080	1.86
Namibia	17,100	1.23	2.1	70,350	0.18	82,438	0.16
Botswana	19,100	1.38	3.3	13,140	0.03	16,500	0.03
Zimbabwe	215,800	15.6	55.2	9,059,850	23.7	11,674,065	22.8
Zambia	577,900	41.6	76.8	8,517,600	22.3	11,979,610	23.4
Tanzania	27,300	1.97	2.9	1,646,400	4.31	2,200,420	4.30
Malawi	110,700	7.97	93.4	13,050,000	34.2	18,071,955	35.3
Mozambique	163,800	11.8	20.5	5,185,600	13.6	6,187,455	12.1

Zambia and Zimbabwe (Table 3.1). The rapid population growth will lead to increased demand for domestic water supply and sanitation services, as well as for food, electricity and jobs. All of these factors may drive and influence the need for greater exploitation of the Zambezi.

The demand for water supply and sanitation services is also fueled by the increasing urbanisation trend in the basin caused by the perception of better economic opportunities in the cities and towns as well as challenges in rural areas. For instance, conflicts and droughts in Mozambique and Angola caused significant migration to urban areas, such as Tete, Mozambique (Figure 3.1), which has continued to grow despite the cessation of hostilities. Consequently, a significant proportion of urban residents in most cities live in unplanned settlements, slums or squatter areas. This phenomenon puts a lot of pressure on the already insufficient urban amenities including water supply and sanitation facilities.

Rapid population growth and urbanisation have increased food demand in a region already beset by food insecurity. The reduced availability of arable land (at least in some sections of the basin) and recurrent and prolonged droughts and floods are a threat to food security. For instance, in Botswana, water scarcity played a role in the decline of the agriculture sector from almost 40 per cent of GDP in the 1960s to only 6 per cent in 2004. In Namibia, water availability is the single greatest factor limiting development. Extreme temporal variability and uneven spatial distribution of water resources constrain livelihoods, particularly for the portion of the population who live in rural areas. This situation calls for intensifying agricultural production through proper water resources development and management interventions.

Figure 3.1 Tete, Mozambique
Photo: Richard Beilfuss

Environmental flow requirements: The Zambezi River and its dense network of tributaries and associated ecosystems constitute one of southern Africa's most important natural resources (Beilfuss 2001). Economic activities that result in water withdrawals must take into account environmental water demands (environmental flows – e-flows), which is the total volume of water (and appropriate hydrological variability mimicking the natural one – in modified rivers) required for maintenance of freshwater ecosystem functions and the services they provide to the basin population. The poorest section of the basin population often relies on aquatic ecosystems services and goods for income and livelihoods. The volume of water required for such purposes is somewhat complex in the Zambezi, varying in space and time. Nonetheless, the 25–30 per cent of mean annual runoff suggested for the Zambezi in the global work of Smakhtin *et al.* (2004) may be considered a conservative assessment.

Integrated development potential: hydropower, irrigation and the environment

As highlighted above, the potential of the Zambezi Basin is immense and the currently developed irrigation and hydropower reflect only a portion of the potential. Many of the currently realised benefits are enabled by the Kariba and Cahora Bassa Reservoirs, which together store about six times the average annual flow at Victoria Falls and twice the average annual discharge flowing to the sea, as well as the Itezhi-tezhi and Kafue Gorge Reservoirs on the Kafue Tributary. The economic value of the storage services associated with these dams is around USD443 million per year.

To identify the potential benefits accruing to hydropower, irrigation and the environment if the basin is fully developed, several management and development scenarios were generated. All scenarios include the power stations and the potential irrigated areas given in Table 3.2.

Table 3.2 Irrigation and hydropower in the basin (Tilmant *et al.* 2012)

Country	Hydropower			Irrigation	
	Name	*Capacity (MW)*	*Existing (E) Planned (P) Extension Planned (EP)*	*Existing area (ha)*	*Potential area (ha)*
Angola	–	–	–	1,989	20,000
Botswana	–	–	–	4	40,000
Malawi	Nkula	279	E	43,987	163,000
	Tedzani		E		
	Kapichira		E		
Mozambique	Boroma	160	P	11,211	49,000
	Mependa	1.5	P		
	Uncua		P		
	Cahorra Bassa	2,925	E/EP		
Namibia	–	–	–	139	15,000
Tanzania	–	–	–	9,070	15,000
Zambia	Itezhi-tezhi	120	P	34,016	117,600
	Kafue Gorge	1,500	EP	–	–
	Victoria Falls	108	E		
	Batoka	1,600	P		
	Kariba	1,980	E/EP		
Zimbabwe				70,850	45,360
Total	–	8,673.5	–	171,266	464,960

Table 3.3 Scenarios

Scenario	Allocation to irrigation	E-flows	Storage	Interpretation
A	Dynamic	No	Yes	Focus on hydropower generation → Energy security
B	Static	Yes	Yes	Focus on irrigated agriculture → Food security
C	Dynamic	Yes	Yes	Water–agriculture–energy–environment nexus
D	Dynamic	No	No	Focus on environmental flows → Environmental integrity

Nonetheless, scenarios differ in three ways: (i) allocation policy for irrigation water; (ii) value attached to environmental flows; and (iii) type of hydroelectric power station (storage versus run-of-river). When it comes to allocating water to the various irrigation demand sites, two different policies were investigated: a static and a dynamic one. As its name indicates, a static policy considers irrigation water as a static asset: farmers receive fixed amounts of water regardless of their economic productivity and the hydrologic status of the system. In other words, this policy reflects a 'food security' concern and would be translated by giving priority to the irrigation sector within each riparian country. If water were considered as a dynamic asset, it would be allocated so as to maximise its productivity; this would also correspond to an economically efficient allocation mechanism. Table 3.3 describes the different scenarios.

Different values for the environmental flows are considered for three of the four scenarios. In scenario A, the value of environmental flows is negligible and ecological services are simply ignored. In this scenario, water is allocated to maximise the benefits from the other two sectors: irrigation and energy. In the second and third scenarios, environmental flows do have a value in February and March in order to force the reservoirs to release more water during the high-flow season and to mimic the natural hydrological regime. The extent to which the hydrological regime can be restored will depend on the value attached to those environmental flows. Based on preliminary runs (Tilmant *et al.* 2010), a value of USD10/1,000 m^3 is given to environmental flows.

Finally, scenario D focuses on environmental integrity by preserving the natural hydrological regime. This is done by replacing all the storage power plants in the system by run-of-river ones. In this imaginary scenario, the absence of storage capacity implies that river discharges are not altered by the power stations and that the impact of the energy sector on the wetlands is minimal. This scenario is, of course, not realistic (the huge reservoirs do exist), but the comparison with other scenarios will help to assess the economic value of storage in the Zambezi.

On average, the potential benefits that can be harnessed through realisation of planned water infrastructure in the Zambezi are around USD2.6 billion per year, with the lion's share (95 per cent) attributed to hydropower. Compared to the current situation, the increase in net benefits is substantial (Figure 3.2). Variation in aggregate benefits across scenarios A, B and C is not as great as one might think; indeed, all three scenarios net greater than USD2.3 billion.

The maximum potential for hydropower generation would be achieved in scenario A only if the riparian countries agree to forgo 28 per cent of the maximum potential net benefits from irrigated agriculture. Comparing scenario B to A provides an estimate of the benefits forgone by the hydropower sector should priority be given to the irrigation sector. In a dynamic allocation scheme, farmers directly compete with downstream power stations and, since they are mostly non-rival water users, their water demands can be summed vertically, meaning that the water value for power generation can become quite high compared to that of irrigated agriculture. If priority is given to agriculture, then this mechanism no longer works and farmers receive

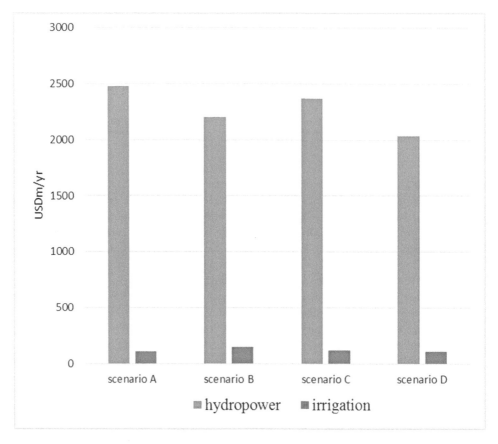

Figure 3.2 Annual average benefits
Source: Authors

their annual entitlements independently of their productivity. With less water available for the power stations, the reduction in net benefits is the opportunity cost associated with the complete development of all irrigation demand sites.

Scenario C is located between B and A by attempting to restore a flow regime in the largest wetlands. Comparison between scenarios A and C reveals the impacts of environmental flows on the production of hydroelectricity and on the number of irrigated hectares that could be developed in the basin. Satisfying environmental flows in a hydropower-dominated basin – depending on implementation – may reduce the power producers' flexibility, that is to say, their ability to adjust power generation, and may also affect the amount of energy that can be generated by altering the drawdown refill cycle.

In scenario D, the storage power plants are replaced by run-of-river ones. In that case, the Zambezi could produce roughly 80 and 70 per cent of the maximum potential benefits in both sectors. The comparison between points A and D shows that downstream irrigation (e.g., in Mozambique) does not benefit from the regulation capacity of this infrastructure. In both cases, about 73 per cent of the potential maximum irrigation benefits can be achieved, indicating that the irrigation sector is independent of the three largest man-made reservoirs in the basin.

Hydropower

Hydropower is a dominant water use in the Zambezi River Basin. The hydropower potential of the Zambezi is sizeable. Currently, the installed capacity is about 5,000 MW – adding Victoria Falls (108 MW), Kariba (1,320 MW), Kafue Gorge (900 MW), Cahora Bassa (2,075 MW) and the cascade of three run-of-river power plants in the Shire River Basin (Tilmant and Kinzelbach 2012; Tilmant *et al.* 2012). The combined capacity of the various projects on the drawing board is at least 13,000 MW (World Bank 2010). The average annual production of future projects is about 33 million megawatt hours (MWh). Assuming a conservative value of USD 60 per MWh, the annual value of that energy is close to USD2 billion. Mozambique has the lion's share of hydropower potential, followed by Zambia, Zimbabwe and Malawi (Table 3.4).

The current energy demand for riparian countries is estimated to be 48 million MWh per year. About 90 per cent of this demand can be satisfied if the full hydropower development potential of the Zambezi Basin is realised. Although hydropower generation is often considered as a non-consumptive water use, the extent of the annual evaporation losses (17 km³) from the large reservoirs in the Zambezi makes it the largest water use in the basin (Euroconsult Mott MacDonald 2007). Yet, despite the importance of the evaporation losses, man-made reservoirs play a key role in the production of hydroelectricity in the Zambezi. The economic value of the storage services, that is to say, the ability to move water from the wet to the dry season, corresponds to some USD443 million each year (Tilmant *et al.* 2012).

Three countries, Mozambique, Zambia and Zimbabwe, have plans to further develop their hydropower potential through new power stations or extensions of existing ones. At the time of writing, Mozambique was about to start construction of the Mphanda Nkuwa project on the Zambezi main stem, some 60 km downstream of Cahora Bassa. This is a 1,300 MW run-of-river power plant, which is expected to be operational in 2017. In Zambia, progress is being made towards the construction of the 750 MW Kafue Gorge Lower Power Plant, another run-of-river plant located downstream from the tailrace tunnel outlet of the Kafue Gorge project. The construction of a 360 MW extension of Kariba North was completed in 2013, while the 300 MW extension of Kariba South in Zimbabwe was initiated in 2014. These projects will add more than 2,700 MW to the electrical grid.

In the medium-term time-horizon, Batoka Gorge and the extension of Cahora Bassa seem to be the most promising projects. The first is a bilateral project under the umbrella of the Zambezi River Authority (ZRA). The project, which would be located 50 km downstream of Victoria Falls, includes a new dam and a 1,600 MW power plant. The extension of Cahora Bassa is an 850 MW project on the left bank of the Zambezi River.

Needless to say, the potential for hydropower development will be increasingly realised. Realising this potential is key not just for basin riparians but for the region since hydropower in the Zambezi is key for the stability of the Southern African Power Pool (SAPP). Hydropower plants have been used to provide spinning and non-spinning reserve, operating reserve and

Table 3.4 Potential hydropower benefits, by country

	Scenario A	Scenario B	Scenario C	Scenario D
Hydropower (USD million/year)	2,480	2,206	2,369	2,037
Malawi (%)	2	2	2	2
Mozambique (%)	55	59	54	52
Zimbabwe (%)	10	6	10	8
Zambia (%)	33	33	34	38

regulation or load following. The flexibility associated with hydropower storage is particularly relevant for load following and to provide spinning reserve. In the SAPP, revenues from these services are not yet fully captured due to the lack of markets for ancillary services.

Irrigated agriculture

Agriculture is an important economic sector in the Zambezi River Basin (Table 3.5). Although its contribution to GDP varies from country to country, it is generally less than 16 per cent of the basin's total production (see Chapter 6). This sector is nonetheless essential for the livelihoods of rural communities, which constitute 70 per cent of the population in the basin (World Bank 2008). At the moment, just over 10 per cent of the total area that could be potentially equipped for irrigation is actually developed.

Altogether 5.2 million hectares (Mha) are cultivated in the basin, mostly in Zambia, Zimbabwe and Malawi. It is estimated that some 183,000 ha have been equipped for irrigation, but the average annual irrigated area is around 260,000 ha due to double cropping (World Bank 2010). Besides these equipped areas, irrigation is also practised within and around the wetlands and floodplains, especially Malawi and Angola. Flood recession agriculture still accounts for about 100,000 ha, mostly in the large flood plains in the upper reaches.

Though fairly underdeveloped, current irrigation in the Zambezi is not without challenges. Some wetlands face fierce competition for access to those marginal lands, which can be observed when the flood recedes. The poor management of these marginal areas contributes to the degradation of the wetlands through overexploitation, affecting not only the production of crops but also the other goods and services derived from those ecosystems such as fishing and hunting (the primary sources of animal proteins), reed harvesting, fuelwood harvesting, and so on. Irrigation reservoirs are found in the tributaries, mostly in Zimbabwe (Kariba and Tete subbasins), Zambia (Kafue subbasin) and Malawi (Shire subbasin). Unfortunately, no study exists on the cumulative impact of these small irrigation reservoirs. Downstream of the large reservoirs on the Zambezi main stem, traditional irrigation practices based on flood recession farming have been negatively impacted by the alteration of the flow regime (Isaacman 2004).

Irrigation development can lead to substantial economic development in the basin. Besides improved food security at both national and household level, irrigation can increase employment levels in the basin. Currently, irrigated agriculture employs more than 60 per cent of the basin's population, yet it only covers less than 10 per cent of the basin's total cultivated area (see

Table 3.5 The economic value of irrigation potential in the basin

	Scenario A	Scenario B	Scenario C	Scenario D
Irrigation (USD million/year)	111	152	120	109
Kafue Flats (%)	1	6	1	7
Upper Kafue (%)	1	16	2	13
Lower Kafue (%)	0.1	0.1	0.2	0.1
Upper Zambezi (%)	10	10	12	10
Mozambique/Zimbabwe (Tete) (%)	8	8	9	8
Malawi/Tanzania (Shire) (%)	51	37	47	38
Mozambique (Delta) (%)	13	10	12	10
Zambia (Luangwa) (%)	3	2	3	2
Zimbabwe (Kariba) (%)	12	11	14	12

Chapter 6). If water is allocated to its most productive uses, such as in scenario A, the upstream irrigation areas would be in a difficult position: farmers there would face a coalition of down-stream consumptive and non-consumptive users, and would therefore be likely to see their entitlements curtailed, especially during dry years when marginal water values increase throughout the basin. Equally, a focus on ecological allocations presented by scenario D may mean that farmers may have their water entitlements curtailed at crucial periods of the cropping season. Therefore, a balance between agricultural water supply and non-consumptive uses has to be negotiated to arrive at more sustainable allocations presented by scenarios B and C.

Mining and industry

Although their levels of water use are not high relative to other sectors, mining and industry are two of the basin's more economically lucrative uses of water. There is a considerable difference between estimates for mining and industrial water uses in the Zambezi. Euroconsult Mott MacDonald (2007) estimated current water uses in the industrial sector at 25 Mm^3/year, which is also negligible when compared to the amount of water available in the basin. In the Program for Infrastructure Development in Africa study (PIDA 2011), industrial water withdrawals derived from FAO-AquaStat reach 350 Mm^3/year. According to the *Integrated Water Resources*

Figure 3.3 Industrial development in Zambia
Photo: Imasiku Nyambe

Table 3.6 Estimate of mining and industrial water uses in Zambezi Basin (Mm³)

Country	Mining	Industrial	Total
Angola	1.43	0.67	2.10
Namibia	0.33	0.28	0.61
Botswana	0.05	0.23	0.28
Zimbabwe	41.9	86.9	128
Zambia	31.2	64.7	95.9
Tanzania	0.42	0.86	1.28
Malawi	18.8	39.0	57.8
Mozambique	5.56	11.5	17.1
Zambezi Basin	99.7	204	303

Management Strategy and Implementation Plan, the total industrial and mining water use in the basin is 145 Mm³/year (Euroconsult Mott MacDonald 2008). Table 3.6 synthesises the data presented in these sources of information.

While the aggregate value of mining activities in different portions of the Zambezi is not known, what is known is that the copper belt, in the Kafue subbasin of Zambia, has been mined for nearly a century and that speculation has begun in several other areas in Zambia – such as the Lower Zambia National Park. Further, there has been considerable actual and exploratory activity in recent years in Mozambican portions of the basin, focused on minerals such as coal. These activities have no doubt led to water-quality issues, particularly in the Kafue subbasin. Draining from mines containing heavy metals and other compounds – known popularly as acid mine drainage – has become an issue, and holds potential to partially offset some of the economic benefits derived from mining (World Bank 2010).

In terms of industry, most industrial activities take place in the large urban centres in the Kafue, Kariba, Mupata and Luangwa subbasins; that is, in the Middle and Lower Zambezi. While the precise monetary value of industry in different portions of the Zambezi is not known, what is known is that industry is a major contributor to the GDP of riparian countries (Table 3.7). Notably, industrial production accounts for more than 30 per cent of the GDP of Botswana, Namibia and Zambia. And industry contributes to greater than 25 per cent of the GDP of Tanzania and Zimbabwe. There is hence little doubt about the importance of industry to riparians of Zambezi.

Table 3.7 Importance of industry in the economies of Zambezi countries

Country	Industry (% contribution to GDP)
Angola	No data
Botswana	33.4
Malawi	16.2
Mozambique	20.1
Namibia	30.4
Tanzania	25.9
Zambia	33.9
Zimbabwe	28.5

Source: World Bank (2016)

Looking forward, SADC has made industrialisation a key priority and the region's heads of state in 2014 called for the region to drive industrialisation as a means to promoting socioeconomic development in the region. A roadmap and strategy for industrialisation were developed and launched in 2015, focused on – among other things – accelerating growth, enhancing comparative and competitive advantages of the region, and diversifying and broadening the industrial base (SADC 2015). The Zambezi is quite likely to play a major role in this regional drive for industrialisation.

Fisheries

According to Shela (2000), at least 200,000 tonnes per year of fish are harvested within the basin each year, with the majority coming from Lake Nyasa/Malawi and from Zambia. In the Lower Zambezi alone, fishing is worth USD66.5 million per year (Fanaian *et al.* 2015). Subsistence and commercial fishing as well as angling tourism take place in lakes and in the highly productive floodplains. The fishery sector provides vital and unique nutritional benefits such as protein, vitamins and minerals. As such, the sector is key for the subsistence of numerous riparian communities.

The two most productive lakes are Lake Nyasa/Malawi and Lake Malombe. In both lakes, catch rates have declined, especially large tilapia species. Annual catches are now about half of

Figure 3.4 Fish catch near Lake Nyasa/Malawi; fishing is a major livelihood activity in the dams and lakes found in the basin
Source: Admire Ndhlovu/SARDC

what they used to be (100,000 tonnes per year in Lake Nyasa/Malawi) due to non-selective fishing. These declines are to some degree offset by increased harvest of smaller fish, a trend that is observed in many water bodies throughout the Zambezi River Basin. In Malawi, subsistence fishing constitutes 85 to 90 per cent of fish catch. Together, subsistence and commercial fishing correspond to 4 per cent of Malawi's GDP (FAO 2006), that is, USD21 million, and support nearly 1.6 million people.

The artificial reservoirs of Kariba and Cahora Bassa are also used for fishing. The potential catch in Kariba Lake is around 40,000 tonnes per year. In Cahora Bassa, the potential yield is around 16,000 tonnes per year (USD5 million) (INIP 2006). In Kariba, the two riparian countries have different approaches to fisheries (Kolding *et al.* 2004). On the Zimbabwean side, fisheries are actively managed, while access on the Zambian side is largely unrestricted. According to Tweddle *et al.* (2015), the unrestricted access policy in Zambia has resulted in the decline of population of the most valuable species such as tilapine cichlids.

Large floodplains are also an important source of fish in the Zambezi. The Barotse floodplain in the Upper Zambezi has a potential yield of 14,000 tonnes per year. Fisheries in the Barotse have reportedly been overexploited, with a shift towards smaller and less-valuable species (Tweddle *et al.* 2015). In Zambia, the Kafue Flats had a potential to generate 10,000 tonnes per year before the construction of Itezhi-tezhi Dam. In Zambia, the contribution to GDP of fisheries and aquaculture as a subsector of the agriculture sector has averaged 3 per cent (FAO 2006).

Management of fisheries in the basin may possess room for improvement. At the end of the International Workshop on the Fisheries in the Zambezi (WorldFish Center 2007), participants concluded that some of the management and policy challenges faced by basin fisheries are, among others, 'a lack of integrated approaches to river basin use' as well as 'inadequate understanding of the economic value of fisheries'. A cross-sectoral approach to food security in which fisheries have a role to play was also advocated. Although broad, these suggestions highlight ways in which fish management in the basin may be improved.

Navigation

The Zambezi has been used for marine transport for centuries (Tumbare 2010). Nonetheless, actual and potential for navigation vary within the basin. In the Upper Zambezi, navigation is difficult due to shallow water and rapids. Ferry crossings can be found in Kazungula, Senanga, Mulilo, Zambezi town and Chavuma. In the Barotse floodplain, navigation with shallow-bottomed vessels is possible during the high-flow season. Further downstream, on both the Zambezi and Chobe Rivers, navigation is mainly used for tourism purposes (Euroconsult Mott MacDonald 2007).

In the Middle Zambezi, navigation is possible and increasing in Lake Cahora Bassa where there is a potential for angling. Navigation on Lake Kariba is used for transport, fisheries and recreation, both in Zambia and Zimbabwe. Ferry crossings also connect Zambia to Zimbabwe near the town of Luangwa. And yet, the levels of large-scale, long-distance navigation in the Middle Zambezi are low.

The Lower Zambezi holds the most potential for navigation (Chirashi 2014). At present, the stretch of the river between Mphanda Nkuwa – about 60 km downstream of the Cahorra Bassa Dam – and the mouth of the river on the Indian Ocean is the longest navigable stretch in the basin. The portion of the river – which stretches nearly 600 km – has been used to transport molasses and coal in the past. Lake Nyasa/Malawi also serves as a major international route between Malawi, Tanzania and Mozambique.

Figure 3.5 River crossing near Mutarara, Mozambique
Source: B. Antonio/SARDC

While the aggregate economic value of navigation in the basin has not been identified, what is clear is that the transport enabled by Zambezi's watercourses holds potential to be expanded – particularly in its lower portions. Various initiatives are under consideration to develop navigation in the Zambezi River Basin. In the Lower Zambezi, the Shire-Zambezi Waterways Project has been proposed to provide a direct navigable link between Nsanje in Malawi and Chinde on the Indian Ocean. The project would include dredging activities as well as the rehabilitation/construction of roads, railways and ports (AfDB 2011; AfDB and SADC 2015). Malawi would have direct access to the sea and see the shipment costs of goods reduced by as much as 60 per cent (World Bank 2010). New mining activities and sugarcane irrigation schemes in Mozambique may also require improved navigation in the Lower Zambezi. More ambitiously, Tumbare (2010) and Chirashi (2014) have highlighted potential for an integrated land and water transport system in the basin, in part to alleviate stress on current land-based transport infrastructure.

Recreation and tourism

The Zambezi River Basin is endowed with scenic landscapes, natural attractions, spectacular game and wildlife. The most important tourist destinations in the Zambezi River Basin are often related to water resources: Victoria Falls, Lake Nyasa/Malawi, the Kafue Flats, the Luangwa National Park, the Mana Pools, the Liwonde National Park. In 2007, the combined value of tourism in the Zambezi River Basin was estimated to be just over USD440 million (World Bank 2010). The contribution of the tourism sector to GDP varies from country to country: from 5.1 per cent in Zambia to 14.5 per cent in Namibia. In absolute terms (Table 3.8), the aggregate value of tourism receipts in Zambezi countries ranges from USD36 million in Malawi to more than USD2 billion in Tanzania. Tourism is clearly an important contributor to the region's economy.

Figure 3.6 South Luangwa National Park of the Luangwa River Basin; wildlife attracts significant numbers of tourists to the basin

Photo: Richard Beilfuss

Table 3.8 Tourism receipts in Zambezi countries, 2014

Country	Tourism (USD millions)
Angola	1,597
Botswana	113
Mozambique	225
Malawi	36
Namibia	517
Tanzania	2,043
Zambia	642
Zimbabwe	827

Source: World Bank (2016)

Given the growth rate of the sector in Africa (between 7 and 10 per cent), the number of tourists and value of their financial injection into basin economies are likely to increase in the future. The Marromeu Complex in the delta, for example, has largely untapped tourism potential. However, some of the tourist attractions might be negatively impacted if upstream developments affect the flow regime. For example, water abstractions in the Caprivi area for irrigated agriculture could have a negative impact on Victoria Falls whose attractiveness is proportional to the river discharges, especially during the summer months. According to Shela (2000), the falls require at least 1,000 m^3/second to remain spectacular. Moreover, certain tourist attractions, for example, whitewater rafting between Victoria Falls and Kariba, as well as the Mana Pools, could cease to exist if planned water resources development is carried out. Already, changes in the flow regime due to Itezhi-tezhi Dam may have affected the attractiveness of the Kafue Flats.

Wetlands

The Zambezi River Basin hosts a series of large wetlands, which are essential to some rural communities in terms of direct and indirect uses. Typical direct uses include flood recession agriculture and grazing, fisheries, wild animals, and so on. Indirect, less tangible, benefits include regulation and storage services, flood attenuation, preventing soil erosion and groundwater recharge. Chapter 6 provides more detail on the various channels through which wetlands generate economic benefits. Turpie *et al.* (1999), as part of an International Union for the Conservation of Nature (IUCN) study, conclude that traditional agriculture and fisheries are the largest contributors to the value of the Zambezi wetlands. Table 3.9 lists the average annual values of these six wetlands in the Zambezi, based on Turpie *et al.* (1999).

Looking forward, there is likely to be substantial potential to expand the value of these wetlands through the use of integrated approaches to wetland management. Designing policies that recognise and prioritise wetlands, and the mainstreaming of wetlands in basin management plans, are examples of such approaches. Given that 50 per cent of the basin population lives in wetlands (see Chapter 7), sustainable management of wetlands is vital for the realisation of cultural, agricultural and other economic benefits.

Discussion: unlocking the potential

This chapter has highlighted that – while small – important progress has already been made toward tapping the economic potential that can be derived from the many beneficial uses of the water resources of the Zambezi Basin. In purely monetary terms, the vast majority of the value of tapped potential has accrued from hydropower development. Improved flow regulation – primarily for hydropower development – has, in turn, created opportunities for irrigation development, while imposing costs on the environment. Varying levels of economic returns –

Table 3.9 Annual values in the Zambezi wetlands

Attribute	Barotse	Chobe-Caprivi	Kafue	Lower Shire	Luangwa	Delta
Area (1,000 ha)	555	220	650	162	250	1275
Total annual value (USD million)	100	123	–	377	–	75

Source: World Bank (2010)

some more quantified than others – have accrued from a set of other areas including mining, navigation and wetlands.

The chapter has also highlighted that there is far more untapped than tapped potential. Indeed, while the economic value of current hydropower and irrigation has been estimated at USD1.27 billion per year, the total additional potential has been estimated to be USD2.6 billion per year. Importantly, the values just specified are estimates resulting from only two water uses. Should other water uses be valued economically and added to hydropower and irrigation, the estimate on the aggregate potential of water-related economic activities would likely resemble a far higher figure.

The vast untapped economic value of the Zambezi's water resources no doubt gives rise to questions about how this value can be tapped most effectively and – given current levels of economic development in the basin – most expeditiously. Critical negotiation may in fact lie in balancing the effective with the expeditious. While the drive for economic development in the region may incentivise progress over process, there is equally a need to understand rewards and risks associated with development pathways – and to incorporate that understanding into decision-making processes.

Unfortunately, integrated decision-making is not always carried out for development activities in transboundary basins, particularly for small projects. Failure to utilise an inclusive decision-making framework, in turn, is likely to result in a 'tyranny of small decisions' whereby the cumulative impact of small, unilateral management decisions renders conditions suboptimal for the basin as a whole. Tilmant and Kinzelbach (2012), for example, identified that unilateral irrigation developments in the Zambezi could cost on average about 10 per cent of basin-wide short-run benefits. Likewise, a piecemeal planning approach was common in the power sector where the hydrologic impact of a modified flow regime on downstream users was often not thoroughly investigated. In the Zambezi, the situation with respect to the new hydropower projects is nonetheless somewhat unique, since planned projects are mostly extensions of existing facilities or run-of-river power plants with limited storage capacity. Whatever the case, this situation should not be interpreted as a blank cheque for a sectoral approach to planning interventions in the hydropower sector; as discussed in Chapter 5, management decisions taken in that sector are likely to influence and be influenced by the decisions made in other water-dependent sectors like agriculture.

One basic impediment to decision-making that integrates the value of water-using activities is clear determination of the current value and future potential associated with such activities. 'You can't manage what you can't measure', goes an old adage. In order to make informed decisions about the basin's optimal future, it is therefore critical to expand knowledge on the current and potential value of such water-related activities as navigation, fisheries, tourism and productive use of wetlands. Determination of quantified value of alternative water uses in turn allows such uses to be directly compared with another.

Understanding not just potential economic benefits, but also costs, is key. In particular, determining the value of environmental flow requirements in ecologically sensitive areas can allow the true costs of not meeting those requirements – which may follow from developments in other water-using sectors – to be captured. Costs of inadequate water quality should also be determined, since increased pollution from point and non-point sources can also contribute to the decline of ecosystems. This exercise will be especially critical in the Lower Zambezi and the delta, where the impacts of upstream management decisions culminate.

Two points should be made before concluding this section. First, uncaptured by conventional assessment of economic potential – such as that undertaken here – but nonetheless quite important is the issue of climate resilience. Covered more extensively in Chapter 4, there is a need to understand how to ensure that the economic potential that is realised can be made resilient to rainfall and temperature patterns. Second, while fostering process is no doubt beneficial and helps to decide on the best course forward, too much process can create inertia and fatigue. There is therefore a need to foster process that outlines constructive paths forward.

Conclusions

This chapter has reviewed and quantified the tremendous and largely unrealised economic potential that can be generated through increased and more effective use of the Zambezi's water resources. Harnessing this potential will undoubtedly require controlling more water for human benefits through investment in hydraulic infrastructure. Each country in the basin has its own plans to further develop water resources for irrigation, hydropower and industrial uses, as well as for in-stream water usage such as wetland and biodiversity conservation, navigation and fisheries. Because water uses are intertwined, coordinated planning will be key to sustainable management of the basin.

Reformulating some of the key areas pointed to above, key recommendations for a basin-wide institute like ZAMCOM are as follows:

- *Foster research that identifies value, potential and sustainable use of the basin's economic assets*. As noted above, one barrier to effective, economically optimal decision-making is quantified assessment of economic values of certain water uses so that those values can be directly compared against values of other water uses. Similarly, work to understand sustainable yield, for example, of fish catch, can foster optimal use of economic assets.
- *Foster integrated perspectives on development opportunities and challenges*. The past development in the Zambezi has been heavily motivated by hydropower. In purely economic terms, hydropower may be the primary driver for continued development. Nonetheless, as noted by this chapter, there are a number of other economically important uses in the basin. A role for ZAMCOM may be to highlight synergies and trade-offs across all water uses and in particular to consider counterbalancing the influence of hydropower on development. This can be done by – among other means – highlighting the value of these other uses, identifying win–win nexus options, and applying a variety of non-monetary metrics to illustrate benefits derived from all various water uses.
- *Promote precautionary approaches that safeguard benefits until their value is determined*. Under the auspices of ZAMCOM, a semi-integrated planning approach could be first proposed in which riparian countries agree on minimum flow thresholds at certain locations in the Zambezi main stem, from the delta to Victoria Falls, that are estimated to preserve the viability of key economic activities. Riparian countries could prioritise interventions based on their own needs, within these thresholds. With flow thresholds in place, ZAMCOM could facilitate build-up of a knowledge base that enables elaboration of the value and thresholds for flow at different points to the basin's economic activities. Such knowledge base may need to be continually updated given the dynamic nature of economic activities.
- *Outline constructive development pathways*. There is danger that overemphasis on complex regional processes – particularly processes that are not necessarily outcome-oriented – can lead to marginalisation of goals that such processes are designed to achieve. Long-winded basin-wide planning, for example, may be deemed to be unnecessary in countries' drive to realise development expeditiously. It is therefore important to foster constructive, goal-oriented processes focused on integration and option-weighing that are geared toward achieving progress toward the development ambitions of riparians and the region.

Note

1 Here and elsewhere in this chapter, the value of a dollar is that in 2010.

References

AfDB (African Development Bank). 2011. Feasibility study for the Shire-Zambezi Waterways Development Project: Appraisal report. Available at www.africanwaterfacility.org/fileadmin/uploads/awf/Projects/AWF-Project-appraisal-report-MULTIN-SHIREZAMBEZI. Pdf

AfDB and SADC. 2015. Feasibility study for the navigability of Shire-Zambezi waterways, final executive summary. Hydroplan. November 2015.

Beck, L. and Bernauer, T. 2011. How will combined changes in water demand and climate affect water availability in the Zambezi river basin? *Global Environmental Change* 21: 1061–1072.

Beilfuss, R. 2001. *Prescribed flooding and restoration potential in the Zambezi delta, Mozambique: Technical report.* Maputo: Int. Crane Foundation.

Beilfuss, R. and Brown, C. 2010. Assessing environmental flow requirements and trade-offs for the Lower Zambezi River and Delta, Mozambique. *International Journal of River Basin Management* 8(2): 127–138.

Brown, A., Beiter, P., Heimiller, D., Davidson, C., Denholm, P., Melius, J., Lopez, A., Hettinger, D., Mulcahy, D. and Porro, G. 2016. *Estimating renewable energy economic potential in the United States: Methodology and initial results.* Golden, Colorado: National Renewable Energy Laboratory.

Chansa, W. and Kampamba, G. 2010. The population status of the Kafue Lechwe in the Kafue Flats, Zambia. *African Journal of Ecology* 48: 837–840.

Chirashi, M.E. 2014. Zambezi River – sea route for the SADC Region: A study on how to extend navigation on the Zambezi River. *Zimbabwe Journal of Science & Technology* 9: 1–20.

Euroconsult Mott MacDonald. 2007. *Integrated water resources management strategy for the Zambezi River Basin – Rapid assessment.* Technical report. Lusaka: Southern African Development Community Water Division/Zambezi River Authority (SADC-WD/ZRA).

Euroconsult Mott MacDonald. 2008. *Integrated water resources management strategy and implementation plan for the Zambezi River Basin.* Technical report. Lusaka: Southern African Development Community Water Division/Zambezi River Authority (SADC-WD/ZRA).

Fanaian, S., Graas, S., Jiang, Y. and van der Zaag, P. 2015. An ecological economic assessment of flow regimes in a hydropower dominated river basin: The case of the lower Zambezi River, Mozambique. *Science of the Total Environment* 505: 464–473.

FAO (Food and Agriculture Organization of the United Nations). 2006. Country fishery profile. Available at www.fao.org/fi/oldsite/FCP/en/ZMB/profile.htm

INIP (Instituto Nacional des Investigacao Pesqueira). 2006. *Research, monitoring and development of the fisheries in the Cahora Bassa Reservoir.* Mozambique: Ministerio Des Pescas.

Isaacman, A. 2004. *Portuguese colonial intervention, regional conflict and post-colonial amnesia: Cahora Bassa Dam, Mozambique 1965–2002.* Ithaca, NY, USA: Institute for African Development, Cornell University.

Kolding, J., Musando, B. and Songore, N. 2004. *Inshore fisheries and fish population changes in Lake Kariba.* The WorldFish Center. Proceeding of the International Workshop on the Fisheries of the Zambezi Basin, Livingstone, Zambia.

Mumba, M. and Thompson, J.R. 2005. Hydrological and ecological impacts of dams on the Kafue Flats floodplain system, southern Zambia. *Physics and Chemistry of the Earth* 30: 442–447.

PIDA (Program for Infrastructure Development in Africa). 2011. *Study on Programme for Infrastructure Development in Africa (PIDA) Phase III: PIDA Study Synthesis.* African Union, Addis Ababa, Ethiopia: SOFRECO-Led Consortium.

SADC (Southern Africa Development Community). 2015. Central role of water in the implementation of the SADC Industrialisation Strategy and Roadmap. Discussion paper for the 7th SADC Multi-Stakeholder Water Dialogue. 2015. Gaborone.

SADC/SARDC and others. 2012. *Zambezi River Basin: Atlas of the changing environment. SADC, SARDC, ZAMCOM, GRID-Arendal, UNEP.* Gaborone, Harare and Arendal.

Shela, O. 2000. Management of shared river basins: The case of the Zambezi River. *Water Policy* 2: 65–81.

Smakhtin, V.U., Revenga, C. and Döll, P. 2004. *Taking into account environmental water requirements in global-scale water resources assessments.* Comprehensive Assessment of Water Management in Agriculture. Research report 2. Colombo, Sri Lanka: International Water Management Institute.

Tilmant, A., Beevers, L. and Muyunda, B. 2010. Restoring a flow regime through the coordinated operation of a multireservoir system: The case of the Zambezi River basin. *Water Resources Research* 46, W07533, doi:10.1029/2009WR008897.

Tilmant, A. and Kinzelbach, W. 2012. The cost of non-cooperation in international river basins. *Water Resources Research* 48(1).

Tilmant, A., Kinzelbach, W., Juizo, D., Beevers, L., Senn, D. and Casarotto, C. 2012. Economic valuation of benefits and costs associated with the coordinated development and management of the Zambezi river basin. *Water Policy* 14(3): 490–508.

Tumbare, M.J. 2010. *The management of the Zambezi River Basin and Kariba Dam*. Oxford, UK: African Books Collective.

Tumbare, M.J. and ZRA. 2004. The Zambezi River: Its threats and opportunities. In: *The management of the Zambezi River Basin and Kariba Dam*. Oxford, UK: African Books Collective.

Turpie, J., Smith, B., Emerton, L. and Barnes, J. 1999. *Economic value of the Zambezi Basin wetlands*. Harare, Zimbabwe: IUCN Publications.

Tweddle, D., Cowx, I.G., Peel, R.A. and Weyl, O.L.F. 2015. Challenges in fisheries management in the Zambezi, one of the great rivers of Africa. *Fisheries Management and Ecology* 22(1): 99–111.

World Bank. 2008. *Zambezi River Basin – Sustainable agriculture water development*. Washington, DC: World Bank.

World Bank. 2010. *The Zambezi River Basin: A multi-sector investment opportunities analysis*. Washington, DC.

World Bank. 2016. Indicators: Agricultural and rural development. Available at http://data.worldbank.org/indicator (accessed 27 September 2016).

WorldFish Center. 2007. Proceedings of the international workshop on the fisheries of the Zambezi Basin, 31 May–2 June 2004, Livingstone, Zambia. The WorldFish Center Conference Proceedings 75, 83 pp. Penang, Malaysia: The WorldFish Center.

4

Climate change vulnerability and risk

Richard D. Beilfuss and Charles Nhemachena

Key messages

- The Zambezi Basin has one of the most variable climates in the world. Extreme floods and droughts are the typical feature of its historic flow record. The coefficient of variation of annual flow ranges from 0.40 in the Upper Zambezi to 0.47 in the Lower Zambezi.

- By 2050, the Zambezi River Basin is expected to become hotter and drier, with a 0.3–0.6°C increase in temperatures per decade (0.8°C in the summer months), a 10–25 per cent increase in evaporation and 10–15 per cent reduction in rainfall across the basin, relative to the 1961–1990 baseline. Zambezi Basin runoff is projected to decrease by 26–40 per cent on average over this period. Impacts will be felt across the entire basin, but will be most pronounced in its western part. A delayed onset of the rainy season is expected, as well as amplified seasonal variations (increased high flows and reduced low flows).
- Climate change in the basin poses serious risks for hydropower. Firm and total energy production is likely to be compromised. Simulations predict that hydropower dams proposed and built now will be negatively affected. Yet energy planning in the basin is not addressing these anticipated risks.
- Climate change is expected to result in substantial reduction in agricultural production in Zambezi countries. Five of the eight countries in the Zambezi River Basin (Botswana, Malawi, Namibia, Zambia and Zimbabwe) face a predicted 15–50 per cent decrease in agricultural productivity by 2080. Such impacts are likely to be felt most acutely in cultivation of rain-fed agriculture, particularly maize. Wetlands used in agricultural production may experience a significant reduction in the depth, duration and extent of flooding.
- Recommendations for improving adaptation include: assessing hydropower development in the context of comprehensive basin-wide planning, incorporating climate change impacts and uncertainties into dam design, promoting crop and power diversification, and implementing environmental flows to improve adaptive capacity.

Introduction

The African continent is highly vulnerable to the emerging impacts of climate change (IPCC 2014). Forecasts for Africa predict that the continent's climate will become more variable, with extreme weather events more frequent and severe, accompanied by increasing risk to health and life (McMichael *et al.* 2006). This includes increasing risk of drought and flooding (Few *et al.* 2004), and coastal inundation due to sea-level rise (Nicholls 2004). The Zambezi Basin faces the 'worst' potential effects of climate change among 11 major African river basins (IPCC 2001). Zambezi runoff is highly sensitive to variations in climate, as small changes in rainfall produce large changes in runoff. Over the next century, climate change is expected to increase this variability, and the vulnerability of the basin to these changes. Yet water and land resources in the basin are being developed without sufficient analysis of the risks from historic hydrological variability as well as from medium- and long-term impacts expected from climate change.

This chapter presents an evaluation of the vulnerabilities and risks associated with observed and projected climate change in the Zambezi Basin, with particular focus on water resources development, agriculture and ecosystem services that sustain human livelihoods and biodiversity. The chapter begins with a review of long-term cycles of droughts and floods, under natural and regulated conditions. The impact of climate change on these hydrological processes and variability is next considered. Risks of climate change and associated hydrological change on hydropower, agriculture and the ecosystem services that sustain rural livelihoods and biodiversity are then examined. The chapter concludes with recommendations for reducing risk by adapting to the realities and uncertainties of climate change in the basin.

Hydrological processes and variability

The Zambezi Basin has one of the most variable climates in the world, both in space and time. An understanding of the hydrological processes and variability in the Zambezi Basin, under natural and regulated conditions, is fundamental to assessing the impact of climate change on water resources, agriculture and the ecosystem services.

The basin climate is largely controlled by the movement of air masses associated with the Inter-Tropical Convergence Zone (ITCZ). As explained in Chapter 2, the heaviest rainfall occurs during the summer (especially December to March), with typically drier winter months and minimum rainfall from May through September. Rainfall is characterised by considerable variation across the basin and over time. Figure 4.1 shows the distribution of mean monthly rainfall at representative gauging stations across the Zambezi Basin, from the Zambezi River headwaters near Mwinilunga to its outlet on the Indian Ocean coast at Quelimane. Rainfall decreases sharply from north to south across the basin interior, except near the coast where coastal systems and cyclones have significant influence.

Rainfall decreases sharply from north to south across the basin. Mean annual rainfall for the entire basin is about 960 mm, but droughts of several years' duration have been recorded almost every decade. Years of exceptional rainfall producing large floods occur with similar frequency.

The natural flow regime of the Zambezi River reflects these rainfall patterns, and is highly variable within and across years. Mean annual runoff for the basin is estimated to be 103 km^3. Upper Zambezi runoff (draining the headwaters from western Zambia and Angola, with minor contributions from Namibia and Botswana), as reflected in the past century of flow records, varies considerably from year to year (0.40 coefficient of variation), ranging from a remarkable

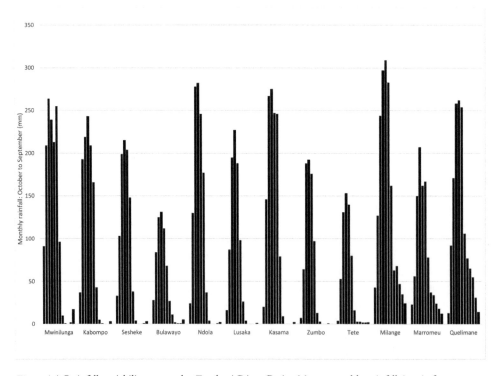

Figure 4.1 Rainfall variability across the Zambezi River Basin. Mean monthly rainfall (mm), from October to September, recorded at various long-term gauging stations located throughout the Zambezi River Basin from headwaters to outlet.

Source: Beilfuss (2002)

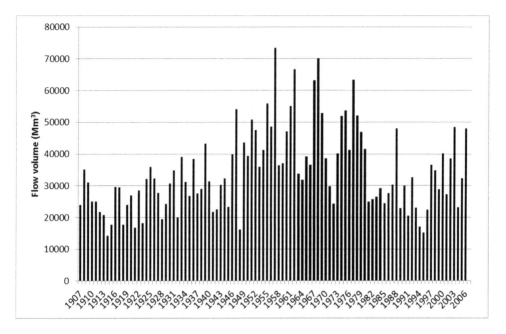

Figure 4.2 Long-term annual flow variability of the Zambezi River. Time series showing natural
variation in mean annual runoff from the unregulated Upper Zambezi region at Victoria Falls
over the past century.

Source: Beilfuss (2012)

72,800 mm^3 in 1957/58 to as low as 12,300 mm^3 in 1995/96 (Figure 4.2) (Beilfuss 2002). Annual
runoff from the Middle Zambezi (draining central/eastern Zambia and Zimbabwe) is even more
variable from year to year than from the Upper Zambezi (coefficient of variation = 0.47). Over
the past century, the highest unregulated runoff volume on record (136,067 mm^3 during 1951/52)
was nearly four times greater than the lowest annual runoff volume (38,687 mm^3 in 1948/49).
The Lower Zambezi (draining central Mozambique, Malawi and southern Tanzania) likewise
displays considerable variability (coefficient of variation = 0.45) (Beilfuss 2002). Mazvimavi and
Wolski (2006) noted multi-year cycles of above-average and below-average runoff in the historical
record. These natural patterns and cycles of variability can mask the effects of climate change
on annual runoff and water availability.

The Zambezi River is a flood pulse system, with strong seasonal fluctuation in flows. Figure
4.3 shows the hydrograph of mean monthly flows for the Zambezi River near its outlet
(Marromeu gauging station in the Zambezi Delta). Zambezi River levels typically begin rising
in late December in response to regional rainfall, peaking between February and April as the
runoff arrives from the Upper and Middle Zambezi catchments, and gradually receding to dry-
season low flows in October and November. This pattern of gradual ebb and flow is repeated,
though much diminished, during drought years – with typically delayed onset of flooding and
more prolonged dry season low flows.

The natural (unregulated) pattern of hydrological variability across the basin, within and across
years, is substantially altered by water resources development projects, especially hydropower dams.
As elaborated in Chapter 3, the Zambezi Basin has currently approximately 5,000 megawatts
(MW) of installed hydropower generation capacity. Major hydropower dams include Kariba and

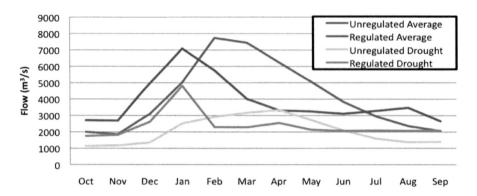

Figure 4.3 Seasonal variability of the Zambezi River. Mean monthly flows for the Zambezi River in the Zambezi Delta region (Marromeu gauging station) during average and drought years, under natural (unregulated) and regulated conditions.

Source: Beilfuss (2012)

Cahora Bassa Dams on the Zambezi River's main stem, Itezhi-tezhi and Kafue Gorge Upper Dams on the Kafue River, and the Kamuzu Barrage that partially regulates Lake Nyasa/Malawi water levels for downstream Shire River hydropower production at Nkula Falls, Tedzani, and Kapichira Stage I hydropower dams. Figure 4.3 shows the Zambezi River hydrograph of mean monthly flows at Marromeu under present regulated conditions during years of average and drought flows. An additional 13,000 MW hydropower potential have been identified (Chapter 3).

Projected climate changes: a review

The general climate picture for southern Africa is increasingly clear based both on observed trends over the past century and increasing confidence in the range of climate change scenarios already developed (IPCC 2014). The following describes the current state-of-the-art predictions for climate change in southern Africa, including temperature, evapotranspiration, rainfall and runoff, based on the IPCC and other peer-reviewed technical reports.

Temperature

The basin is expected to experience a significant warming trend over the next century. The general consensus, emerging from modeling and direct observation, suggests an increase of 0.3–0.6°C per decade (IPCC 2014). Figure 4.4 shows observed and simulated trends in temperature for the previous century, and projected temperature trends over the next century for southern Africa.

Direct observations over the period 1960–2000 in southern Africa indicate a warming trend of 0.1–0.3°C per decade. Under a medium to high emissions scenario (A1B) from the Special Report on Emissions Scenarios[1] (SRES), and using the average of 20 General Circulation Models (GCMs) for the period 2080–2099, annual mean surface air temperature is expected to increase by 3–4°C relative to the 1980–1999 period, with less warming in equatorial and coastal areas (Christensen *et al.* 2007). Other models (e.g., Ruosteenoja *et al.* 2003), assuming more intensive use of fossil fuels and corresponding emissions, indicate warming over this period up to 7°C for southern Africa (which equates to approximately 0.7–1.0°C per decade). Downscaled regional climate models predict smaller but still significant temperature increases for southern

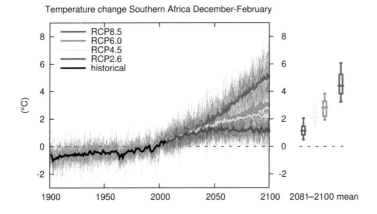

Temperature change Southern Africa December-February

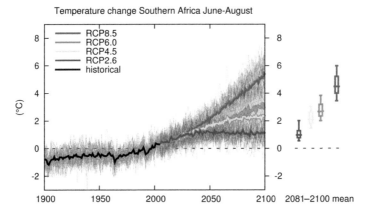

Temperature change Southern Africa June-August

Figure 4.4 Regional warming trends, in different seasons. Time series of temperature change relative to 1986–2005 averaged over land grid points in southern Africa (35°S to 11.4°S, 10°W to 52°E) for wet season December to February (upper) and dry season June to August (lower). Thin lines denote one ensemble member per model and thick lines denote the CMIP5 multi-model mean.[2] On the right-hand side the 5th, 25th, 50th (median), 75th and 95th percentiles of the distribution of 20-year mean changes are given for 2081–2100 for the four greenhouse gas concentration trajectories (RCP).

Source: IPCC (2014)

Africa (Kamga *et al.* 2005). Schlosser and Strzepek (2015) projected that by 2050 the western half of the Zambezi Basin would experience more dramatic temperature increases than the eastern half. Temperature increases are projected to be most significant for the highly arid south/southwestern portions of the Zambezi River Basin.

Climate models for southern Africa predict more significant warming during the winter months than summer ones. Hudson and Jones (2002) forecast a 3.7°C increase in mean surface air temperature in summer (December to February) and a 4°C increase in winter (June to August) by 2080.[3]

Evapotranspiration

The increase in temperatures across the Zambezi Basin will result in higher rates of evaporation and transpiration. Over the next century, the Zambezi River Basin is expected to experience a significant increase in the rate of potential evapotranspiration, based on projected increases in temperature coupled with decreased humidity associated with reduced rainfall (below). Arnell (1999, as cited in IPCC 2001) projected an increased rate of evapotranspiration in the basin of 10–25 per cent over the next 100 years.

Rainfall

Three significant trends in rainfall for the Zambezi Basin are apparent from direct observations over the past 40 years (IPCC 2007) and projected by recent modelling efforts (e.g., Schlosser and Strzepek 2015).

i   A slight reduction in annual precipitation.
ii Increased interannual variability with more intense and widespread droughts.
iii A significant increase in heavy rainfall events in many Zambezi Basin countries (including Angola, Malawi, Mozambique, Namibia and Zambia), including evidence for changes in seasonality and extreme weather events.

Multiple studies cited in IPCC (2007) estimate that rainfall across the Zambezi Basin will decrease by 10–15 per cent over the next century. The predicted decrease in rainfall is associated with a reduction in the number of rainy days and in the average intensity of rainfall. Based on the average of six GCMs, Shongwe *et al.* (2009) project a decreasing rainfall trend with more extreme droughts in northern Botswana, western Zimbabwe and southern Zambia; generally drier conditions in Zambia and Malawi; and less clear precipitation trends in eastern Zimbabwe and central Mozambique during the twenty-first century. Schlosser and Strzepek (2015) projected that by 2050 the reduction in rainfall would be more pronounced in the western portion of the Zambezi River Basin relative to the eastern portion, noting that improvements in CO_2 emissions scenarios could greatly reduce climate impact on rainfall in the basin. Figure 4.5 shows the latest projection in rainfall for southern Africa (IPCC 2014).

Significant changes in the seasonal pattern of rainfall over the Zambezi River Basin are also predicted, although the magnitude of change is less certain. Shongwe *et al.* (2009) indicate a 10–16 per cent reduction in rainfall during autumn (March–May), 31–35 per cent reduction during winter (June–August) and spring (September–November), and a slight 1 per cent reduction in summer (December–February). The simulated annual climatic cycles suggest that the rainfall season may begin one month later than the recorded norm, effectively shortening the duration of the rainy season in the northern parts of the Zambezi Basin.

Tadross *et al.* (2005) and New *et al.* (2006) noted evidence of increasing weather extremes in several Zambezi Basin countries, including Malawi, Mozambique and Zambia. Usman and Reason (2004) predicted a significant increase in heavy rainfall events over southern Africa (including Angola, Malawi, Mozambique, Namibia and Zambia). According to the IPCC models, the frequency of extremely dry austral winters and springs will increase to roughly 20 per cent, while the frequency of extremely wet austral summers will double in southern Africa. There is an emerging consensus that the intensity of tropical cyclones will increase, with less certainty about whether the frequency of these events will increase.[4]

Runoff

Zambezi runoff is highly sensitive to variations in climate, as small changes in rainfall produce large changes in runoff. Of the 11 African basins reviewed by IPCC (2001),[5] the Zambezi

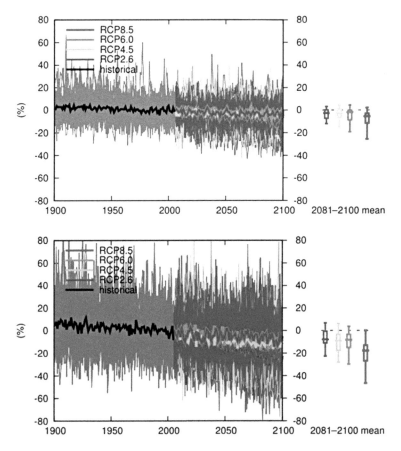

Figure 4.5 Declining rainfall in southern Africa, in different seasons. Time series of relative change relative to 1986–2005 in precipitation averaged over land-grid points in southern Africa (35°S to 11.4°S, 10°W to 52°E) for the wet season (October to March) and dry season (April to September). Thin lines denote one ensemble member per model and thick lines denote the CMIP5 multi-model mean. On the right-hand side the 5th, 25th, 50th (median), 75th and 95th percentiles of the distribution of 20-year mean changes are given for 2081–2100 for the four greenhouse gas concentration trajectories (RCPs).

Source IPCC (2014)

exhibited the most extreme (and thereby 'worst') effects in response to climate change, due to the resonating effect of increases in temperature and decreases in rainfall on potential evaporation and runoff. The Zambezi catchment is characterised by low runoff efficiency, low drainage densities and relatively high aridity, indicating a high sensitivity of runoff to climate change. Given the non-linearity of rainfall-runoff processes, a small change in annual precipitation or annual potential evaporation can have a large impact on annual river flows. Observed impacts of rising temperatures on runoff in other, comparable, basins, for example, indicate that an increase of 1°C leads to an approximate 15 per cent reduction in annual flows, exacerbating flow reductions resulting from decreasing rainfall in the catchment (Cai and Cowan 2008).

Based on 10 scenarios, derived by using five different climate models in conjunction with the SRES-A2 and B2 emissions scenarios, Strzepek and McCluskey (2006) indicate that all Zambezi Basin countries will experience a significant reduction in streamflow. Multiple studies cited in IPCC (2001) estimate that Zambezi Basin runoff will be reduced by 26–40 per cent by 2050. Cambula (1999) projected a decrease in surface and subsurface runoff for the Zambezi in Mozambique, under various climate change scenarios, while Swain *et al.* (2012) suggest that the Zambezi Basin is already experiencing reduced annual flow levels resulting from changes in climate and annual rainfall. Arnell (1999) noted that as water demand increases and water availability declines in the coming decades, countries such as Zimbabwe will shift into the high water-stress category.

The World Bank (2010) assessed the percentage change in runoff for each of the major Zambezi subbasins by 2030, relative to the 1961–1990 baseline. Using the mid-range of 23 GCMs with emissions scenario SRES-A1B, they estimated a 16 per cent reduction in runoff from the Upper Zambezi, 24–34 per cent reduction in the Middle Zambezi and 13–14 per cent reduction in the Lower Zambezi. Norconsult (2003) carried out a sensitivity analysis of climate change on Lake Nyasa/Malawi using a simple water balance to show that small changes in temperature and evaporation could have a significant impact on outflow to the Shire River, the largest tributary of the Lower Zambezi River.

De Wit and Stenkiewicz (2006) assessed changes in surface water supply (especially perennial water availability) across Africa with predicted climate change. They noted that most of southern Africa (including the Zambezi River Basin) is an 'unstable' rainfall region that receives between

Figure 4.6 Communities on river banks are at risk of floods during extreme weather events. Shown here is the Zambezi near Sesheke, where the river forms the boundary between Zambia and Namibia.

Photo: Richard Beilfuss

Figure 4.7 Rivers at risk of drying up
Photo: Leonard John Abrams

400 and 1,000 mm rainfall per annum with high seasonality. Their models examine perennial drainage density and suggest that a 10 per cent drop in rainfall would result in a 17 per cent reduction in surface drainage for regions receiving ~1,000 mm rainfall and a shocking 50 per cent reduction in surface drainage for regions receiving 500 mm rainfall. They note also that the Zambezi subbasins currently receiving 500–600 mm per year could switch from perennial to seasonal surface water supply under climate change forecasts.

Based on average annual rainfall throughout the Zambezi River Basin (about 960 mm), a ~20 per cent reduction in basin-wide runoff is expected. But rainfall is distributed very unevenly across the basin, with the southern and western parts receiving much less rainfall than the northern and eastern parts. Regions around Chipata, Harare, Zambia and Zimbabwe are each predicted to have a 19 per cent reduction in perennial drainage corresponding to a 10 per cent reduction in rainfall. Maun, Botswana, just west of the Zambezi River Basin in the Okavango River Basin, is predicted to have a 72 per cent reduction in runoff corresponding to the same 10 per cent reduction in rainfall. Some tributaries of the Middle Zambezi (draining from Zimbabwe) and Lower Zambezi (draining the Mozambique highlands) could likewise experience severe reductions in perennial drainage, perhaps shifting to seasonal periods without flow. As the authors note, the extent to which reduced flow in major rivers reflects direct changes in rainfall-runoff discharge and groundwater flow, rather than reduced perennial drainage, requires further study. However, the results indicate that future availability of water, especially in headwater streams, is a serious concern in many parts of the Zambezi Basin.

In summary, the Zambezi River Basin is characterised by climate cycles and natural hydrological variations, including long-term cycles of wet and dry periods over the past century. Zambezi runoff is highly sensitive to these variations in climate, as small changes in rainfall produce large changes in runoff. By 2050, the Zambezi River Basin is expected to become hotter and drier, with a 0.3–0.6°C increase in temperatures per decade (0.8°C in the summer months), and a 10–25 per cent increase in evaporation and 10–15 per cent reduction in rainfall across the basin, relative to the 1961–1990 baseline. Impacts will be felt across the entire basin, but will be most pronounced in the western region. Runoff in the Zambezi Basin is projected to decrease by 26–40 per cent on average over this time period. A shift in the timing (a delayed onset) of the rainy season is expected, as are more amplified seasonal variations (increasing high flows and reducing low flows). The intensity of rainfall will increase, compounded by a high likelihood of more frequent and intense tropical cyclones. Overall, the Zambezi will be both drier and more variable, experiencing more prolonged drought periods and more extreme floods. These climate change predictions, based on the average (not extreme) of diverse climate models, have profound implications for future development of hydropower, agriculture, and other land and water resources in the basin.

Climate change and hydropower

Climate change will have a profound effect upon many aspects of water resources development, including hydropower and water supply, and will exacerbate regional and transboundary challenges in water management. According to the World Commission on Dams (2000), climate change has the potential to affect hydropower installations in at least five important ways:

i   Reduced reservoir inflows on a seasonal and annual basis, due to decreased basin runoff and more frequent and prolonged drought conditions, reducing energy generation capacity.
ii   Increased surface water evaporation, especially from upstream reservoirs and floodplains, further reducing energy generation capacity.
iii Increased extreme flooding (inflow) events, due to higher rainfall intensity and more frequent and intense tropical cyclones, affecting dam safety and operational rule curves designed to prevent overtopping.
iv   Altered timing of the wet season flows, especially delayed onset of the rainy season, affecting dam operations as well as downstream release patterns.
v   Increased sediment load to reservoirs, resulting from higher rainfall intensity and corresponding erosion, resulting in reduced reservoir capacity (life span) and water quality.

In addition, climate change is expected to reduce groundwater recharge, and resulting groundwater-fed baseflows, that contribute to stable year-round hydropower production (Treidel *et al.* 2011). Numerous studies have assessed the impact of climate change on hydropower development in the Zambezi River Basin, most recently summarised in Beilfuss (2012). Some of the earliest studies of climate change in the Zambezi Basin, using first generation climate change models, suggested the potential for significant reductions in hydropower generation (Salewicz 1996), with one study suggesting that Kariba would fail to meet its generation capacity due to low water levels, even in tandem with the proposed Batoka Gorge (Urbiztondo 1992). IPCC (2001) found that hydropower production at the Kariba Dam decreased under two different climate change scenarios due to the reduction in river flows caused by higher surface temperatures and associated increase in evapotranspiration.

World Bank (2010) assessed the potential impact of climate change on multisector development scenarios for the Zambezi River Basin. They simulated modest basin development with a system of new hydropower production plants as envisaged under the Southern African Power Pool, using moderate climate change scenarios. The projected impact on energy productivity is substantial. Compared to baseline, firm energy falls by 32 per cent from 30,013 to 20,270 GWh per year. Similarly, a significant reduction is seen in the average annual energy production, falling by 21 per cent from 55,857 to 44,189 GWh per year. With less optimistic climate change assumptions, more substantial reductions in firm power (43 per cent) and average energy (25 per cent) are predicted.

The SWRSD[6] Zambezi Joint Venture (2010) study by the Southern Africa Development Community (SADC) and the German Organization for Technical Cooperation (GTZ) generated a series of simple models to test the sensitivity of hydropower production to climate change and hydrological variability at Kariba and Cahora Bassa Dams, for the period 2030–2050. The model simulated more extreme variability in the predicted flow series, by taking the long-term historic inflow series for each dam and multiplying the deviation of the historical flow series from the long-term mean by a constant factor for years drier than the mean and another constant factor for years wetter than the mean (effectively making the dry years drier and wet years wetter). The model results suggest that very substantial reductions in inflows to Kariba (Table 4. 1) and Cahora Bassa (Table 4. 2) would occur under widely accepted climate forecasts, resulting in significant reductions in generating capacity.

The African Dams Project (Beck and Bernauer 2010) examined the effects of three different localised climate change scenarios, coupled with different levels of water demand for agriculture, municipalities and other uses, for the Zambezi River Basin, 2000–2050, including effects on hydropower. The scenario results point to significant reductions in hydropower generation for Kariba and Cahora Bassa Dams on the Zambezi mainstem. For the worst-case scenario, hydropower is reduced by 60 per cent at Cahora Bassa and by 98 per cent at Kariba. Kafue Gorge Dam, a run-of-river operation, is only minimally affected.

Beilfuss (2010) developed a simulation model using a 97-year historical flow series, aimed at assessing trade-offs between environmental flow scenarios and firm power reliability and total power generation from Cahora Bassa Dam. The flow series captures the full range of natural

Table 4.1 The effect of a selected number of combinations of temperature, precipitation and evapotranspiration on inflows to Kariba Reservoir, for the period 2030–2050 (SWRSD Zambezi Joint Venture 2010)

Temperature change (°C)	Precipitation change (%)	Potential evaporation change (mm/yr)	Runoff coefficient change (%)	Total runoff change (%)
0	−30	0	−50	−65
0.5	−30	25	−52	−66
1	−30	45	−53	−67
1.5	−30	70	−55	−68
2	−30	90	−56	−69
0	−15	0	−26	−37
0.5	−15	25	−28	−39
1	−15	45	−30	−40
1.5	−15	70	−32	−42
2	−15	90	−34	−44
0	0	0	0	0
0.5	0	25	−3	−3
1	0	45	−5	−5
1.5	0	70	−8	−8
2	0	90	−10	−10

Table 4.2 The effect of a selected number of combinations of temperature, precipitation and
evapotranspiration on inflows to Cahora Bassa Reservoir, for the period 2030–2050

Temperature change (°C)	Precipitation change (%)	Potential evaporation change (mm/yr)	Runoff coefficient change (%)	Total runoff change (%)
0	−30	0	−53	−67
0.5	−30	25	−55	−68
1	−30	45	−56	−69
1.5	−30	70	−58	−70
2	−30	90	−59	−71
0	−15	0	−27	−38
0.5	−15	25	−30	−40
1	−15	45	−32	−42
1.5	−15	70	−34	−44
2	−15	90	−36	−45
0	0	0	0	0
0.5	0	25	−3	−3
1	0	45	−5	−5
1.5	0	70	−8	−8
2	0	90	−10	−10

Source: SWRSD Zambezi Joint Venture (2010)

variability observed over the past century. The sensitivity of model output to a reduction in
mean monthly inflows was also tested. The impact of a 10 per cent reduction in mean monthly
flows was moderate; firm power reliability remained at an industry-acceptable 95 per cent level,
with a 3.9 per cent reduction in total power generation. More substantial reductions in runoff
resulted in unacceptable levels of firm power reliability, however. For a 20 per cent flow
reduction, for example, firm power reliability fell to 91.8 per cent with a 13.7 per cent reduction
in total power production. These results indicate that firm power contracts and other energy
commitments will require renegotiation for modest reductions in future Zambezi River runoff,
with corresponding reduction in revenue generation.

Collectively, these diverse studies suggest that future hydropower development in the
Zambezi Basin could be very risky from a hydrological perspective, especially given the long
life of dams, the scale of these investments compared to the size of many African energy-sector
budgets and the hydrological uncertainty that climate change is surely bringing. Substantial
economic risks are associated with reduced mean annual flows, more extreme flood and
drought cycles, and increased evaporative water loss – including risk of structural failure if the
design flood is underestimated, and financial risk associated with overestimated firm power
generation, reduced revenue from total energy production and other uncertainties. Water-
dependent ecosystem services affected by over-designed hydropower development are also at
risk. The financial implications of these risks are discussed below.

Financial implications of hydropower risk

Hydropower economics are sensitive to changes in precipitation and runoff (Mimikou and Baltas
1997; Gjermundsen and Jenssen 2001; Harrison and Whittington 2001, 2002; Alavian *et al.*
2009). Uncertainty about future hydrology presents a great challenge for infrastructure planning
and engineering. Most hydropower projects are designed on the basis of recent climate history

(typically a 30–50-year historic time series of flow data) and the assumption that future hydrological patterns (average annual flows and their variability) will follow historic patterns. This notion that hydrological patterns will remain 'stationary' (unchanged) in the future, however, is no longer valid (Milly *et al.* 2008). Under future climate scenarios, a hydropower station designed and operated based on the past century's record of flows is unlikely to deliver the expected services over its lifetime. It may be over-designed relative to expected future water balances and droughts, as well as under-designed relative to the probability of extreme inflow events in the future.

Over-designed projects, resulting from reduced and more variable inflows relative to the historical time series, incur financial risk by generating lower levels of power production than forecast, leading to reduced electricity sales and revenue, including failure to meet firm energy commitments. Capital costs for hydropower are high compared with alternative energy options, and the financial risk of over-design is significant (World Bank 2010). Development of the hydropower sector according to the generation plan of the Southern African Power Pool (Nexant Consultants 2007), for example, will require an investment of USD10.7 billion over an estimated 15-year period. A comparable investment in energy efficiency and renewable technologies, including biomass, solar, wind and small-scale hydro, would aggressively expand decentralised (on- and off-grid), clean energy access and markets in Africa (Hankins 2009).

Financial and technical analyses to assess the feasibility of hydropower projects typically evaluate the financial impacts of a range of factors on the ability to generate a positive cash flow; these analyses apply traditional engineering cost/financial analysis to characterise construction and operational costs (e.g., size and location of the project) and future trends that could affect project revenues (e.g., changing demand, new supply and economic drivers affecting the price of electricity). These assessments rarely evaluate potential power generation and associated revenue changes associated with climate change. When climate considerations are incorporated, the financial risks may significantly undermine the feasibility of existing and future hydropower projects.

The regional economic impacts of reduced hydropower generation from the Kariba Reservoir during the 1991/92 drought, for example, included an estimated USD102 million reduction in GDP, a USD36 million reduction in export earnings, and the loss of 3,000 jobs (Magadza 2006). Droughts of this magnitude (or worse) will occur more frequently with regional climate change.

Harrison and Whittington (2002) examined the susceptibility of the proposed Batoka Gorge hydroelectric scheme to climate change, with emphasis on financial risks associated with the project. They reconstructed a flow series for inflows to Batoka Gorge, using the US Army Corps of Engineers HEC-5 reservoir routing programme. Inflows to the model were generated using rainfall-runoff models based on precipitation according to three different climate change scenarios (IPCC 2001). Their simulations suggest a strong sensitivity of the Batoka Gorge project to changes in climate. The models indicate significant reductions in river flows (mean monthly flows fell between 10 and 35 per cent, and both wet season and dry season flows declined), declining power production (mean monthly production fell between 6 and 22 per cent), reductions in electricity sales and revenue, and consequently an adverse impact on a range of investment measures. Harrison *et al.* (2006) note that climate change scenarios alter not only the financial performance of hydropower schemes such as Batoka, but also the financial risks they face. Changes in climate lead to significant variability in economic performance – reducing not only the mean values for energy production, but also the reliability of electricity sales income.

In the face of hydropower blackouts caused by low water levels, governments are often forced to buy expensive emergency power, which is not included in the risk analysis for large-dam hydropower. For example, after the 2009 drought in Kenya brought reservoirs to their lowest levels in 60 years, the government brought in Aggreko PLC, a UK firm that supplies temporary diesel generators. For an extended period, reports the *New York Times*,[7] Aggreko was delivering roughly 140 MW at a cost of USD30 million per year, not including fuel purchases. Meeting future needs through diesel generation could cost the Kenyan government more than USD780 million a year – a key reason Kenya is now building wind farms and geothermal plants to bring its hydro-dependency down from 60 to 35 per cent.

Hartmann (2008) notes that hydropower planners have been aware of climate change for years, but until recently it was assumed that climate trends were too uncertain, and the range of natural variability too high, to make reliable predictions. From a financial point of view, it was argued that changes beyond 20–30 years from the present would have little impact on the financial return of hydropower investments – introducing a mismatch between financial time horizons and water resource management implications, as the physical life span of hydropower assets is much longer than the payback period. Large and financially powerful hydropower operators from the temperate regions, who might be expected to lead the way in terms of new policy and research, are also the ones expected to be less affected by climate change. Environmental impact assessments and other planning guidelines still do not usually include guidance on hydrological variability and climate change, beyond the impact of extreme flood events on dam safety. Together, these factors have led to a neglect of climate change in hydropower planning – in an approach which might be called either 'wait-and-see' or 'head-in-the-sand' (Hartmann 2008).

Among the major hydropower projects in operation or planning for the Zambezi River, the financial risks of climate change were considered by hydropower developers only for the Kafue Gorge Lower project (Stenek and Boysen 2011). This analysis, for the International Finance Corporation (IFC), combined three GCM models and two SRES emission scenarios to project a set of temperature and precipitation levels over four time periods (base, early-, mid- and late-century) for the Kafue River Basin. The outputs from each GCM/emission scenario combination were used as inputs for the hydrologic flow modelling of the Kafue River Basin, which provided climate-modified flow rates across four time horizons for each of the GCM/emission scenarios. The flow series was routed through a reservoir model to assess energy production, and a financial risk model. IFC results indicate that future emission projections have a significant impact on the operations, and therefore on the financial viability, of the Kafue Gorge Lower project. None of the scenarios exceeded the average annual generation of about 2,450 GWh needed to satisfy investor requirements, and most of the scenarios considered did not yield acceptable returns to investors. The study notes that, 'given the significance of water flow on the financial viability of hydropower projects, adaptation planning should include considerations such as climate change, conservation, and development that introduce variability into available water flow to the project'. The study concluded that climate change will significantly impact the financial performance of the Zambian Electricity Supply Corporation's (ZESCO) hydropower plants, with the financial viability of hydropower investment dependent on the relative severity of climate change on the basin. These impacts highlight the importance of considering changes in water supply due to climate change when implementing financial analyses for hydropower projects. Governments and investors must become better informed about climate change risks to future hydropower projects by analysing projects for projected changes in available water flow and power generation, rather than assuming constant flows and power generation rates.

The financial risks of climate change are not under serious consideration for other proposed hydropower projects in the Zambezi River Basin. The design and operation of Mphanda Nkuwa Dam in Mozambique, for example, assumes the continued validity (stationarity) of the mean and variability of the historic flow series, despite climate change forecasts to the contrary. The project has not been evaluated for the risks associated with reduced mean annual flows and more extreme flood and drought cycles, which include the risk of structural failure if the design flood is underestimated, financial risk associated with overestimated firm power generation, reduced revenue from total energy production and other uncertainties.

Under-design of hydropower projects also poses significant financial risk with respect to future climate change scenarios. The occurrence of extreme flooding events on a more frequent basis (Boko *et al.* 2007) may threaten the stability of large dams and/or force more frequent spillage, which exacerbates downstream flood damage.[8] The design flood rule curve that governs the risk associated with overtopping Kariba and Cahora Bassa Dams, for example, is based on the historical hydrological record and may not result in adequate reservoir storage capacity for large flood events. The financial and social impact of a major dam failure in the Zambezi River Basin would be nothing short of catastrophic.

Overall, climate change in the Zambezi Basin poses serious risks for hydropower and other water resources development, with decreasing runoff, worsening droughts and more extreme floods. Hydropower dams being proposed and built now will be negatively affected; yet energy planning in the basin is not taking serious steps to address these huge hydrological uncertainties. The result could be dams that are uneconomic, disruptive to the energy sector and possibly even dangerous to downstream communities and livelihoods.

Climate change and agriculture

Climate change can be expected to have profound impacts on agricultural activities in the Zambezi Basin. Rising temperatures will shorten the crop-growth period and increase plant transpiration rates, both of which hold potential to reduce crop production (Ludwig and Asseng 2006; Springate and Kover 2014). Furthermore, increasing temperatures will contribute to reductions in soil water available for plant uptake. Coupled with anticipated heat waves, reductions in soil moisture may substantially reduce agricultural production. Lobell *et al.* (2011), for example, identified that maize yield is reduced by 1.7 per cent each degree day above 30°C under drought conditions in Africa.

Agricultural activities are also likely to be substantially affected by increasing rainfall variability manifested most commonly in recurrent droughts (SARDC and HBS 2010; Swain *et al.* 2012). Recent droughts in southern Africa (including basin countries), for example, have resulted in annual yield losses of between 10 to 50 per cent on 80 per cent of the area planted with maize in the region (Swain *et al.* 2012). Such effects have been most strongly felt in semi-arid areas in the western parts of the basin. Eastern and low-lying areas of the Zambezi Basin have also experienced devastating floods in recent years with destructive impacts on agricultural activities (SARDC and HBS 2010).

Notably, the impacts of climate change on agriculture may not be entirely negative. Crop yield may improve, for example, due to increased concentration of carbon dioxide (CO_2) in the atmosphere (Ludwig and Asseng 2006). Nonetheless, maize, the main staple cereal crop in southern Africa, is unlikely to benefit from increased CO_2 concentrations (Taylor *et al.* 2014). Further, the poor soil nutrient availability on highly weathered sandy soils, comprising a major portion of smallholder farming areas, may negate any yield benefit of elevated CO_2 (Tubiello and Ewert 2002). Ultimately, the negative impacts of increased temperatures and changing rainfall are likely to far outstrip any positive effects of increased CO_2 on crop yields in southern Africa.

Efforts have been made to identify the impacts of increased temperatures and declining rainfall on agricultural production. Lobell *et al.* (2008) predicted that maize production will drop by

Figure 4.8 Livestock grazing in the Middle Zambezi. Climate change poses a high risk to agriculture, including the availability of pastures for grazing livestock.

Photo: Richard Beilfuss

20 to 40 per cent in southern Africa due to a combination of warming temperatures and changing rainfall patterns. Brown *et al.* (2012) found that, if no adaptation measures are taken, yields from rain-fed agriculture in Zimbabwe may decrease by up to 50 per cent by 2020; maize is identified to be particularly vulnerable due to its intolerance to drought. USAID (2012) reported declining crop yields, especially maize, in Zambia. Nkomwa *et al.* (2014) highlighted substantial declines in yield/ha of maize, cotton, sesame and sorghum in Malawi; notably, this study and one other (Dinesh *et al.* 2015) identify the proliferation of pests due to climate change as a factor contributing to declining agricultural production.[9]

Climate change may also impact the degree to which irrigation water requirements are met. Fant *et al.* (2015) predicted that runoff may actually increase in some northern areas of Malawi and Zambia, resulting in sufficient water availability to meet irrigation demands into the future there. However, irrigation in Zimbabwe and Mozambique is affected negatively by the predicted drying; this drying is predicted to result in unmet irrigation water demand by the 2040s. There is nonetheless considerable uncertainty in such predictions.

Figure 4.10 presents the projected changes in agricultural productivity due to climate change by 2080. Five of the eight countries in the Zambezi River Basin (Botswana, Malawi, Namibia, Zambia and Zimbabwe) expect a 15–50 per cent decrease in agricultural productivity by 2080, while the other three (Angola, Mozambique and Tanzania) project reduced agricultural productivity of up to 15 per cent. In addition, the IPCC AR5 reports with high confidence that projected increases in warming and changes in precipitation patterns would have significant impacts on the performance of the agriculture sector in Africa (including in the Zambezi Basin), with some crops expected to experience yield losses as high as 50 to 80 per cent (IPCC 2014).

Importantly, the impacts of climate change on water resources also affect livestock production. USAID (2012) noted how climate change can affect the quality of grazing grass and availability of drinking water for livestock in Zimbabwe; this has resulted in longer walking distances to obtain drinking water, resulting in reduced live-weight as animals expend greater energy travelling. Dinesh *et al.* (2015) noted how warmer temperatures may reduce livestock food intake, which may also reduce their weight. Nkomwa *et al.* (2014) identified a shift from cattle to goats in Malawi, due to their greater adaptability to water shortage.

There is a growing evidence base on climate change adaptation in agriculture. Dinesh *et al.* (2015) explained how there are both autonomous adaptations (e.g., shifts in planting dates, cultivar substitution) and transformational changes (e.g., climate-smart breeding, livelihood diversification). In Zambia, there is evidence that autonomous adaptation is taking place such as adopting different maize varieties, conservation farming, crop rotation to improve soil fertility and staggering planting of crops to reduce risk (USAID 2012). In Malawi, farmers have adopted more drought-tolerant crops and early yielding varieties, using more manure, and planting on ridges rather than on flat areas (Nkomwa *et al.* 2014). In Zimbabwe, Rurinda *et al.* (2013) determined that improved timing and planting, and adjusting soil nutrient inputs, can stabilise

Figure 4.9 Poor harvests from climate-induced weather variations in Hwange, Zimbabwe. Rural communities are especially vulnerable to climate change because their livelihoods are mostly dependent on natural resources.

Photo: Charles Nhemachena

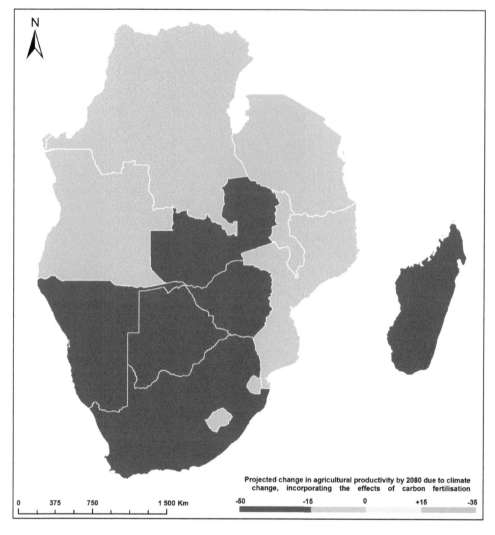

Figure 4.10 Projected changes in agricultural productivity by 2080 due to climate change
Source: Hugo Ahlenius (2008). UNEP/GRID-Arendal Adapted from GRID-Arendal

maize yields under variable rainfall conditions. However, Rurinda *et al.* (2015) suggest that improvements to crop and soil fertility management will offset the effects of climate change only temporarily; by 2100, the effects of climate change are predicted to result in substantial yield losses without broader transformational adaptation efforts.

Climate change and ecosystem services

Ecosystem services are the benefits derived from our natural capital of water, land, air and biota. They include: provisioning services, such as production of food and water; regulating services, such as control of climate and disease; supporting services, such as nutrient cycles and crop pollination; and cultural services, such as spiritual and recreational benefits. Scientific understanding of the effects of climate change on the provision and value of ecosystem services is improving rapidly. Several recent studies have assessed the impact of climate change on key ecosystem services and the human well-being (Nelson *et al.* 2013; Pedrono *et al.* 2016). In specific settings, climate change is linked to reduced fisheries and seafood production, increased wildfires, increasing extreme weather and rising sea levels, reduced water quality (e.g., temperature, acidity, salinity) and increased water scarcity. Conversely, ecosystem services also play a vital role in protecting against the impact of climate change, sequestering carbon and providing flood storage, coastal storm surge protection and many other benefits. These and other studies emphasise the cumulative impacts of climate change stresses coupled with other development pressures.

As highlighted in Chapter 7, Zambezi wetlands play a particularly important role in providing these services (McCartney *et al.* 2015). The Barotse Floodplain has an annual gross financial value estimated to be USD417 per household with a total annual economic value (from fish, crops, cattle, wildlife, reeds and papyrus) of USD12.2 million (Turpie *et al.* 1999). Barotse fisheries provide the bulk of the protein in the diet of about 200,000 people (Hughes and Hughes 1992). The Kafue Flats support more than 250,000 cattle during the dry season each year, with a market value of USD4 million (Seyam *et al.* 2001). Guveya and Sukume (2008) estimate that the annual total value of ecosystem services in the Zambezi Delta ranges between USD0.93 billion and USD1.6 billion. Many thousands of smaller, lesser-known wetlands, such as the dambos, also play a vital role in the everyday lives of poor rural communities, through the provision of clean drinking water and, because they retain extensive wet regions during the dry season, as a valuable agricultural resource in the semi-arid regions of the basin (Scoones 1991). Zambezi Basin wetlands also support considerable biodiversity and productivity in terms of plants, large mammals, birds and fish, and other groups (Timberlake 2000; Beilfuss *et al.* 2000).

Zambezi Basin wetlands are highly vulnerable to the impact of climate change, as in much of sub-Saharan Africa, threatening the benefits they provide (Mitchell 2013). As the Zambezi Basin climate becomes hotter and drier, with a projected 26–40 per cent reduction in runoff, floodplain wetlands will experience a significant reduction in the depth, duration and extent of floodwaters. Rainfall-dependent dambos will dry up faster. Based on the observed impacts of severe drought in the Zambezi Basin, these changes are expected to have a direct, negative impact on water supply, water quality, freshwater fisheries, dry-season grazing lands and the availability of wetland plant and animal resources (e.g., Tiffen and Mulele 1994).

The potential loss of other ecosystem services, more difficult to quantify, has a profound effect on community life. Reduced presence of floodplain waterbodies and shallow ground-water tables, due to diminished recharge from annual floods, forces villagers to use the main Zambezi River channel rather than floodplain waterbodies for their bathing, drinking and other domestic uses – where they are more vulnerable to crocodile attacks and waterborne disease. The encroachment of permanent settlements and fishing camps on riverbanks and sandbars – an adaptation to the reduction in floodplain inundation – results in higher social and economic costs, including injury and death, during very large (uncontrollable) floods (Hanlon 2001). Important cultural values linked to Zambezi waters – including ceremonial, recreational, aesthetic and spiritual values – are also affected by changes in the flow regime (Beilfuss 2002). Cumulatively, the economic value of water for downstream ecosystem services exceeds the value of water for strict hydropower production – even without valuation of biodiversity and culture.

Climate change will also exacerbate the trade-offs between water allocations for hydropower development and ecosystem services. In their study of the impact of climate change on the financial feasibility of further hydropower development in the Kafue River Basin, Stenek and Boysen (2011) noted that operation of the Itezhi-tezhi Dam for hydropower will result in higher levels of conflict between the current operating rules for power generation and the need for water releases for downstream users and conservation purposes on the Kafue Flats. Anticipated increases in temperature and changes in precipitation, combined with increasing development and population growth, will increase water demands for irrigation, fisheries and floodplain conservation. Heavy reliance on hydropower in the Zambezi River Basin will also be increasingly challenged by growing water needs for addressing conservation goals in light of existing impacts and the potential impact of climate change and climate variability on water supply and evaporation.

Conclusions

The Intergovernmental Panel on Climate Change (IPCC) has categorised the Zambezi as the river basin most vulnerable to climate change impacts in Africa. Zambezi runoff is highly sensitive to variations in climate, as small changes in rainfall produce large changes in runoff. By the end of the century, climate change is expected to increase this variability, and the vulnerability of the basin to these changes. The following are key risks predicted for the Zambezi Basin:

- The basin is expected to experience a significant warming trend of 0.3–0.6°C per decade.
- Multiple studies cited by IPCC estimate that rainfall across the basin will decrease by 10–15 per cent.
- Significant changes in the seasonal pattern of rainfall across the basin are predicted, including delayed onsets, as well as shorter and more intense rainfall events.
- All Zambezi Basin countries will experience a significant reduction in average annual streamflow. Multiple studies estimate that Zambezi runoff will decrease by 26–40 per cent by 2050.
- Increasing water stress is anticipated in the semi-arid parts of the basin.

These changes will place profound constraints on the development of water resources and agriculture in the basin, while stressing human livelihoods and biodiversity linked to ecosystem services. Conversely, the impacts of climate change will be exacerbated by existing and planned hydropower and other water and land resources development.

Adaptation attempts to reduce the vulnerability of human livelihoods, economies and natural systems to the impact of climate-induced changes. The United Nations Framework Convention on Climate Change (UNDP 2004) states:

> The most effective climate change adaptation approaches for developing countries are those addressing a range of environmental stresses and factors. Strategies and programs that are more likely to succeed need to link with coordinated efforts aimed at poverty alleviation, enhancing food security and water availability, combating land degradation and reducing loss of biological diversity and ecosystem services, as well as improving adaptive capacity.

Important opportunities for climate change adaptation in the Zambezi Basin include the following:

Prioritise investments that increase climate resilience

An estimated 60 to 120 million people in southern Africa face water stress in the next 50 years due to climate variability and governance issues (Arnell 2004). Climate models warn about the impact of changing rainfall and runoff patterns on grain yields, water availability and the survival of plant and animal species that are expected to shift production seasons, alter productivity, and modify the set of feasible crops. A large part of the population is engaged in subsistence agriculture on marginal lands that are particularly vulnerable to the adverse effects of climate change (Ndaruzaniye *et al.* 2010). By the 2080s, a significant decrease in suitable rain-fed land for agriculture is estimated due to climate change (Boko *et al.* 2007). Wheat production is likely to disappear from southern Africa, and notable reductions in maize production are expected (Fischer *et al.* 2005; Stige *et al.* 2006).

In this context, it is essential that future investments in the Zambezi River Basin increase the resiliency of agriculture and water sectors to climate change. Efforts to strengthen climate resilience are often coupled with development of large hydropower dams, which brings some management complexity. Indeed, there often are inherent incompatibilities between generation of electricity and provision of water supply during the dry season, when water is scarce but most needed. When dam operators must prefer one to the other, electricity generation almost always supersedes water supply (Harrison *et al.* 2007). Hydropower dams diminish or eliminate the annual flood pulse downstream, reducing the productivity and extent of floodplain and riverbank agricultural systems, an important alternative to drought-prone rain-fed cropping practices (Scudder 1989). Evaporative water loss from large reservoirs further decreases water availability for downstream use.

Integrated river basin development investments should be prioritised to enhance climate resilience by helping poor and vulnerable communities prepare for, withstand and recover from the negative effects of climate change (African Development Bank *et al.* 2003). While more water storage will be needed (World Bank 2006), decentralised solutions that preserve river-based ecosystem services are better suited to the needs of the rural majority, who face the greatest adaptation challenges. Resilience strategies should be an integral part of research, development, planning, training, capacity-building and implementation in Zambezi Basin countries.

Assess hydropower development in the context of comprehensive basin-wide planning

More than 13,000 MW of additional hydropower potential exist in the Zambezi River Basin (see Chapter 3), but development of that potential would come at significant social and economic cost to many water users and concerns in the basin and entail substantial financial risk in the face of climate change. Holistic approaches to future developments are essential to ensure the sustainability of the basin. Planners need to carefully consider how climate change will shape the supply of water in terms of future river flows (and shifts in their mean and variability), as well as the demand for power, conservation, domestic use, agriculture, industry and other water services. Basin-wide approaches to hydropower and land-use planning are increasingly adopted by decision-makers in other major river basins of the world, notably including the Mekong (King *et al.* 2007; ICEM 2010).

Comprehensive basin-wide planning must consider a full accounting of the values of ecosystem services supported by river flows. Community- and ecosystem-based adaptation approaches that integrate the use of biodiversity and ecosystem services into an overall strategy aimed at empowering people to adapt to climate change must be central to any comprehensive planning efforts (Girot *et al.* 2012). When these values are fully considered and integrated along with all other management objectives, the prospects for optimising both dam- and ecosystem-related objectives are greatly enhanced (Krchnak *et al.* 2009).

Incorporate climate change scenarios into dam design

The major implication of climate change for dams and reservoirs is that the future is uncertain, and can no longer be assumed to mirror the past. Until now, the design and operation of hydropower dams have been based on the best historic river discharge data obtainable. For the Zambezi River Basin, a substantial time series of monthly flow data is available dating back to 1907. These flow data provide a useful picture of the natural variability of river flows over the past century, including several cycles of wet and dry periods. These data are unreliable, however, for predicting the variance of future flows under climate change, including fundamental design criteria such as mean annual runoff and maximum probable floods. Milly *et al.* (2008) argue that *stationarity* – the idea that hydrological systems fluctuate within an unchanging envelope of variability, a foundational concept that permeates training and practice in water-resource engineering – is no longer valid, and should not serve as a central assumption in water-resource risk-assessment and planning. Hallegatte (2009) notes that new infrastructure will have to be able to cope not only with new climate states but also with a large range of changing climate conditions over time, which will make design more difficult and construction more expensive.

The reality of climate change demands more adaptive, flexible water management, which includes the use of both moderate and strong climate change scenarios for estimating future dam safety and reservoir reliability for individual dams and cascades of them. The risk assessment must include the safety and operation of cascades of dams, given the heightened potential for catastrophic failure of structures under new climate realities. Uncertainty in the future climate makes it impossible to directly use the output of a single climate model as an input for infrastructure design, and the needed climate information will not be available soon (Hallegatte 2009). New models must be developed to incorporate climatic uncertainty into dam design and management, combining historical records of past flow volumes and periodicities (often insufficiently known, due to poor historic records) with projections of multiple climate models using stochastic (probabilistic) elements, driven by multiple climate-forcing scenarios. Research is needed into statistical techniques for separating climate change impacts from natural variability; and improvements are needed in regional climate models, with a stronger focus on prediction in the short to the medium term and the inclusion of land-use and ecosystem expertise in the prediction of hydrological impacts on hydropower and reservoirs (Harrison *et al.* 2007). The information base for developing these models is likely to change rapidly as climate science advances during the coming decades, and will require innovative training of hydrologists, engineers and managers (Milly *et al.* 2008).

Projects should be approached with extreme caution. New developments should be subject to substantial analysis of the hydrological and financial risks, performed by expert teams including hydrologists, energy economists and climate-change scientists. As an example, HydroTasmania is already downrating their power production due to climate change.[10]

Hallegatte (2009) provided a useful decision-making framework for adapting uncertainty-management methods to hydropower development:

- Selecting 'no-regret' strategies that yield benefits even in the absence of climate change.
- Favouring reversible and flexible options.
- Buying 'safety margins' in new investments.
- Promoting soft adaptation strategies, including long-term prospective.
- Reducing decision-time horizons and projected lifetime of investments.

Diversify the regional power pool to reduce hydropower dependency

Climate change adaptation requires diversified investments to 'avoid putting all eggs into one basket' at a time of increasing hydrological uncertainty (Goodland 2011). The Southern African Power Pool (SAPP) was created to provide a reliable and economical electricity supply to power consumers across southern Africa, and provides an excellent framework for diversifying power production in southern Africa and reducing dependency on hydropower.[11] The SAPP vision includes ensuring sustainable energy development through sound economic, environmental and social practices, as part of a competitive electricity market for the southern African region. In practice, however, the SAPP has emphasised large-scale coal and hydropower development to feed the regional grid, without serious consideration of climate change impacts (Hankins 2009).

The SAPP can play a key leadership role in adapting the regional power grid to the realities of climate change and water scarcity by promoting decentralised energy technologies, energy efficiency standards, demand-side management and feed-in tariff pricing to encourage the adoption of renewable technologies. Region-wide funds are needed to develop renewable energy projects that benefit the SAPP. Many SAPP countries have a huge untapped potential for solar, wind, geothermal and other renewable energy technologies that are well-suited for both urban and rural energy development. In failing to integrate these technologies with the regional grid, southern Africa is missing out on critical global developments in new clean sources of energy that could benefit its population, create new industry, jobs and capacities, and bring clean power to its own population (Hankins 2009).

Promote adoption of planting schedules and crop varieties that reduce risk

There is a growing body of techniques that fosters adaptation to higher temperatures and less reliable rains. Drought-tolerant and early-yielding crop varieties, as well as crop diversification, may help mitigate risks associated with these changes. At a basin-wide level, there may be opportunities to identify hot spots where climate changes are expected to be greatest, such as in western parts of the basin where drought has already wielded adverse impacts on agriculture. Promotion of greater knowledge, and adoption, of adaptation measures in such areas may partially mitigate impacts in such areas. Further, certain areas of Mozambique and Malawi may wish to proceed cautiously with irrigation expansion given the predicted impacts of climate change on irrigation there.

Implement environmental flows for climate adaptation

Environmental flows are an important tool for restoring river systems and the goods and services they provide (Arthington *et al.* 1992; Postel and Richter 2003; King and Brown 2006). Environmental flows describe the quantity, timing and quality of water flows required to sustain freshwater and estuarine ecosystems, and the human livelihoods and well-being that depend on these ecosystems. Maintaining and strengthening the delivery of ecosystem goods and services is an important aspect of adaptation to climate change (Bergkamp *et al.* 2003; Le Quesne *et al.* 2010). Environmental flow requirements will be critical to help communities living downstream of dams adapt to a changing climate, and therefore should be incorporated into existing hydropower operations, as well as future infrastructure planning and design. Two recent World Bank documents provide recommendations for integrating environmental flows into hydropower dam planning, design and operations (Krchnak *et al.* 2009), and supporting improved protection of environmental flows across projects, plans and policies (Hirji and Davis 2009).

Reoperation of existing infrastructure to realise environmental flows may include redistributing the spillage of excessive reservoir waters to better mimic seasonal fluctuations, or setting specific targets for outflows to meet stakeholder-defined goals for ecological, social or economic outcomes. For cascades of dams, dam operators and water managers should investigate opportunities to re-regulate flows by capturing flows in the lowest dam of the cascade and then releasing flows to mimic natural patterns. Opportunities for integrating groundwater storage with dam storage should also be investigated. Releases may be timed to coincide with periods when downstream tributaries are contributing peak flows, or 'piggy-backing' water releases with water diversions for human use, to increase opportunities for overbank flow to reach floodplains and wetlands. Conversely, environmental flow strategies may target dry-season releases to enhance water security.

Future structures should be designed to ensure compatibility with environmental flow releases, including: adequate outflow capacity to realise a range of target outflows; multilevel intakes to allow for water releases corresponding to a range of reservoir storage levels, to improve downstream water quality; and designing dams that enable movement of fish and other organisms and sediments around dam walls. Where possible, existing dams should be retrofitted to achieve these outcomes.

Environmental flows are under consideration in many African river basins (e.g., Acreman 1994). Within the Zambezi River Basin, environmental flows were first considered in the Kafue River as early as the 1960s. Itezhi-tezhi Dam was designed to generate a flood of 300 m^3/s during a four-week period in March for the maintenance of agricultural and biological productivity in the Kafue Flats (Scudder and Acreman 1996). Although the additional reservoir storage capacity increased project costs by 15 per cent, the Ministry of Power, Transport and Communication agreed to the plan because of the importance of the annual floods for aquifer recharge, alluvial deposition, flood recession agriculture, livestock grazing and floodplain fisheries (Handlos and Williams 1985).

The importance of environmental flows for restoring the Lower Zambezi Basin below Cahora Bassa Dam was first proposed to the Government of Mozambique by consultants SWECO/ SWED POWER (1983). They recommended an environmental flow release (*freshet*) from Cahora Bassa to coincide with high flows from downstream tributaries, aimed at reducing the impact of soil salinisation on natural vegetation, improving agricultural productivity and the carrying capacity of grasslands, expanding floodplain waterbodies and reducing the growth of invasive aquatic macrophytes in river channels. In 1997, under the auspices of the Zambezi Valley Planning Authority, the operators of Cahora Bassa Dam hosted a Workshop on the Sustainable Management of Cahora Bassa Dam and the Zambezi Valley (Beilfuss 1997). More than 50 participants from government agencies, academic institutions and development NGOs concluded that environmental flow releases from Cahora Bassa Dam were necessary to restore human livelihoods and ecosystems downstream (Davies 1998).

Most recently, the SADC recognised six objectives that can be addressed through environmental flow management in the Zambezi River Basin in addition to hydropower objectives (SWRSD Zambezi Joint Venture 2010):

- Dam safety: Managing releases to avoid the reservoir reaching unsafe levels. Provide adequate capacity to safely store and pass the design flood.
- Flood management: Avoiding loss of life and reducing socioeconomic impact.
- Environmental management: Providing quantity and quality of water required to maintain ecosystems and enabling them to provide sustainable services and good quality water.
- Dry-season floodplain agriculture: Accommodating the harvest period in release management.

- Plantation irrigation: Providing adequate yield for crop production.
- Water supply: Setting priorities based on economic or social considerations, including poverty alleviation.

Simulation modeling of the Zambezi system dam operation (Beilfuss 2010) indicates that modest environmental flow releases from Cahora Bassa Dam can be realised without a significant reduction in hydropower production, by revisiting the operational rule curve to redirect the spillage of excess reservoir waters from the dry season to early wet season. Beilfuss and Brown (2010) demonstrate that the majority of Lower Zambezi water users/concerns would benefit from annual flood releases, the trade-offs among different water users is minimal in terms of the timing, magnitude or duration of releases, and the economic value of releases to downstream users exceeds the value of waters used solely for hydropower production.

In practice, dams of the Zambezi Basin have been operated fairly independently, without regard to economic requirements of other stakeholders in the basin. Dam operations have focused primarily on dam safety and maximisation of hydropower production on a one-year operating window. New modes of operation, which consider multiple-objective environmental flows over a multi-year operating window, should be considered for the Zambezi River system.

A unique partnership between the Zambezi River water authorities, dam operators and power companies, NGOs (the World Wide Fund for Nature, International Crane Foundation), and regional universities is uniquely positioned to build on these findings and implement environmental flows in the Zambezi River Basin. The partnership seeks to incorporate environmental flows into the operating rules of hydropower dams in the Zambezi River Basin, and ensure that essential freshwater resource areas in the Zambezi River Basin are well protected and properly managed. This partnership could play a vital role in facilitating climate change adaption for vulnerable Zambezi Basin communities, and illustrates the potential for environmental flows to overcome conflict in shared water resources and create opportunities for cooperation.

www.solutionsforwater.org/solutions/joint-zambezi-river-basin-environmental-flows-programme.

Strengthen institutional capacity for climate change adaptation

The development of strong institutional capacity may be the single most important factor in the successful adaptation of water resources management frameworks to cope with climate change. Significant technical, financial and social capacity is required, at different scales, from strong and well-governed national water ministries and river basin operators, through regional departments and basin councils, to local river basin offices and water user associations (Matthews and Le Quesne 2009). As new risks and uncertainties arise with climate change, a water resources management style is needed that is flexible enough to adjust to ongoing change (Bergkamp *et al.* 2003). Those responsible for hydropower management at all levels must be trained in new modes for dam operation and equipped with models and tools for implementation, including flood forecasting systems, routing models, conjunctive management systems and monitoring and adaptive management protocols. Substantial investment in water management institutions is essential to facilitate new perspectives and proficiencies. For example, climate change adaptation in Rwanda includes a series of training and technical assistance activities with hydropower operators and managers to improve operation and maintenance of the stations, and with decision-makers in the Ministry of Infrastructure to facilitate the integration of climate change considerations into the management of Rwanda's hydroelectric sector.[12] Training opportunities for water resource managers, authorities and users in the Zambezi River Basin may be provided through innovations in curricula at training facilities that already service hydropower professionals, such as the International Centre for Hydropower, the Global Water Partnership and UNESCO's Institute for Water Education.

Notes

1 The IPCC Special Report on Emissions Scenarios (SRES) describes four global emissions scenarios used to make projections about future climate change (Nakićenović *et al.* 2000). The SRES scenarios were used in the IPCC Third Assessment Report (2001) and IPCC Fourth Assessment Report (2007). The SRES scenarios were replaced by four greenhouse gas concentration trajectories (called RCPs) for the Fifth Assessment Report (2014).
2 The Coupled Model Intercomparison Project (CMIP) is used as a standard experimental protocol for studying the output of coupled atmosphere-ocean general circulation models (GCMs), under the World Climate Research Program.
3 Major climate simulation models and their sources for this analysis include the CSIRO2 (Commonwealth Scientific and Industrial Research Organization, Australia), HadCM3 (Hadley Centre for Climate Prediction and Research, UK), CGCM2 (Meteorological Research Institute, Japan), ECHAM (Max Plank Institute for Meteorology, Germany), GISS-NASA (US National Aeronautics and Space Agency/Goddard Institute for Space Studies), GFDL (US Department of Commerce/NOAA/ Geophysical Fluid Dynamics Laboratory) and PCM (National Center for Atmospheric Research, US).
4 Cyclonic events are not explicitly modelled by existing Global Circulation Models (GCMs).
5 Other African river basins assessed by IPCC Third Assessment Report (2001) include the Congo, Limpopo, Ogooue, Orange, Niger, Nile, Rufiji, Ruvuma, Schebeli and Volta.
6 The SWRSD Zambezi Joint Venture consulting firms include Deltares, Rankin, SEED, SSI and WRNA.
7 www.nytimes.com/gwire/2010/05/10/10greenwire-droughts-turn-out-the-lights-in-hydro-dependen-40458.html?pagewanted=all
8 The need to adapt infrastructure to more extreme flooding resulting from climate change extends well beyond hydropower design. For example, the magnification of the intensity/severity of flooding events in Mozambique could repeatedly destroy road stocks and other infrastructure, with negative implications for growth (Chinowsky *et al.* 2015).
9 Pests were also identified more broadly in IPCC (2014).
10 See www.dpac.tas.gov.au/__data/assets/pdf_file/0005/154427/FINAL_Hydro_Tasmania_Case_Study_2.pdf and www.nccarf.edu.au/content/climatefuturestasmania
11 See www.sapp.co.zw
12 Rwanda Environment Management Authority (2011) *Guidelines to mainstream climate change adaption and mitigation in the energy and infrastructure section.* www.rema.gov.rw/rema_doc/IMCE_Doc/Guide lines-Energy&Infrastructure.pdf

References

Acreman, M. 1994. The role of artificial flooding in the integrated development of river basins in Africa. In: *Integrated river basin development*, (eds.), Kirby, C. and White, W.R., 35–44. Chichester: John Wiley & Sons.
African Development Bank, Asian Development Bank, Department for International Development, UK, European Commission, Federal Ministry for Economic Cooperation and Development, Germany, Ministry of Foreign Affairs – Development Cooperation, The Netherlands, Organisation for Economic Cooperation and Development, United Nations Development Programme, United Nations Environment Programme and World Bank. 2003. *Poverty and climate change: Reducing the vulnerability of the poor through adaptation.* Washington, DC: World Bank.
Alavian, V., Qaddumi, H.M., Dickson, E., Diez, S.M., Danilenko, A.V., Hirji, R.F., Puz, G., Pizarro, C., Jacobsen, M. and Blankespoor, B. 2009. *Water and climate change: Understanding the risks and making climate-smart investment decisions.* Final Report. Washington, DC: World Bank.
Arnell, N.W. 1999. Climate change and global water resources. *Global Environmental Change* 9: S31–S49.

Arnell, N.W. 2004. Climate change and global water resources: SRES emissions and socio-economic scenarios. *Global Environmental Change* 14: 31–52.

Arthington, A., King, J., O'Keeffe, J., Day, D., Pusey, B., Bluhdorn, D. and Tharme, R. 1992. Development of a holistic approach for assessing environmental flow requirements of riverine ecosystems. In: *Proceedings of an international seminar and workshop on water allocation for the environment*, (eds.), Pilgram, J. and Hooper, B., 69–87. Armidale, Australia: The Center for Water Policy Research.

Beck, L. and Bernauer, T. 2010. *Water scenarios for the Zambezi River Basin, 2000–2050.* Zurich: African Dams Project, ETH University of Zurich.

Beilfuss, R.D. 1997. Restoring the flood: A vision for the Zambezi Delta. *The ICF Bugle* 23(4): 1–2. Available at www.savingcranes.org

Beilfuss, R.D. 2002. Hydrological degradation, ecological dynamics, and restoration potential: The story of an African floodplain. PhD dissertation. Madison: University of Wisconsin.

Beilfuss, R.D. 2010. Modelling trade-offs between hydropower generation and environmental flow scenarios: A case study of the Lower Zambezi River Basin, Mozambique. *International Journal of River Basin Management* 8(3): 331–347.

Beilfuss, R.D. 2012. *A risky climate for Southern African Hydro: Assessing hydrological risks and consequences for Zambezi River Basin dams.* Berkeley, CA: International Rivers Network.

Beilfuss, R.D. and Brown, C. 2010. Assessing environmental flow requirements and tradeoffs for the Lower Zambezi River and Delta, Mozambique. *International Journal of River Basin Management* 8(2): 127–138.

Beilfuss, R.D., Dutton, P. and Moore, D. 2000. Land cover and land uses in the Zambezi Delta. Volume III, Chapter 2. Land Cover Change Zambezi Delta. In: *Biodiversity of the Zambezi Basin wetlands*, (ed.), Timberlake, J. Occasional Publications in Biodiversity No. 8. Famona, Bulawayo Zimbabwe: Biodiversity Foundation for Africa, PO Box FM 430.

Bergkamp, G., Orlando, B. and Burton, I. 2003. *Change: Adaptation of water management to climate change.* Gland, Switzerland and Cambridge, UK: International Union for Conservation of Nature (IUCN). ix + 53 pp.

Boko, M., Ning, I., Nyong, A., Vogel, C., Githeko, A., Medany, M., Osman-Elasha, B., Tabo, R. and Yanda, P. 2007. Africa. Climate change 2007: Impacts, adaptation, and vulnerability. In: *Contribution of Working Group II to the Fourth Assessment Report of the Intergovernmental Panel on Climate Change*, (eds.), Parry, M.L., Canziani, O.F., Palutikof, J.P., van der Linden, P.J. and Hanson, C.E., 433–467. Cambridge, UK: Cambridge University Press.

Brown, D., Chanarikia, R., Chatiza, K., Dhliwayo, M., Dodman, D., Masiyiwa, M., Muchadienyika, D., Mugabe, P. and Zvigadza, S. 2012. *Climate change impacts, vulnerability and adaptation in Zimbabwe.* IIED Working Paper no. 3. London, UK: International Institute for Environment and Development.

Cai, W. and Cowan, T. 2008. Evidence of impacts from rising temperature on inflows to the Murray-Darling Basin. *Geophysical Research Letters* 35.

Cambula, P. 1999. *Impacts of climate change on water resources of Mozambique.* Final report of the Mozambique/US Country Study Program Project on Assessment of the Vulnerability of the Economy of Mozambique to Projected Climate Change. Maputo, Mozambique (unpublished).

Chinowsky, P.S., Schweikert, A.E., Strzepek, N.L. and Strzepek, K. 2015. Infrastructure and climate change: A study of impacts and adaptations in Malawi, Mozambique, and Zambia. *Climatic Change* 130(1): 49–62.

Christensen, J.H., Hewitson, B., Busuioc, A., Chen, A., Gao, X., Held, I., Jones, R., Koli, R.K., Kwon, W.-T., Laprise, R., Rueda, V.M., Mearns, L., Menéndez, C.G., Räisänen, J., Rinke, A., Sarr, A. and Whetton, P. 2007. Regional climate projections. In: *Climate change 2007: The physical science basis. Contribution of Working Group I to the Fourth Assessment Report of the Intergovernmental Panel on Climate Change*, (eds.), Solomon, S., Qin, D., Manning, M., Chen, Z., Marquis, M., Averyt, K.B., Tignor, M. and Miller, H.L., 847–940. Cambridge: Cambridge University Press.

Davies, B.R., (ed.) 1998. *Sustainable use of the Cahora Bassa Dam and the Zambezi Valley. Final report.* Maputo, Mozambique: Arquivo do Patrimonio Cultural and Ford Foundation.

De Wit, M. and Stankiewicz, J. 2006. Changes in surface water supply across Africa with predicted climate change. *Science* 311(5769): 1917–1921.

Dinesh, D., Bette, B., Boone, R., Grace, D., Kinyangi, J., Lindahl, J., Vishnumurthy, M., Ramirez-Villegas, J., Robinson, T., Rosenstock, T., Smith, J. and Thornton, P. 2015. *Impacts of climate change on African agriculture: Focus on pests and diseases.* CCAFS Info note. Copenhagen, Denmark: CGIAR Research Program on Climate Change, Agriculture and Food Security (CCAFS).

Fant, C., Gebretsadik, Y., McCluskey, A. and Strzepek, K. 2015. An uncertainty approach to assessment of climate change impacts on the Zambezi River Basin. *Climatic Change* 130(1): 35–48.

Few, R., Ahern, M., Matthies, F. and Kovats, S. 2004. *Floods, health and climate change: A strategic review.* Working paper 63. Norwich: Tyndall Centre for Climate Change Research, University of East Anglia, 138 p.

Fischer, G., Shah, M., Tubiello, F.N. and van Velthuizen, H. 2005. Socio-economic and climate change impacts on agriculture: An integrated assessment, 1990–2080. *Philos. T. Roy. Soc. B.* 360: 2067–2083.

Girot, P., Erhart, C., Ogelthorpe, J., Reid, H., Rossing, T., Gambarelli, G., Jeans, H., Barrow, E., Martin, S., Ikkala, N. and Phillips, J. 2012. Integrating community and ecosystem-based approaches in climate change adaptation. *Ecosystems & Livelihoods Adaptation Network.* www.elanadapt.net

Gjermundsen, T. and Jenssen, L. 2001. Economic risk and sensitivity analyses for hydropower projects. *Hydropower in the New Millennium: Proceedings of the 4th International Conference on Hydropower Development,* 23–28. Bergen, Norway, June 20–22, 2001.

Goodland, R. 2011. *Ten 'rules-of-thumb' to select better hydroelectricity projects.* Burlington, Vermont: Institute for Environmental Diplomacy and Security, Univ. of Vermont. Available at http://ieds.newsvine.com/ _news/2011/12/20/9584548-ten-rules-of-thumb-to-select-better-hydroelectricity-projects. Updated at http://goodlandrobert.com

Guveya, E. and Sukume, C. 2008. *The economic value of the Lower Zambezi Delta.* Report to WWF Mozambique Country Office. Maputo, Mozambique: World Wide Fund for Nature.

Hallegatte, S. 2009. Strategies to adapt to an uncertain climate change. *Global Environmental Change* 19(2): 240–247.

Handlos, W.L., and Williams, G.J. 1985. The Zambian sector of the Zambezi catchment – an overview. In Handlos, W.L., and Howard, G.W., (eds.) *Development prospects for the Zambezi Valley in Zambia,* 1–28 Kafue Basin Research Committee, University of Zambia, Lusaka.

Hankins, M. 2009. *A renewable energy plan for Mozambique.* Maputo, Mozambique: Justiça Ambiental, 64 p.

Hanlon, J. 2001. Floods displace thousands in Mozambique. *The Guardian.* 28 March.

Harrison, D., Opperman, J. and Richter, B. 2007. Can hydropower be sustainable? *International Water Power & Dam Construction.* 17 September 2007.

Harrison, G.P. and Whittington, H.W. 2001. Impact of climate change on hydropower investment. In: *Hydropower in the new millennium: Proceedings of the 4th International Conference on Hydropower Development,* 257–261. Bergen, Norway, June 20–122, 2001.

Harrison, G.P. and Whittington, H.W. 2002. Susceptibility of the Batoka Gorge hydroelectric scheme to climate change. *Journal of Hydrology* 264: 230–241.

Harrison, G.P., Whittington, H.W. and Wallace, A.R. 2006. Sensitivity of hydropower to climate change. *International Journal of Power and Energy Systems* 26(1).

Hartmann, J. 2008. Climate change: Implications for hydropower sustainability. Presentation at HSAF Meeting 5. Itaipu. 8 December, 2008.

Hirji, R. and Davis, R. 2009. *Environmental flows in water resources policies, plans, and projects.* Washington, DC: World Bank.

Hudson, D.A. and Jones, R.G. 2002. *Regional climate model simulations of present day and future climates of southern Africa.* Technical note 39. Bracknell: Hadley Centre, 42 p.

Hughes, R.H. and Hughes, J.S. 1992. *A directory of African wetlands.* Gland, Switzerland and Cambridge, UK: IUCN; Nairobi, Kenya: UNEP; Cambridge, UK: World Conservation Monitoring Centre, 820 p.

ICEM (International Center for Environmental Management). 2010. *Mekong River Commission Strategic Environmental Assessment (SEA) of hydropower on the Mekong mainstream: Final report.* Hanoi, Vietnam.

IPCC (Intergovernmental Panel on Climate Change). 2001. Climate change 2001: Impacts, adaptation, and vulnerability. In: *Contribution of Working Group II to the Third Assessment Report of the Intergovernmental Panel on Climate Change,* (eds.), McCarthy, J.J., Canziani, O.F., Leary, N.A., Dokken, D.J. and White, K.S. Cambridge: Cambridge University Press, 1032 p.

IPCC. 2007. Climate change 2007: The physical science basis. In: *Contribution of Working Group I to the Fourth Assessment Report of the Intergovernmental Panel on Climate Change,* (eds.), Solomon, S., Qin, D., Manning, M., Chen, Z., Marquis, M., Averyt, K.B., Tignor, M. and Miller, H.L. Cambridge: Cambridge University Press, 996 p.

IPCC. 2014. *Climate change 2014 – Impacts, adaptation and vulnerability: Regional aspects.* Cambridge: Cambridge University Press.

Kamga, A.F., Jenkins, G.S., Gaye, A.T., Garba, A., Sarr, A. and Adedoyin, A. 2005. Evaluating the National Center for Atmospheric Research climate system model over West Africa: Present-day and the 21st century A1 scenario. *J. Geophys. Res.–Atmos.* 110.

King, J.M. and Brown, C.A. 2006. Environmental flows: Striking the balance between development and resource protection. *Ecology and Society* 11(2): 26.

King, P., Bird, J. and Haas, L. 2007. *The current status of environmental criteria for hydropower development in the Mekong region: A literature compilation.* Vientiane: Asian Development Bank; Mekong River Commission; WWF.

Krchnak, K., Richter, B. and Thomas, G. 2009. *Integrating environmental flows into hydropower dam planning, design, and operations.* Washington, DC: World Bank.

Le Quesne, T., Matthews, J., Von der Heyden, C., Wickel, B., Wilby, R., Hartmann, J., Pegram, G., Kistin, E., Blate, G., Kimura de Freitas, G., Levine, E., Guthrie, C., McSweeney, C. and Sindorf, N. 2010. *Flowing forward: Freshwater ecosystem adaptation to climate change in water resources management and biodiversity conservation.* Water Working Notes. Washington, DC: World Bank.

Lobell, D.B., Burke, M.B., Tebaldi, C., Mastrandrea, M.D., Falcon, W.P. and Naylor, R.L. 2008. Prioritizing climate change adaptation needs for food security in 2030. *Science* 319(5863): 607–610.

Lobell, D.B., Schlenker, W. and Costa-Roberts, J. 2011. Climate trends and global crop production since 1980. *Science* 333(6042): 616–620.

Ludwig, F. and Asseng, S. 2006. Climate change impacts on wheat production in a Mediterranean environment in Western Australia. *Agricultural Systems* 90(1): 159–179.

Magadza, C.H.D. 2006. Kariba Reservoir: Experience and lessons learned. *Lakes & Reservoirs: Research and Management* 11(4): 271–286.

Matthews, J.H. and Le Quesne, T. 2009. *Adapting water management – a primer on coping with climate change.* Surrey, UK: WWF-UK.

Mazvimavi, D. and Wolski, P. 2006. Long-term variations of annual flows of the Okavango and Zambezi rivers. *Phys Chem Earth* 31(15–16): 944–951.

McCartney, M.P., Rebelo, L.M. and Sellamuttu, S.S. 2015. Wetlands, livelihoods and human health. In: *Wetlands and human health,* (eds.), Finlayson, C.M., Horwitz, P., and Weinstein, P., 123–148. Wetlands: Ecology, Conservation and Management 5. Netherlands: Springer.

McMichael, A.J., Woodruff, R.E. and Hales, S. 2006. Climate change and human health: Present and future risks. *Lancet* 367: 859–869.

Milly, P.C.D., Betancourt, J., Falkenmark, M., Hirsch, R.M. and Zbigniew, W. 2008. Climate change – stationarity is dead: Whither water management? *Science* 319: 573–574.

Mimikou, M. and Baltas, E.A. 1997. Climate change impacts on the reliability of hydroelectric energy production. *Hydrol. Sci. J.* 42(5): 661–678.

Mitchell, S.A. 2013. The status of wetlands, threats and the predicted effect of global climate change: The situation in sub-Saharan Africa. *Aquat Sci* (2013) 75: 95–112.

Nakićenović, N., Alcamo, J., Davis, G., de Vries, B., Fenhann, J., Gaffin, S., Gregory, K., Grübler, A., Jung, T.Y., Kram, T., Lebre la Rovere, E., Michaelis, L., Mori, S., Morita, T., Pepper, W., Pitcher, H., Price, L., Riahi, K., Roehrl, A., Rogner, H.H., Sankovski, A., Schlesinger, M., Shukla, P., Smith, S., Swart, R., van Rooijen, S., Victor, N. and Dadi, Z. (eds.) 2000. *Emissions scenarios: A special report of the Intergovernmental Panel on Climate Change (IPCC).* Cambridge: Cambridge University Press, 509 pp.

Nda, J., Mapfumo, P., van Wijk, M.T., Mtambanengwe, F., Rufino, M.C., Chikowo, R. and Giller, K.E. (2013). Managing soil fertility to adapt to rainfall variability in smallholder cropping systems in Zimbabwe. *Field Crops Research,* 154, 211–225.

Ndaruzaniye, V., Volkmann, E., Lipper, L., Demeke, M., Capaldo, J., Fiott, D., Kantu, P.Y.T., Flavell, A. and Clover, J. 2010. *Climate change and security in Africa: Vulnerability discussion paper.* Brussels: German Federal Government and Swedish International Development Agency (Sida).

Nelson, E.J., Kareiva, P., Ruckelshaus, M., Arkema, M., Geller, G., Goodrich, D., Matzek, V., Pinsky, M., Reid, W., Saunders, M., Semmens, D. and Tallis, H. 2013. Climate change's impact on key ecosystem services and the human well-being they support in the US. *Frontiers in Ecology and the Environment* 11(9): 483–893.

New, M., Hewitson, B., Stephenson, D.B., Tsiga, A., Kruger, A., Manhique, A., Gomez, B. and Coelho, C.A.S. 2006. Evidence of trends in daily climate extremes over southern and west Africa. *Journal of Geophysical Research: Atmospheres* 111(D14)

Nexant Consultants. 2007. SAPP regional generation and transmission expansion plan study. Draft final report. Main Report, Volume 2, submitted to SAPP Coordination Center.

Nicholls, R.J. 2004. Coastal flooding and wetland loss in the 21st century: changes under the SRES climate and socio-economic scenarios. *Global Environmental Change* 14: 69–86.

Nkomwa, E., Joshua, M., Ngongondo, C., Monjerezi, M. and Chipungu, F. 2014. Assessing indigenous knowledge in agriculture: A case study of Chagaka Village, Chikhwawa, southern Malawi. *Physics and Chemistry of the Earth* 67–69: 164–172.

Norconsult. 2003. *The integrated water resources development plan for Lake Malawi/Nyasa/Niassa and Shire River System - Stage 2.* Final feasibility report. Republic of Malawi: Ministry of Water Development.

Pedrono, M., Locatelli, B., Ezzine-de-Blas, D., Pesche, D., Moranda, S. and Binot, A. 2016. Impact of climate change on ecosystem services. In: *Climate change and agriculture worldwide*, (ed.), Torquebiau, E., 251–261. New York: Springer.

Postel, S. and Richter, B. 2003. Rivers for life: Managing water for people and nature. Washington, DC: Island Press.

Ruosteenoja, K., Carter, T.R., Jylhä, K. and Tuomenvirt, H. 2003. *Future climate in world regions: An intercomparison of model-based projections for the new IPCC emissions scenarios.* Helsinki: Finnish Environment Institute, 83 p.

Rurinda, J., Mapfumo, P., van Wijk, M.T., Mtambanengwe, F., Rufino, M.C., Chikowo, R. and Giller, K.E. 2013. Managing soil fertility to adapt to rainfall variability in smallholder cropping systems in Zimbabwe. *Field Crops Research* 154: 211–225.

Rurinda, J., van Wijik, M., Mpfumo, P., Descheemaker, K., Supit, I. and Giller, K. 2015. Climate change and maize yield in southern Africa: What can farm management do? *Global Change Biology* 21(12): 4588–4601.

Salewicz, K.A. 1996. Impact of climate change on the Lake Kariba hydropower scheme. In: *Water resources management in the face of climatic/hydrological uncertainties*, (eds.), Kaczmarek, Z., Strzepek, K.M., Somlyody, L. and Priazhinskaya, V., 200–321. Rotterdam: Kluwer Academic Publishers.

Schlosser, C.A. and Strzepek, K. 2015. Regional climate change of the Greater Zambezi River Basin: A hybrid assessment. *Climate Change* 130: 9–19.

Scoones, I. 1991. Wetlands in drylands: Key wetlands in drylands: Key resources for agricultural and pastoral production in Africa. *Ambio* 20(8): 366–371.

Scudder, T. 1989. River basin projects in Africa: Conservation vs. development. *Environment* 31: 4–32.

Scudder, T. and Acreman, M.C. 1996. Water management for the conservation of the Kafue wetlands, Zambia, and practicalities of artificial flood releases. In: *Water management and wetlands in sub-Saharan Africa*, (eds.), Acreman, M.C. and Hollis, G.E., 101–106. Gland, Switzerland: IUCN.

Seyam, I.M., Hoekstra, A.Y. and Ngabirano, H.H.G. 2001. *The value of freshwater wetlands in the Zambezi basin.* Delft, The Netherlands: UNESCO-IHE Institute for Water Education, 22p.

Shongwe, M.E., van Oldenborgh, G.J., van den Hurk, B.J.J.M., de Boer, B., Coelho, C.A.S. and van Aalst, M.K. 2009. Projected changes in mean and extreme precipitation in Africa under global warming. Part I: Southern Africa. *Journal of Climate* 22(13): 3819–3837.

Southern African Research and Documentation Centre (SARDC) and Heinrich Boll Stiftung (HBS). 2010. *Responding to climate change impacts: Adaptation and mitigation strategies as practised in the Zambezi River Basin.* Harare and Cape Town: SARDC and HBS.

Springate, D.A. and Kover, P.X. 2014. Plant responses to elevated temperatures: A field study on phenological sensitivity and fitness responses to simulated climate warming. *Global Change Biology* 20(2): 456–465.

Stenek, V. and Boysen, D. 2011. *Climate risk and business – hydropower: Kafue Gorge Lower, Zambia.* Zambia: International Finance Corporation.

Stige, L.C., Stave, J. and Chan, K. 2006. The effect of climate variation on agro-pastoral production in Africa. *Proceedings of the National Academy of Sciences* 103(9): 3049–3053.

Strzepek, K. and McCluskey, A. 2006. *District level hydro-climatic time series and scenario analysis to assess the impacts of climate change on regional water resources and agriculture in Africa.* Discussion Paper No. 13. Centre for Environmental Economics and Policy in Africa (CEEPA). Pretoria: University of Pretoria, 59 p.

Swain, A., Bali Swain, R., Themner, A. and Krampe, F. 2012. Zambezi River Basin: A risk zone of climate change and vulnerability. *New Routes* 17(3): 17–20.

SWECO/SWED POWER Consultants. 1983. *Cahora Bassa hydroelectric power scheme – State II, Pre-investment report, Part 5: Ecology.* Stockholm, Sweden.

SWRSD Zambezi Joint Venture. 2010. *Dam synchronization and flood releases in the Zambezi River Basin project.* Consultancy report for the German Federal Ministry for Economic Cooperation and Development (GTZ) and the UK Department for International Development (DFID). Gaborone, Botswana.

Tadross, M., Jack, C. and Hewitson, B. 2005. On RCM-based projections of change in southern African summer climate. *Geophysical Research Letters* 32. 15 December 2005.

Taylor, A., de Bruin, W.B. and Dessai, S. 2014. Climate change beliefs and perceptions of weather-related changes in the United Kingdom. *Risk Analysis* 34: 1995–2004.

Tiffen, M. and Mulele, M.R. 1994. *The environmental impact of the 1991–92 drought on Zambia.* Gland, Switzerland and Lusaka, Zambia: IUCN, 118 p.

Timberlake, J. 2000. *Biodiversity of Zambezi Basin wetlands: Review and preliminary assessment of available information.* Phase 1. Final report. Bulawayo: Biodiversity Foundation for Africa and Harare: The Zambezi Society.

Treidel, H., Martin-Bordes, J.L. and Gurdak, J.J. 2011. *Climate change effects on groundwater resources: A global synthesis of findings and recommendations.* IAH – International Contributions to Hydrogeology. Leiden, The Netherlands: CRC Press, 414 p.

Tubiello, F.N. and Ewert, F. 2002. Simulating the effects of elevated CO_2 on crops: Approaches and applications for climate change. *European Journal of Agronomy* 18(1): 57–74.

Turpie, J., Smith, B., Emerton, L. and Barnes, J. 1999. *Economic value of the Zambezi Basin wetlands.* Cape Town: IUCN Regional Office for Southern Africa, 346 p.

UNDP (United Nations Development Programme). 2004. *Adaptation policy frameworks for climate change: Developing strategies, policies and measures.* Cambridge: Cambridge University Press.

Urbiztondo, R.J. 1992. *Modelling of climate change impacts on the Upper Zambezi River Basin.* MSc thesis. USA: University of Colorado.

USAID (United States Agency for International Development, 2012. *Climate change impact on agricultural production and adaptation strategies: Farmers' perception and experiences.* Summary results of focus group interviews in Zambia, 2012. USAID Project 'Improved Modeling of Household Food Security Decision-Making and Investment Given Climate Change Uncertainty'. Accessed at http://fsg.afre.msu.edu/climate_change/Climate_change_FGD_synthesis_Zam.pdf.

Usman, M.T. and Reason, C.J.C. 2004. Dry spell frequencies and their variability over southern Africa. *Climate Research* 26: 199–211.

World Bank. 2006. *Zambezi River Basin – Sustainable water resources development for irrigated agriculture.* Trust Fund for Environmentally & Socially Sustainable Development (TFESSD) Africa Poverty and Environment Program. Washington, DC: World Bank.

World Bank. 2010. *The Zambezi River Basin. A multi-sector investment opportunities analysis.* Washington, DC: World Bank.

World Commission on Dams. 2000. *Dams and development: A new framework for decision-making. The report of the World Commission on Dams.* London: Earthscan Publications Ltd.

5

Hydropower and the water-energy-food nexus

Amaury Tilmant

Key messages

- The Zambezi River Basin is an important regional water resources system in terms of energy generation and food production. As the demands for water, energy and food increase due to population growth and rising living standards, so will the interconnectedness between the corresponding sectors; this is the so-called water-energy-food nexus.

- In the near future, the irrigated area is expected to double and exceed 500,000 ha. In terms of power, ongoing and planned projects will add 2,700 MW to the electrical grid. Projects in both sectors – agriculture and energy – are all located in the Lower and Middle Zambezi.
- A two-pronged approach is needed to address the nexus challenge in the Zambezi Basin: first, to improve the management of water resources at the basin scale; second, to enhance cross-sectoral planning.
- The ultimate goal of a nexus approach in the Zambezi is to manage the trade-offs between new irrigation projects, flood recession agriculture and hydropower generation.
- Because ZAMCOM is the only institution overlooking the entire situation in the basin, its mandate could be expanded to explicitly include the promotion of a nexus approach. ZAMCOM is particularly well placed to manage trade-offs and maximise co-benefits through intersectoral water allocation in the Zambezi Basin. Through enhanced cooperation with the Southern Africa Power Pool, ZAMCOM could assist countries in reforming their energy and water policies by making them more coherent.

Introduction

The Zambezi River Basin is an important regional water resources system in southern Africa in terms of food production and energy generation. Historically, hydropower generation has been the largest economic use of water in the basin (Euroconsult Mott MacDonald 2007) with an average annual generation of 30 terawatt hours (TWh). Assuming a value of 60 USD/MWh (megawatt hour) this amount of energy corresponds to USD1,800 million/year. Hydropower has also been a factor of regional integration with the establishment of the Zambezi River Authority (ZRA) for the operation of the Kariba Reservoir, and the interconnection of most of the hydropower stations with the Southern African Power Pool (SAPP). The second largest economic use of water is irrigated agriculture, which mainly occurs in the Lower and Middle Zambezi (World Bank 2008). Despite the evaporation losses from the large man-made reservoirs and irrigation consumptive uses, the Zambezi is still a largely open river basin where the amount of renewable water exceeds demands (with the notable exception of the Kafue, a tributary flowing through Zambia).

In their quest for food and energy security, riparian countries have plans to further develop the water resources in the Zambezi Basin (World Bank 2010); the irrigated area is expected to double in the near future while more than 2,000 MW of power will be added to the electrical grid. This will inevitably increase the interconnectedness between water, food production and energy generation; this is the so-called water-energy-food (WEF) nexus (World Economic Forum 2011; WWAP 2014). The presence of this nexus implies that changes in one sector are likely to impact the others. For example, the growth in agricultural production will require more water and energy, either as direct input or indirectly through processed inputs like fertilisers. If the energy needed in the agriculture sector is produced by using hydropower, even more water must be mobilised to increase food production. Another notable example is that of biofuels, which may require large amounts of water and land, and, therefore, compete with food production and/or with other forms of energy generation like hydropower (FAO 2013).

Like many other regional water resource systems, the development in the Zambezi River Basin requires careful planning to simultaneously achieve water, food and energy security. The presence of competing and intertwined uses makes this basin sensitive to unilateral developments, thereby increasing the risk of collateral damages downstream. Unfortunately, water resources development in the Zambezi has traditionally been undertaken at country level, with little consultation and cooperation among riparian countries (World Bank 2008). Traditionally, riparian countries have not seized the opportunities for joint water resources management, except in isolated cases like ZRA (Shela 2000). A nexus approach should help water managers and policy-makers in the Zambezi to mitigate the risks of collateral damages by engaging with other sectors, identifying the interconnections between sectors, quantifying the positive and negative external-ities across sectors, and designing cooperative institutions to share the benefits of cooperation.

This chapter starts with a review of the WEF nexus concepts and continues with the main drivers of the WEF nexus in the Zambezi River Basin, that is to say, hydropower and irrigation developments. The chapter then provides a description of physiographic, institutional and environ-mental factors affecting the WEF nexus in the Zambezi, discussion of challenges and opportun-ities associated with the WEF nexus approach to planning interventions, and conclusions that outline ways forward.

Drivers of the WEF nexus within the Zambezi Basin

Background: understanding the nexus

Over the past 10 years, the discourse on the WEF nexus has gained attention worldwide (Marsh and Sharma 2007). One of the first works on the nexus is a 2004 World Bank report on the WEF nexus in Central Asia (World Bank 2004), which was examined in the context of regional cooperation among the riparian countries of the Syr Darya River where the mismatch between upstream power and downstream irrigation demands was (and still is) a source of tension. In 2006, the US Department of Energy released a report for the United States Congress on the interdependence between water and energy in the country (DoE 2006). More recently, the United Nations chose to dedicate the World Water Development Report to the WEF nexus (WWAP 2014). This report provides a comprehensive overview of the concept with examples taken from all continents.

Despite being increasingly studied, there is no clear understanding as yet on how the concept can be operationalised to ensure water, energy and food security (Hussey and Pittock 2012). One of the key issues comes from the fact that energy and water policies are developed separately, largely in isolation from one another. The result is a lack of policy integration, which makes it difficult to identify and then manage the links between sectors.

To counteract the reality of silos-driven policy development, scholars argue that what is needed is a more integrated, cross-sectoral assessment of interventions required to meet the rising demands for water, food and energy (Biggs *et al.* 2015). Various types of interventions can be envisaged: structural (e.g., hydraulic infrastructures, power plants) and/or non-structural - (e.g., improved operation, institutional restructuring, insurance mechanisms, demand management, and so on). Regardless of the sector in which these interventions are needed, the planning process should highlight the trade-offs and synergies associated with the proposed interventions across sectors and over the appropriate spatial and temporal scales (Rasul and Sharma 2015). This nexus thinking was first proposed by the World Economic Forum as a new approach for fostering policy coherence and coordination across sectors and stakeholders (World Economic Forum 2011). However, turning this general principle into practice will be challenging as water and energy communities have significantly different views and conceptual approaches when planning interventions in their respective sectors (WWAP 2014).

In the energy sector, most interventions focus on production and distribution; that is, power plants, transmission lines and distribution networks. In the water sector, most of the interventions deal with the capture, use and discharge of water. In terms of management, power and water systems are also quite different. Various mechanisms are available for water allocation:

administrative, market-based, cost-based or community-based. Dinar *et al.* (1997) review the pros and cons as well as the conditions under which a particular allocation mechanism can develop. In general, water allocation is undertaken through a combination of top-down and bottom-up approaches; large infrastructures are managed by government agencies whereas daily allocations to end-users are usually determined locally, either individually or through a users' association, and so on. In the energy sector, electricity is either traded through a wholesale market or managed by a vertically integrated utility responsible for production, transmission and distribution of electricity. Moreover, because of its larger economic weight, the energy sector usually receives greater political attention.

The issue of scale is a delicate, albeit often overlooked, one. Every planning process requires that boundaries in space and time be defined. When dealing with water-related interventions, the analysis should be done at the river-basin scale over a period of several decades. In the energy sector, the spatial boundaries are usually the limits of the interconnected electrical system, which rarely (if ever) coincide with a river basin. In the agriculture sector, the boundaries vary from local to international depending on the type of agriculture (subsistence versus industrial). These differences mean that energy and food tend to be managed at the national-international level whereas water is managed at the local-national level.

Even though water is managed more locally and has received less political attention, there is a general consensus among professionals that water plays a central role in the nexus as it is needed to achieve water, food and energy security. Water, as a resource, has some important characteristics that are directly relevant to the nexus:

- Because it is a fugitive resource, its management generates unidirectional externalities (from upstream to downstream) and, therefore, it creates asymmetrical relationships between water users/sectors. In other words, the allocation of water to one sector upstream is likely to impact another sector downstream, meaning that there is a 'spatial' dimension associated with the nexus.
- There is a large diversity of water uses, which can fall into two categories: rival versus non-rival uses. Non-rivalry is observed when users are not in competition for the same unit of water. The consumptive nature of irrigation water use, even in the presence of return flows, implies that water in irrigated agriculture is often considered a rival good. In contrast, hydropower companies are closer to non-rival users since most water stored and channeled through turbines for electricity generation can in turn be used by a downstream user. Notably, however, the water is consumed through evaporation losses from reservoirs while it is stored, and the release patterns of water for electricity generation may adversely affect the timing of water availability for downstream uses. Ultimately, the distinction between rival and non-rival uses is important in order to understand the synergies and identify trade-offs between the three sectors.
- In the energy sector, water is a universal coolant. When electricity is generated from thermo-electric power plants, a certain amount of water is needed to cool the power-producing equipment. The cooling of thermoelectric power plants is a consumptive use because, depending on the cooling method, a fraction of the water withdrawal will be lost through evaporation.

Hydropower development

The sequence of development in the Zambezi River Basin is typical of the twentieth-century evolution of many southern African river basins (Burke 1994). The main effort was given to the energy sector, with the construction of hydropower plants and the power utilities holding the principal water rights, while increased irrigation and municipal water demands were dealt with locally.

Victoria Falls, the first power station commissioned in 1938, has an installed capacity of 108 MW. This power station, which has been upgraded several times, is essentially a run-of-river scheme, with water uptakes located upstream of the falls. During low flows, water abstractions upstream of the falls are restricted in order to maintain a minimum discharge at the falls.

In the 1950s, the intensification of copper mining activities in the region became the main driver for the Kariba project, a hydroelectric plant located a few hundred kilometres downstream of Victoria Falls. The first stage of the Kariba Dam was completed at the border between Northern Rhodesia (Zambia) and Southern Rhodesia (Zimbabwe). It consisted of the dam wall and the Kariba South power station. Stage 2, the North power station, was commissioned in 1977. The project was planned with a total installed capacity of 1,320 MW for an expected annual energy output of 6,400 GWh. Kariba, with its huge storage capacity (180 km^3), is arguably the largest man-made reservoir in the world. The management of Kariba is under the responsibility of the Zambezi River Authority (ZRA), a binational organisation equally owned by the governments of Zambia and Zimbabwe.

During the 1960s, the Zambian government launched the Kafue Gorge project, a high-head 900 MW run-of-river power plant, recently upgraded to 990 MW. This project was followed by the construction of the Itezhi-tezhi Dam further upstream. This dam was designed to store water for the Kafue Gorge project and regulate the flows at the expense of the Kafue Flats, a large wetland located in between, whose ecosystem relies on a natural flow regime. Itezhi-tezhi has recently been equipped with a 120 MW power plant. Both infrastructures are operated by ZESCO, the Zambian power utility.

The construction of the largest hydropower plant in the Zambezi started in 1969. Located in the Cahora Bassa Gorge on the Zambezi main stem in Mozambique, the hydropower scheme has an installed capacity of 2,075 MW and a storage capacity of 51 km^3. The project was designed as a single purpose hydroelectric scheme to be financed by the sale of electrical power to South Africa. For decades, the dam was managed by Hidroeléctrica de Cahora Bassa (HCB), a company whose ownership was shared between Portugal (82 per cent) and Mozambique (18 per cent). In 2007, Mozambique bought Portugal's shares to obtain control over HCB.

In the Shire subbasin, a tributary flowing from Lake Nyasa/Malawi, three run-of-river stations exist: Nkula Falls (124 MW), Tedzani (90 MW) and Kapichira (64 MW). These three power plants constitute the bulk of ESCOM's (Electricity Supply Corporation of Malawi) generation capacity in Malawi. Water that flows through these stations is partially regulated by the Kamuzu Barrage in Liwonde.

These existing hydropower plants currently exploit less than one-third of the total hydropower potential of the basin; indeed, about 5,000 MW has been tapped whereas 13,000 MW remains unexploited. Most of the planned projects lie in Mozambique, Zambia and Zimbabwe. They consist of either new projects or extensions of existing infrastructures. Figure 5.2 lists the existing and planned projects.

At the time of writing, Mozambique had started the construction of the Mphanda Nkuwa project on the Zambezi main stem, some 60 km downstream of Cahora Bassa. This is a 1,300 MW run-of-river power plant, expected to be operational in 2017. In Zambia, progress is being made towards the construction of the 750 MW Kafue Gorge Lower power plant, another run-of-river plant located downstream from the tail race tunnel outlet of the Kafue Gorge project. A 360 MW extension of Kariba North was recently commissioned, while the 300 MW

Figure 5.1 Hydropower in the basin. (top) Hydropower production in Malawi; (bottom) Cahora Bassa, the second largest source of hydropower production in the basin, after Kariba

Photo: (top) Admire Ndhlovu/SARDC) (bottom) Richard Beilfuss

extension of Kariba South in Zimbabwe is in an advanced planning stage. These projects will add more than 2,700 MW to the electrical grid.

Moving forward, the most serious contenders for future development are Batoka Gorge and the extension of Cahora Bassa. The first is a bilateral project under the umbrella of ZRA. The project, which would be located 50 km downstream of Victoria Falls, includes a new dam and a 1,600 MW power plant. The extension of Cahora Bassa is an 850 MW project on the left bank of the Zambezi River.

Other, less-promising projects have been sidelined due to excessive financial and/or environmental costs. One of them is Devils Gorge, a 1,200 MW power plant that would be shared by Zambia and Zimbabwe. The Katombora Reservoir and the Muptata Gorge are two hydro projects on the Zambezi main stem that will not be developed in the foreseeable future due to their large environmental impacts.

As can be seen in Figure 5.2, existing and planned hydropower plants are concentrated in the Lower and Middle Zambezi, that is, from Victoria Falls to the river mouth. In the Upper Zambezi, the low hydraulic gradient makes this region unattractive to large-scale hydropower projects.

The interconnection between power utilities in southern Africa means that the energy generated by the hydropower stations in the Zambezi Basin can be exported over long distances. The SAPP indeed coordinates the planning and operation of the electric power system among the 12 member utilities and provides a forum for regional solutions to electric energy problems. The objective of the SAPP is to provide reliable and economical electricity supply to the consumers of each of the SAPP members consistent with reasonable utilisation of natural resources and effect on the environment (Musaba 2005). Due to their inherent flexibility, the hydropower plants in the Zambezi not only supply energy to the pool but also provide the much-needed

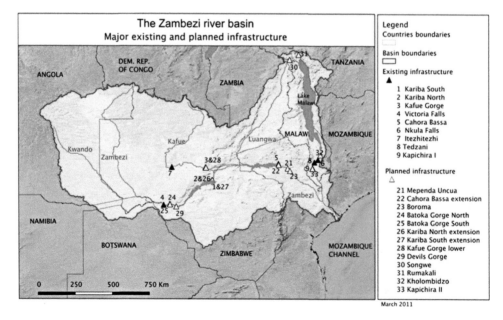

Figure 5.2 Existing and planned dams in the Zambezi Basin
Source: Tilmant and Kinzelbach (2012)

Table 5.1 Characteristics of existing and planned dams

Name	Country	Capacity (MW)	Life storage (km³)	Existing (E) Under Construction (C) Planned (P)
Nkula+Tedzani +Kapichira	Malawi	279	ROR	E
Mphanda Uncua	Mozambique	1,500	2.32	C
Cahora Bassa	Mozambique	2,925	51	E+ extension P
Kariba	Zambia/Zimbabwe	1,980	65	E+ extension P/C
Itezhi-tezhi	Zambia	120	5.3	E
Kafue Gorge	Zambia	1,650	ROR	E+ extension C
Batoka Gorge	Zambia/Zimbabwe	1,600	0.58	P
Victoria Falls	Zambia	108	ROR	E

Note: ROR = run-of-river.

ancillary services that are required to maintain the stability and security of the electric power system. This is an example of regional, cross-sectoral, impacts associated with local water resources allocation decisions (the amount of water released through the turbines of a particular power plant). A nexus approach to water resources planning and management would therefore need to consider regional and cross-sectoral benefits and impacts even if these extend beyond the basin.

It must also be stressed here that hydropower is considered as a major source of renewable energy in the SADC region, with most of the projects located in the Zambezi and Congo River Basins (EECG 2012). Bagasse, a byproduct of sugarcane, is another renewable energy source already used to generate power and steam in some countries like Zimbabwe. Generally speaking, producing bioenergy from agricultural wastes or residues can save land otherwise needed to produce energy crops as well as contribute to value-added within the supply chain (IRENA 2015). Yet, despite these obvious advantages, the trade-offs between food and fuel are not entirely resolved because of indirect land-use changes, and due to the potentially huge market demand for renewable energy in comparison to agriculture (FAO 2013). Whereas solar and wind energy sources have minimal water needs, bioenergy projects can have a substantial water footprint that needs to be adequately considered in energy sector planning.

Irrigation development

As indicated in Chapter 3, agriculture is an important economic activity in each riparian country. The development of the agriculture sector is also a key component in strategies to achieve food security and poverty reduction. Previous analyses (Denconsult 1998; World Bank 2010) have already shown that, in terms of available resources, there is scope to expand irrigated agriculture in the basin.

According to the Food and Agriculture Organization of the United Nations (FAO), the irrigation potential in the Zambezi River Basin is more than 3 million ha (Mha), of which less than 5 per cent is currently developed. Most of the existing and planned irrigation schemes are located in just three of the riparian countries: Malawi, Zambia and Zimbabwe (96 per cent of the total of about 259,039 ha). About 70 per cent of the basin population relies more or less directly on agriculture and the vast majority of the farming community are smallholder farmers (World Bank 2008).

According to the World Bank (2008), the lands with the highest productive potential are found within the large tributaries of the Zambezi River and not on the main stem of the Zambezi itself: Tete, Kafue, Kariba and Shire. It is therefore no surprise that this is where most of the basin's irrigation is concentrated (Table 5.2/Figure 5.3). In these subbasins, current water

Table 5.2 Irrigation areas in the Zambezi River Basin (World Bank 2010)

Subbasin	Irrigated area (ha)	Projects (ha)
Kafue	46,538	20,520
Kariba	44,531	184,388
Luangwa	17,794	11,063
Mupata	21,790	8,566
Shire	60,960	101,166
Tete	52,572	55,621
Delta	7,664	99,110
Others	7,190	4,207
Total	259,039	514,641

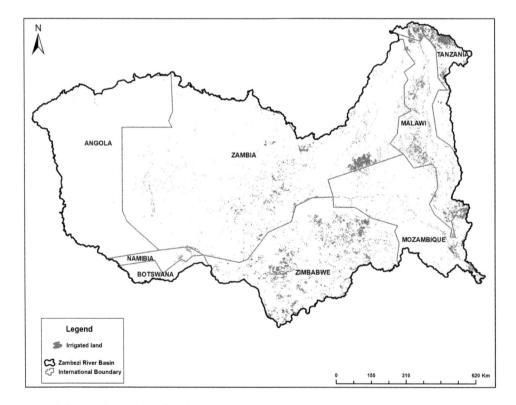

Figure 5.3 The irrigated land of the basin
Source: Luxon Nhamo/IWMI

abstractions for irrigated agriculture correspond to 3.2 km³, of which 46 per cent take place in Malawi (Shire subbasin), 27 per cent in Zimbabwe (Tete and Kariba subbasins) and 15 per cent in Zambia (Kafue subbasin). Assuming an average annual discharge of 95 km³, current irrigation withdrawals only account for about 3 per cent of the total. Because these subbasins are managed locally, upper limits on irrigation expansion must be imposed to avoid the potentially large opportunity cost associated with reduced discharges downstream. In other words, a strategic basin-wide study should provide the boundary conditions within which irrigation development can occur in each national subbasin.

The MSIOA (World Bank 2010) provides a list of ongoing irrigation projects. In the near future, it is expected that the irrigation area will double and exceed 500,000 ha. Most new irrigation projects will also be located in the subbasins in the Middle and Lower Zambezi. They would consume slightly more than 5 per cent of the average annual discharge of the Zambezi.

Factors affecting the water-energy-food nexus

As discussed earlier, the two largest economic activities in the Zambezi Basin – hydropower generation and irrigated agriculture – heavily rely on water. At a regional scale, water is a renewable but finite resource linking both energy and food production. Specific institutional arrangements and mechanisms are therefore needed to consider the impact that water policies and regulations may have on energy and food production. At the same time, we also need to assess the impacts that food and energy policies have on water demands and availability. In the Zambezi, those arrangements and mechanisms need to consider specific factors, ranging from physiographic to institutional, when planning water-related interventions in both sectors.

The topology of the Zambezi River system

Most of the existing and planned projects in the agricultural and energy sectors are concentrated in the Middle and Lower Zambezi. They form a network with a complex topology whereby irrigation schemes are intertwined with hydropower plants (Figure 5.4). As a result, increased water abstraction due to consumptive use in irrigated agriculture and/or evaporation losses from man-made reservoirs are likely to reduce the availability of water downstream not only for both sectors but also for the ecosystems. However, as discussed earlier, since most of the hydropower projects do not involve additional storage, much of the threat comes from the developments in the agriculture sector. It is worth noting here that the nature of the nexus in the Zambezi differs from that often evidenced elsewhere (e.g., in the Syr Darya) where the mismatch between *upstream* power demand and *downstream* irrigation demand is the main source of tension. In a sense, we have the inverse situation in the Zambezi where irrigation schemes are located upstream of the power stations, creating a 'volumetric' risk for the latter. Further, two other trade-offs must be managed in the Zambezi: (i) a temporal one between hydropower generation and the preservation of ecosystems; and (ii) a 'volumetric' one between irrigated agriculture and the ecosystems.

Even if the development potential is located in the tributary rivers, the assessment of new irrigation schemes cannot be carried out locally but should rather be part of a holistic approach whereby all downstream uses are considered. In practice, this might turn out to be challenging if a piecemeal approach is implemented by the planning agencies in the respective countries. The cumulative impact of unilaterally developed small irrigation projects might be serious and will increase with the number of hydropower plants located downstream. A cross-sectoral planning approach is especially relevant for those irrigation projects located upstream of a cascade of

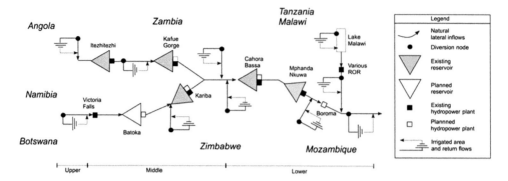

Figure 5.4 Topology of the Zambezi River system
Source: Tilmant and Kinzelbach (2012)

hydropower plants because of the potentially large impact in terms of foregone hydropower revenue. Here, the benefits foregone are essentially due to: (i) lower energy output as the amount of water available decreases; and (ii) lower ability to provide ancillary services following a reduced operational flexibility. As shown in Tilmant *et al.* (2012) and the MSIOA (World Bank 2010), expanding the irrigated areas in the upstream countries at a rate of 20,000 ha/year over the next 20 years would cost 9 per cent of the total hydropower benefits that can be reaped from the basin (assuming realisation of power stations that are in an advanced planning phase).

A reduction of power output in the Zambezi will have regional-wide consequences because the hydropower stations are part of the SAPP. In a power pool, the output from different power plants is pooled, scheduled according to increasing marginal cost, and dispatched according to merit in order to meet the load. If the northern part of the SAPP is hydropower-dominated, the southern region is mostly thermal with a significant portion of coal-fired power plants. Reducing the power output in the Zambezi implies that the energy will have to be generated elsewhere, most likely through thermal and other sources. Consequently, provided there is no bottleneck in the transmission system, unilateral irrigation expansions in the Zambezi will have basin-wide consequences in terms of water availability, and regional-wide consequences in terms of energy exchanges and prices.

Storage

A large number of man-made reservoirs can be found in the Zambezi River Basin. Reservoirs are important hydraulic infrastructures needed when water supply and demand do not coincide both in space and time. Small dams are primarily used to meet more immediate demands whereas large dams are better suited to deal with larger spatiotemporal imbalances between supply and demand (typically multi-season to multi-year at a regional scale). Regardless of the size, the basic principle remains the same: to store water when supply exceeds demand (when the marginal water value is low) in order to make it available when demand is greater than supply.

The ability to move water in time is the essential service offered by storage and, as such, this service can generate substantial benefits in terms of energy generation, food production, flood control and municipal and industrial water supply. However, storage also negatively impacts those water uses relying on a natural flow regime such as flood recession agriculture and riverine wetlands. Impacts of storage on the Zambezi Delta are well documented (see, e.g., Beilfuss

2001; Tilmant *et al.* 2010). Likewise, the impact of the Ithezi-tezhi Reservoir on the Kafue Flats has been extensively studied (see, e.g., Burke 1994; Mumba and Thompson 2005; Smardon 2009).

In the Zambezi, evaporation losses from the basin's major reservoirs are significant and much larger than current consumptive use of all irrigation schemes (Euroconsult Mott MacDonald 2007; World Bank 2008). Yet, reservoir services are highly valuable to the energy sector in the Zambezi with an average annual worth of about USD440 million (Tilmant *et al.* 2012). The highly contrasted natural flow regime of the Zambezi and the erratic rainfall characterised by multi-year cycles require that storage be built in order to supply the SAPP with a more or less constant amount of energy throughout the year. However, the contribution of these reservoirs to the agriculture sector is limited as most of the irrigation schemes are located in the main tributaries, outside the hydraulic influence of the reservoirs. Growth of irrigated agriculture in some subbasins (e.g., Kafue, Kariba, Tete) will rather require the addition of many small dams as dry-season flows are negligible. Again, the cumulative impact of these small dams on downstream water uses might be significant.

The provision of ancillary services by hydropower plants is also particularly important for the stability and security of a power system. Hydropower plants have been used to provide spinning and non-spinning reserve, operating reserve and regulation or load following.[1] The flexibility associated with hydro storage is particularly relevant for load following and to provide spinning reserve. In the SAPP, revenues from these services are not yet fully captured due to

Figure 5.5 Lower Zambezi Gorge below Cahora Bassa
Photo: Richard Beilfuss

the lack of markets for ancillary services. But this might change in the future as the SAPP is evolving from a cooperative to a fully competitive pool.

Even though the large reservoirs have been built for the power sector, fishing activities have developed over time. In terms of fish production, Lake Kariba comes second after Lake Nyasa/Malawi (Euroconsult Mott MacDonald 2007). Other man-made reservoirs like Cahora Bassa and Itezhi-tezhi have potential for more intense fisheries. The many small irrigation reservoirs could also be used for fisheries provided they are not completely depleted at the end of the irrigation season, but no study exists on their productivity.

Wetlands and hydroelectric power

Flood recession irrigation is practised over 100,000 ha, primarily in the large wetlands located not only in the Upper Zambezi (World Bank 2010) but also along the Zambezi River banks (riverine wetlands). In these regions, when flooding occurs, it can extend over large areas, leaving a rich deposit of nutrients along the shoreline when floodwaters recede. With the notable exception of the Kafue Flats, the wetlands in the upper reaches have not been affected by hydropower projects and the flow regime is still largely unregulated.

For river stretches located downstream of a dam, the picture is different. Local communities have developed farming strategies to cope with the seasonality of the Zambezi River. Decisions regarding the spatial and temporal patterns of food production were fine-tuned to changes in the river's discharge rates as well as variations in soils and sunlight. After the construction of Cahora Bassa, for example, farmers living down the river on both banks of the Zambezi were forced to abandon the fertile lands adjacent to the river and to cultivate in upper lands only. These lands are appreciably less fertile, dependent on uncertain rains and yield only one harvest a year (Isaacman and Sneddon 2003).

Wetlands also provide local communities with animal proteins through fisheries, floodplain grazing for cattle and wildlife. Most fish species move onto the floodplain to breed at the time of the first floods in November and December. Other species inhabit the system more or less permanently, living among the weeds in the marshes. In general, the productivity of the wetlands is adversely impacted by upstream storage as the ecosystems rely on a natural flow regime. This issue has been extensively studied in the Zambezi Delta and in the Kafue Flats (see Chapter 7).

Various studies have shown that a re-operation of the reservoirs to restore a flow regime close to the pristine conditions in the delta would be too costly for the power sector (World Bank 2010; Tilmant *et al.* 2010). However, flood releases that balance the demands for hydropower and the needs of ecosystems and subsistence communities are generally technically feasible and financially sound, especially if the operation of the power plants is coordinated. There are two main advantages associated with the coordinated operation of the multi-reservoir system in the Zambezi:

- Through a system-wide approach, synergies between the hydraulic infrastructures can be identified and ultimately yield substantial operational benefits. In other words, in the context of environmental flows, the coordinated operation ensures that the benefit foregone for the power sector is minimised;
- Provided there is an adequate institutional arrangement in place, the coordinated operation can be used to design policies to equitably distribute the benefit foregone among the power companies (Tilmant and Marques 2016). As a matter of fact, the typical approach to implement hydropower-to-environment water transfers focuses on the reoperation of the dam located immediately upstream of the environmentally sensitive area, meaning that only

one power station will bear the brunt of the benefits foregone for the power sector. By ignoring the contribution of infrastructures further upstream to the alteration of the flow regime, the opportunity cost associated with the restoration of a flow regime is not equitably distributed among the power companies in the river basin, thereby slowing the establishment of environmental flow programmes.

To sum up, a nexus approach in the Zambezi should seek to promote the coordinated operation of the multi-reservoir system in order to minimise the impact of storage on ecosystems and subsistence communities, while at the same time maximising the power output.

Traditional approaches to planning energy and food production

As in many transboundary river basins, the long-term planning of energy and food production is still fragmented and largely done independently (WWAP 2014). Power planning studies typically seek to determine future short-run marginal costs for various supply and demand scenarios, taking into account fuel prices, transmission constraints, the characteristics of all power stations, and so on. (Stoft 2002). These studies could easily accommodate scenarios of irrigation development and assess their impacts on the performance of the power pool.

In the agriculture sector, planning has not been seen by policy-makers as either a continuing or important function (World Bank 2008). A piecemeal approach has indeed often been implemented in the Zambezi Basin (Burke 1994); because they were limited in size, individual irrigation projects were assessed locally and independently, that is to say, at best within the boundaries of the watershed. This is an example of the tyranny of small decisions, a situation where small, incremental, decisions taken independently can lead to a suboptimal outcome for the society as a whole. In the Zambezi, the consequences have, so far, been marginal (at least from a basin-wide perspective), but as the prospect of river basin closure increases so will the cross-sectoral impacts. This threat is compounded by the current institutional restructuring of the water sector that is taking place in several riparian countries where a gradual process of decentralisation is underway. By empowering local authorities to manage water and agriculture, there is a risk of negative externalities should the government be unable to coordinate policies across departments and ministries on the one hand, and at a strategic, basin-wide, level on the other.

It is worth noting that collaborative initiatives already exist in the Zambezi Basin. For example, the ZRA is responsible for the planning and operation of hydropower stations in the Middle Zambezi, along the border between Zambia and Zimbabwe. However, in Article 9 of the 1989 Zambezi River Authority Act, there is no provision for cross-sectoral planning; most of the listed functions are related to reservoir operation, planning of new dams, hydrologic monitoring, and so on.

Another example is the establishment of ZAMCOM by the eight riparian states under the auspices of SADC. The purpose of ZAMCOM is to facilitate the management of the Zambezi River on a basin-wide basis, while implementing IWRM principles and policies for the sustainable development and utilisation of the water and other natural resources of the Zambezi River (Tumbare and ZRA 2004). To achieve this, ZAMCOM will prepare and update a basin development plan and strategy based on countries' expectations.

Challenges associated with a nexus approach

As illustrated earlier in this chapter, the production of food and energy in the Zambezi River Basin is interconnected through water. Hence, to address food and energy security, all sectors

Figure 5.6 (top) Household food production in the basin. Farming is planned at fragmented individual levels and assessed only locally; (bottom) Fishing in Lower Zambezi, Mozambique

Photos: (top) Admire Ndhlovu/SARDC (bottom) Richard Beilfuss

must acknowledge and understand the pivotal role played by water, as well as the importance of a cross-sectoral approach to intervention planning in their respective sectors. In other words, a two-pronged approach is needed to address the nexus challenge in the Zambezi Basin: first, to improve the management of water resources at the basin scale; second, to enhance cross-sectoral planning.

In a transboundary river basin, the ultimate goal of cross-sectoral planning is to achieve efficient use of competing resources such as land, water and fuel through the development of portfolios of interventions that are perceived as fair by the riparian countries. Promoting cross-sectoral planning might turn out to be challenging as the planning processes have evolved separately in both sectors for many decades without much interaction. In the energy sector, there is a tradition to consider water as a free resource, and planning studies of large-scale hydrothermal electrical systems rarely consider the interdependence between hydroelectricity and irrigated agriculture. In the water sector, multi-objective planning approaches have been used for decades but they usually fail to properly capture the complex feedbacks with the power system.

To support ZAMCOM and the riparian countries in addressing trade-offs and promoting synergies among the concerned sectors, the development of integrated analytical tools and of a nexus knowledge base is required. This could include the development of a shared decision support system (DSS), upgrading the monitoring network, cross-sectoral capacity-building activities to train professionals and to strengthen the collaboration between energy and water agencies in the region. To assess the water needs of the energy sector, water planners and decision-makers must be knowledgeable about electricity generation, fuel extraction, power system operation and their potential impact on water resources. On the other hand, energy planners and investors must be aware of the competing water uses, the specificities of the hydrologic cycle when assessing plans and investments in power stations and/or transmission lines. Political and economic frameworks need to be adapted to promote cooperation and cross-sectoral planning approaches.

In the Zambezi Basin, formulation of hydrologic data in a nexus framework could be improved. This issue should be addressed through the development of a nexus knowledge base, which should include, among other things, detailed data on the supply and demand of both water and energy. The idea here is to collect enough information to build reliable water accounts for all water uses, including irrigated agriculture, hydropower generation, the ecological services, and so on. Such information is a prerequisite for informed decision-making on water allocation.

Several factors make the development of a nexus-based DSS difficult: cultural differences between the energy and the water communities, the mismatch between the boundaries of the respective systems (interconnected grid versus river basin), the fundamentally different management approaches (wholesale market versus administrative allocation mechanism), and so on. Moreover, as already observed with integrated water resources management (IWRM), a higher level of integration usually means increased complexity, which may in turn aggravate the decision-making inertia with analysts and policy-makers influenced by outdated planning paradigms.

One of the challenges faced by ZAMCOM will be to help countries reconcile upstream and downstream interests by revealing the upstream-downstream linkages throughout the basin. In terms of the nexus, this is especially critical in the Lower and Middle Zambezi where most riparian countries have hydropower facilities and irrigation schemes. Even though irrigation projects are located in the subbasins, a cross-sectoral, basin-wide planning process is needed to assess the trade-off relationship between food production in that subbasin, and both energy generation and irrigation in the main stem of the Zambezi.

Another challenge is to improve the operational effectiveness of the two large hydroelectric reservoirs (Kariba and Cahora Bassa), especially with regard to environmental flows, which are

Figure 5.7 Sugar factory on the Zambezi River bank
Photo: Richard Beilfuss

also needed to sustain food production through, for example, flood recession agriculture and fisheries. Here again, a cross-sectoral planning process is needed because the potential re-operation will affect the production of hydroelectricity and hence the energy exchanged in the SAPP.

The management of Lake Nyasa/Malawi also presents similar challenges as a trade-off must be found between developments in Tanzania's Nyasa Basin on the one hand, and both food production and hydropower generation in the Shire, on the other. Recall that much of Malawi's power plants are in the Shire River and that their energy production depends on the outflow of Lake Nyasa/Malawi.

To unlock the potential of a nexus-based approach to water-related investments planning in the Zambezi River Basin, the riparian countries could adopt a benefit-sharing framework. There is indeed growing consensus among water professionals that the cooperative management of shared river basins should provide opportunities to increase the scope and scale of benefits (Sadoff and Grey 2002), which could then be shared according to an agreed-upon distribution key, which may involve a variety of factors such as side-payments, financing investments, the provision of non-water-related goods and services across sectors, and so on.

In the Zambezi, cooperative and cross-sectoral management can yield substantial benefits in terms of increased food and energy production without undue impacts on fragile ecosystems (World Bank 2010). To facilitate this cross-sectoral planning process, water accounts can be developed. Hydrologists are now able to track water fluxes in complex river basins thanks to the availability of both sophisticated hydrologic models and remote sensing data. When linked to productivity indicators, detailed water accounts can be established in which various watershed processes are represented (Karimi *et al.* 2013).

In a benefit-sharing exercise, the ultimate goal of a water-accounting framework is to measure the contribution of each water user, infrastructure and management decision to the overall economic value of water resources in a given basin. Once this information becomes available, it can be used to design a mechanism whereby the benefits of cooperation are shared between riparian countries and economic sectors. How the benefits will be shared depends entirely on the definition of fairness as agreed by water users/riparian countries. This could range, for example, from a simple proportional sharing of the benefits to more sophisticated approaches involving a mix of water and non-water-related goods and services.

The objective of ZAMCOM is 'to promote the equitable and reasonable utilization of the water resources of the Zambezi Watercourse as well as the efficient management and sustainable development thereof'. Because ZAMCOM is the central institution tasked with advancing sustainable development in the basin-as-a-whole, its mandate could be expanded to explicitly include the promotion of a nexus approach. One of the key outputs of this effort could be a joint multi-sectoral investment programme at the basin scale, which would be endorsed by the heads of state. Such an investment programme would comprise a portfolio of structural and non-structural interventions in the relevant sectors including the environment, and would have to be updated on a regular basis (Cogels 2014). ZAMCOM is particularly well placed to manage trade-offs and maximise co-benefits through intersectoral water allocation in the Zambezi Basin. Within such a joint investment programme, benefit-and-cost-sharing arrangements can be negotiated and measures taken to protect local stakeholders who are not involved in decision-making fora, and the environment. Through enhanced cooperation with the SAPP, ZAMCOM could assist countries in reforming their energy and water policies by making them more coherent. In the long term, these services could be financed by charging bulk water supplies to both consumptive and non-consumptive users.

Conclusions

The increased interdependence between water, energy and food production in the Zambezi River Basin implies that traditional, sectoral-based, planning approaches must be replaced by a more holistic one whereby synergies and trade-offs between sectors can be identified and managed. This is particularly challenging in a transboundary river basin where asymmetric relationships between riparian countries, the contrasted economies, the already-fragmented national decision-making, the unequal endowment of water, and land and energy resources, further complicate the management of trade-offs. Adopting a holistic planning approach is easier said than done; policy-makers, planners and professionals in water and energy need to take steps to overcome the barriers that exist between their sectors.

Since water is at the heart of the WEF nexus in the Zambezi, water governance, which is the range of political, social, economic and administrative systems that are in place to manage water resources at different levels (Rogers and Hall 2003), must be critically assessed with respect to its inclusiveness vis-à-vis the other sectors. This critical assessment may trigger reforms of a potentially wide variety of activities such as planning processes and procedures, allocation policies, legislation, data collection and modelling, and so on.

This governance restructuring could accompany two major ongoing institutional developments in the region: the strengthening of the SAPP and the emergence of ZAMCOM. Although these two initiatives are different in scope and scale, they seek to strengthen cooperation in the SADC region through the energy and water sector, respectively. Hydropower generation, which is already the largest water use in the Zambezi and a major source of hydroelectricity for the SAPP, is sensitive to the uncoordinated, unilateral developments of consumptive water uses in the riparian countries. Unwise water allocation could potentially affect downstream water uses, including ecosystems, as well as the rest of the SADC region through the SAPP.

Note

1   The spinning reserve corresponds to an amount of power that is available from generating units in order to quickly serve additional demand and/or to compensate for transmission or power outages. The operating reserve is an amount of power that can be made available after a short delay once the units are connected to the grid (online).

References

Beilfuss, R. 2001. *Prescribed flooding and restoration potential in the Zambezi delta.* Mozambique, technical report. Maputo: Int. Crane Foundation.

Biggs, E., Bruce, E., Boruff, B., Duncana, J., Horsley, J.M.A., Pauli, N., McNeill, K., Neef, A., Van Ogtrop, F., Curnow, J., Haworth, B., Duce, S. and Imanari, Y. 2015. Sustainable development and the water–energy–food nexus: A perspective on livelihoods. *Environmental Science & Policy* 54: 389–397.

Burke, J. 1994. Approaches to integrated water resources development and management – The Kafue Basin, Zambia. *Natural Resources Forum* 18(3): 181–192.

Cogels, O. 2014. Hydro-diplomacy: Putting cooperative investment at the heart of transboundary water negotiations. In: *Hydro diplomacy: Sharing water across borders,* (ed.), Pangare, G. New Delhi, India: Academic Foundation.

Denconsult. 1998. Water consumption and effluent from food and agriculture sector including fisheries and livestock – Final report. Sector Studies no. 2 under ZACPLAN. Prepared for the Zambezi River Authority.

Dinar, A., Rosegrant, M. and Meinzen-Dick, R. 1997. *Water allocation mechanisms – Principles and examples.* Policy Research Working Paper 1779. Washington, DC: World Bank.

DoE (US Department of Energy). 2006. *Energy demands on water resources – Report to Congress on the interdependency of energy and water.* Washington, DC: DoE.

EECG (Energy, Environment, Computing and Geophysical Applications). 2012. *The SADC Regional Infrastructure Master Plan – Energy Sector Plan Report.* Gaborone: EECG Consultants.

Euroconsult Mott MacDonald. 2007. *Integrated water resources management strategy for the Zambezi River Basin – Rapid assessment.* Technical report. Lusaka: SADC-WD/Zambezi River Authority, SIDA, DANIDA, Norwegian Embassy, Lusaka.

FAO (Food and Agriculture Organization of the United Nations). 2013. *Biofuels and the sustainability challenge: A global assessment of sustainability issues, trends and policies for biofuels and related feedstocks.* Available at www.fao.org/docrep/017/i3126e/i3126e.pdf.

Hussey, K. and Pittock, J. 2012. The energy–water nexus: Managing the links between energy and water for a sustainable future. *Ecology and Society* 17(1): 31.

IRENA (International Renewable Energy Agency). 2015. *Renewable energy in the water, energy and food nexus.* Report prepared for the International Renewable Energy Agency.

Isaacman, A. and Sneddon, C. 2003. Portuguese colonial intervention, regional conflict and post-colonial amnesia: Cahora Bassa Dam, Mozambique 1965–2002. *Portuguese Africa Review* 11: 207–236.

Karimi, P., Bastiaanssen, W.G.M. and Molden, D. 2013. Water accounting plus (WA+) – A water accounting procedure for complex river basins based on satellite measurements. *Hydrol. Earth Syst. Sci.* 17: 2459–2472. doi:10.5194/hess-17-2459-2013, 2013.

Marsh, D. and Sharma. 2007. Energy–water nexus: An integrated modelling approach. *International Energy Journal* 8: 235–242.

Mumba, M. and Thompson, J.R. 2005. Hydrological and ecological impacts of dams on the Kafue Flats floodplain system, southern Zambia. *Phys. Chem. Earth* 30(6–7): 442–447.

Musaba, L. 2005. The development of the SAPP competitive electricity market. Inaugural IEEE PES 2005 Conference and Exposition in Africa, Durban, South Africa.

Rasul, G. and Sharma, B. 2015. The nexus approach to water–energy–food security: An option for adaptation to climate change. *Climate Policy*. doi: 10.1080/14693062.2015.1029865.

Rogers, P. and Hall, A.W. 2003. *Effective water governance*. TEC Background Papers No. 7. Technical committee. Stockholm, Sweden: Global Water Partnership.

Sadoff, C. and Grey, D. 2002. Beyond the river: The benefits of cooperation on international rivers. *Water Policy* 4: 389–403.

Shela, O. 2000. Management of shared river basins: The case of the Zambezi River. *Water Policy* 2: 65–81.

Smardon, R. 2009. The Kafue Flats in Zambia, Africa: A lost floodplain? In: *Sustaining the world's wetlands*, doi: 10.1007/978-0-387-49429-6-4. USA: Springer.

Stoft, S. 2002. *Power system economics – Designing markets for electricity*. New York, USA: John Wiley.

Tilmant, A., Beevers, L. and Muyunda, B. 2010. Restoring a flow regime through the coordinated operation of a multireservoir system: The case of the Zambezi River Basin. *Water Resources Research* 46. W07533. doi:10.1029/2009WR008897.

Tilmant, A. and Kinzelbach, W. 2012. The cost of noncooperation in international river basins. *Water Resources Research* 48. W01503. doi:10.1029/2011WR011034.

Tilmant, A., Kinzelbach, W., Juizo, D., Beevers, L., Senn, D. and Cassarotto, C. 2012. Economic valuation of benefits and costs associated with the coordinated development and management of the Zambezi Basin. *Water Policy* 14: 490–508.

Tilmant, A. and Marques, G. 2016. Sharing the opportunity cost among power companies to support hydropower-to-environment water transfers. *Geophysical Research Abstracts* 18, EGU2016–17187.

Tumbare, M.J. and Zambezi River Authority. 2004. The Zambezi River: Its threats and opportunities. In: *The management of the Zambezi River Basin and Kariba Dam*. Oxford, UK: African Books Collective.

World Bank. 2004. *Water energy nexus in Central Asia – Improving regional cooperation in the Syr Darya Basin*. Washington, DC: World Bank.

World Bank. 2008. *Zambezi River Basin – Sustainable agriculture water development*. Washington, DC: World Bank.

World Bank. 2010. *The Zambezi River Basin: A multi-sector investment opportunities analysis*. Volumes 1–4. Washington, DC: World Bank.

World Economic Forum. 2011. *Water security: The water-food-energy-climate nexus: The World Economic Forum Water Initiative*. Washington, DC: Island Press.

WWAP (World Water Assessment Programme). 2014. *The United Nations World Water Development Report 2014: Water and energy*. Paris: United Nations Educational, Scientific and Cultural Organization (UNESCO).

6

Towards sustainable agricultural water management

Emmanuel Manzungu, Aidan Senzanje
and Justin Mutiro

Key messages

- The agriculture sector contributes significantly to the socioeconomic development of the riparian countries of the Zambezi Basin and the livelihoods of its inhabitants. More than 60 per cent of the basin's population is actively engaged in agriculture.
- While the vast majority of agriculture is rain-fed, most of the water used in the basin is for irrigation. Ambitious plans exist to scale up irrigation in the basin. Such plans have serious implications on water use.

- Small-scale agricultural water management technologies relevant to the basin have met with mixed success. Evidence of success in terms of increased yields and income clearly exists, yet challenges – often related to management and governance that foster maintenance and sustainability – are also present. Improving performance of such technologies is key to reducing rural poverty and improving livelihoods.
- The emergence of ZAMCOM presents new opportunities for improving agricultural water management. ZAMCOM may seek to foster: i) improvements in rain-fed agriculture as a means to mitigating potential future disruptions to water withdrawal; ii) exploration of groundwater sources as an alternative to surface water on which there will likely be more future demand; iii) improvements to water productivity where appropriate.
- The need for improvements in the areas of governance and gender go without saying. Effectiveness and sustainability of large-scale irrigation and small-scale technologies rest on enhancing the governance and management of interventions. One way for governance to be strengthened is forging a more explicit focus on gender, which is currently confounding successful implementation of small-scale technologies.

Introduction

Agriculture contributes significantly to the socioeconomic development of riparian countries in the Zambezi Basin, and to the livelihoods of the majority of its 40 million inhabitants (IFRC 2009). Realisation of this agricultural contribution is achieved through a diversity of farming types and systems, using a wide range of technologies for abstracting and distributing water, across the heterogeneous biophysical and socioeconomic geography of the basin. Crops are grown under rain-fed and irrigated conditions as well as in wetlands and floodplains, for example, and in market-oriented large-scale farms and subsistence-oriented smallholder farms.

There has been scant effort to address the totality of agricultural water management – including large- and small-scale irrigation and rain-fed cultivation – in the Zambezi from a basin-wide perspective. World Bank (2008; 2010, in particular volume II) focused mainly on large-scale irrigation development in the Zambezi, while Nanthambwe (2015) examined agricultural trends in the basin with little focus on related water use. Mloza-Banda (2006) and Mloza-Banda *et al.* (2010) examined agricultural development in individual countries in the Zambezi, such as Malawi. Further, a notable body of literature (e.g., Kadyampakeni *et al.* 2004; Daka 2006; Sullivan 2008) focuses on small-scale agricultural interventions in particular sites in one or more of the basin's eight countries. A thorough stock-take of agricultural water management in the Zambezi, including both rain-fed and irrigated activities at different scales, is not known to exist.

This chapter reviews agricultural water uses and evaluates agricultural water management technologies in the Zambezi Basin. Then it uses this review to infer when and how basin-level approaches may be used to enhance conditions inside and outside the agriculture sector, and concludes with six provisional recommendations for strengthening agricultural water management in the basin.

Background

Agricultural Water Management (AWM): terms and definitions

AWM refers to the management of water in agriculture in a continuum from rain-fed systems to irrigated agriculture, and includes the capture, storage and drainage of any water used for agricultural production (Merrey *et al.* 2006). AWM has also been described as the planned development, distribution and use of water resources to meet predetermined agricultural objectives (CAWMA 2007). AWM can include direct rain as well as water supplied from surface water and underground sources, for agricultural purposes (Mati 2007).

AWM is practised in a variety of farming types (Figure 6.1). It extends from full irrigation to field-based water harvesting, with supplemental irrigation and water harvesting falling in between. Notably, each farming type requires different organisational skills and infrastructure. Within the farming types, there are in turn different farming systems, which include the production and consumption decisions taken at household level and beyond. Complexity associated with farming systems is reflected in differences between women and men regarding crop choices and the use of income generated. Such gender issues have implications on how AWM and associated productivity levels are operationalised and assessed.

AWM is increasingly viewed in the context of broader ecological systems, as part and parcel of diverse agroecosystems (Molden *et al.* 2010). Placing AWM in environmental, economic and social contexts improves AWM sustainability. This underlines the importance of understanding and assessing how water flows in and around the farm, and how farming practices affect water flows at farm and other levels, such as the catchment and basin level (Molden *et al.* 2010).

Investments in AWM are critical to enhancing local agriculture-based livelihoods. Such investments are typically manifested in interventions that cover a range of technologies and practices whose objective is to ensure that adequate water is available in the root zone of crops when needed. This objective includes: water capture and storage (in dams or groundwater) as well as drainage of any water used for agriculture (crops, livestock, fish); lifting and transporting water from where it is captured to where it is used for agricultural production or removing excess water from where agriculture is practised; and in-field application and management of water, including land management practices that affect availability of water to crops. In general,

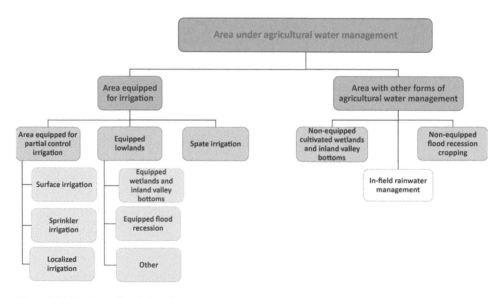

Figure 6.1 Typology of agricultural water management
Source: Delaney (2012)

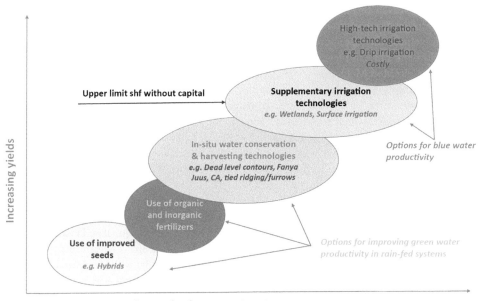

Figure 6.2 Options for improving agricultural water management in cropping systems
Source: Nyagumbo *et al.* (2013)

the management of areas equipped for irrigation with 'blue water' call for greater capital injections than unequipped areas that rely mainly on 'green water' (Figure 6.2). Further, investments to improve the productivity of rain-fed agriculture may have equal or greater positive impacts on poverty reduction, agricultural growth and food security than conventional irrigation investments (Merrey and Sally 2008).

AWM interventions in southern Africa hold potential to increase economic growth, reduce poverty and foster climate resilience. AWM practices come in many forms but the benefits they bring about include:

- Harnessing and storing water in the field for improved soil water content leading to successful crop production.
- Enabling mixed crop-livestock farming that provides a buffer against a failure of one or the other.
- Enabling intensified agricultural production leading to higher crop yields.
- Allowing growing out of season crops in flood recession plains; and enabling an early start to the cropping season.

Data sources and methods used

Three approaches were used to assess AWM in the Zambezi. The first approach focused on collecting and analysing macro-level data to generate an overview of AWM in the basin, at a high level, based on aggregated figures on agriculture and associated water use. The second approach focused on assessing the performance of a set of formal irrigation schemes in the basin, drawing from the broader SADC-wide data set compiled by Mutiro and Lautze (2015).

The third approach focused on identifying and understanding the impact of specific AWM interventions in Zambezi countries.

To implement the first approach, key sources include the FAO AQUASTAT database and the World Bank Human Development Indicators database. Zambezi-specific sources consisted of EuroConsult/Mott McDonald (2008), World Bank (2008; 2010), and Zambezi Environmental Outlook (2015).

To implement the second approach, an irrigation scheme database, established by Mutiro and Lautze (2015), was filtered for those schemes in the Zambezi Basin. For each scheme, success or failure was determined according to five criteria (Table 6.1). Three analyses were then undertaken: i) the aggregate success rate of irrigation schemes; ii) the success rate of the irrigation scheme, stratified by irrigation method; and iii) the success rate of the irrigation scheme, stratified by type of financier.

To implement the third approach, collection, classification and analysis of literature on particular AWM technologies and interventions in Malawi, Mozambique and Zambia were undertaken. Experiences in these countries highlight some of the potential and challenges with AWM interventions in the basin. Altogether, 32 documents were collected and examined. Information was more abundant in Malawi (13) and Zambia (13), while in Mozambique (2) the information was relatively thin. Four documents reported on experiences in more than one country. Sources and documents were examined according to parameters that included type of intervention, type of technology, impacts (income and other), gender impacts (male vs female beneficiaries), level of adoption and water source. The foci of subsequent analysis were on the impact of technologies and gender. The impacts (positive or negative) were explored according to several criteria. Documents were first examined for evidence of change in net farm income associated with a technology or intervention. Technologies with a positive net farm income were considered to have a positive impact on the beneficiaries. When possible, change in agricultural yield due to the introduction of a certain technology was also used as the basis of evaluating impact.

Information on the number of women or youth that benefitted from each of the technologies analysed was recorded when possible, in order to determine whether the adoption rate by women was affected by the approach used by the implementers of that project and also to see if the implementers were gender-sensitive. This was done by extracting the actual number of women who benefitted as compared to the number of men. If the absolute numbers were not provided and the percentages were given, then the percentages were used instead. If the document covered gender issues, it was equally noted.

Table 6.1 Criteria used to measure success

Criteria	Success	Failure
Economic Internal l Rate of Return	>10%	<10%
Gross margin	Positive gross margin	Negative gross margin
Net income	Positive net income/ha	Negative net income/ha
Yield	Greater than 50% of maximum potential of the area	Less than 50%
Area actually irrigated/area equipped for irrigation	Greater than 50%	Less than 50%

Source: Mutiro and Lautze (2015)

Agricultural water management in the Zambezi: an overview

Agriculture is a key contributor to the basin's economies

Agriculture accounted for approximately USD6.5 billion of production in the Zambezi Basin in 2015. This amounts to about 16 per cent of the basin's total production, though this contribution is greater than 25 per cent in Malawi, Mozambique and Tanzania. The real value of agricultural production slightly increased between 1996 and 2015, despite notable fluctuations from year-to-year (Figure 6.3). Across countries, Malawi and Zambia have seen steady, albeit fluctuating, growth in their agricultural production since 2000. Agricultural production in the Zambezi portion of Zimbabwe stands roughly where it did in 1996, despite a notable decline in between. Review of agricultural production trends in Mozambique, Tanzania and Angola suggests slow-to-moderate growth. Agricultural production in Zambezi portions of Namibia and Botswana appears very low.

Employment of women and men in agriculture

Perhaps more important than its contribution to GDP, agriculture also makes a significant contribution to the livelihoods of the majority of people who live in the basin. Review of national-level statistics in Zambezi riparian countries reveals that between approximately 26 and 80 per cent of the populations work in agriculture, with a cross-country average of just over 60 per cent (Table 6.2). Agriculture employed a higher percentage of women than men across the basin, though this varied by country. A substantially greater percentage of women than men

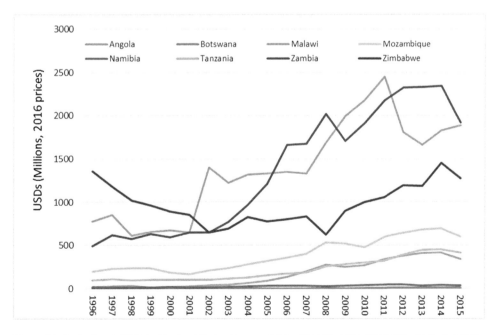

Figure 6.3 Agricultural GDP in Zambezi Basin-Country Units (BCUs), 1996–2015 (World Bank 2016). GDP at a BCU-level were derived from population ratios.

Source: Authors

Table 6.2 Employment in agriculture, Zambezi countries

	Employment in agriculture as percentage of total employment	Female employment in agriculture as percentage of total female employment	Male employment in agriculture as percentage of total male employment
Angola	–	–	–
Botswana	26.4	21.3	30.7
Malawi	64.1	69.9	58.5
Mozambique	80.5	89.9	69.2
Namibia	31.4	30.9	31.9
Tanzania	66.9	70	64
Zambia	52.2	53.4	51
Zimbabwe	65.8	71.6	59.9
Population-weighted average	61.3	65.9	56.6

Source: World Bank (2016). Percentages generally reflect conditions at a country level in 2014. When data were not available for 2014, data from the most recent available year were used.

are active in agriculture in Malawi, Mozambique and Zimbabwe, whereas more men are active in agriculture in Botswana. In other countries, percentage differences are not major.

Geographic distribution of agricultural activities in the basin

AWM activities in the Zambezi Basin are most concentrated in Malawi, Mozambique, Tanzania, Zambia and Zimbabwe; there is comparatively less activity in Angola, Botswana and Namibia (Figure 6.4). Dambos, or water-managed wetlands, evidenced in blue on the map below, are found in most of the basin's countries though particularly in Malawi, Zimbabwe and Zambia.

Land and water use in agriculture and irrigation

Irrigated land area comprises only a small portion of the total cultivated area in the countries of the Zambezi Basin (Table 6.3). While estimates for both irrigated and cultivated areas are likely to contain substantial approximation, it is safe to state that less than 10 per cent of cultivated land is formally irrigated at present. More than 90 per cent of the cultivated area in the basin is instead flood- and rain-dependent; indeed, the majority of the people in the basin practise agriculture along floodplains, swamps, wetlands and margins of large water bodies. It is nonetheless important to note that while there is very little irrigation compared to other forms of agriculture in the Zambezi, irrigation is by far the most water-intensive form of agriculture. Because other forms of agriculture require little to no artificial water regulation or withdrawal, the volume of water used outside of irrigation is often viewed as negligible in basin-wide assessments – and agricultural water use is often treated *de facto* as synonymous with irrigation water use.

Current and potential irrigation in the Zambezi

While assessing irrigated area is not straightforward, the most recent assessment of irrigated land identified that approximately 259,000 ha were irrigated in the basin (Table 6.4). Nearly half of

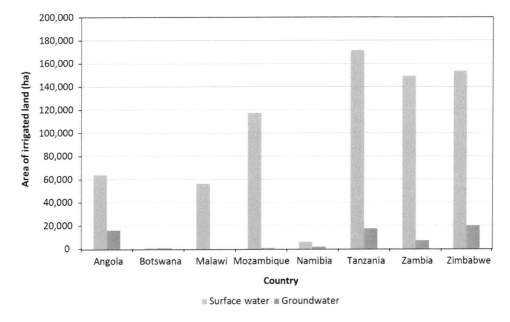

Figure 6.4 Cropped areas in the Zambezi River Basin by agricultural system
Source: IWMI (2014)

Table 6.3 Irrigated and cultivated area, country level

Country	Area equipped for irrigation (1,000 ha)	Total cultivated area (1,000 ha)
Angola	80	5,190
Botswana	1.4	274
Malawi	56.4	2,940
Mozambique	118.1	5,950
Namibia	7.6	809
Tanzania	189.0	15,650
Zambia	155.0	3,736
Zimbabwe	173.5	4,100

Source: FAO (2016)

this aggregated area is in the Zimbabwean portion of the basin, and more than 90 per cent of the basin's irrigated area is contained in the four countries of Malawi, Tanzania, Zambia and Zimbabwe. To foster economic growth in a way that is more insulated from erratic rains, there are ambitious plans for nearly tripling the basin's irrigated area by 2025 (World Bank 2010). While it goes without saying that such ambitions may not be fully achieved, progress toward the established target may still foster meaningful, discernible improvements for the basin's rural inhabitants.

Water requirements for irrigation

Current and future irrigation no doubt has implications for water use. At present, approximately 3,235 million m³ of water are utilised in irrigation in the basin (Table 6.5). As noted in Chapters

Table 6.4 Area equipped for irrigation in the Zambezi Basin, by country

Country	Irrigated area at present (ha)	Irrigated area projected for 2025 (ha)	Increase (%)
Angola	6,125	10,625	173
Botswana	0	20,300	–
Malawi	37,820	78,026	206
Mozambique	8,436	137,410	1,629
Namibia	140	450	321
Tanzania	23,140	23,140	100
Zambia	74,661	61,259	82
Zimbabwe	108,717	183,431	169
Total	259,039	514,641	199

Source: World Bank (2010)

Table 6.5 Current and projected irrigation water use in the Zambezi, by country

Country	Year 2010		Year 2025 (projected)	
	Abstraction to meet current irrigation water requirements (mcm)	Percentage of Zambezi Basin renewable water resources (%)	Abstraction to meet current and future irrigation water requirements (mcm)	Percentage of Zambezi Basin renewable water resources (%)
Angola	76	<0.05	207	0.1
Botswana	0	0	254	0.1
Malawi	495	0.2	2,312	1.0
Mozambique	134	0.1	1,515	0.7
Namibia	2	<0.05	8	<0.05
Tanzania	154	0.1	308	0.1
Zambia	879	0.4	1,601	0.7
Zimbabwe	1,496	0.6	4,019	1.7
Total	3,235	1.4	9,661	4.1

Adapted from World Bank (2010); Zambezi renewable water resources equal 233 km^3 (see Chapter 2)

2 and 5, abstraction for irrigation currently comprises only a small proportion (<2 per cent) of the basin's renewable water resources. Nonetheless, to provide for the targeted expansion in irrigated areas by 2025, the proportion of water abstracted for irrigation will likely need to increase substantially. While the total required by irrigation may still appear low (i.e., just over 4 per cent), there is clear potential for the timing of such requirements to present challenges inside and outside the agriculture sector (see Chapter 5).

Groundwater vs surface water use in irrigated agriculture

As elsewhere in Africa, irrigation draws heavily from surface water sources and scantly from groundwater in the Zambezi's countries (Figure 6.5). Indeed, while reflecting conditions in the entire basin rather than portions of countries in the basin, more than 90 per cent of irrigated area uses surface water rather than groundwater resources. Groundwater remains an important source of water, especially for rural households where it is used for domestic purposes and watering

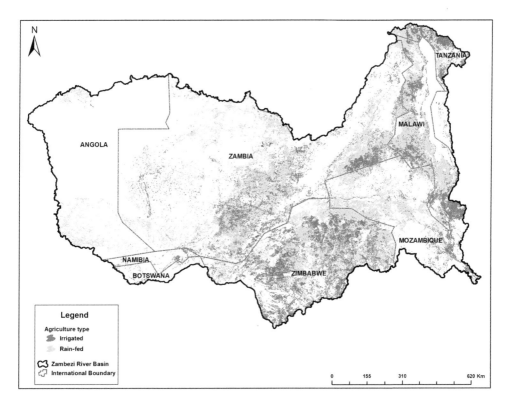

Figure 6.5 Area cultivated with surface water vs groundwater, country level
Source: FAO (2016)

livestock. As elaborated in Chapter 2, the low groundwater use should be considered in the context of abundant groundwater resources in the basin that remain largely untapped.

Performance of formal irrigation in the Zambezi

Aggregate level of performance

Sixteen irrigation schemes in the Zambezi Basin (one in Zambia; six in Mozambique; four in Zimbabwe; five in Malawi) were evaluated. Out of these 16 schemes, eight were successful while eight were not. In terms of irrigation system used, all the Mozambican schemes were surface/flood irrigated with pumping, The Malawi projects were all flood without pumping, Zambia's scheme was flood-based, while Zimbabwe's four schemes were a mixture of one flood with no pumping and three sprinklers. The 50 per cent success rate is a cause for concern.

Irrigation system type

It has been noted that the irrigation system type has a direct effect on the performance of the irrigation scheme in the Zambezi Basin. Type and complexity of the irrigation system – and associated variation in operation and maintenance costs – also play a role in the success of the

Figure 6.6 Irrigation fields in Zambia
Photo: S. de Silva/IWMI

irrigation scheme. In particular, flood irrigation schemes relying on pumping have very low success rates. This is evidenced by scheme performance in Mozambique and Malawi and partly in Zimbabwe. Results reported on the limitations of pump-based systems are fairly consistent with other evidence (FAO 1997), which point to higher operating costs and shorter life spans. However, findings related to the reasonable performance of other irrigation methods may be somewhat at odds with other evidence that has, for example, highlighted challenges of drip irrigation (Tren and Schur 2000; Fanadzo *et al.* 2009; van Averbeke 2011).

Crop selection

Performance of irrigation schemes in the Zambezi is also linked to crop selection. Irrigation schemes that cultivate cereal crops (maize and wheat) tend to perform poorly. This is supported by evidence on the general decline in the international prices of cereals (Innocencio *et al.* 2007), which tends to negatively affect the profit margins of most farmers growing mainly cereals. While economies of scale may, to some extent, enhance returns on cereal production on larger schemes, it may also be necessary to think carefully when deciding to cultivate cereals – perhaps balancing their cultivation with other, more lucrative crops such as vegetables.[1] However, irrigated rice has shown a high failure rate especially in Mozambique and Malawi.

Crop selection vs irrigation type

While schemes with crops such as vegetables have shown a high success rate, especially under flood with no pumping and even under sprinkler, they have shown a dismal performance if under flood-based methods reliant on pumping because of higher operating costs (that erodes the high gross margin generated by vegetable crops) and shorter life spans. To offset the high operational costs one needs to look at very high-value crops to improve the performance of such schemes.

Financier

A scheme's financier also has an effect on performance. Performance of government (public)-financed irrigation schemes has been found to be poorer in comparison to farmer-managed schemes, which are consistent with other evidence (FAO 1996). Underlying factors for such poor performance include inadequacy of budgetary allocations, lack of maintenance of facilities, inadequate consideration of institutional constraints, inadequate capability of local contractors and lack of capacity building of various players in the sector (Kin'ombe 2008). Government-funded projects also tend to have a weaker monitoring mechanism (FAO SAFR 2000). This has seen flood-irrigated projects, especially in Mozambique and Malawi under rice cultivation, failing to perform well while similar schemes under the same conditions but with different financiers other than the government have proven to do much better.

Agricultural water management technologies in Malawi, Mozambique and Zambia

Identifying technologies and interventions

Review of documents focused on AWM in Malawi, Mozambique and Zambia suggests that approaches and technologies can be divided into the following six groups: i) river diversion (gravity-fed earth or lined canals); ii) treadle pumps; iii) motor pumps; iv) dambo cultivation; v) buckets/watering cans; and vi) small reservoirs/irrigation dams.

River diversion

River diversion is one of the most popular and oldest approaches to AWM. This is perhaps the most common approach to AWM in the three countries. River diversion, typically community-managed, usually consists of temporary or semi-permanent weirs and earthen canals that divert surface water from rivers. Such schemes are often managed by farmers without external support. Where river diversion schemes have been improved, the farmers earn considerably more than those in unimproved schemes (Evans *et al.* 2012). High net farm income, increased area under irrigation and high crop intensity are some of the benefits that have been realised as a result of the use of river diversion techniques. Nonetheless, maintenance is an issue as deteriorating infrastructure, leading to water management challenges and low yields, has been noted.

Treadle pumps

Treadle pumps have received considerable focus in Malawi, Mozambique and Zambia. They are human-powered suction pumps that sit on top of a well and are used for irrigation. Benefits associated with treadle pumps include high cropping intensity and increased net income, increased area under irrigation and improved yields. In Malawi, for example, since the treadle pumps were introduced in 1994, there has been an annual increase in the adoption rate up to 2005 (Mangisoni 2006). In some parts of Mozambique, Malawi and Zambia, improved crop intensity and yields with treadle pumps were recorded (Daka 2006). More income was realised by farmers and area under irrigation increased significantly, especially for high-value crops. However, evidence from Zambia highlights how treadle pumps were distributed but not used by farmers due to their high labour demand. Men and women were found to prefer water technologies that require less labour (Adeoti 2009). Low adoption rates and abandonment of

Figure 6.7 Farm plots on the Barotse Plain, Zambia
Photo: Richard Beilfuss

Figure 6.8 Treadle pump, Zambia
Photo : S. de Silva/IWMI

treadle pumps are also due to lack of spare parts, farmers going for the less labour-intensive motorised pumps, and lack of after-sales service.

Motorised pumps

Motorised pumps have achieved a high adoption rate among the rich and those with more disposable income and larger irrigated areas in Malawi and Zambia. As with treadle pumps, high net income, increased cropping intensity, increased water abstraction and increase in area under irrigation have been recorded, especially in Zambia and Malawi. In terms of net farm income per hectare, Zambia recorded up to USD1,650/ha while in Malawi a negative gross margin of negative amount of USD155/ha, was recorded for the farmers using motorised pumps (Kadyampakeni *et al.* 2004). Usage of motor pumps in Zambia is limited because of financial constraints and access to the pumps. Knowledge limitations about the pumps – for example, pump capacity, operational requirement, pumping head, lack of proper training in the selection of the best pumps – have also constrained their adoption. If water is available and management capacity improved, adoption of the motorised pumps has the potential to increase and sustain agricultural yields.

Drip irrigation

Low-cost drip irrigation technology (drip kits) has been promoted in southern Africa. Drip irrigation is a form of irrigation that saves water and fertiliser by allowing water to drip slowly to the roots of many different plants, either onto the soil surface or directly onto the root zone. While positive impacts such as greater income, improved crop intensity, increased water use efficiency and yields have been realised within a short period after adoption of drip irrigation,

Table 6.6 Comparison of technologies with respect to adoption and sustainability

Technology	Adoption	Sustainability
River diversion	High adoption rate due to low operation and maintenance costs	Highly sustainable only in cases where there is improved infrastructure and availability of water
Treadle pumps	High adoption rate due to low operational costs and increase in yield and net farm income	Highly sustainable where labour is available
Motor pumps	Medium adoption rate due to high maintenance costs	Sustainability depends on availability of spare parts
Drip irrigation (drip kits)	Low adoption rate due to complexity of the system	Low sustainability due to limited training on usage and maintenance
Bucket system	High adoption rate due to low operational costs	Highly sustainable because it is cheaper
Dambo cultivation	High adoption rate due to low operational costs and increase in yield and net farm income	Highly sustainable only if there is no overabstraction of water and soil erosion in the sub-catchment
Small reservoirs/ irrigation dams/ earth dams	Low adoption rate due to conflicts over usage and ownership	Low sustainability due to conflicts over water usage and ownership

Figure 6.9 Bucket system irrigation in Chigome, Angonia District, Mozambique
Photo: Everisto Mapedza

sustainability challenges have been noted (Belder *et al.* 2007; Sullivan 2008; Mugabe *et al.* 2008; Merrey *et al.* 2008). In Zimbabwe, the adoption of drip kits was a failure and most drip kits were abandoned because of lack of water, lack of seeds and maintenance challenges. For example, in Zimbabwe, out of 400 drip kits distributed, only 40 (10 per cent) were still being used three to four years after distribution (Sullivan 2008). Discontinued use of drip kits was attributed to inadequate training and uncertainty about how the kits should be used and where to get spare parts, limited access to water, lack of follow-up or backstopping, but not to a simple and labour-saving technology as anticipated.

Bucket system

The bucket system (also called watering cans) is a technology that is very common among the poorest farmers who have very small irrigation plots. It has the highest adoption rate among the poor farmers, while better-off farmers with more disposable income or assets and large plots are abandoning it for the more advanced technologies such as the treadle pump and motorised pump irrigation. Of particular importance is that wealthier families make less use of bucket systems and make more use of advanced technologies such as river diversion and motor pumps. The high labour intensity of the bucket system/watering can is a big challenge to women and the sick as they will not be able to sustainably operate these systems.

Dambo cultivation

Dambos are shallow wetlands found in higher rainfall flat plateau areas or bordering rivers. They are used for grazing, fishing, seasonal cropping and increasingly for upland rice, representing a possible low-cost, high-potential option. Evidence suggests that dambo cultivation boosts harvests, increases crop intensity and generates higher yields in the three countries. For example, the crop intensity in Malawi increased from one crop per year in rain-fed agriculture to three crops per year in dambos. Unfortunately, precise figures on yields and incomes in dambo-cultivated areas are in short supply. In Malawi, land clearing in the uplands for maize production in the rainy season resulted in soil erosion, siltation and lowering of the water table in the wetland areas. This raises the question of sustainability of dambo cultivation.

Small reservoirs

Small reservoirs comprise one of the most important water sources for livestock in semi-arid areas, particularly for traditional farmers who aim to stabilise production and improve nutrition rather than increase production for sale. This technology aims to provide water for multiple uses, that is to say, cropping, livestock water and domestic purposes. Despite high potential, there appears poor management of small reservoirs. In Malawi, for example, it was found that out of 200 small dams built between the 1950s and 2010, only six were still functional (Nkhoma 2011). Many small dams have been abandoned due to issues such as conflicts over the uses of the dams, lack of sense of ownership, poor siting of the dams and corruption. Results obtained with small dams contrast with the benefits of medium to large dams; this is a cause for concern considering the high investment cost of building even the small dams. The multifunctional nature of the small dams is crucial to contribute to reducing vulnerability to shocks and increasing resilience and therefore to alleviate poverty.

Improvements to rain-fed agriculture

While not emerging as commonly as the technologies just listed, it is critical to focus also on soil and water conservation (SWC) practices that help in managing water resources for crop production. SWC practices aim to make the best use of rainwater, preferably where it falls, that is, in-field rainwater harvesting (IRWH). In situations where water is harvested from outside the cropped field, for example, runoff water from the roadside, it is called ex-field rainwater harvesting (ERWH). Associated with soil and water conservation practices is the concept of conservation agriculture (CA) based on the three tenets of minimum soil disturbance, mulching and the practice of crop rotations. CA seeks to conserve, improve and make more efficient use of natural resources through integrated management of available soil, water and biological resources combined with external inputs.

Conservation agriculture: from theory to reality

Although CA is widely considered as a no-lose option for improving AWM, realities on the ground have been disappointing as adoption of CA practices has not met expectations. Andersson and D'Souza (2014) revealed that the challenges faced by smallholder farmers, with respect to the adoption of CA practices, were related more to the challenges encountered with the CA practices than to the socioeconomic state of the farmers. Giller et al. (2009) expressed reservations with regard to the applicability of CA to smallholder farmers in sub-Saharan Africa, namely that their physical and socioeconomic conditions constrain successful adoption of CA.

In-situ rainwater harvesting

In-field rainwater harvesting practices come in many forms and include technologies such as tied ridges, zero tillage, micro-basins, fanya juu terraces, stone bunds, zai pits and dead-level contours. Most of these practices are simple, require minimum investment, are applicable across many farming spatial scales and produce benefits within a season or two. Examples exist where in-situ rainwater harvesting practices have successfully boosted crop production, food security and rural development (Daka 2006; Merrey and Sally 2008). In-situ rainwater harvesting is widely practised in the Zambezi Basin. The initial investment in the technology can be slightly higher than in-field rainwater harvesting because of the need to put some basic infrastructure (e.g., storage tanks and canals) in place for collecting and conveying water to the field. As in-situ rainwater harvesting, ex-field rainwater harvesting practices can be simple, take advantage of existing facilities or features such as rock faces and roof tops, do not require too much new knowledge, and are applicable on a small scale in general. Typically, these practices are suited to vegetable gardening in and around the home as well as in small field portions.

Evaluating impacts of technologies

Adoption and sustainability

Having reviewed technologies and approaches in the three countries, it would appear that relatively greater potential rests in treadle pumps, motor pumps, river diversions and dambo cultivation (Table 6.7). Adoption is greater in these areas, though sustainability is likely to be a challenge – across-the-board challenges must be addressed as far upstream as possible in intervention-planning and technology-distribution processes. Maintenance of individually managed technologies, such as motor pumps, and governance of collectively owned infrastructure appear critical to fostering sustainable rather than ephemeral improvements. In any event, the reality is that some form of pumping (treadle or motorised) is often required, often in conjunction with infrastructure that enables diversion of rivers and improved exploitation of dambos. Fostering sustainable improvements to agricultural production will no doubt benefit from a balanced approach to upscaling different technologies and interventions.

Comparative performance of AWM interventions

Interventions centred on river diversion and treadle pumps appear to perform comparatively stronger than others. More importantly, however, the performance of AWM interventions is dependent on a range of factors – such as the crops being grown, market linkages, quality of post-harvest food storage – that may be unrelated to the particular water management technologies. Pieces of evidence on performance of drip irrigation, motorised pumps and small reservoirs were somewhat mixed. Information on impacts of dambo exploitation was either not as available or not as clear-cut.

River diversion and treadle pumps

The river diversion system is often in two parts, the gravity-fed public system, which is more formal, and the informal diversion by individual farmers. In Malawi, reliable yields from formal river diversion schemes like Camaco and Nega Nega were realised due to financial, technical and credit support as well as market access, agribusiness support and input credit facilities from commercial partners. While irrigation in most cases brings about improved yields and crop intensity, this has not been the case with the Chokwe irrigation scheme (Mozambique) where yields are very low because fertilisers are very expensive and farmers have no access to credit facilities. In terms of treadle pumps, the highest net farm income per hectare was recorded in

Table 6.7 Comparison of technologies with respect to impacts

Technology	Impacts	
	Positive	*Negative*
River diversion	Increased cropping intensity Increased yield Increased net farm income	Increased competition for water Overabstraction of water Water conflicts due to increased competition for available water
Treadle pumps	Increased cropping intensity Increased yield Increased net farm income Maintenance of food security Increased area under irrigation	Increased competition for water Overabstraction of water Water conflicts due to increased competition for available water Labour-intensive
Motor pumps	Increased cropping intensity Increased yield Increased net farm income	Increased carbon emissions Negative gross margin realised in some areas Overabstraction of water
Drip irrigation (Drip kits)	Water saving Increased net farm income Increased yield	Labour-intensive High failure rate
Bucket system	Increased cropping intensity Increased yield Increased net farm income Low operational costs	Labour-intensive Time consuming, hence farmers have less time to do other work
Dambo cultivation	Increased cropping intensity Increased yield Increased net farm income Low operational costs	Overabstraction of water Lowering of the water table Distraction of biodiversity Increased competition among multiple users Overexploitation of dambos
Small reservoirs/ irrigation dams/ earth dams	Increased area under irrigation as more water is available Increased cropping intensity Improved yields	Conflicts over water usage Conflicts over ownership of the dams

eastern Zambia (USD3,020/ha). In another area of Zambia, income rose from USD125, achieved with bucket irrigation on 0.25 ha of land, to USD850–1,700 using treadle pumps, due to the ability to irrigate a large area, improved crop yield and quality (Kay and Brabben 2000).

Gender

Differentiated impacts

Only about half of the reports reviewed on AWM interventions in the three countries consider gender, a critical variable influencing impacts of AWM interventions, which is often masked in theory and practice. Among those reports that consider gender, a central finding is that the bucket system is far more widely used among women. The treadle pump, by contrast, is disliked by women due to its high labour requirements. In both Malawi (Mangisoni 2006) and Zambia (van Koppen *et al.* 2013), men were found to be far more likely to adopt treadle pumps. In both cases, labour associated with the operation of treadle pumps resulted in very few women – and female-headed households – adopting this technology.

International aid and gender

It may be that the purchase of equipment, like motorised and treadle pumps, contains an embedded bias toward men. Cultural values in the rural areas may ascribe disproportionate power to the men, as head of the household, to make decisions related to selection of new technologies. Adoption rates on treadle and motorised pumps may in turn lag because the preferences of those acquiring technologies do not necessarily match the preferences of those ultimately using them. This not only constrains efforts to realise benefits of AWM technologies and interventions, but indicates that female-headed households are less likely to benefit from available irrigation opportunities and as such there is a need to address the gender imbalance (Gebregziabher 2012).

Addressing the gender imbalance

To promote the uptake of certain technologies by women, some non-governmental organisations (NGOs) specifically targeted women when distributing the technologies. For example, in Zambia 30 pumps were delivered by an NGO specifically targeting women free-of-charge (van Koppen *et al.* 2013). In general, men tend to have a high adoption rate because they have the added advantage of having access to public support, input stores, credit facilities, transport, markets, land, technical training and high-performing irrigation equipment. Women's equal access to these assets would accelerate irrigation adoption even further (van Koppen *et al.* 2013). However, while a lot has been said about the adoption rate with respect to gender, very little has been said about the sustainability of the technologies with respect to gender.

Conclusions

This chapter provided both a broad overview of agricultural water management in the Zambezi as well as a specific review of particular AWM technologies and interventions that have been evidenced in the basin. This chapter is believed to be the first to focus on both irrigated and rain-fed agricultural water management in the Zambezi Basin. From this review, it is clear that there are both tremendous opportunities and challenges associated with agricultural water management in the basin. Opportunities include high potential to contribute to food security, livelihoods and economic growth. Challenges include governance and management of development efforts to achieve sustainability.

The primary purpose of this chapter was to review the state of agricultural water management in the basin in order to generate suggestions for how agricultural water management may be improved moving forward. While it is certainly possible to point to standard recommendations for improving AWM in Africa, most of which are applicable in the Zambezi, it is worth noting the emergence of basin-level management manifested in the recent creation of ZAMCOM generates opportunities for improving AWM that may not necessarily have existed in the past. In the spirit of providing somewhat 'fresh' suggestions for AWM in the basin, six recommendations are presented that are specifically aimed at answering the question: what can basin-level water management do to strengthen AWM in the Zambezi? These six recommendations are as follows:

- *Promote focus on improvements to rain-fed and small-scale agriculture as a means to reduce proliferation of more water-intensive large-scale irrigation.* Clearly, there is substantial scope – and substantial need – for fostering improvements in AWM in the Zambezi. Much of this focus, particularly at a basin level, has been placed on irrigation. Against this backdrop, basin-wide approaches may seek to foster relatively greater emphasis on rain-fed agriculture given the more direct linkages to poverty reduction and livelihoods, as well as the lower intensity of water use in rain-fed agriculture. While traditionally not central to the purview of basin-wide management, promotion of rain-fed agriculture as part of a more balanced agricultural development plan may be seen as conserving water withdrawal for other uses.

- *Foster linkages between large, multipurpose agriculture-hydropower developments and local water uses such as pumping for small-scale agricultural production.* Related in some ways to the initial recommendation, a basin-wide organisation such as ZAMCOM may help foster improvements in small-scale AWM by promoting linkages between forthcoming large water developments that it envisions to facilitate, and more local populations in surrounding communities. High-tension electricity lines stretching from dams to capitals while by-passing adjacent villages have been evidenced elsewhere. The Zambezi may seek to follow a path in which large-scale developments also foster small-scale improvements.

- *Given potential future scarcity in surface water availability, consider fostering exploration of opportunities for use of groundwater in agriculture.* Increasing water use in agriculture and other sectors (namely hydropower) will place greater stress on the basin's water resources. One way to alleviate some of this stress is through greater exploration of opportunities for groundwater use. Hydropower development, for example, is presumed to require increased surface water use, which may render less surface water available to agriculture. While one option may be to optimise surface water management to satisfy both agriculture and energy requirements through a systems approach to the degree possible, another option may be to draw more extensively on groundwater to satisfy agricultural water requirements. These options are not mutually exclusive but can be used in conjunction.

- *Propose measures to improve water productivity – strategically.* While water use relative to availability is low in the basin, future development is likely to drive the need for greater emphasis on improving water productivity. Care needs to be taken so that calls for enhancing water productivity are accurately targeted to areas in need of water productivity improvements, as there is a danger that roll-out of 'best practices' is undertaken without sufficient consideration to context. A role for basin-wide management may therefore be to: i) highlight specific areas in which productivity improvements are most needed, that is, areas of acute water stress; and ii) propose ways to incentivise water productivity improvements in those areas.

- *Encourage water governance improvements at multiple scales.* While strengthening governance associated with small-scale water infrastructure at the community scale is likely infeasible for a basin-wide organisation such as ZAMCOM, there is little doubt that the sustainability of small-scale water institutions is a major challenge in the basin. Further, evidence from a SADC-level report (Mutiro and Lautze 2015) suggests that, while irrigation performance has been reasonable, there is certainly room for governance improvements that foster greater sustainability. A basin-wide organisation such as ZAMCOM may seek to identify incentives that can be used to foster greater institutional support for AWM interventions at all scales.

* **Raise the profile of gender in water**. Variation in impacts of AWM across gender lines is clear. Acknowledging these differential impacts and incorporating such varied impacts into planning holds potential to strengthen the efficacy of interventions. A role for basin-wide planning is to foster gender disaggregation when possible, and perhaps more importantly to raise the profile of gender so that gender considerations trickle down and are factored into planning at all scales.

Note

1 Greater use of hybrid crop varieties (see Fanadzo *et al.* 2009) may also help enhance performance on cereal schemes.

References

Adeoti, A.I. 2009. *Factors influencing irrigation technology adoption and its impact on household poverty in Ghana*. IWMI Research Report 117. Colombo, Sri Lanka: International Water Management Institute (IWMI).

Andersson, J.A. and D'Souza, S. 2014. From adoption claims to understanding farmers and contexts: A literature review of Conservation Agriculture (CA) adoption among smallholder farmers in southern Africa. *Agriculture, Ecosystems & Environment* 187: 116–132.

Belder, P., Rohrbach, D., Twomlow, S.J. and Senzanje, A. 2007. *Can drip irrigation improve the livelihoods of smallholders? Lessons learned from Zimbabwe: Global theme on agroecosystems*. Report no. 33. Bulawayo: ICRISAT.

CAWMA (Comprehensive Assessment of Water Management in Agriculture). 2007. *Water for food, water for life: A comprehensive assessment of water management in agriculture (Summary)*. London: Earthscan and Colombo: International Water Management Institute (IWMI).

Daka, A.E. 2006. Experiences with micro agricultural water management technologies: Zambia. *Report submitted to the International Water Management Institute, Southern Africa Sub-regional Office*. Available at http://sarpn.org.za/documents/d0002066/Zambia_AWM_Report.pdf (retrieved 2 September 2016).

Delaney, S. 2012. *Field experiences: Challenges and opportunities for agricultural water management in West and Central Africa: Lessons from IFAD Experience No. 3*. Rome: IFAD.

Euroconsult/Mott MacDonald. 2008. *Integrated water resources management strategy and implementation plan for the Zambezi River*. Lusaka, Zambia: SIDA/DANIDA.

Evans, A.E.V., Giordano, M. and Clayton, T. (eds.) 2012. *Investing in agricultural water management to benefit smallholder farmers in Zambia. AgWater Solutions Project country synthesis report*. IWMI Working Paper 150. Colombo, Sri Lanka: IWMI. 37p. doi: 10.5337/2012.212.

Fanadzo, M., Chiduza, C. and Mnkeni, P.N.S. 2009. Investigation of agronomic factors constraining productivity of grain maize (Zea mays L.) at Zanyokwe irrigation scheme, Eastern Cape, South Africa. *Journal of Applied Biosciences* 17: 948–958.

FAO (Food and Agriculture Organization of the United Nations). 1996. *Guidelines for planning irrigation and drainage investment projects*. Technical Paper No. 11. Rome: FAO Investment Centre.

FAO. 1997. *Irrigation technology transfer in support of food security*. Water Report 14. Rome.

FAO. 2016. Global pap of irrigation areas. Statistics Division. Available at http://faostat3.fao.org/download/R/RL/E (accessed on 2 September 2016).

FAO SAFR. 2000. *Socio-economic impact of smallholder irrigation development in Zimbabwe: Case studies of ten irrigation schemes*. Harare, Zimbabwe: SAFR/AGLW/DOC/002.

Gebregziabher, G. 2012. *Water lifting irrigation technology adoption in Ethiopia: Challenges and opportunities*. AgWater Solutions Project. Colombo, Sri Lanka: IWMI.

Giller, K.E., Witter, E., Corbeels, M. and Tittonell, P. 2009. Conservation agriculture and smallholder farming in Africa: The heretics' view. *Field Crops Research* 114: 23–34.

IFRC (International Federation of Red Cross and Red Crescent Societies, Southern Africa). 2009. Zambezi river basin initiative. Southern Africa zone plan, 2009–2010. Available at www.ifrc.org/where/plan_budget/index.asp.

Innocencio, A., Kikuchi, M., Tomosaki, M., Maruyama, M., Merrey, D., Sally, H. and de Jong, I. 2007. *Costs and performance of irrigation projects: A comparison of sub-Saharan Africa and other developing regions*. IWMI Research Report 109. Colombo, Sri Lanka: IWMI, 81 p.

IWMI (International Water Management Institute). (2014). Irrigated area map of Asia and Africa. Colombo, Sri Lanka: IWMI. Available at http://waterdata.iwmi.org/applications/irri_area/ (accessed on 31 September 2016).

Kadyampakeni, D.M., Kazombo-Phiri, S., Mati, B. and Fandika, I.R. 2004. Impacts of small-scale water management interventions on crop yield, water use and productivity in two agro-ecologies of Malawi. *Agricultural Sciences* 2014(5): 454–465.

Kay, M. and Brabben, T. 2000. *Treadle pumps for irrigation in Africa. International Programme for Technology and Research in Irrigation and Drainage*. Knowledge Synthesis Report No. 1. Rome: FAO.

Kin'ombe, L.M. 2008. Analysis on performance of irrigation projects in Tanzania (case study of public funded schemes in Pangani and Rufiji river basins). MSc thesis, Universita degli Studi di Firenze Facolta di Agraria.

Mangisoni, J.H. 2006. *Impact of treadle pump irrigation technology on smallholder poverty and food security in Malawi – A case study of Blantyre and Mchinji districts*. IWMI Report. Colombo, Sri Lanka: IWMI.

Mati, B. 2007. *100 ways to manage water for smallholder agriculture in eastern and southern Africa: A compendium of technologies and practices*. SWMNET Working Paper 13. Nairobi, Kenya: Improved Management of Agricultural Water in Eastern and Southern Africa (IMAWESA).

Merrey, D.J., Namara, R. and de Lange, M. 2006. *Agricultural water management technologies for small scale farmers in southern Africa: An inventory and assessment of experiences, good practices and costs*. Report submitted to USAID and FAO Investment Center. IWMI, Pretoria, South Africa (available on CD).

Merrey, D.J. and Sally, H. 2008. Micro-agricultural water management technologies for food security in southern Africa: Part of the solution or red herring? *Water Policy* 10: 515–530.

Merrey, D.J., Sullivan, A., Mangisoni, J., Mugabe, F. and Simfukwe, M. 2008. *Evaluation of USAID/OFDA small-scale irrigation programs in Zimbabwe and Zambia 2003–2006: Lessons for future programs*. Food, Agriculture and Natural Resources Policy Analysis Network (FANRPAN) Final Report. Pretoria: FANRPAN.

Mloza-Banda, H. 2006. *Experiences with micro agricultural water management technologies: Malawi*. IWMI Research Report. Colombo: IWMI.

Mloza-Banda, H.R., Makwiza, C. and Kadyampakeni, D. 2010. Improving smallholder irrigation performance in Malawi. Research Application Summary/Second RUFORUM Biennial Meeting 20–24 September 2010, Entebbe, Uganda.

Molden, D., Owels, T., Steduto, P., Bindraban, P., Hanjira, M.A. and Kinjine, J. 2010. Improving agricultural water productivity: Between optimism and caution. *Agricultural Water Management* 97(4): 528–535.

Mugabe, F.T., Chivizhe, J. and Hungwe, C. 2008. *Quantitative assessment of the effectiveness of drip irrigation kits in alleviating food shortages and its success in Zimbabwe: A case study of Gweru and Bikita districts*. FANRPAN Final Report. Pretoria: FANRPAN.

Mutiro, J. and Lautze, J. 2015. Irrigation in southern Africa: Success or failure? *Irrigation and Drainage*. doi:10.1002/ird.1892.

Nanthambwe, S. 2015. Land and agriculture. Chapter 3 in *Zambezi environmental outlook – Towards strengthening environmental cooperation and integration in the Zambezi River Basin*. Harare: Zimbabwe Watercourse Commission/Southern African Development Community/Southern African Research and Documentation Centre.

Nkhoma, B.G. 2011. The politics, development and problems of small irrigation dams in Malawi: Experiences from Mzuzu ADD. *Water Alternatives* 4(3): 383–398.

Nyagumbo, I., Munamati, M., Chikwari, E. and Gumbo, D. 2013. In-situ water harvesting technologies in semi-arid southern Zimbabwe: Part I. The role of biophysical factors on performance in Gwanda district. Paper presented at the 10th WaterNet/WARFSA/GWP-SA Annual Symposium, Entebbe, Uganda, 2009. Amsterdam, Netherlands: WaterNet.

Sullivan, A. 2008. *Qualitative assessment of USAID/OFDA small-scale irrigation programs: Zimbabwe drip irrigation kits 2003–2006*. FANRPAN Report. Pretoria: FANRPAN.

Tren, R. and Schur, M. 2000. *Olifants River irrigation schemes: Reports 1 and 2* (Vol. 3). Colombo, Sri Lanka: IWMI.

Van Averbeke, W., Denison, J. and Mnkeni, P.N.S. 2011. Smallholder irrigation schemes in South Africa: A review of knowledge generated by the Water Research Commission. *Water SA* 37(5): 797–808.

Van Koppen, B., Hope, L. and Colenbrander, W. 2013. Gender aspects of smallholder private groundwater irrigation in Ghana and Zambia. *Water International* 38(6): 840–851.

World Bank. 2008. *Zambezi river basin sustainable agriculture water development.* Washington, DC: World Bank.

World Bank. 2010. *The Zambezi river basin: A multi-sectoral investment opportunities analysis:* Vol 1. Summary report. Washington, DC: World Bank.

World Bank. 2016. Employment in agriculture. Available at http://data.worldbank.org/indicator/SL.AGR.EMPL.ZS (accessed 2 September 2016).

Zambezi Environmental Outlook. 2015. *Towards strengthening environmental cooperation and integration in the Zambezi River Basin.* Harare: ZAMCOM/SADC/SARDC.

7

Ecosystem services

Opportunities and threats

Matthew McCartney and Imasiku A. Nyambe

Key messages

- The social and economic value of ecosystem services in the Zambezi River Basin is immense. They support the livelihoods of between 30 and 35 million people – particularly small-scale subsistence farmers who dominate the basin population – and make significant contributions to the economies of all eight riparian countries. A crude but conservative estimate gives a value of USD1.3–1.6 billion annually.
- An assessment of the ecological footprint in the basin indicates that, currently, overall demands on ecosystem services do not exceed what they can supply. Nevertheless, despite their value, pressures on ecosystems in the basin are growing. Multiple factors, not least economic development, climate change and population increase, are driving changes in

125

the state of ecosystems. Degradation (e.g., deforestation, soil erosion and deteriorating water quality) is increasing and ecosystem services are increasingly under threat with potentially serious implications for the livelihoods of the poor.

- The predominantly rural population (approximately 75 per cent) and the high proportion (approximately 80 per cent) of the basin covered in near-natural ecosystems means that safeguarding ecosystem services must be central to strategies for poverty reduction, food security and economic development in the basin.
- As an institution with a basin-wide mandate and a remit 'to promote the equitable and reasonable utilization of the water resources of the Zambezi', it is vital that the Zambezi Watercourse Commission (ZAMCOM) plays a prominent role in fostering the concept of ecosystem services and emphasises the importance of including them explicitly in national policies and strategies, as well as in the planning and management of all future water resources development.
- The future development trajectory of the basin is yet to be determined. There is scope for much greater consideration of 'nature-based solutions' for climate change adaptation and for more sustainable development. Approaches to safeguarding ecosystem services in the basin are dependent on: i) better identification, quantification and valuation of ecosystem services; ii) in-depth strategic and environmental impact assessments prior to construction of major infrastructure; iii) operation of dams in a coordinated manner to provide adequate environmental flows for downstream ecosystem services; iv) strengthened community involvement in environmental protection and management; and v) regional cooperation and research on holistic natural resources management.

Introduction

Ecosystem services are the benefits that people obtain from ecosystems. As defined by the Millennium Ecosystem Assessment (MEA 2005) these include provisioning services such as food and water, regulating services such as flood and disease control, cultural services such as spiritual, recreational and cultural benefits, and supporting services such as nutrient cycling (Table 7.1).

Until recently, the value of ecosystem services largely went unrecognised in economic and financial decision-making. They were typically overlooked or viewed simply as 'free' or 'public goods'. Now there is increasing recognition that ecosystem services are valuable economically

Table 7.1 Classification of different types of ecosystem service (MEA 2005)

Provisioning services	The products obtained from ecosystems, including, for example, genetic resources, food and fibre and freshwater.
Regulating services	The benefits obtained from the regulation of ecosystem processes, including, for example, the regulation of climate, water and some human diseases.
Cultural services	The non-material benefits people obtain from ecosystems through spiritual enrichment, cognitive development, reflection, recreation and aesthetic experience, including, for example, knowledge systems, social relations and aesthetic values.
Supporting services	Ecosystem services that are necessary for the production of all other ecosystem services. Some examples include biomass production, production of atmospheric oxygen, soil formation and retention, nutrient cycling, water cycling and provisioning of habitat.

and increasingly the case is being made to maintain and invest in 'natural capital' to ensure that ecosystem services continue to sustain both human well-being and national economies (MEA 2005; Costanza *et al.* 2014).

The Zambezi River Basin, with eight riparian countries (that is, Angola, Botswana, Malawi, Mozambique, Namibia, Tanzania, Zambia and Zimbabwe), is one of the most valuable natural resources in southern Africa. The population of the basin is approximately 40 million. Of this population, 75 per cent live in rural areas, mostly as subsistence farmers with limited access to basic human needs, such as food and water. The vast majority of these people depend, for a very significant part of their livelihoods and well-being, on the services that the river and the ecosystems of the basin provide (World Bank 2010; ZAMCOM *et al.* 2015).

This chapter briefly describes the major ecosystems in the basin and the key services they deliver. To the extent possible the services are quantified. Although attaching a monetary value to ecosystem services is not always possible or necessarily desirable, an attempt is made to provide an estimate of the overall economic value of the basin ecosystem services. The drivers of change and the threats to the continued provision of ecosystem services in the basin are discussed. The ecological footprint is determined as an overall measure of human impact on ecosystems in the basin. Finally, the challenges faced by decision-makers who must find an appropriate balance, weighing the consequences of interventions that contribute to national priorities for economic development against the likely impacts on vital ecosystem services, are discussed.

Major ecosystems

With a total drainage area of approximately 1.34 million km^2, the Zambezi River Basin is the largest river basin in southern Africa. Mean annual discharge is 103.2 km^{3}y^{-1}. The river has three distinct stretches: the Upper Zambezi from its source to Victoria Falls; the Middle Zambezi from Victoria Falls to Cahora Bassa Gorge; and the Lower Zambezi from Cahora Bassa to the delta. Currently, due to the absence of large dams and water diversions, the Upper Zambezi remains the most natural portion of the river. Further downstream the flow is regulated by two large dams on the Zambezi main stem – Kariba and Cahora Bassa – as well as a number of tributary dams, most notably Kafue Gorge and Itezhi-tezhi on the Kafue River.

The Zambezi River Basin comprises a mosaic of miombo woodland, grassland, savannah, agricultural land and wetlands (Figure 7.1; Table 7.2). Miombo woodland (i.e., closed/open deciduous woodland dominated by the genera *Brachystegia*, *Julbernadia* and/or *Isoberlinia*) is the most extensive tropical seasonal woodland and dry forest formation in Africa and covers a substantial part (607,523 km^2, 45 per cent) of the basin. Other widespread vegetation types are mopane woodland (dominated by mopane, *Colophospermum mopane*), mosaics of various types of woodland, dry forest (including that dominated by Zambezi teak, *Baikiaea plurijuga*) with grassland and open woodland dominated by various species of *Acacia* (Timberlake 2000).

Wetlands, comprising swamps, marshes and seasonally inundated floodplains, are also a major feature of the basin, covering an area of at least 63,266 km^2 (4.7 per cent) (Lehner and Döll 2004). However, this is certainly an underestimate since, in addition to the major wetlands (Table 7.3), smaller wetlands, called dambos, are widespread, but typically unmapped (Bullock 1992). Dambos are clay-based, low-lying areas flooded by a combination of direct precipitation, surface runoff and seepage from higher ground (Acres *et al.* 1985). They occur under a wide range of ecological conditions and their shape and areal extent vary considerably but a common attribute is poor drainage.

Riparian reed swamps, dominated by *Phragmites mauritianus* and *Typha domingensis*, occur along the upper courses of many tributary rivers with riverine forest occurring at lower altitudes

127

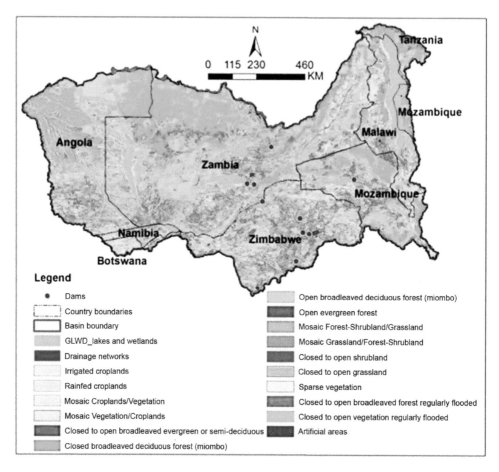

Figure 7.1 Land cover, dams and the riparian country boundaries of the basin
Source: McCartney *et al.* (2011)

(e.g., along parts of the Kafue and Zambezi above Victoria Falls where dense stands of *Syzgium spp* characterise the riverbanks). Further downstream, several tributaries flow into large depressions, which contain permanent swamps each of which cover tens of thousands of hectares and across which water flow is diffuse, often taking place in the absence of discrete channels. At even lower elevations the river and its tributaries (e.g., Kafue and Shire) have formed huge seasonally inundated floodplains (McCartney *et al.* forthcoming).

Twenty million people (ca. 50 per cent of the population) of the basin are estimated to be concentrated around wetlands (ZAMCOM *et al.* 2015), largely because of the wide range of ecosystem services they provide, including provision of water and fertile soils for agriculture.

The role and value of ecosystem services

The woodlands, wetlands and other ecosystems of the Zambezi River Basin, including the river itself and its tributaries, provide a wide range of ecosystem services that support the livelihoods and well-being of millions of rural and urban dwellers in, and to a lesser extent outside, the basin.

Table 7.2 The characteristics of land use (km²) in the 13 major sub-catchments (see Figure 2.4 in Chapter 2) of the Zambezi River Basin

Land use	Zambezi Delta	Tete	Shire	Mupata	Luangwa	Kariba	Kafue	Cuando/ Chobe	Barotse	Luanginga	Lungue Bungo	Upper Zambezi	Kabompa	Total
Rain-fed croplands	196	12	720	8	20	6.9	58	0	0	0	0	0	0	1,020
Mosaic cropland (50–70%)/ vegetation (grass/ shrub/forest) (20–50%)	189	18	593	3.5	5	2.2	64	0	0	0	0	0	0	874
Mosaic vegetation (grass/shrub/forest) (50–70%)/cropland (20–50%)	1,816	39,374	30,737	5,643	25,869	33,016	7,419	21,704	8,558	1,839	1,167	2024	544	179,710
Closed to open (>15%) broad-leaved semi-deciduous forest (>5 m)	522	18	1,948	0	7	0	2.7	0.9	2.8	103	2.7	52	11	2,669
Closed (>40%) broad-leaved deciduous forest (>5m) (miombo)	6,454	25,054	32,641	4,891	25,290	5,292	36,153	11,135	5,366	7,781	18,486	34,230	40,563	253,336
Open (15–40%) broad-leaved deciduous forest (>5m) (miombo)	1,888	49,092	17,851	11,590	53,309	36,553	49,989	25,945	40,416	7,043	10,036	35,925	14,552	354,187
Closed (>40%) needle-leaved evergreen forest (>5m)	0	0	1	0	0	0	0	0	0	0	0	0	0	1

continued . . .

Table 7.2 Continued

Land use	Zambezi Delta	Tete	Shire	Mupata	Luangwa	Kariba	Kafue	Cuando/ Chobe	Barotse	Luanginga	Lungue Bungo	Upper Zambezi	Kabompa	Total
Open (15–40%) needle-leaved deciduous forest (>5m)	156	24	1,705	1.9	41	0.1	0.8	0.4	0	0	0	0	0	1,929
Closed to open (>15%) mixed broad-leaved forest (>5m)	0	0.5	2.2	0	0	0.1	0.1	0	0	0	0	0	0	3
Mosaic forest or shrubland (50–70%)/ grassland (20–50%)	2.3	1,586	869	244	829	5,248	2,179	6,421	3,869	2,851	4,647	4,846	389	33,981
Mosaic grassland (50–70%)/forest or shrubland (20–50%)	0.6	1,007	566	49	504	690	259	3,627	2,179	289	105	314	62	9,650
Closed/open (>15%) (broad-leaved deciduous) shrubland (<5m)	1,057	47,658	18,971	10,022	34,347	41,999	31,529	31,877	26,815	5,299	6,409	7,481	10,634	274,098
Closed/open (>15%) herbaceous vegetation (grassland)	13	18,031	2,668	1,878	4,694	29,707	8,094	28,920	12,417	4,871	4,064	2,107	400	117,863

														Total
Sparse (<15%) vegetation	0.1	29	2	1.1	43	19	59	0	0.4	0.1	0	0.2	4	157
Closed/open (>15%) broad-leaved forest regularly flooded	0	0	32	0	17	0	110	0	0	0	0	49	18	226
Closed/open (>15%) grassland/woody vegetation regularly flooded	0	25	75	0	252	0	0.9	25	746	538	2,571	3,332	107	7,672
Artificial surfaces and associated areas (urban areas >50%)	0	603	209	59	29	452	512	0	0	0	0	0	0	1,864
Bare areas	0	0.2	0	0	0.2	1.6	0.6	0.2	0.2	0	0	0	0	3
Water bodies	270	4,949	29,573	215	198	5,003	1,763	17	268	40	3.2	119	9.7	42,428
Wetlands	2,123	978	4,251	0	2,156	0	15,520	11,993	13,177	5,424	2,499	3,538	1,608	63,266
Total	14,687	188,458	143,412	34,605	147,610	157,990	153,712	141,665	113,815	36,075	49,989	94,017	68,902	1,344,936

Source: McCartney et al. (2013)

Table 7.3 Major wetlands in the basin

Name	Location (latitude and longitude and subbasin)	Area (km²)	Description (e.g., wetland type)
Zambia			
Swamps of the Kabompo River	Kabompo River	180	Small riparian swamps, extending in narrow strips
Swamps of the Lungue-Bungo River	The Lungue-Bungo River and two tributaries (Litapi and Lutembwe)	1,000	Large permanent swamp in the triangle of land between the two tributaries (papyrus, phragmites and floodplain grasslands)
Luena Flats	Luena River	897	Papyrus and phragmites swamps with grass floodplains fed by several small streams (i.e., Nkala, Luambua, Lukuti and Ndanda).
Nyengo Swamps	Luanginga River	700	Seasonal flood waters spread between the Luanginga, Ninda and another tributary.
Lueti and Lui Swamps	Lueti and Lui Rivers	375	Floodplain wetlands + patches of permanent swamp that merge with Barotse Floodplain
Barotse Floodplain	Upper course of the Zambezi River 14°19' −16°32'S/23°15' −23°33'E	7,700	Floodplain wetland located on Kalahari Sand
Sesheke Maramba Floodplain	Zambezi along the northern border of the Caprivi Strip	1,500	Floodplain
Busanga Swamp	Kafue River 14°05' −14°21'S/25°46' −25°57'E	600	Permanent shallow swamp
Lukanga Swamp	Lukanga but with spill from Kafue 14°00' −14°40'S/27°19' −28°00'E	2,100	Reed/papyrus swamp
Kafue Flats	Kafue River 15°11' −16°11'S/26°00' −28°16'E	7,000	Floodplain swamps and marshes located between Itezhi-tezhi Dam and Kafue Gorge Dam
Zimbabwe			
Mid Zambezi Valley and Mana Pools	Zambezi River 15°36' −16°24'S/29°08'–30°20'E	360	Floodplain – pans and pools

continued . . .

Table 7.3 Continued

Name	Location (latitude and longitude and subbasin)	Area (km²)	Description (e.g., wetland type)
Malawi			
Shire Marshes	Shire River draining Lake Nyasa/Malawi 16°11'–17°05'S/34°59' –35°19'E	740	Two tracts of permanent swamp and lagoons in the Chikwawa and Bangula areas plus floodplain
Namibia			
Cuando-Linyanti-Chobe-Zambezi (including Linyanti Swamp, Eastern Caprivi Wetland, Chobe Swamps)	Cuando, Linyanti (Chobe) Rivers 17°39'–18°40'S/ 23°18'–25°10'E	Total 3,930 900 (Linyanti Swamp)	Floodplain, swamps and shallow lakes through the Caprivi Strip. Near the Chobe-Zambezi, confluence in phase flooding of both rivers may inundate 1,700 km² of floodplain
Mozambique			
Lower Zambezi	Downstream of Tete, particularly in the vicinity of the Shire River	>325	Floodplain, swamps and shallow lakes (e.g., Lake Mimbingue and Lake Tanie)
Zambezi Delta	Zambezi downstream of Caia	1,300	Zambezi discharges via distributaries through wide delta; swampy floodplain and areas of mangrove forest extending up to 23 km inland along the main channels

Source: Adapted from Hughes and Hughes (1992)

Provisioning services

The provisioning services represent the most fundamental way in which natural ecosystems benefit people, supporting basic human needs: food, water and shelter. They are 'extractive' and so most easily quantified and valued. As a result, to date most studies of ecosystem services, both in the Zambezi and elsewhere, have tended to focus on them.

Water provision

As everywhere else, quality of life in the Zambezi River Basin is underpinned by access to freshwater. Only a very small proportion of the basin population (mostly living in the urban centres) have a piped water supply, and even access to an 'improved' water source is limited. For example, in Angola, Mozambique, Zambia and Zimbabwe only 34, 35, 49 and 69 per cent of the rural population, respectively, have access to an improved water source (World Bank 2015).[1] As a result, most of the people depend on unprotected groundwater and surface water sources: shallow hand-dug wells, springs, rivers and wetlands. In many places water abstracted directly from these sources is essential for basic human survival, domestic uses, watering of livestock and small-scale irrigation.

A study of four wetlands in Zambia – three of which were in the Zambezi – found that at all locations a significant proportion (i.e., between 35 and 100 per cent) of the population used them as a source of domestic/drinking water. Access to water was usually via shallow hand-dug wells in seepage zones. In some of the case studies, there were boreholes located in the uplands, and these served as alternative sources for domestic water supply. The availability of these alternatives and the distance to them determined whether householders walked to the wetland or used these boreholes for domestic water. In some places villagers stated that the wetlands were a more reliable source of water in the dry season and during droughts (Masiyandima *et al.* 2004).

The river and its tributaries also convey water to places where it is used for industry, irrigation and hydropower generation. It is not well monitored but, currently, consumptive use in the basin is estimated to be a little under 20 per cent of mean annual discharge, with evaporation from reservoirs (17 km^{3}y^{-1}) being by far the single largest anthropogenic consumer of water (Table 7.4). Anthropogenic demand for water is anticipated to increase in future due to rising population, increased mining, industrial and commercial activities, proposed increase in irrigation (including biofuels), growing economies and the impacts of climate change.[2]

Table 7.4 Average annual water consumption in the Zambezi River Basin

	Annual consumption (Mm³)	*% of mean annual runoff*
Rural domestic consumption	24	0.02
Urban domestic consumption	175	0.17
Industrial consumption	25	0.02
Mining	120	0.11
Irrigated agriculture	1,478	1.43
Livestock consumption	113	0.11
Reservoir evaporation	16,989	16.5
Total	18,924	18.3

Source: Adapted from ZAMCOM *et al.* (2015)

Recession agriculture

Throughout the Zambezi River Basin, populations have to cope with both seasonal and inter-annual shortages of water as a matter of course. Under such circumstances, floodplain and wetland environments that retain water close to or at the ground surface represent a water reserve that can be used to bridge mid-season droughts and extend the length of the agricultural growing season.

So-called recession agriculture (i.e., fertile land cultivated as floodwater recedes) is practised on approximately 113,000 ha. This accounts for just 2 per cent of the total cultivated land in the basin (ca. 5.2 million ha) and compares to a total of 259,039 ha of irrigated agriculture (World Bank 2010). However, it is a major contributor to agricultural production in some subbasins and exceeds the area equipped for formal irrigation in some countries (i.e., Zambia, Namibia, Botswana and Mozambique) (Table 7.5).

In addition, cultivation in dambos, also effectively a form of recession agriculture, is widespread though largely unquantified. The water resources of dambos are widely utilised as an alternative, or supplement, to rain-fed agriculture. Although there are no data on the total extent, it is known that many thousands of hectares are cultivated throughout the basin (e.g.,

Table 7.5 Main areas of flood recession agriculture in the Zambezi River Basin

Subbasin	Country	Floodplain extent (ha)	Area of recession cultivation (ha)	Area equipped for irrigation in subbasin (ha)	Area equipped for irrigation in country (ha)
Barotse	Zambia	900,000	28,000	200	56,542
Kafue	Zambia	650,000	13,000	40,158	
Luangwa	Zambia	1,080,000	17,000	10,100	
Cuando/Chobe	Namibia/Botswana	220,000	9,000	620	120
Shire	Malawi	1,510,000	21,000	42,416	30,816
Zambezi Delta	Mozambique	1,940,000	25,000	6,998	7,413
Total		6,300,000	113,000	100,492	94,891

Source: Adapted from World Bank (2010)

in Malawi, Zambia, Zimbabwe and Mozambique). Most often, this takes the form of cultivation of maize, rice and vegetables in relatively small plots. The intensity of cultivation varies considerably, but in some communal regions of Zimbabwe typically 5–75 per cent of the dambo area is cultivated (McCartney *et al.* 1997).

Livestock grazing

For many communities in the basin, livestock and nomadic pastoralism are the main economic activities. The head of cattle in the basin was estimated to be about 41 million in 2011 (ZAMCOM *et al.* 2015). Driven by the seasonal availability of pasture and water, the majority of herds are managed under a system of transhumance and move between floodplains in the dry season and adjacent uplands in the wet season (Table 7.6). For example, in the Western Province of Zambia, over three-quarters of the cattle are pastured in the Barotse Floodplain during the dry season and moved to higher ground in the wet season. Annual transhumance is important for the distribution of manure, and across many floodplains there is a strong interaction between herding, cropping and fishing activities (Simwinji 1997).

Dambos and smaller wetlands are also widely used for grazing livestock but there is no quantitative information on the extent of this use. Cattle can be a vital source of wealth for people, providing owners with drought-coping strategies, access to community rights as well as other intangible benefits (World Bank 2010). The financial value of cattle is derived from meat and milk as well as their role as draught animals for plowing.

Table 7.6 Cattle grazing in the major wetlands of the Zambezi

Wetland	Dry-season head of cattle	Estimated financial gross value (USD million)
Barotse	435,000[1]	3.32[1]
Kafue Flats	250,000[2]	4.0[2]
Caprivi Floodplain	124,000[1]	1.94[1]
Lower Shire Floodplain	104,450[1]	1.77[1]
Luangwa	N/A	0.90[1]
Lukanga	Unknown	N/A
Zambezi Delta	0	0

[1] World Bank (2010); [2] Seyam *et al.* (2001)

Globally, there have been relatively few studies of the impacts of cattle grazing in wetlands but it is a common perception that they are a major cause of degradation. Certainly large herds in relatively confined spaces are a cause for concern in the Zambezi Basin (ZAMCOM *et al.* 2015). However, the effects of grazing for biodiversity and ecosystem services are not easy to predict (Reeves and Champion 2004). They depend not only on site-specific characteristics but also on stocking intensities and management regimes, as well as on the grazing behaviour and feeding preferences of different livestock species. There is some evidence that African wetland grasslands are able to withstand extremely heavy grazing over the dry season without becoming degraded because, during the wet season flooding, they are inaccessible to livestock (and wild grazers) (Fynn *et al.* 2015).

Fisheries

Subsistence and commercial fishing, as well as angling tourism, are major activities throughout the basin. Because of the varied habitats, fisheries are also diverse. On floodplains, largely subsistence fisheries exploit the natural seasonal cycles (Figure 7.2), while the man-made reservoirs are the focus of commercial-scale fisheries for kapenta (*Limnothrissa miodon*), a pelagic fish introduced from Lake Tanganyika (Tweddle 2010).

As in many other tropical rivers (e.g., the Amazon and the Mekong) seasonal flooding is a major driver of ecological transformation and fisheries productivity in the Zambezi (Junk *et al.* 1989). Many fish species migrate onto floodplains to breed during the first floods in November/December. Spawning on the floodplains provides juveniles the advantages of abundant food, well-oxygenated conditions and habitat that provides enhanced security from predation (World Bank 2015). Thus, the flood pulse contributes significantly to fish production in the basin, which then supports a large fishery that is a major source of rural livelihoods, both as a source of cheap, yet high-value protein and the primary source of income for some. With the exception of the larger fisheries in lakes and on floodplains (Table 7.7), the fishing effort and catches go unrecorded and hence undervalued, but the contribution of fish to nutrition in villages bordering the rivers, wetlands and lakes is without doubt substantial.

Throughout the basin there is considerable pressure on fisheries and evidence that most are being overexploited. As a result of overfishing, catch rates are decreasing, fish communities are changing and larger, more valuable species are being replaced by smaller, much less valuable species (Tweddle *et al.* 2015). Where data are available, annual yields in recent years have been considerably lower than those presented in Table 7.7. Lack of alternative livelihoods means that impoverished rural fishing communities are trapped in a cycle of declining individual catches resulting from increased effort, reduced mesh sizes and ultimately use of destructive fishing practices (e.g., the use of large beach seine nets, lined with cloth, to catch the few remaining small fish) (Tweddle *et al.* 2015).

In addition to artisanal fisheries, significant commercial fisheries have been established in both the Kariba and Cahora Bassa Reservoirs. On Lake Kariba, to maximise the use of the deep water habitat, the Zambian Department of Fisheries introduced kapenta into the reservoir in 1968/69 and within five years the species had completely colonised the lake. Now a total of 98 registered operators fish with 295 boats (Tweddle 2010). The total kapenta catch from Lake Kariba peaked at around 35,000 tons per year (ty^{-1}) (valued at USD25 million) in 1990 and has since declined to approximately 20,000 ty^{-1} (Magadza 2006). The trends in Magadza (2006) agree with other published statistics (WCD 2000) but differ in total yields (Figure 7.3a). Kapenta catches have reportedly declined further to approximately 7,820 ty^{-1} by 2005 (FAO 2007). In Cahora Bassa, the commercial kapenta fishery started in 1994 and expanded rapidly to more

Figure 7.2 Subsistence fishing is a major livelihood activity. (top) Fishing village by the river bank, Kafue Flats; (bottom) Fisherman with a catch

Photos: Richard Beilfuss

Table 7.7 Major fisheries (excluding kapenta) in the Zambezi Basin (adapted from Tweddle 2010 with additional data from Tweddle *et al.* 2015)

	Fishery	Annual yield (metric tons)	Numbers of fishers	Value USD million ++	Comment
Upper Zambezi	Barotse Floodplain	6,000–7,000	>1,000	4.94	Excessively overfished – shift from large, high-value to small, low-value fish
Middle Zambezi	Lake Kariba	8,000–9,000	~1,300		Evidence of severely degraded fishery particularly on the Zambian side of the reservoir
	Kafue Flats	6,000	~4000	13.3	In recent years catch per unit of effort has declined significantly: 20 fish per gillnet set in the mid-1980s to 2 fish per set in 2005.
	Lukanga	1,000–2,600	N/A		The relative inaccessibility of the wetland has prevented the development of commercial fishing but overfishing is still a threat.
	Itezhi-tezhi	1,200	1,250		Inshore lake fisheries are heavily exploited and the numbers of fishers have declined.
	Lusiwashi	2,000–2,450	N/A		
	Lake Liambezi	~2,700	N/A		Illegal fishing methods by fishers from outside the locality mean that fishing levels are unsustainable.
	Caprivi	~1,500	>2,000	1.49	Estimated stock decline in large commercial species by >90% between 2010 and 2012
	Cahora Bassa +	>6,000	>1,200		
Lower Zambezi	Lower Shire	5,000–7,000	N/A	3.27	
	Delta	10,000#	N/A	5.0★	Declines associated with the reduced flooding caused by the Cahora Bassa Dam
	Marine	22,000		21.7#	Since the mid-1980s declines in shallow water landings are attributed to over-fishing in combination with environmental effects, including flow regulation.

+Source: IIP and IIDA (2006); ++Source: World Bank (2015); #Source: Praagman (2013)
★Freshwater and estuarine fish

than 200 boats in 2005. The number of people estimated to be employed by 42 companies that operate in the lake is 1,500 (IIP and IIDA 2006). Catches peaked in 2004, with an apparent subsequent decline (Figure 7.3b) attributed to either overfishing or environmental factors (Mafuca 2008).

Both commercial and artisanal near-shore estuarine and marine fisheries in the vicinity of the mouth of the Zambezi River are influenced by river flows. Studies have shown that total

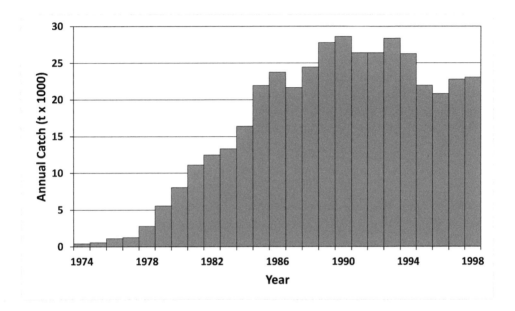

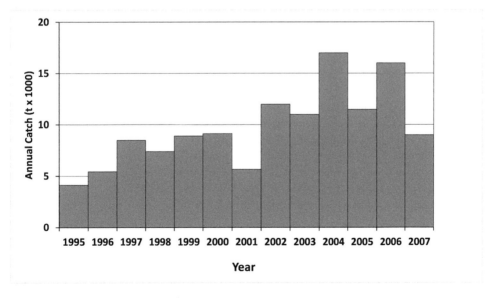

Figure 7.3 Annual catches of kapenta from (a) Lake Kariba and (b) Lake Cahora Bassa
Sources: Adapted from data in WCD (2000); Mafuca (2008)

annual catches, which average 22,000 ty^{-1}, are positively correlated with annual discharge (Hoguane and Armando 2015). This is attributable to land-based nutrient input into the sea via river or coastal rainfall leaching, which effectively fertilises the coastal water thereby providing food for fish. Hence, the higher and the longer the freshwater supply, the greater the primary production and the fish production. However, some species (e.g., prawns) have life cycles that migrate between estuarine and coastal waters. In these cases production is favoured by high wet-season flows and low dry-season flows (Gammelsrød 1992). In the case of the Zambezi, increased regulation of river flows (primarily by Cahora Bassa Dam) has adversely impacted the commercial prawn (*Penaeus indicus*) fishery, which in the early 1980s was Mozambique's second largest earner of foreign exchange (Blythe *et al.* 2013). Amounts of between USD10–30 million are reported as being lost each year due to decreased catch rates. This is attributed to lower floods and higher dry-season flows, which prevent juvenile prawn larvae migrating into mangroves and other freshwater areas of the delta (Ribeiro undated). It has been proposed that operation of the Cahora Bassa Dam could be modified to improve the prawn fishery. Without using additional water, but by simulating a more natural distribution of flow, especially in drought years, it is estimated that prawn catch could be increased by approximately 20 per cent (Gammelsrød 1992).

Other provisioning services

In addition to those described above, a wide range of other provisioning services support rural living throughout the basin. Some act as subsidies to agriculture (browse, leaf mulch) and others provide for basic needs such as food, shelter and health. Important products include poles and construction materials (e.g., timber and thatching for houses) and materials for tool handles and household utensils. Trees in miombo woodlands also provide a range of tanins, dyes, oils, resins and gums that are used for a wide range of purposes (Clarke *et al.* 1996).

Wild foods, including fruits, honey, vegetables, mushrooms, leaves, roots and certain grasses, as well as some insects (e.g., certain caterpillars) and meat from wild animals (e.g., antelopes, hares, birds and mice) are important both for food security and nutrition (i.e., protein, vitamins and energy) and, in places, commercially (Clarke *et al.* 1996). For example, chikanda, a vegetarian meatloaf made from peanuts and the boiled tubers of orchids (genera: *Disa*, *Satyrium*, *Habenaria*, *Brachycorythis* and *Eulophia*), is a popular delicacy in Zambia and elsewhere in the basin. At Mabumba wetland in Zambia, the harvesting of wild orchid tubers for household consumption and for sale is a common practice. In recent years, orchids have been collected in ever-increasing numbers and are reported to be declining as a consequence of unsustainable harvesting practices (Masiyandima *et al.* 2004).

Despite the fact that the river is a major source of hydropower, the majority of the basin population continue to rely on biomass as energy. Fuelwood is used for cooking and lighting, and in some rural industries (i.e., brick-making, lime production, smoking fish, brewing beer and the drying of tea and tobacco (ZAMCOM *et al.* 2015)).

The roots, leaves and bark of many different wetland and woodland species are used as medicines. The general lack of formal health facilities in rural areas means that people are very dependent on plant medicines. Commonly, plant material combinations are used in self-treatment of common ailments, such as coughs, headaches, sores and diarrhoea, and people are generally very knowledgeable about which plants can be used and how to prepare them. The efficacy of such remedies is likely to be highly variable but they are often perceived as more effective than 'western' medicines by local people (Clarke *et al.* 1996).

Regulating services

By regulating biophysical cycles and processes, natural ecosystems make a vital contribution to livelihoods and economic development through the prevention and mitigation of damage that inflicts costs on society. However, compared to provisioning services, the regulating services are much less understood and even more neglected in policy appraisal, and natural resources and development planning and management. One reason for the failure to include them is lack of a detailed understanding of the processes occurring, their dynamic nature and the interaction of these functions with the catchments within which the ecosystems are located. Very often, it is unclear exactly which functions are performed and how these functions change over time (i.e., between seasons and between years). Furthermore, both the lack of quantitative information and a recognised method to incorporate them in decision-making processes make it very difficult to integrate them into the planning and management of natural resources.

Flow regulation

By affecting transpiration and evaporation, and influencing how water is routed and stored, natural ecosystems play a crucial role in the hydrology of a basin. A key service widely attributed to many natural systems (forests and wetlands) is regulating river flow: effectively storing water when it is wet and then releasing it slowly when it is dry (Blumenfeld *et al.* 2009). By reducing the frequency and damaging impacts of floods and simultaneously ensuring that water is available (i.e., for domestic supply, irrigation, industry, and so on) at times when it would normally be unavailable, this natural regulation of flows translates into benefits for human populations living downstream. Notwithstanding the fact that if natural ecosystems regulated flows in an ideal way for society there would be no need to build storage reservoirs, natural ecosystems are increasingly perceived to play a role akin to human-made reservoirs. In recent years, this has led to the proposition that natural ecosystems should be considered as 'natural infrastructure' and more explicitly incorporated in water resources planning (Emerton and Bos 2004).

A recent evaluation of the flow-regulating functions of natural ecosystems in the Zambezi Basin developed a method for quantifying the extent to which natural ecosystems (i.e., wetlands, floodplains and miombo woodland) influence flow (McCartney *et al.* 2013). The method utilises observed streamflow records and standard hydrological techniques to derive a simulated time series of flow in the absence of an ecosystem. This can then be compared with an observed time series to evaluate the impact of the ecosystem on the flow regime (Figure 7.4). The method was applied to 16 locations in the basin. Results indicate that the different ecosystems affect flows in different ways. Broadly: i) floodplains decrease flood flows and increase low flows; ii) headwater wetlands increase flood flows and decrease low flows; and iii) miombo forest, when covering more than 70 per cent of the catchment, decreases flood flows and decreases low flows. However, in all cases there were examples that produced contrary results and simple correlations between the extent of an ecosystem type within a catchment and the impact on the flow regime were not found. This confirms that effects on flow are a function not just of the presence/absence of different ecosystem types, but also of a range of other biophysical factors, including topography, climate, soil, vegetation and geology. Hence, the hydrological functions of natural ecosystems depend to a large extent on location-specific characteristics that make it difficult to generalise.

Water purification

Water treatment facilities are limited in the Zambezi River Basin. Most cities in the basin have inadequate sewerage treatment plants and very few of the small towns and villages have any

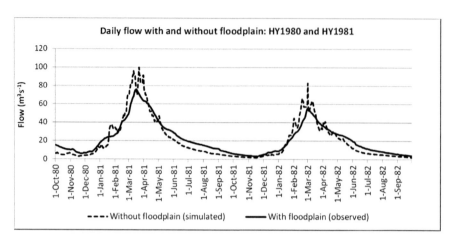

Figure 7.4 Example of the impact of the Luswishi Floodplain on river flow, illustrating flow regulation: decreases in flood flow and increases in low flow

treatment facilities (World Bank 2010). Other water-quality pressures are exerted by the discharge of industrial, mining and agricultural effluents (World Bank 2010). Under these circumstances, the water purification services provided by ecosystems are critical for many people dependent on unprotected water sources.

The ability of wetlands to improve water quality arises from natural purifying processes including: dilution, sedimentation, filtration, physical and chemical immobilisation, microbial interactions and uptake by vegetation and aquatic organisms (Kadlec and Knight 1996). The effectiveness of these processes varies considerably between ecosystems and within ecosystems (e.g., wetlands and buffer strips along rivers) and may be highly ephemeral as plants grow and die. Furthermore, if pollutant loadings occurring naturally or in anthropogenic effluents exceed the physiological tolerances of key microbial and/or plant species, the effectiveness in terms of water purification will decline. In such circumstances the health of people reliant on water from the ecosystem may be severely compromised. The total economic value of the water purification role of Zambezi Basin wetlands (based on the cost of replacement with water treatment schemes) is estimated at USD12.7 million per year (My^{-1}) (Turpie *et al.* 1999).

Chivero Reservoir, the main source of water for Harare, provides an example of how wetlands could be used more widely to improve water quality. The reservoir is highly polluted as a result of population growth, industrialisation and increased livestock on the inflowing tributaries. Although improved wastewater treatment facilities could contribute to improvement of the water quality, the fact that much of the pollutant loading is from non-point sources means that not only are they very expensive (estimated cost USD353 million) but in isolation they will not solve the problem. Studies on the Mukuvisi River, one of the major contributors to the reservoir, have shown that the wetlands connected to the river have considerable capacity to improve the water quality and reduce treatment costs (Machena 1997). As a result, ecological approaches to protect and restore wetland functions have been proposed (Magadza 2008).

Carbon sequestration

Ecosystem structure and function are fundamentally linked to carbon cycling, storage and emissions. Consequently, grasslands, forests and wetlands (Figure 7.5) are important elements

Figure 7.5 Wetland mosaic on the Kafue Flats
Photo: Richard Beilfuss

of the biosphere with respect to climate change. Degradation of natural ecosystems can result in the release of large amounts of stored carbon and so exacerbate climate change. Understanding the **carbon sequestration** potentials of ecosystems (both above and below ground) is important to develop strategies for climate change mitigation and adaptation. Conserving or enhancing carbon stocks (particularly of forests but also of rangelands and wetlands) is perceived as a way both to reduce carbon emissions (e.g., from deforestation, conversion to agriculture or wetland drainage) and to offset emissions elsewhere.

Within the Zambezi Basin there is relatively little quantitative information on carbon sequestration and fluxes but a crude estimate of the total value of carbon sequestration by wetlands alone is USD64 My^{-1} (Turpie *et al.* 1999). A number of ambitious projects have been established to better understand carbon stocks and fluxes in the basin, to put a value on carbon and reduce greenhouse gas emissions. For example, the Kariba REDD project is estimated to have reduced greenhouse gas emissions by over 5.6 million tons of CO_2 equivalent (MtCO$_2$e) (through reduced deforestation) since it started in 2011. The intention is that carbon revenues achieved through the project will be shared among community institutions and the project developers (CGI 2014).

Cultural services

In addition to the tangible benefits provided by provisioning and regulating services, the ecosystems of the Zambezi River Basin also provide a wide range of intangible, cultural services.

Such services are difficult to quantify and value but can contribute significantly to social cohesion and so are important for both individual well-being and community solidarity.

Social systems

In many places in the Zambezi Basin, communities have developed customs, rituals and philosophies that are synchronic with, and reflective of, the natural rhythms of forest and wetland ecosystems. For example, the Lozi people in western Zambia celebrate the flooding of the Barotse Floodplain with the Kuombokav ceremony. Every year the community makes a ceremonial move to higher ground at the end of the rainy season. When the king decides that it is time to leave, all the people pack their belongings into canoes and the whole tribe leaves together: the king, in his barge with his family and a troop of traditionally dressed paddlers, in the lead. It takes about six hours to cover the distance between the dry-season capital Lealui and the wet-season capital Limulunga. There the successful move is celebrated with traditional singing and dancing. This ceremony is known to date back more than 300 years.

Territorial cult religions in which natural resources are believed to be guarded by spirits of the ancestors are common in many of the indigenous people of the basin. In miombo woodlands, sacred groves are used for a variety of important cultural and religious ceremonies (Clarke *et al.* 1996). In such instances the ecosystems may be integral to community perspectives of the world, create a sense of place and are part of important cultural heritage.

Tourism

Tourism is a major contributor to the economies of sub-Saharan Africa and is one cultural service that is relatively easy to quantify. The Zambezi Basin is well endowed with wildlife, scenic, cultural and adventure attractions that draw large numbers of tourists. In 2007, the annual direct value of tourism in the river basin was estimated to be USD457 million, representing between 12 and 20 per cent of the tourism economy of the riparian countries (World Bank 2010). The total varies substantially between countries. For example, in Angola very few tourists visit the Zambezi Basin. In contrast, in Zambia it is estimated that 54 per cent of tourists want primarily to visit the Victoria Falls and another 34 per cent want to experience wildlife, adventure activities, sport fishing (largely based on exploitation of the Tiger fish (*Hydrocynus vittatus*)) and hunting in areas that lie within the basin. The Caprivi/Chobe/Kasane/Victoria Falls area is the most significant tourism destination in the basin (World Bank 2010).

Tourism does not always bring benefits to local people. Often, the financial benefits accrue to tour operators, hotel owners and government, with limited opportunities for local people. Consequently, it is unsurprising that local people are often sceptical of plans for increased tourism (McCartney *et al.* 2011). Benefit-sharing mechanisms, intended to ensure that local people gain from tourism, have been developed. For example, Zimbabwe's Communal Areas Management Programme (CAMPFIRE) was until recently regarded as highly successful. Between 1989 and 2001, the programme generated over USD20 million for local communities. However, more recently the scheme has been riven with conflicts, and accusations of misappropriation of funds and lack of benefit-sharing (Leach and Scoones 2015).

The overall value of ecosystem services

As indicated above, the ecosystems of the Zambezi Basin provide a wide range of services. As elsewhere, determining the true economic value of these services is difficult. There have

Figure 7.6 Endemic Kafue lechwe on the Kafue Flats
Photo: Richard Beilfuss

been past attempts to value specific ecosystems and some specified ecosystem services (Turpie *et al.* 1999; Seyam *et al.* 2001; World Bank 2010), mostly in relation to wetlands. However, to date there has been no attempt to estimate (even a ballpark figure) the overall value of ecosystem services throughout the basin. One difficulty is that, with the exception of wetlands, there has been very little analyses of economic value in relation to specific ecosystem types. Rather there is very limited information available on certain sectors (e.g., fisheries, charcoal manufacture and wood production), predominantly at national level.

Starting with the estimates for wetland ecosystem services available, information on both sector and ecosystem was combined, and using a very simple 'benefits transfer'[3] approach, a preliminary estimate of the overall economic value of ecosystem services in the basin was developed.

Wetlands

Seyam *et al.* (2001) estimated the total economic value of ecosystem services from 10 major wetlands in the basin, excluding the delta, at USD123 My[-1]. The World Bank (2010) drew on the Seyam *et al.* report, and others, to derive minimum estimates of the value of ecosystem services for six large wetlands in the basin, categorised into direct and indirect uses (Table 7.8). Direct use values are those associated with benefits derived from 'planned use' of an ecosystem, such as grazing of livestock, extraction of papyrus and grass (Figure 7.7), hunting and provision of water. Indirect use values are those associated with services that are supported by an ecosystem rather than used directly, such as flood attenuation, sediment retention, groundwater recharge, shoreline protection and carbon sequestration. The data in the World Bank (2010) report explicitly excludes commercial fisheries and tourism values.

The direct use values were derived for all six wetlands and estimated to total USD94 My[-1]. The indirect use values were estimated for four of the wetlands and were estimated to

Figure 7.7 Social and cultural ecosystem benefits: reed harvest from Barotse Plain
Photo: Richard Beilfuss

Figure 7.8 Subsistence forestry is common in the basin
Photo: Richard Beilfuss

Table 7.8 Direct and indirect use values for selected wetlands (derived from data presented in World
　　　　Bank 2010)

Wetland	Area (km²)	Direct use value (USDMy⁻¹)	Indirect use (USDMy⁻¹)
Barotse	5,550	11	44
Chobe–Caprivi	2,220	5	22
Lower Shire	1,620	24	37
Kafue Flats	6,500	28	
Luangwa	2,500	11	
Zambezi Delta	12,750	15	79.3
Total	31,140	94	182

total USD182 My⁻¹. Based on the area of the wetlands, this enables estimates of direct use and indirect use values of USD3,021 and USD8,211 per km², respectively. Given that the total area of wetlands in the basin exceeds 63,226 km² (Table 7.8) and assuming the same average values across the entire area of wetlands, this provides an estimate of USD191 My⁻¹ of direct use benefits and USD 519 My⁻¹ of indirect use benefits (i.e., a total of USD710 My⁻¹).

Miombo woodland

Miombo woodland is of low productivity and, although there are some valuable hardwoods in places, it is generally not well endowed with high-value timber. Nevertheless, throughout southern Africa, including in the Zambezi Basin, it plays a crucial role in their livelihoods and so is of high local value to millions of poor households (Figure 7.8) (Campbell *et al.* 2007). Consequently, the cumulative economic value is relatively high (Table 7.9).

Additional values

Commercial fisheries are an additional high-value ecosystem service (Table 7.10) while tourism also adds considerably to the value with, as noted above, the annual direct value of tourism in the basin estimated to be USD450 My⁻¹.

Total value

Hence a rough but, because a lot of both use and non-use values have been omitted, conservative estimate of the total value of ecosystem services in the basin is USD1,341–1,542 My⁻¹. Although imperfect, this highlights the extraordinary value of ecosystem services in the basin. It is also important to bear in mind that much (though by no means all) of this value accrues to the very poorest rural communities in the region. As such, though clearly not eliminating poverty, the ecosystem services help mitigate it.

Threats to ecosystem services

Threats to the continued provision of ecosystem services in the basin relate particularly to pressures arising from economic development, climate change and increasing population. These threats pose complex, interrelated challenges for the ecology of the basin, and hence for the ecosystem services provided.

Table 7.9 Direct use values for some Miombo woodland ecosystem services

Ecosystem service	Value USD My⁻¹	Comment
Timber	10–25	Timber for housing construction and other purposes (e.g., furniture, poles, tool handles, carvings). In Zambia, production of industrial round wood from all forest types is estimated to be 1.15 million m³y⁻¹ with a value of USD 12.2 My⁻¹ (Ng'andwe *et al.* 2015). The forestry sector in Tanzania contributes a total of USD31 My⁻¹ (Abaza and Jha 2002).
Charcoal	62–232★	Assuming a value of USD511 ha⁻¹ (Luoga *et al.* 2000) and assuming an annual clearance of 0.2–0.75% (see below) of total Miombo area in the basin is for charcoal production.
Honey	2–3	Official figures indicate a production of 390, 600 and 27,000 ty⁻¹ in Mozambique, Zambia and Tanzania, respectively. Some proportion of this (especially in Zambia) will be produced in the Zambezi Basin. In 2008, exports of about 200 t of honey from Zambia were worth USD670,000 (Kommerskollgium 2009). Domestic use will add to the total value.
Medicinal plants	15–30	Based on Shackleton and Gumbo (2010), total value of medicinal plants in southern Africa was estimated to be USD75–150 My⁻¹. A significant proportion of this will come from the Zambezi Basin.
Total	89–290	

★ These are conservative estimates since for just four urban areas in Malawi an estimate of charcoal value is USD41.3 My⁻¹ (Kambewa *et al.* 2007). Between 70 and 80 per cent of urban households across southern Africa still rely on charcoal/fuelwood for domestic use. No allowance has been made for opportunity costs (associated with resource depletion), which ultimately threaten the sustainability of charcoal production.

Table 7.10 Value of major commercial fisheries

Fishery	Value (USD My⁻¹)
Offshore prawn	20
Kariba	25
Cahora Bassa	34
Lower Zambezi	13
Total	92

Source of data: Fanaian *et al.* (2015)

Economic development

The Zambezi River is critical to the economic development of the riparian countries and southern Africa generally. Accounting for half of the installed hydropower capacity and supporting mining, agriculture and fisheries, it plays a vital role in stimulating economic opportunities for 250 million people in the region. However, changes in the basin intended to boost economic development have, inevitably, wrought changes to the environment and, hence, to the ecosystem services. As development pressures intensify, national governments are keen to further exploit the economic opportunities that the basin provides.

The hydrology of the middle and lower basin has been greatly modified by the construction of large hydropower dams. The natural variability in flow has been reduced, with much less variation between wet- and dry-season flows (Beilfuss *et al.* 2002). There are now ambitious plans for several more hydropower schemes and large-scale irrigation on both the main river and its tributaries (see Chapters 5 and 6). If built, these will further alter the hydrology and are likely to exacerbate many of the changes in ecosystem services.

Although the economies of the riparian states have gained overall from the construction of the dams, there have been significant impacts on downstream ecosystems and the services that they provide. Arguably the most significantly altered part of the basin is the river delta which, as a consequence of the modified flow regimes and the trapping of sediment in the reservoirs, is experiencing desiccation and salinisation of alluvial soils, increasing terrestrialisation of vegetation, reduced herbivore carrying capacity of the floodplains, reduced fisheries and coastal shelf erosion (Beilfuss *et al.* 2001).

Data presented in Fanaian *et al.* (2015) indicate that although the net benefits of the Cahora Bassa Dam exceed USD60 My^{-1}, reduction in downstream fisheries (both in the estuary and off-shore) and lost opportunities in wildlife tourism cost Mozambique approximately USD57 My^{-1}. The same analyses indicate that total economic benefits could be substantially increased with small changes to the dam operation. For example, releasing so-called 'environmental flows' at critical times of year to simulate the natural pattern of flooding, would result in significant increases in fisheries and wildlife tourism and only marginal declines in electricity generation. As a result the total economic benefit could increase by USD28 My^{-1}.

Pollution from mines and industry is an increasing problem in the basin. Subbasins such as the Luangwa River, Lake Kariba and the Kafue and Kabompo Rivers have high concentrations of mining, which are adding significantly to river pollution. For example, water quality in the Kafue River, which provides domestic water supply to over 40 per cent of the Zambian population, is of increasing concern. Heavy metals such as copper, cobalt, arsenic, lead and zinc, originating primarily from the Copperbelt mining region, a significant part of which lies within the basin, have been detected in many rivers and streams. Recent studies have concluded that water pollution is largely a consequence of: i) industrial and mine water discharged into the water courses; ii) seepage and overflow from tailing impoundments; and iii) erosion and washout of fine-grained particulates from spoil banks and tailings impoundments (Kříbek *et al.* 2010). The town of Kabwe (population 300,000), which lies in the basin, is considered one of the 10 most polluted cities in the world, with lead poisoning particularly prevalent. There is concern that, although there is no evidence as yet, bioaccumulation of heavy metals in fish could have serious health implications for people in the future (World Bank 2010).

Pollution is not only a direct threat to the health of those people who depend on the water for drinking and domestic use, it also threatens biota and hence other ecosystem services. Increasing nutrient inputs to water (primarily from agriculture) has, in places, resulted in infestation by aquatic weeds (e.g., water hyacinth, water lettuce and water fern). In Kafue, Lake Kariba, Lake Chivero, Kwando-Linyanti and the Lower Shire the infestation of aquatic weeds has caused problems such as hypoxia leading to fish kills, blockage of channels, irrigation and hydropower intakes, and the spread of aquatic invertebrates that cause disease (ZAMCOM *et al.* 2015).

Climate change

The climate of the Zambezi Basin is extremely variable. Although the impacts of climate change remain uncertain most climate models indicate a drying trend for much of the twenty-first century. Among 11 major sub-Saharan African river basins, the Zambezi exhibits the worst potential effects of climate change, and will experience the most substantial reduction in rainfall and runoff, according to the Intergovernmental Panel on Climate Change (IPCC). Multiple studies cited by the IPCC estimate that rainfall across the basin will decrease by 10–15 per cent and runoff by as much as 40 per cent or more (Beilfuss 2012). There may be seasonal shifts in rainfall and hence flow (World Bank 2010). It is also likely that the uneven distribution of rainfall, both spatially and temporally, will increase and the frequency of extremes (floods and droughts) will rise.

By increasing temperature, changing patterns of rainfall and modifying flow regimes, climate change will have significant impacts on the ecology of river, wetland, forest and grassland ecosystems and inevitably ecosystem services will be affected. Although there has been some effort to predict the implications of changing climate on some ecosystem services (e.g., kapenta fish stocks in Lake Kariba (Ndebele-Murisa *et al.* 2011), there has been little systematic analyses of likely impacts to date. Still, in a basin in which rainfall and runoff are projected to decline, it seems probable that there will be a substantive reduction in the overall value of the ecosystem services.

Furthermore, interventions to mitigate and adapt to climate change may also have significant impacts on ecosystems. For example, mitigation measures such as afforestation (for carbon sequestration) and the planting of bioenergy crops (to replace fossil fuels) can, by changing land-use and modifying hydrological regimes, have major impacts on wetlands and other ecosystems. Similarly, increased water storage in dams, widely promoted as an important contribution to adaptation, can, as has already been seen in the Zambezi, have major impacts on downstream hydrology and hence on ecosystems. Clearly, such interventions need to be carefully planned and managed to limit potential adverse impacts.

Population growth

The population of the basin is growing rapidly and is estimated to increase from 40 million in 2008 to 51 million in 2025 (ZAMCOM *et al.* 2015). This will inevitably increase competition for resources, adding to pressure on the basin ecosystems. Increased population pressure manifests itself in many ways but for the ecosystem services the most significant are direct degradation of forests, wetlands, grasslands and the river itself.

Across the riparian countries loss of miombo woodland is reported to be occurring at a rate of between 0.2 and 1.7 per cent a year, with the greatest rates of loss (> 1 per cent of remaining forest cover per annum) in Tanzania, Zambia and Zimbabwe (ZAMCOM *et al.* 2015). Unlike other places in the world, where commercial logging and clearing land for cattle ranching are the primary causes, in the Zambezi Basin deforestation is predominantly a consequence of the need for fuelwood/charcoal for domestic needs and land clearing by subsistence and commercial farmers. Deforestation in conjunction with poor cultivation practices, cultivation of marginal and unsuitable areas and increased encroachment into environmentally fragile areas such as steep slopes, river banks and, in some places, wetlands is reported to have led to increased soil erosion, which has implications for agricultural productivity and food security, as well as turbidity of river water and siltation of reservoirs, diversion channels and irrigation schemes.

Pollution from domestic waste is causing localised problems within the basin in the vicinity of some urban populations (e.g., Harare, Lusaka, Livingstone and Kafue). Sewerage effluent, and seepage from landfills and pit latrines, all degrade water quality. For example, the dolomite karstic aquifer that supplies Lusaka is threatened by large numbers of pit latrines and septic tanks, and some boreholes that produce drinking water have been contaminated (De Waele and Follesa 2003). As urban populations increase this is likely to worsen but currently, largely because of high levels of dilution and natural water purifying processes (see above), there is no evidence that domestic waste pollution is likely to reach problematic levels generally in the basin (World Bank 2010).

Increasing population is increasing the pressure on wetland ecosystems. Wetland degradation arises from unsustainable utilisation of wetland resources (e.g., fish, water and plants) and conversion of wetlands for agriculture and, in peri-urban areas, construction. With the exception of the impacts on fish (described above) the direct impacts on wetlands are relatively localised and not widely reported. Consequently, it is difficult to assess the direct implications of increased population but it is likely that, though still important for local people, impacts will be relatively small compared to the indirect pressures arising from human activities (see above).

With some exceptions (e.g., fisheries and deforestation) overall increase in population is not as significant a threat to the basin ecosystems and hence ecosystem services as economic development and climate change. Nevertheless, in some places, such as Lusaka, increasing population could significantly aggravate the pressures arising from these other threats.

Ecological footprint

The ecological footprint is a systematic measure of human impact on ecosystems at national, regional and global levels (WWF 2014). Here, national-level data have been used to develop a crude indicator of the overall pressure on ecosystems in the Zambezi Basin.

The ecological footprint is a measure of how much area of biologically productive land and water a country, region or individual requires to produce all the resources it consumes and to absorb the waste (primarily carbon dioxide) it generates, using prevailing technology and resource management practices. Because trade is global, an individual's or country's footprint includes land or sea from all over the world (Borucke *et al.* 2013).

To determine if demand exceeds supply the footprint can be compared with the 'biocapacity' of a specific region. The biocapacity of a region is a measure of the ability of ecosystems in that region to regenerate biological materials used, and to absorb wastes generated, by people. Both biocapacity and ecological footprint are expressed in a common unit called a global hectare (gha): a biologically productive hectare with world average biological productivity.[4] If in a given region the ecological footprint exceeds the biocapacity, this means that the biological resources of that area are being used at a rate that exceeds their ability to recover in a single year; effectively natural resources are being exploited at an unsustainable rate.

Figure 7.9 presents the Human Development Index (HDI), per capita GDP, ecological footprint and biocapacity of each of the riparian countries of the Zambezi Basin (Table 7.11). The graph plots HDI vs ecological footprint for each country. It also displays an estimate of the ecological footprint and biocapacity for the Zambezi Basin, computed as the areal weighted average based on the proportion of the basin in each of the riparian countries. This shows that: i) currently, the estimated ecological footprint (1.12 gha) is less than the basin biocapacity (1.96 gha), which means that, notwithstanding impacts on fish and forests, overall demands on ecosystem services do not currently exceed what they can supply; ii) the current biocapacity of the basin (1.96 gha) slightly exceeds the global average (1.70 gha); and iii) with the exception of two countries (Namibia and Botswana) the ecological footprints of riparian countries are currently less than the biocapacity of the basin.

To achieve sustainable development it is necessary to create a decent standard of living while having a per capita footprint that is smaller than the per capita biocapacity of the planet. The former can be defined as an HDI score of 0.71 or above. The latter is 1.70 gha – the maximum that can be replicated worldwide without demand exceeding supply. The results indicate that, currently, none of the riparian countries are achieving a high level of human development in a sustainable manner. Those countries with the highest HDI (i.e., Botswana and Namibia) have the highest ecological footprints, greatly exceeding not only the global average biocapacity but also that of the Zambezi Basin. The other riparian countries have ecological footprints that are lower than the biocapacity of both the basin and the planet, but in these countries standards of living fall significantly below the HDI target of 0.70. The sustainability challenge for these countries is to raise living standards without exceeding the biocapacity targets.

Table 7.11 Ecological footprints of riparian countries

Country	HDI	GDP per capita (USD)	Ecological footprint per capita (gha)	Biocapacity per capita (gha)
Angola	0.52	4,666	0.9	2.6
Botswana	0.69	7,744	3.8	3.5
Malawi	0.43	494	0.8	0.7
Mozambique	0.41	539	0.9	2.1
Namibia	0.62	5,881	2.5	6.9
Tanzania	0.48	765	1.3	1.1
Zambia	0.58	1,741	1	2.2
Zimbabwe	0.49	866	1.4	0.6
Average			1.58	2.46

Source: Derived from data provided in the Global Footprint Network (2016)

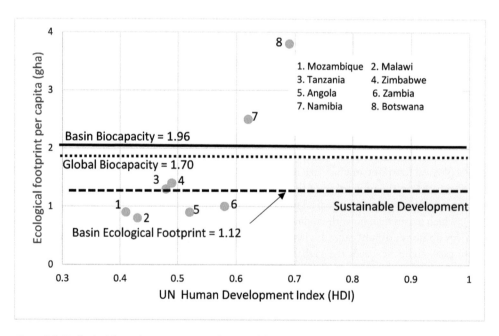

Figure 7.9 Ecological footprint per person and HDI of the countries in the Zambezi Basin, in 2012

Note: Basin biocapacity and ecological footprint were determined using areal weighted averages based on the proportion of the basin in each of the riparian countries.

Source: Derived from data provided in Global Footprint Network (2016)

Conclusions

The social and economic value of ecosystem services in the Zambezi River Basin is vast; directly and indirectly supporting the livelihoods of millions of people and making significant contributions to the economies of all eight riparian countries. Despite this, largely because they are provided for free, ecosystem services have rarely been given due consideration in past development planning. As this chapter has described, despite their value, pressures on ecosystems are accumulating, ecosystem services are increasingly under threat and the gap between supply and demand is narrow and closing.

Multiple factors are driving changes in the state of ecosystems and the services that they provide. In addition to significant environmental pressures, prevailing high levels of poverty and food insecurity, reflected in relatively low values of HDI in all riparian countries, suggest that current economic growth is not sufficiently inclusive and is unlikely to be sustainable in the long term. Continued depletion of ecosystem services will likely translate into fewer livelihood benefits and reduced well-being for much of the basin population. Ultimately, the future of the river basin and the people who live in it will depend in large measure on the stewardship of its ecosystems and the benefits that they provide.

In the basin, the predominantly rural population and the fact that near-natural ecosystems represent a significant proportion of the basin landscape make a strong case for the centrality of ecosystem services in strategies for poverty reduction, food security and economic development. However, ecosystem services represent the outcomes of dynamic social-ecological systems that are characterised by change and variability. In such circumstances, no single policy instrument or strategy can deal with the complexity, which is further exacerbated by the transboundary nature of the basin. Rather, safeguarding the benefits derived from ecosystems will depend on a mix of policies and strategies that foster sustainable development by recognising and giving proper weight to ecosystem services.

The challenge for policy- and decision-makers is that poverty reduction requires the identification and implementation of opportunities to improve livelihoods through economic activities: moving beyond subsistence to using the available resources in an efficient and productive manner. This inevitably requires some change to the environment. However, significantly altering ecosystems for economic development can adversely affect the very ecosystem services on which the poor most depend and often results in unintended, negative consequences for the most vulnerable. Striking an appropriate balance is a far from trivial task.

As an institution with a basin-wide mandate and a remit 'to promote the equitable and reasonable utilization of the water resources of the Zambezi . . .', it is vital that ZAMCOM plays a prominent and active role in fostering the concept of ecosystem services and emphasises the importance of including them explicitly in the planning of all water resources development. The environment and the need to mainstream ecosystem approaches are given prominence in the final IWRM strategy and implementation plan for the Zambezi (SADC 2008). This needs to be taken seriously, moving beyond fine words to on-the-ground action.

The following are some possible approaches for safeguarding ecosystem services in the basin.

- Better identify, quantify and value the ecosystem services of the basin. Generate maps that show where ecosystem services are produced and used. Maps can contribute to better understanding of the synergies and trade-offs among different ecosystem services and are important communication tools to initiate discussions with stakeholders, visualising the locations where valuable ecosystem services are located within the basin. Conduct research to better understand: i) how services link to hydrological and ecological functioning; and ii) who derives benefits and their value.

- Conduct in-depth strategic and environmental impact assessments prior to the construction of any new infrastructure in the basin, including assessment of cumulative impacts. Recognise that despite the economic benefits of water resources development, hydraulic structures and related flow alterations also pose an equity problem as the people directly affected rarely benefit from the investment. These conflicting interests should be thoroughly evaluated prior to finalising the planning and design of the numerous water infrastructure projects currently proposed for the basin.
- Ensure environmental flows and coordinate dam operation. Research has shown that maintaining more natural flow regimes – particularly wet season floods – downstream of the large hydropower dams in the Zambezi can significantly improve total economic returns with only modest implications for electricity generation. Furthermore, coordinated operation of the existing hydropower facilities in the basin could increase energy production, thereby cancelling out the losses associated with environmental flow releases and possibly removing the need for some of the currently proposed future investment.
- Strengthen community involvement in environmental protection and management with appropriate legislation on local resource access rights, effective community resource management programmes and regional cooperation and research on holistic natural resource management.

Notes

1   The *Zambezi Environment Outlook* (ZAMCOM *et al.* 2015) states that 77 per cent of the Zambezi River Basin population has access to an adequate and safe water supply (Table 2.5, p. 32) but this is unlikely given the national figures provided in World Bank (2015).
2   Rising temperatures will result in increased potential evapotranspiration and hence rising demand for water in irrigation and other sectors, including evaporation from reservoirs.
3   Benefits transfer applies economic values that have been generated in one context to another similar context for which the values are required. In this case we transfer values determined for some wetlands in the basin to the total area of wetlands in the basin.
4   Global hectares are needed because different ecosystems/landscapes have different productivities. For example, because pasture is less biologically productive than cropland, a global hectare of cropland occupies a smaller physical area than that of pasture.

References

Abaza, H. and Jha, V. 2002. *Integrated assessment of trade liberalization and trade-related policies.* UNEP Country Projects – Round II. A Synthesis Report. New York and Geneva: United Nations.

Acres, B.D., Rains, A.B., King, R.H.B., Lawton, R.M., Mitchell, A.J.B. and Rackham, L.J. 1985. African dambos: Their distribution, characteristics and use. *Zeitschrift für Geomorphologie* 52: 63–86.

Beilfuss, R.D. 2012. *A risky climate for southern African hydro: Assessing hydrological risks and consequences for Zambezi River Basin dams.* Berkeley, CA: International Rivers Network.

Beilfuss, R., Chilundo, A., Isaacmen, A. and Mulwafu, W. 2002. *The impact of hydrological changes on subsistence production systems and socio-cultural values in the Lower Zambezi Valley.* Working Paper #6. Program for the sustainable management of Cahora Bassa Dam and the Lower Zambezi Valley. Available at http://bscwapp1.let.ethz.ch/pub/nj_bscw.cgi/ d11576983/Beilfuss_2002_The_impact.pdf; (accessed January 2015).

Beilfuss, R., Moore, D., Bento, C. and Dutton, P. 2001. *Patterns of vegetation change in the Zambezi Delta.* Working paper of the program for the sustainable management of Cahora Bassa Dam and the Lower Zambezi Valley, 78p. Available at www.xitizap.com/zambeze-hydrochanges.pdf (accessed November 2016).

Blumenfeld, S., Lu, C., Christophersen, T. and Coates, D. 2009. *Water, wetlands and forests: A review of ecological, economic and policy linkages.* CBD Technical Series No. 47. Montreal: Secretariat of the Convention on Biological Diversity; Gland: Secretariat of the Ramsar Convention on Wetlands.

Blythe, J.L., Murray, G. and Flaherty, M. 2013. Historical perspectives and recent trends in the coastal Mozambican fishery. *Ecology and Society* 18(4): 65. Available at http://dx.doi.org/10.5751/ES-05759-180465 (accessed 1 May 2016).

Borucke, M., Moore, D., Cranston, G., Gracey, K., Iha, K., Larson, J., Lazarus, E., Morales, J.C., Wackernagel, M. and Galli, A. 2013. Accounting for demand and supply of the biosphere's regenerative capacity: The National Footprint Accounts' underlying methodology and framework. *Ecological Indicators* 24: 518–533.

Bullock, A. 1992. Dambo hydrology in southern Africa – review and reassessment. *J Hydrol.* 134: 373–396.

Campbell, B.M., Angelsen, A., Cunningham, A., Katerere, Y., Sitoe, A. and Wunder, S. 2007. Miombo woodlands – opportunities and barriers to sustainable forest management. Available at www.cifor.org/miombo/docs/Campbell_BarriersandOpportunities.pdf (accessed 25 June 2016).

CGI (Carbon Green Investments). 2014. Kariba REDD+ Project Zimbabwe. Project Implementation Report. 43p.

Clarke, J., Cavendish, W. and Coote, C. 1996. Rural households and miombo woodlands: Use, value and management. In: *The miombo in transition: Woodlands and welfare in Africa*, (ed.), Campbell, B., 101–135. Bogor, Indonesia: Centre for International Forestry Research.

Costanza, R., de Groot, R., Sutton, P., van der Ploeg, S., Anderson, S.J., Kubiszewski, I., Farber, S. and Turner, R.K. 2014. Changes in the global value of ecosystem services. *Global Environmental Change* 26: 152–158.

De Waele, J. and Follesa, R. 2003. Human impact on karst: The example of Lusaka (Zambia). *International Journal of Speleology* 32(1/4): 71–83.

Emerton, L. and Bos, E. 2004. *Value: Counting ecosystems as an economic part of water infrastructure.* Gland, Switzerland; Cambridge, UK: International Union for Conservation of Nature (IUCN), 88p.

Fanaian, S., Grass, S., Jiang, Y. and van der Zaag, P. 2015. An ecological economic assessment of flow regimes in a hydropower dominated river basin: The case of the lower Zambezi River, Mozambique. *Science of the Total Environment* 505: 464–473.

FAO (Food and Agriculture Organization of the United Nations). 2007. Report of the third Technical Consultation on the Development and Management of the Fisheries of Lake Kariba. Siavonga, Zambia, 26–27 October 2006. Rome: *FAO Fisheries Report.* No. 824, 13p.

Fynn, R.W.S., Murray-Hudson, M., Dhliwayo, M. and Scholte, P. 2015. African wetlands and their seasonal use by wild and domestic herbivores. *Wetlands Ecology and Management.* doi: 10.1007/s112733-015-9430-6.

Gammelsrød, T. 1992. Variation in shrimp abundance on the Sofala Bank, Mozambique, and its relation to the Zambezi River Runoff. *Estuarine, Coastal and Shelf Science* 15: 91–103.

Global Footprint Network. 2016. Available at www.footprintnetwork.org/ (accessed 25 June 2016).

Hoguane, A.M. and Armando, E.V. 2015. The influence of the river runoff in the artisanal fisheries catches in tropical waters – the case of the Zambezi River and the fisheries catches in the northern Sofala Bank, Mozambique. *Journal of Integrated Coastal Zone Management* 15(4): 9. doi: 10.5894/rgci600.

Hughes, R.H. and Hughes, J.S. 1992. *A directory of African wetlands.* Gland, Switzerland and Cambridge, UK: IUCN; Nairobi: United Nations Environment Programme; Kenya: World Conservation Monitoring Centre (WCMC). 820 pp.

IIP (Fisheries Research Institute of Mozambique) and IIDA (The Icelandic International Development Agency). 2006. *Research, monitoring and development of the fisheries in the Cahora Bassa Reservoir – Phase-II 2007–2010.* Available at www.iceida.is/media/verkefnagagnabanki/Mozambique-Cahorra-Bassa-II-Project-Document-2007-2010.pdf (accessed 26 March 2016).

IPCC (Intergovernmental Panel on Climate Change). 2007. Climate change 2007: The physical science basis. In: *Contribution of Working Group I to the Fourth Assessment*, (eds.), Solomon, S., Qin, D., Manning, M., Chen, Z., Marquis, M., Averyt, K.B., Tignor, M. and Miller, H.L. Cambridge: Cambridge University Press.

Junk, W.J., Bayley, P.B. and Sparks, R.E. 1989. The flood pulse concept in river-floodplain systems. In: *Proceedings of the International Large River Symposium Can*, (ed.), Dodge, D.P. *Spec. Publ. Fish Aquat. Sci* 106: 110–127.

Kadlec, R.H. and Knight, R.L. 1996. *Treatment wetlands.* Boca Raton, Florida: Lewis Publishers, CRC Press.

Kambewa, P., Mataya, B., Sichinga, K. and Johnson, T. 2007. *Charcoal: The reality – a study of charcoal consumption, trade and production in Malawi.* Small and Medium Forestry Enterprise Series No. 21. London, UK: International Institute for Environment and Development.

Kommerskollgium. 2009. A case study of Zambia honey exports. Available at www.kommers.se/Documents/dokumentarkiv/publikationer/2009/rapporter/report-case-study-of-zambian-honey-exports.pdf (accessed 13 October 2016).

Křibek, B., Majer, V., Veselovský, F. and Nyambe, I.A. 2010. Discrimination of lithogenic and anthropogenic sources of metals and sulphur in soils of the central-northern part of the Zambian Copperbelt Mining Districts: A topsoil vs. subsurface soil concept. *Journal of Geochemical Exploration* 104: 69–86.

Leach, M. and Scoones, I. 2015. Ecologies of carbon in Africa. In: *Carbon conflicts and forest landscapes in Africa online,* (eds.), Leach, M. and Scoones, I. Available at www.routledge.com/products/9781138824836 (accessed 6 May 2016).

Lehner, B. and Döll, P. 2004. Development and validation of a global database of lakes, reservoirs and wetlands. *Journal of Hydrology* 296(1–4): 1–22.

Luoga, E.J., Witkowski, E.T.F. and Balkwill, K. 2000. Economics of charcoal production in miombo woodlands of eastern Tanzania: Some hidden costs associated with commercialization of the resources. *Ecological Economics* 35: 243–257.

Machena, C. 1997. The pollution and self-purification capacity of the Mukuvisi River. In: *Lake Chivero: A polluted lake,* (ed.), Moyo, N.A.G., 75–91. Harare: University of Zimbabwe.

Mafuca, J.M. 2008. The kapenta fishery in the Cahora Bassa Dam – Mozambique: The past, present and the future. Poster presentation, PAFFA Conference, Addis Ababa, Ethiopia, September 2008.

Magadza, C.H.D. 2006. Kariba reservoir: Experience and lessons learned. On-line ILEC publication. Available at www.ilec.or.jp/eg/lbmi/pdf/14 Kariba Reservoir 27 February 2006.pdf. (accessed 30 April 2016).

Magadza, C.H.D. 2008. Management of eutrophication in Lake Chivero: Success and failures. A case study. In: *Proceedings of Taal 2007: The 12th World Lake Conference,* (eds.), Sengupta, M. and Dalwani, R., 790–798. Penang: World Fish Center.

Masiyandima, M., McCartney, M.P. and Van Koppen, B. 2004. *Wetland contributions to livelihoods in Zambia.* FAO Netherlands Partnership Program: Sustainable Development and Management of Wetlands 50 p. Rome: FAO.

McCartney, M.P., Beilfuss, R. and Rebelo, L-M. Forthcoming. The Zambezi River Basin. In: *The wetland book: Distribution, description, and conservation,* (eds.), Finlayson, M.C., Milton, R.G, Prentice, R.C. and Davidson, N.C. New York: Springer.

McCartney, M.P., Cai, X. and Smakhtin, V. 2013. *Evaluating the flow regulating functions of natural ecosystems in the Zambezi Basin.* IWMI Research Report 148. Colombo, Sri Lanka: International Water Management Institute. doi: 10.5337/2013.206, 51pp.

McCartney, M.P., Chigumira, F. and Jackson, J.E. 1997. *The water-resource opportunities provided by dambos for small-scale farming in Zimbabwe.* Paper presented at a workshop on the Management and Conservation of the Wetlands of Zimbabwe, Harare, Zimbabwe, 12–14 February 1997.

McCartney, M., Rebelo, L-M., Mapedza, E., de Silva, S. and Finlayson, M. 2011. The Lukanga Swamps: Use, conflicts, and management. *Journal of International Wildlife Law & Policy* 14(3–4): 293–310.

MEA (Millennium Ecosystem Assessment). 2005. *Millennium Ecosystem Assessment General Synthesis Report.* Washington, DC: Island Press.

Ndebele-Murisa, M.R., Mashonjowa, E. and Hill, T. 2011. The implications of a changing climate on the Kapenta fish stocks of Lake Kariba, Zimbabwe. *Transactions of the Royal Society of South Africa* 66(2): 105–119.

Ng'andwe, P., Mwitwa, J., Muimba-Kankolongo, A., Kabibwa, N. and Simbangala, L. 2015. Contribution of the forestry sector to the national economy. In: *Forest policy, economics and markets in Zambia,* (eds.), Ng'andwe, P., Mwitwa, J. and Muimba-Kankolongo, A. Oxford: Academic Press, Elsevier.

Praagman, E. 2013. Trade-offs between ecosystem services and a changing flow regime in the Zambezi Delta, Mozambique. MSc thesis. Wageningen University. 63 p.

Reeves, P.N. and Champion, P.D. 2004. Effects of livestock grazing on wetlands: Literature review. Environment Waikato. NIWA Client Report HAM2004–059. Hamilton, New Zealand: National Institute of Water & Atmospheric Research Ltd., 33 p.

Ribeiro, D.L. Undated. *The Zambezi Valley: damned by dams.* Justica Ambiental. 19 pp.

SADC (Southern Africa Development Community) 2008. Integrated Water Resources Management Strategy for the Zambezi Basin, Zambezi Action Plan Project 6.2 ZACPRO 6.2, SADC Water Division, Danida, Sida, Norwegian Embassy Lusaka, Zambezi River Authority.

Seyam, I.M., Hoekstra, A.Y. and Ngabirano, H.H.G. 2001. *The value of freshwater wetlands in the Zambezi basin.* Delft, The Netherlands: IHE, 22 p.

Shackleton, S. and Gumbo, D. 2010. Contribution of non-wood forest products to livelihoods and poverty alleviation. In: *The dry forests and woodlands of Africa: Managing for products and services*, (eds.), Chidumayo, E.N. and Gumbo, D.J. London: Earthscan.

Simwinji, N. 1997. Summary of existing relevant socio-economic and ecological information on Zambia's Western Province and Barotseland, IUCN – The World Conservation Union Regional Office for Southern Africa, Harare.

Timberlake, J. 2000. Biodiversity of the Zambezi Basin. Bulawayo, Zimbabwe: Biodiversity Foundation for Africa. Occasional Publications in Biodiversity No. 9. 23 pp.

Turpie, J.K., Smith, B., Emerton, L. and Barnes, J. 1999. Economic value of the Zambezi Basin wetlands. Report to IUCN ROSA, Harare.

Tweddle, D. 2010. Overview of the Zambezi river system: Its history, fish fauna, fisheries and conservation. *Aquatic Ecosystem Health and Management* 13: 224–240.

Tweddle, D., Cowx, I.G., Peel, R.A. and Weyl, O.L.F. 2015. Challenges in fisheries management in the Zambezi, one of the great rivers of Africa. *Fisheries Management and Ecology* 22: 99–111.

WCD (World Commission on Dams). 2000. *Dams and development: A new framework for decision-making*. London: Earthscan Publications Ltd.

World Bank 2010. *The Zambezi River Basin: A multi-sector investment opportunities analysis*. Volume 3 – State of the Basin. Washington, DC: World Bank. 182p.

World Bank 2015. *The little green data book 2015*. Washington, DC: World Bank. doi:10.1596/978-1-4648-0560-8. License: Creative Commons Attribution CC BY 3.0 IGO.

WWF (Worldwide Fund for Nature). 2014. *Living Planet Report 2014*. Gland: WWF.

ZAMCOM (Zambezi Water Commission), SADC (Southern African Development Community) and SARDC (Southern African Research and Documentation Centre). 2015. *Zambezi Environment Outlook 2015*. Harare, Gaborone.

8

Urbanisation, water quality and water reuse

*Munir A. Hanjra, Pay Drechsel and
Hillary M. Masundire*

Key messages

- Urbanisation and human activities like mining affect both water quality and quantity in the Zambezi River Basin.
- Domestic water consumption and wastewater loads are projected to increase by about 50 per cent between 2005 and 2020, and to double between now and 2050.
- Benchmarking the compliance of local authorities with set water quality targets, wastewater treatment standards and regulations across the basin countries could provide incentives for basin-level investment to spur environmental protection.

- Basin-states are encouraged to develop a water reuse framework to support the development of national reuse guidelines and data monitoring in view of Sustainable Development Goal 6.3, which seeks, inter alia, to improve water quality by reducing pollution and wastewater treatment, and to increase the share of safe water reuse.

Introduction

Urbanisation is widely recognised as an important issue in Africa (World Bank 2016). At present, only 40 per cent of the continent's population lives in urban areas (United Nations 2015). However, the population is set to more than double between now and 2050, reaching 2.4 billion, (Haub and Kaneda 2013) and the urban proportion of this population will rise to 56 per cent. This increase will put immense pressure on already challenged service provision (Capps *et al.* 2016).

Urbanisation has, in particular, a key impact on the quantity and quality of available water (Drechsel *et al.* 2015). Urbanisation typically leads to increased water demand in the form of direct potable supplies for household and industrial use, as well as for water in peri-urban agriculture.[1] Urbanisation also leads to greater production of wastewater, which can have adverse effects on water quality and pose health risks (Nhapi and Hoko 2004; Gutierrez 2007; Parnell and Walawege 2011; Hanjra *et al.* 2012). Population pressure on limited service provision capacity, and the proliferation of informal settlements which are not serviced by sewerage systems, are some of the major contributors to poor water quality, and public and environmental health challenges (Nhapi 2009). Hove *et al.* (2013) conclude that conditions in sub-Saharan Africa's urban areas contribute to poor sanitation and the spread of infectious diseases.

There may be a role for basin-level management in enhancing urban water management, and, indeed, connections between cities and transboundary water management have been identified (Earle 2013). Basin-level planning can facilitate improved urban water supply through effective water resources management, for example, through the sequencing of infrastructure development (World Bank 2015). Further, the mandates of river basin organisations (RBOs) have expanded to cover a range of new issues, such as malaria control by the Organisation pour la Mise en Valeur du fleuve Sénégal (OMVS) in the Senegal Basin (Lautze and Kirshen 2007). There may, therefore, be opportunities for RBOs to influence water management associated with urbanisation even if primary institutions tasked with such issues operate at more local levels.

The objective of this chapter is to synthesise existing knowledge on urbanisation, water quality and water reuse in the Zambezi River Basin (hereafter the Zambezi) in order to offer recommendations on how basin-wide management by the Zambezi Watercourse Commission (ZAMCOM) may foster improvements in these areas. The chapter will review urbanisation in the Zambezi, its water quality and health impacts, as well as the formal and informal use of urban wastewater for productive activities. Of these focal areas, wastewater use may merit special focus. It is also important to consider the potential for wastewater reuse to provide a significant source of water in view of possible impacts of climate change on water demand and supply in the Zambezi Basin (see Chapter 4). Importantly, wastewater use, water reuse and wastewater reuse are treated synonymously and defined as the intentional or unintentional use of untreated, treated, partially treated or mixed wastewater.

Materials and methods

Materials utilised in this chapter were assembled from a range of sources, and statistical databases from riparian countries (e.g., Malawi, Mozambique, Zambia) were utilised to generate trends relevant to the chapter. The somewhat sparse data available in the Zambezi called for thoroughly mining all relevant sources. As such, while scrutiny was applied to data utilised, extensive filtering based on quality of data was not possible. Ultimately, the findings presented below may be best viewed as estimates based on certain assumptions, and known or unknown risk factors, rather than an exact depiction of conditions and trends in the Zambezi.

The distinction between formal and informal water use is worth clarifying here. Formal water reuse is presumed to be practised under a regulatory framework designed to ensure the safety of the resulting water for the intended use, whereas informal use is not. Informal wastewater use for agricultural irrigation is widespread in the developing world (Scheierling *et al.* 2010). It is often officially prohibited, yet unofficially tolerated because many people derive their livelihoods from access to untreated or partially treated wastewater (Hanjra *et al.* 2015a; Rao *et al.* 2015).

Urbanisation trends in the Zambezi

While the population of the Zambezi Basin is predominantly rural at present, migration is increasing due to new socioeconomic opportunities in urban areas. Urbanisation will likely accelerate in the decades ahead, due to better access to water and sanitation, education, employment opportunities, healthcare and other amenities. Indeed, urban population is projected to cross the 50 per cent benchmark by 2050 in all the Zambezi Basin countries, except Malawi (Figure 8.1, based on the population database of the United Nations).

Specific manifestations of rapid urbanisation are abundant in the basin's towns. The population of Solwezi in Zambia has more than tripled since 2000; in Malawi, Lilongwe's population rose from 99,000 in 1977 to 782,000 in 2012; and the population of Tete in Mozambique grew from 56,000 in 1986 to 156,000 in 2008 (SADC *et al.* 2012). Table 8.1 shows the population growth rate in selected major towns in the basin.

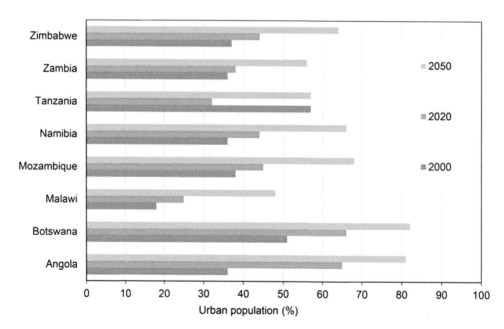

Figure 8.1 Urban population (percentage of total) in the Zambezi Basin countries
Source: Authors

Table 8.1 Population growth in the main towns of the Zambezi Basin

Country	Town	Urban population (2005)	Urban population (2015)	% change per year (2010–15)
Malawi	Blantyre	562,000	661,000	2.86
	Lilongwe	522,000	675,000	4.46
Mozambique	Tete	124,000	221,000	4.07
Zambia	Kitwe	406,000	648,000	3.27
	Lusaka	1,211,000	2,330,000	4.89
Zimbabwe	Harare	1,976,000	2,123,000	1.14
	Kwekwe	82,000	110,000	0.75

Source: Author's own synthesis, based on Euroconsult (2008), Central Statistical Office Zambia, Zimbabwe National Statistics Agency, National Statistical Office of Malawi, and Instituto Nacional de Estatistica Moçambique (National Institute of Statistics Mozambique), cited in the database www.citypopulation.de (accessed 8 December 2015)

Table 8.2 Urban domestic water demand and wastewater generated in key urban centres in the Zambezi Basin

Urban centre	Population 2005	2020 Business-As-Usual scenario			2020 Optimistic scenario		
		Population	Domestic water consumption (million m³)	Wastewater effluent generated (million m³)	Population	Domestic water consumption (million m³)	Wastewater effluent generated (million m³)
Lusaka	1,211,000	2,295,000	52.77	47.50	2,179,000	50.12	45.10
Harare	1,976,000	2,311,000	53.15	47.83	2,220,000	51.06	45.95
Lilongwe	522,000	1,090,000	25.07	22.56	1,012,000	23.28	20.95

Source: Own calculations, based on the population database of the United Nations

Rapid urban population growth and general urban expansion are driving both increased domestic water consumption and increased wastewater generation (Table 8.2). Whether water consumption and wastewater production are directly extrapolated at current rates – as shown in the Business-As-Usual (BAU) scenario – or even if efficiency gains are made in the Optimistic scenario, the bottom line is that both water consumption and wastewater production are likely to increase by at least 50 per cent in the period from 2005 to 2020, and to double between now and 2050.

Water quality challenges

Water quality impacts associated with urbanisation arise from waste disposal challenges, use of groundwater, proliferation of informal settlements, mining operations and irrigated urban and peri-urban agriculture (Figure 8.2).

Waste disposal

Wastewater

While the basin's larger cities and towns have sewage treatment works, the volume of wastewater generated by such cities far exceeds the capacities that such works were designed to handle.

Figure 8.2 Poor water quality in Lake Chivero, near Harare. Disposal of untreated or partially treated wastewater as well as siltation are major threats to water quality in the basin.

Photo: Admire Ndhlovu/SARDC

For instance, wastewater treatment plants (WWTPs) in Lilongwe only connect 15 per cent of the population (Table 8.3). As a result, major cities including Lusaka, Kafue, Livingstone, Harare, Blantyre and smaller towns still depend on on-site systems, like septic tanks, or discharge their collected but only partially treated or untreated sewage into the tributaries of the Zambezi River system. Sanyanga and Masundire (1999) found that wastewater treatment plants in Kasane and Kazungula (Botswana), Livingstone and Siavonga (Zambia), and Victoria Falls and Kariba (Zimbabwe) were poorly working or overloaded, which fact was also reported from Harare amid urbanisation and service delivery challenges (Muzondi 2014) and other towns and cities in the Zambezi Basin in Zimbabwe (Bulawayo, Chitungwiza, Hwange, Chinhoyi, Kwekwe, Kadoma, Gweru, Mazowe and Karoi).

Specific examples of wastewater disposal challenges associated with urbanisation can be found in Livingstone in Zambia, Victoria Falls and Chitungwiza in Zimbabwe (ZAMCOM *et al.* 2015). In Livingstone, raw sewage was discharged into the river prior to the commissioning of six wastewater oxidation ponds in 1995. Despite this, some limited discharge into the river still occurs. In Victoria Falls, about 8,000 m^3 of wastewater were discharged daily into the Zambezi River until 2000 since the population was considered to be small. Since then, the sewage system has become overloaded, triggering intermittent breakdowns that cause raw sewage discharge into the Zambezi. In Chitungwiza, which has expanded rapidly (3.6–7 per cent per annum) since 1980, sewage facilities have received triple the volume of sewage relative to their capacity,

Table 8.3 Sanitation status for capital cities in the Zambezi River Basin

Item	Lusaka (Zambia)	Harare (Zimbabwe)	Lilongwe (Malawi)
Water supply	Daily water supply at 201,000 to 260,000 m³; nearly half water supply from Kafue River, and half from groundwater.	Mainly from Lake Chivero and Manyame, very high water use leading to very high wastewater volumes.	About 85,000 m³/day from two dams, groundwater for isolated peri-urban villages.
Sanitation access	Only 17% of city's population served by sewerage or septic tanks, much below national average for urban areas (34%); majority use pit latrines (judged to pollute hand-dug well/groundwater), others use shared latrines. Frequent cholera outbreaks.	No consistent data on sanitation access. Flush toilets connected to sewers in formal residential districts; pit latrines most common; open defecation widespread in informal settlements; dry composting latrines recently introduced.	Statistics from national agencies report about 80% of the city's population receiving sanitary waste treatment services, actually 30% by WHO standards (9% piped sewers, 20% septic tanks); pit latrines are the dominant fecal disposal measure but unsafe.
Sewerage system	Only some districts have sewerage systems covering 30% of the area covered with water supply; only 10–15% of the Lusaka population benefit from access to sewerage (just 480 km long with 8 pumping stations); others depend on on-site sanitation.	Sewerage system for 80% of city population but largely exceeding design limits and dysfunctional; informal settlements not served by sewers and use septic tanks or open drains.	Only 15% of city population connected to a sewage system; inadequate treatment causes severe water pollution; others have septic tanks (5%) and sanitary latrines (38%).
Septage management	No formal system for safe disposal of effluent and sludge into the environment, sludge not treated adequately before disposal to landfills, and potential exists to generate electricity from wastewater and sludge.	Almost no institutional support; private tankers provide septic tank emptying services but are high cost.	Data needed on septage management; city council empties septic tanks but had inadequate vehicles.
Sewage treatment	Manchinchi and Chunga WWTPs, and oxidation ponds in Chelstone, Ngwerere and Chunga; stabilization ponds in Kaunda Square areas of Lusaka; low capacity, poor repair, some non-operational; most effluent discharged into Ngwerere, Chongwe and Chunga rivers; impacts	Five WWTPs but overloaded and inadequately treated wastewater discharged to Marimba and Mukuvisi Rivers; sludge partly applied to pastures.	City has four wastewater treatment plants: Kauma Sewage Treatment Plant (biggest, 6,100 m³/day), Kanengo Industrial Treatment Plant, Cold Storage Treatment Plant, and Lumbadzi Sewage Treatment Plant; treatment efficiency lower than WHO standards; effluent discharged to Lilongwe River, with

continued . . .

Table 8.3 Continued

Item	Lusaka (Zambia)	Harare (Zimbabwe)	Lilongwe (Malawi)
	likely to render these rivers unsustainable for future use.		heavy organic loadings and risks to communities using the river.
Sanitation in low-income districts of the city (equality aspect)	About 70% of population in low-income districts live in informal settlements, with no specific policy for sanitation improvement.	Low-quality pit latrines and open defecation are common; needs mapping of districts with high sanitation needs, and specific policy for sanitation in informal settlements.	Pit latrines common; unsafe sanitation in informal settlements poses risks; high population density determines sewage system, low density areas excluded, and managed through on-site septic tanks.

Source: Own synthesis, based on literature (IWA 2010a, b, 2012; Msilimba and Wanda 2012; GoM 2013; Muserere *et al.* 2014; AfDB 2015; Chidya *et al.* 2016). The data for Tete City in Mozambique are not reported here as these are available for water access 'broad definition' only (JMP) and there are no data on other aspects (IWA 2012).

resulting in the pollution of Manyame River (Kibena *et al.* 2014), while others report high levels of ammonia and phosphates in the Umguza River, Zimbabwe (Chinyama *et al.* 2016).

Solid waste

The amount of solid waste generated in the Zambezi Basin's towns and cities also far exceeds their capacity for collection, treatment and disposal (ZAMCOM *et al.* 2015). Most urban towns are still using crude dumping methods as the emphasis is not on safe disposal. For example, the city of Lusaka produces about 1,400 tons of waste daily, yet only 10 per cent of this amount is collected by the municipality and 16 per cent by private companies (Table 8.4).

Compounding matters, when waste is collected by the municipal authorities, disposal is generally inadequate as they are financially overstretched due to low levy collection rates. The uncollected waste is carried to streams by precipitation runoff, where its heavy metal content and hydrocarbon loads alter water quality. Solid waste disposed of in landfills can also cause pollution of groundwater when microbial decomposition produces leachate.

Table 8.4 Municipal solid waste disposal in Lusaka city – key benchmarks (2006)

Item	Value
Total municipal solid waste generated per year	381,850 tons
Generation rate per capita per year	201 kg
Coverage rate for waste collection	45%
Disposal in environmentally sound landfills or controlled disposal sites	26%
Municipal solid waste incinerated	None
Diverted and valorised of total waste generated	6%

Source: Lusaka City Report 2007, cited in ZAMCOM *et al.* (2015)

Industrial waste

Industrial waste is also a major source of pollution of both surface water and groundwater. The surge in industrial activity that follows from urbanisation increases waste discharges into the river system. Industries in most urban areas dump hazardous waste directly into streams, negatively affecting water quality. Waste containment, availability of and access to safe sanitation, pathogen emission control, nutrient emission control, resources management, and resource recovery and reuse (RRR) are nascent but represent emerging solutions (Hanjra *et al.* 2015b).

A major factor in much urban industry is the lack of on-site facilities for treatment before discharging effluents into the environment. While lack of data makes it difficult to assess the pollution load from industries located within the Zambezi tributaries, a few examples of such pollution can be found. The sugar industry in Marromeu, Mozambique discharges large volumes of biodegradable waste and wastewater into the Zambezi River system (Chenje 2000). The Mukuvisi River, which flows through both industrial and residential areas of Harare and drains into the Manyame River, is considered the most heavily polluted river system in Zimbabwe. Data show that aluminum residues from Morton Jaffray Water Works in Harare were affecting the water quality of the Manyame River and Lake Manyame. This, in turn, creates *Al* toxicity risk in Nile Tilapia, of importance to the commercial fisheries industry in Zimbabwe (Muisa *et al.* 2011). Pollution of the Kiwira River by the coal mining industry, and the Songwe River by the cement industry, also affects the Lower Zambezi in Tanzania (SADC *et al.* 2012).

An example of industrial groundwater contamination is found in Zambia. Heavy metals contaminate water, soils and crops in peri-urban wastewater irrigation farming in Mufulira and Kafue towns in Zambia (Kapungwe 2013). The Kafue Flats' industries – sugar estates, chemical plants for fertiliser, leather and integrated pig and fish farms – have caused nitric and phosphorous pollution of groundwater (Euroconsult 2008). In addition to groundwater pollution, the deterioration of water quality along the Kafue River has been detected. The river supplies water to 40 per cent of Zambia's population, including that in the city of Lusaka. Water supply for Lusaka is abstracted downstream of these industries, posing serious risks for urban water users. The eutrophic conditions, increased suspended solids and heavy metals in the river have resulted in complaints of alleged loss of taste and a decrease in both catch and size of fish by the fishermen along the Kafue Gorge stretch of the river (Kambole 2003). Small-scale industries located in the basin's residential areas also pose complex water-quality challenges. Data from two high-density suburbs in Harare show that home-based industries discharge higher pollution loads into the Marimba River due to higher runoff volumes from the industrial area (Mvungi *et al.* 2003). As a result, the sewage treatment plants in Harare are overloaded – the total design capacity is 219,500 m^3 per day, yet inflows now average 287,000 m^3 per day.

Informal settlements and groundwater

Informal settlements mainly rely on groundwater for domestic water supply. While large-scale impacts on water quality are minimal because groundwater is not overused at a basin level, groundwater use for domestic purposes poses a water pollution risk at local levels. Poor communities do not have the capacity to develop shallow wells in ways that allow them to be classified as 'improved' in terms of the Sustainable Development Goals (SDGs). For example, the majority of well users in Ndola do not protect their wells from contamination or treat their water (Liddle *et al.* 2014). Reducing risk requires the careful planning and regulation of the proliferation of wells in urban areas and investment in public education for protecting water quality and the wells (ibid.).

Mining operations

The mining activities that dot the basin are important in terms of poverty reduction and shared prosperity (Hilson 2012) but they are also a challenge to water quality. These range from small-scale artisanal mining at local levels to aggregate impact at basin level (SADC *et al.* 2012). Mining operations are concentrated in subbasins such as the Luangwa, Kafue and Kabompo Rivers and Lake Kariba, which contribute specifically to water pollution and quality issues in the Zambezi. All the streams that drain the mining areas of the copperbelt region in Zambia release waste into the Kafue River and its tributaries (SADC *et al.* 2012). Chegutu, Kadoma and Kwekwe towns in Zimbabwe are heavily involved in mining gold, platinum and other precious metals, with notable impacts on water resources and quality, especially in the immediate vicinity of mines. About 6,000 mining operations in the Zambezi are listed for Zimbabwe (Ashton *et al.* 2001). Major impacts arise from alluvial gold mining along the Mazowe and Gairezi Rivers and their tributaries. The mining of precious metals (*Au*, *AG*) and industrial minerals (calcite, fluorite, mica, and so on) in Zimbabwe, coal mining in Mozambique, especially downstream of the Cahora Bassa Dam, all affect the quality of surface water and groundwater in the basin (Ashton *et al.* 2001; Nhantumbo *et al.* 2015). Acid mine drainage is the most common and serious problem, which contaminates both surface water and groundwater resources.

Environmental and public health impacts of water quality

The discharge of poor-quality water and untreated sewage into the environment can pose major risks to environmental and public health (Hanjra *et al.* 2012). Examples include the excess nutrient loadings resulting in eutrophication of river water and insanitary conditions leading to the spread of diseases such as cholera, dysentery and typhoid.

Waterborne diseases are often caused by consuming contaminated water due to a lack of alternatives. The disease burden associated with contaminated water consumption could be reduced by improving access to water and sanitation, as well as through improvement of water quality and better hygiene behaviours among the population. Improved access to water supplies and sanitation facilities makes it easier to practise hygiene (hand-washing, safe-containment and disposal of excreta). For instance, in relation to sanitation, the 2009 cholera epidemic in Zimbabwe killed about 4,300 people (Chirisa *et al.* 2015). None of the municipal water samples tested in Kadoma City (Zimbabwe) showed contamination with *Escherichia coli*. However, samples of shallow well water (52 per cent) and borehole water (20 per cent) tested positive for *Escherichia coli*. As such, it would appear that an outbreak of watery diarrhoea in children under five resulted from 'inadequate clean water and use of contaminated water' associated with shallow wells and boreholes in communities (Maponga *et al.* 2013). Cholera outbreaks are almost an annual occurrence in the basin's low-income areas of Blantyre and Lilongwe. Some 1,478 cholera cases were recorded in Lilongwe in 2009, out of 2,487 countrywide. A previous cholera epidemic in Lusaka affected more than 4,000 people, due mainly to 'consumption of raw vegetables'. This highlights the importance of food-borne transmission, which also illustrates the protective role of hand-washing. There was minimal contribution from direct waterborne transmission – no water source or treatment practice was significant (Dubois *et al.* 2006). While some of these vegetables might have been produced using waters contaminated with wastewater, it is more the absence of basic sanitary conditions at the town markets, which had almost no infrastructure suitable for fresh produce (FAO 2012). These markets lack latrines and running water and are flooded due to blocked drains causing unhygienic conditions.

Waterborne diseases bring economic and social costs. Costs of diarrhoea are large in the basin's capital cities like Lusaka. The average cost of providing outpatient service was USD3 per visit, while the cost per outpatient visit attributed to children under five was USD26. For inpatients, the average cost of hospitalisation was USD78 per bed/day at a public health centre in the capital, Lusaka (Chola and Robberstad 2009). The cost of prevention is less than USD1 per person per year for household water treatment and safe storage (Mudenda 2012). The benefits of diarrhoea prevention and improvements in water quality do not accrue to health alone but extend to include overall improvements in the quality of life and labour-saving from time spent on drawing water and open defecation.

Despite the links between safe water and sanitation and improved public health, huge funding gaps continue as the global emphasis continues to be water supply, rather than sanitation or hygiene. For example, Zambia seems to have a large funding gap on the national urban water and sanitation programme as 73 per cent of the allocation had been directed solely towards water supply for the period 2006 to 2010 (Mudenda 2012). Similarly, the national urban water and sanitation programme for 2011 has 61 per cent allocation to water supply, 14 per cent to sanitation, and 25 per cent to other functions. There is a need to revisit the budget allocation criteria among rural and urban areas and between water supply and sanitation and hygiene. Adjustments in favour of increased sanitation could potentially enhance the river system and human health.

Opportunities for wastewater reuse

To address issues of resource security amid population growth, urbanisation, agricultural expansion and mining, and to put environmental change on a more sustainable development pathway, there is a need for a mutually agreed and shared framework to:

- enhance water quality, promote waste reduction and resource reuse, protect public and environmental health and increase public confidence in water reuse across the basin communities, and
- assist riparian states to formulate policy and positions on their sustainable development objectives such as climate change, sustainable water resources management, and water and sanitation for all.

A central challenge is how to make safe reuse of wastewater, human excreta and fecal sludge for nutrient reuse and energy recovery from waste, while minimising impacts on water quality. Putting wastewater back to the service of communities and ecosystems, in turn, requires evidence-based solutions that link science, business models, social change, local acceptability and culture, and public policies for promoting safe reuse (Hanjra *et al.* 2015b).

Urban and peri-urban agriculture is common practice in the basin and produces food for family consumption and sale to urban residents (FAO 2012). It is generally practised on small plots and home gardens, as well as larger open spaces and infrastructure fringes within and around cities. Open-space urban and peri-urban agriculture is a major, but informal, user of polluted water, which, due to its nutrient content, helps farmers save fertiliser costs and overrides constraints to accessing freshwater.

Urban agriculture is a significant economic activity that contributes to household income. In Zambia, a quarter of urban households engage in urban agriculture; households grow vegetables and other crops and low-income city gardeners make USD230 per year from sales (FAO 2012). Home gardening accounts for nearly half of fruit and vegetable production in Zambia. A recent survey in Zambian cities in the basin, including Lusaka, Kabwe, Kitwe and Ndola, found that backyard gardening and crop production on communal lands was the most common form of agriculture; maize was the most frequently grown crop, and half of the production consisted of horticultural crops, including pumpkins, beans, onions and tomatoes (FAO 2012). Surplus produce is sold on the open market. For instance, 80 per cent of Lusaka's supply of leafy vegetables is produced locally and marketed through small vendors in city streets and neighbourhoods. Annual profits range from USD67 in Lusaka to USD230 in Kibwe, while revenue from sales accounts for 18 per cent of annual household income in Lusaka, and about 50 per cent in the basin cities of Kabwe, Kitwe and Ndola (FAO 2012).

In Zimbabwe around 70 per cent of urban households practise some form of urban agriculture on residential land in the capital city of Harare, with about 17 per cent practised outside their homes in the vicinity of water bodies (ZAMCOM *et al.* 2015). The streams, canals and wetlands around towns and cities often receive untreated or partially treated wastewater – for example, as shown in Figure 8.3 – and this commingled water supports agricultural activities, which make a notable contribution to food security and nutrition of the urban poor. Data on peri-urban agriculture around Bulawayo in Zimbabwe for 2006 show that some 500 farmers are using highly polluted water for irrigation of vegetable crops on small plots of half a hectare each (Mutengu *et al.* 2007). Bulawayo also used wastewater to maintain its public parks and gardens. Harare used wastewater to irrigate maize and pasture for dairy cows.

For urban agriculture to optimally benefit from water reuse while reducing risks, it must be integrated into urban planning. Most cities have not yet integrated market gardening into urban planning, although some have with great success. Mozambique has officially encouraged market gardens for decades, while urban agriculture is illegal in Harare, and Zimbabwe has regulated urban market gardens since 1912. The Harare Declaration[2] of 29 August 2003, signed by five ministers of local government from east and southern Africa, called, however, for the promotion of a new shared vision of urban agriculture. The city of Ndola in Zambia recognised crop and

Figure 8.3 Drainage challenges in Norton, Zimbabwe
Photo: Leonard John Abrams

livestock production as legitimate land uses in its strategic plan. In Malawi, Lilongwe was among the 'greenest' of capital cities, with 35 per cent of households engaged in horticulture (FAO 2012). However, according to the *Urban Structure Plan of Lilongwe City* (GoM 2013) 'urban agriculture mainly consists of illegal farming practiced seasonally in open spaces in the city' and 'it should be regulated land use' for 'commercial farms in the future' (p.26). While wastewater reuse is important in urban food systems, as about 50 per cent of the urban population use wastewater for irrigated agriculture, the use of raw wastewater is against the policy framework in Malawi (Msilimba and Wanda 2012).

Ideally, all waterborne sewage must be conveyed to treatment plants before discharge. Any encouragement of urban agriculture or wastewater reuse that is based on the malfunctioning sewage systems has potential to exacerbate public and environmental health risk in and around urban centres. Legislation and other supportive measures are required to match wastewater quality with end reuse. This is a major challenge in the Zambezi Basin given financial burdens and governance issues at various levels. Investing in waste management – both liquid and solid – may be viewed as a 'waste', yet this would be beneficial to the basin's environment and population as waste management and wastewater reuse could open new livelihood opportunities. Wastewater reuse could also become a tool for adaption in the face of climate change.

Wastewater reuse for peri-urban agriculture should be practised with caution, as it poses notable health risks. Data on farmers, effluents, fields and vegetables show that 70 per cent of the respondents around Bulawayo in Zimbabwe were aware of the health-related risks (Mutengu *et al.* 2007) but reported no major disease outbreaks. Despite some health-related risks to farmers due to effluent use in the vegetable fields, for consumers there appears to be no risk. Long-term use of wastewater in urban horticulture can lead to heavy metal accumulation in soils, posing potential environmental and health risks. For example, potential health risks due to cadmium intake existed for daily consumers of leafy vegetables grown using wastewater for irrigation around Harare (Mapanda *et al.* 2007). Data from Firle Municipal Farm in Harare show higher concentrations of four regulated metals, (cadmium, copper, lead and zinc) in maize, beans, pepper and sugarcane. This highlights the potential risks from cultivation and consumption of vegetables irrigated with mixtures of wastewater and sewage sludge (Muchuweti *et al.* 2006). Other risks associated with reuse of wastewater for urban agriculture include creating favourable sites for mosquitoes other than those transmitting malaria or dengue, as both need in general very clean water for breeding.

Nevertheless, these health risks can be mitigated through the treatment of wastewater and health-protection measures. While conventional methods of wastewater treatment may be expensive, low-cost unconventional methods can be implemented, such as stabilisation ponds, sedimentation tanks and oxidation ditches (Jiménez *et al.* 2010). Diseases related to the use of wastewater in agriculture, like diarrhoea, typhoid and hepatitis A, can also be reduced by both on-farm and post-harvest interventions, for example, drip irrigation, ceasing irrigation before harvest, on-farm treatment, sanitising/washing produce, and so on (Bos *et al.* 2010; Amoah *et al.* 2011).

Conclusions and recommendations

This chapter is perhaps the first to synthesise a basin-wide perspective on urbanisation, water quality, health risks and water reuse in the Zambezi. The chapter compiled raw data and secondary information to characterise urbanisation trends, waste disposal challenges, health risks and opportunities for more productive water reuse in the basin. These findings lay the basis for more informed interventions, and bring awareness to stakeholders of the need for action on

Figure 8.4 Rapid urbanisation is a challenge to water quality and waste water disposal in Lusaka
Photo: Fabian Niggeman

waste and wastewater challenges. Furthermore, opportunities presented by wastewater reuse are expected to catalyse basin-level investment that can spur sustainable water use.

This chapter produced four major findings. First, water quality and wastewater treatment are major issues in the Zambezi Basin. Population growth and economic activities are driving urbanisation, which, in turn, is placing pressure on wastewater treatment capacities and adversely affecting water quality in the basin. Second, solid waste disposal is a major challenge. This is not confined to major urban centres but extends to the entire basin. The current urbanisation rate will, nonetheless, intensify the problem. Third, economic and social costs caused by diseases related to water quality and waste disposal are already evident. Institutional efforts aimed at containing the challenges are costly and therefore actions for improved waste containment, treatment and disposal for safe reuse are not abundant in the basin. Last, there is an opportunity for greater wastewater reuse, especially where freshwater is in short supply. Reuse of wastewater for productive ends has been practised in the basin, but often outside of regulatory frameworks. The practice has to be streamlined into policy and planning to better manage potential risks while building on the benefits of reuse.

As ZAMCOM and other relevant actors (e.g., including national agencies) seek to foster socioeconomic development in the basin, this chapter offers the following recommendations:

- ***Put wastewater treatment for reuse on the table for basin-scale management.*** In keeping with increasingly integrated principles of basin-level management that consider the whole hydrological cycle, water reuse can play an important role. With an understanding that different types of use require different water qualities, ZAMCOM is well positioned to develop a reuse framework in support of the development of national reuse guidelines and data monitoring in view of SDG 6.3.

- ***Recognise the benefits of irrigated urban and peri-urban agriculture.*** Only if this sector moves from informal into formal agricultural planning and capacity development that the associated health hazards can be fully addressed.
- ***Consider inter-sectoral water needs and challenges.*** Understanding the degree to which water supply and sanitation capacities of the basin's cities can absorb additional population growth without undermining other sectors in need of water will help guide sustainable growth and investment needs.
- ***Promote cleaner production approaches in urban water supply and sanitation to reduce waste generation.*** Water conservation, treatment and reuse strategies for various land uses must start from water-saving technologies, regulation, leak detection and repairs to wastewater treatment and safe reuse. Modelling results show that the application of cleaner production approaches could ease the production and treatment of wastewater.
- ***Monitor the degree to which regulations for water supply, treatment and reuse are adhered to.*** Benchmarking the compliance of local authorities with set targets and regulations across the basin can provide incentives for investment. ZAMCOM can play a key role in this effort.

Acknowledgements

This review chapter was financially supported by the International Water Management Institute (IWMI), funded through the CGIAR Research Program on Water, Land and Ecosystems (WLE). We are thankful to the editors and anonymous reviewers who helped improve the quality of the manuscript.

Notes

1 There are also linkages with urbanisation, water and energy. Cities require electricity, which requirement is often satisfied through hydropower generation, yet there are equally other ways to satisfy growing electricity demands of cities.
2 www.ruaf.org/sites/default/files/ministers_conference.pdf

References

AfDB (African Development Bank). 2015. Lusaka Sanitation Program, African Development Bank, Reference: P-ZM-E00–010. Available at www.afdb.org/en/projects-and-operations/project-portfolio/project/p-zm-e00-010/ (accessed on 14 December 2015).
Amoah, P., Keraita, B., Akple, M., Drechsel, P., Abaidoo, R.C. and Konradsen, F. 2011. Low-cost options for reducing consumer health risks from farm to fork where crops are irrigated with polluted water in West Africa. IWMI Research Report Series 141. Colombo, Sri Lanka: IWMI. Available at www.iwmi.cgiar.org/publications/iwmi_research_reports/pdf/pub141/rr141.pdf (accessed on 24 June 2016).
Ashton, P., Love, D., Mahachi, H. and Dirks, P.H.G.M. 2001. An overview of the impact of mining and mineral processing operations on water resources and water quality in the Zambezi, Limpopo and Olifants catchments in southern Africa. Report No. ENV-P-C 2001–042. xvi + 336 pp. Pretoria, South Africa: CSIRE Environmentek.
Bos, R., Carr, R. and Keraita, B. 2010. Assessing and mitigating wastewater-related health risks in low-income countries: An introduction. Chapter 2. In: *Wastewater irrigation and health: Assessing and mitigating risk in low-income countries*, (eds.), Drechsel, P., Scott, C.A., Raschid-Sally, L., Redwood, M. and Bahri, A. London: Earthscan.
Capps, K.A., Bentsen, C.N. and Ramírez, A. 2016. Poverty, urbanization, and environmental degradation: Urban streams in the developing world. *Freshwater Science* 35: 429–435.
Chenje, M. 2000. *State of the environment: Zambezi Basin 2000.* Maseru, Harare, Zimbabwe: SADC/IUCN/SARDC.

Chidya, R.C.G., Mulwafu, W.O. and Banda, S.C.T. 2016. Water supply dynamics and quality of alternative water sources in low-income areas of Lilongwe City, Malawi. *Physics and Chemistry of the Earth*. doi: 10.1016/j.pce.2016.1003.1003.

Chinyama, A., Ncube, R. and Ela, W. 2016. Critical pollution levels in Umguza River, Zimbabwe. *Physics and Chemistry of the Earth*. doi: 10.1016/j.pce.2016.1003.1008.

Chirisa, I., Nyamadzawo, L., Bandauko, E. and Mutsindikwa, N. 2015. The 2008/2009 cholera outbreak in Harare, Zimbabwe: Case of failure in urban environmental health and planning. *Reviews on Environmental Health* 30: 117–124.

Chola, L. and Robberstad, B. 2009. Estimating average inpatient and outpatient costs and childhood pneumonia and diarrhoea treatment costs in an urban health centre in Zambia. *Cost Effectiveness and Resource Allocation* 7: 1–8.

Drechsel, P., Qadir, M. and Wichelns, D. (eds.). 2015. *Wastewater: Economic asset in an urbanizing world*. New York, London, Heidelberg, Dordrecht: Springer. On behalf of IWMI/CGIAR/UNU INWEH.

Dubois, A.E., Sinkala, M., Kalluri, P., Makasa-Chikoya, M. and Quick, R.E. 2006. Epidemic cholera in urban Zambia: Hand soap and dried fish as protective factors. *Epidemiology and Infection* 134: 1226–1230.

Earle, A. 2013. The role of cities as drivers of international transboundary water management processes. Chapter 7. In: *Water security: Principles, perspectives and practices*, (eds.), Lankford, B., Bakker, K., Zeitoun, M. and Conway, D. New York: Routledge.

Euroconsult. 2008. *Integrated water resources management strategy and implementation plan for the Zambezi River Basin*. Final Report, Rapid Assessment. Gaborone, Botswana and Lusaka, Zambia: South African Development Community Water Division and Zambezi River Authority, Euroconsult Mott MacDonald, UK.

FAO (Food and Agriculture Organization of the United Nations). 2012. *Growing greener cities in Africa. First status report on urban and peri-urban horticulture in Africa*. Rome: FAO.

GoM (Government of Malawi). 2013. *Urban structure plan of Lilongwe City*. Lilongwe, Malawi: GoM.

Gutierrez, E. 2007. Delivering pro-poor water and sanitation services: The technical and political challenges in Malawi and Zambia. *Geoforum* 38: 886–900.

Hanjra, M.A., Blackwell, J., Carr, G., Zhang, F. and Jackson, T.M. 2012. Wastewater irrigation and environmental health: Implications for water governance and public policy. *International Journal of Hygiene and Environmental Health* 215: 255–269.

Hanjra, M.A., Drechsel, P., Mateo-Sagasta, J., Otoo, M. and Hernandez-Sancho, F. 2015a. Assessing the finance and economics of resource recovery and reuse solutions across scales. Chapter 7. In: *Wastewater: Economic asset in an urbanizing world*, (eds.), Drechsel, P., Qadir, M. and Wichelns, D. New York, London, Heidelberg, Dordrecht: Springer. On behalf of IWMI/CGIAR/UNU NWEH.

Hanjra, M.A., Drechsel, P., Wichelns, D. and Qadir, M. 2015b. Transforming urban wastewater into an economic asset: Opportunities and challenges. Chapter 14. In: *Wastewater: Economic asset in an urbanizing world*, (eds.), Drechsel, P., Qadir, M. and Wichelns, D. New York, London, Heidelberg, Dordrecht: Springer. On behalf of IWMI/CGIAR/UNU INWEH.

Haub, C. and Kaneda, T. 2013. *World population data sheet*. Washington, DC: Population Reference Bureau.

Hilson, G. 2012. Family hardship and cultural values: Child labor in Malian small-scale gold mining communities. *World Development* 40: 1663–1674.

Hove, M., Ngwerume, E.T. and Muchemwa, C. 2013. The urban crisis in sub-Saharan Africa: A threat to human security and sustainable development. *Stability: International Journal of Security and Development* 2. doi: http://doi.org/10.5334/sta.ap.

IWA (International Water Association). 2010a. *Harare: Sanitation status. Sanitation status of African cities*. London. UK: IWA Water Wiki.

IWA. 2010b. *Lusaka: Sanitation status. Sanitation status of African cities*. London, UK: IWA Water Wiki.

IWA. 2012. *Water supply and sanitation in Mozambique: Sanitation status*. London, UK: IWA Water Wiki.

Jiménez, B., Mara, D., Carr, R. and Brissaud, F. 2010. Wastewater treatment for pathogen removal and nutrient conservation: Suitable systems for use in developing countries. Chapter 8. In: *Wastewater irrigation and health: Assessing and mitigating risk in low-income countries*, (eds.), Drechsel, P., Scott, C.A., Raschid-Sally, L., Redwood, M. and Bahri, A. London: Earthscan.

Kambole, M.S. 2003. Managing the water quality of the Kafue River. *Physics and Chemistry of the Earth* 28: 1105–1109.

Kapungwe, E.M. 2013. Heavy metal contaminated water, soils and crops in peri urban wastewater irrigation farming in Mufulira and Kafue towns in Zambia. *Journal of Geography and Geology* 5: 55–72.

Kibena, J., Nhapi, I. and Gumindoga, W. 2014. Assessing the relationship between water quality parameters and changes in landuse patterns in the Upper Manyame River, Zimbabwe. *Physics and Chemistry of the Earth, Parts A/B/C* 67–69: 153–163.

Lautze, J. and Kirshen, P. 2007. Dams, health, and livelihoods: Lessons from the Senegal, suggestions for Africa. *International Journal of River Basin Management* 5: 199–206.

Liddle, E.S., Mager, S.M. and Nel, E. 2014. Water quality awareness and barriers to safe water provisioning in informal communities: A case study from Ndola, Zambia. *Bulletin of Geography* 26: 167–181.

Mapanda, F., Mangwayana, E.N., Nyamangara, J. and Giller, K.E. 2007. Uptake of heavy metals by vegetables irrigated using wastewater and the subsequent risks in Harare, Zimbabwe. *Physics and Chemistry of the Earth, Parts A/B/C* 32: 1399–1405.

Maponga, B.A., Chirundu, D., Gombe, N.T., Tshimanga, M., Shambira, G. and Takundwa, L. 2013. Risk factors for contracting watery diarrhoea in Kadoma City, Zimbabwe, 2011: A case control study. *BMC Infectious Diseases* 13: 1–8.

Msilimba, G. and Wanda, E.M.M. 2012. *Wastewater production, treatment, and use in Malawi.* Luwinga, Mzuzu, Malawi: Water and Sanitation Centre of Excellence.

Muchuweti, M., Birkett, J.W., Chinyanga, E., Zvauya, R., Scrimshaw, M.D. and Lester, J.N. 2006. Heavy metal content of vegetables irrigated with mixtures of wastewater and sewage sludge in Zimbabwe: Implications for human health. *Agriculture, Ecosystems & Environment* 112: 41–48.

Mudenda, C.G. 2012. *Financing water supply and sanitation in Zambia: 2007–2012 study to establish levels and trends of sector financing.* Lusaka, Zambia: Zambia NGO Water, Sanitation and Hygiene Forum.

Muisa, N., Hoko, Z., Chifamba, P. 2011. Impacts of alum residues from Morton Jaffray Water Works on water quality and fish, Harare, Zimbabwe. *Physics and Chemistry of the Earth, Parts A/B/C* 36: 853–864.

Muserere, S.T., Hoko, Z. and Nhapi, I. 2014. Characterisation of raw sewage and performance assessment of primary settling tanks at Firle Sewage Treatment Works, Harare, Zimbabwe. *Physics and Chemistry of the Earth, Parts A/B/C* 67–69: 226–235.

Mutengu, S., Hoko, Z. and Makoni, F.S. 2007. An assessment of the public health hazard potential of wastewater reuse for crop production. A case of Bulawayo city, Zimbabwe. *Physics and Chemistry of the Earth, Parts A/B/C* 32: 1195–1203.

Muzondi, L. 2014. Urbanization and service delivery planning: Analysis of water and sanitation management systems in the city of Harare, Zimbabwe. *Mediterranean Journal of Social Sciences* 5: 2909–2915.

Mvungi, A., Hranova, R.K. and Love, D. 2003. Impact of home industries on water quality in a tributary of the Marimba River, Harare: Implications for urban water management. *Physics and Chemistry of the Earth, Parts A/B/C* 28: 1131–1137.

Nhantumbo, C.M.C., Larsson, R., Juízo, D. and Larson, M. 2015. Key issues for water quality monitoring in the Zambezi river basin in Mozambique in the context of mining development. *Journal of Water Resource and Protection* 7: 430–447.

Nhapi, I. 2009. The water situation in Harare, Zimbabwe: A policy and management problem. *Water Policy* 11: 221–235.

Nhapi, I. and Hoko, Z. 2004. A cleaner production approach to urban water management: Potential for application in Harare, Zimbabwe. *Physics and Chemistry of the Earth, Parts A/B/C* 29: 1281–1289.

Parnell, S. and Walawege, R. 2011. Sub-Saharan African urbanisation and global environmental change. *Global Environmental Change* 21, Supplement 1, S12-S20.

Potts, D. 2009. The slowing of sub-Saharan Africa's urbanization: Evidence and implications for urban livelihoods. *Environment and Urbanization* 21: 253–259.

Rao, K., Hanjra, M.A., Drechsel, P. and Danso, G. 2015. Business models and economic approaches supporting water reuse. In: *Wastewater: Economic asset in an urbanizing world*, (eds.), Drechsel, P., Qadir, M. and Wichelns, D. New York, London, Heidelberg, Dordrecht: Springer. On behalf of IWMI/CGIAR/UNU-INWEH.

SADC, SARDC, ZAMCOM, Global Resource Information Database (GRID)-Arendal and United Nations Environment Programme (UNEP). 2012. *Zambezi River Basin – Atlas of the changing environment.* Gaborone, Harare and Arendal: SARDC, SADC, Water Division, ZAMCOM, GRID-Arendal, UNEP.

Sanyanga, R.A. and Masundire, H.M. 1999. Waste management in the major population centres in the Zambezi Valley: Botswana, Zambia and Zimbabwe. In: *Cleaner production and consumption opportunities in east and southern Africa*, (ed.), Yap, N.T., 1–16. Harare, Zimbabwe: Weaver Press.

Scheierling, S.M., Bartone, C., Mara, D.D. and Drechsel, P. 2010. *Improving wastewater use in agriculture: An emerging priority.* World Bank Policy Research Working Paper 5412. Washington, DC: World Bank.

United Nations. 2015. *United Nations, Department of Economic and Social Affairs, Population Division (2015). World Urbanization Prospects: The 2014 Revision.* Available at http://esa.un.org/unpd/wup/ (accessed on 27 April 2016).

World Bank. 2015. *Integrated urban water management.* Washington, DC: World Bank. Available at http://water.worldbank.org/iuwm (accessed on 31 March 2016).

World Bank. 2016. *Urban development. Urban development in Africa.* Washington, DC: World Bank. Available at www.worldbank.org/en/topic/urbandevelopment/x/afr (accessed on 23 June 2016).

ZAMCOM, SADC and SARDC. 2015. *Zambezi environment outlook (ZEO) – Towards strengthening environmental cooperation and integration in the Zambezi River Basin.* A report by ZAMCOM, SADC and SARDC. Harare, Zimbabwe; Gaborone, Botswana.

9

Transboundary water cooperation

Taking stock and looking forward

*Davison Saruchera, Jonathan Lautze, Juliet Mwale,
Claudious Chikozho and Osborne N. Shela*

Key messages

- More than 10 transboundary water agreements – increasingly multilateral and increasingly water-centred – have been concluded on the Zambezi over the last 130 years. Despite variation, common threads are apparent, such as using the basin as a vehicle for trade and regional integration, and as a driver of economic growth.

- The recent entry into force of the Zambezi Watercourse Commission Agreement (2011) and subsequent emergence of the Zambezi Watercourse Commission (ZAMCOM) presents a critical opportunity to consolidate and expand past cooperative efforts. The ZAMCOM framework presents a robust mechanism to advance cooperation in the basin.
- There are, nonetheless, risks which may constrain cooperation. The main risks relate to equity and access, and sovereignty and autonomy. Cooperation may present the greatest risks to Angola, Malawi and Zambia. Risks are partially mitigated through basin-level, regional and customary international water law. Nonetheless, uncertainty related to the interpretations of equitable use principles, as well as a lack of clarity on potential impacts on national development plans, may deter cooperative engagement from certain countries.
- Efforts to advance cooperation may benefit by responding to riparians' varying motivations for basin-wide engagement given their geographic position. For example, safeguards can be proposed that protect the interests of less-motivated states. Further, efforts could be made to strengthen capacity to leverage riparians' geographic position through a cooperative framework.

Introduction

Cooperative development and management of the Zambezi Basin is widely viewed as critical to advancing the socioeconomic and sustainable development aspirations of its inhabitants and the environment. The *Multi-Sector Investment Opportunities Analysis* (World Bank 2010) determined that cooperative development of multipurpose infrastructure in the Zambezi Basin has potential to enhance electricity and agriculture production as well as flood control. Beck and Bernauer (2010) highlighted the need to achieve cooperative allocation rules in order to avert conflict due to drastically reduced dry-season runoff. GIZ (2011) described how cooperative management of the Kariba and Cahora Bassa Dams creates opportunities for improved environmental conservation. Finally, Tillmant and Kinzelbach (2012) highlighted how coordinated and cooperative development in the Zambezi is key to tackling the basin's food security and poverty challenges.

Despite progress, cooperation in the Zambezi is a long-term endeavour that is far from complete. Cooperation in the Zambezi can be evidenced in the bilateral management of the Kariba Dam, as well as recent efforts toward basin-wide institutional development (Jensen and Lange 2013). Nonetheless, the state of cooperation remains far from optimal. Shela (2000) noted that, except in isolated cases, riparians have not seized opportunities for joint water resources management. Swain (2012) suggested that the Zambezi's riparians remain more interested in unilateral than cooperative water development and management. Söderbaum (2015) noted a significant failure to cooperate, both historically and presently, in the Zambezi.

Systematic reviews of the past legal evolution and future outlook for cooperation in the Zambezi are not extensive. Tumbare (1999) considered water sharing in the Zambezi in the context of international principles of water law. Nakayama (1998) and Fox and Sneddon (2007) focused on transboundary treaties and environmental issues in the Zambezi. Shela (2000) provided a review of water management in the Zambezi, yet legal issues comprised a relatively small portion of this review. Subramanian *et al.* (2012; 2014) undertook a cursory analysis of the Zambezi context, along with several other basin contexts, in order to validate the assertion that country risk is a major impediment to achieving substantive cooperation – in the Zambezi and elsewhere. Petersen-Perlman (2016), based on numerous interviews with actors in the basin, speculated that intensifying cooperation in the Zambezi may be hindered by the inability to accommodate geographic variations in a political framework; in other words, Zambia's relatively powerful geographic position in the basin may be somewhat compromised by entering a basin-wide framework as a presumably equal riparian.[1]

This chapter reviews the evolution of interstate cooperation in the Zambezi, assesses the benefits and risks for intensifying cooperation, and proposes ways to catalyse cooperation. Structurally, the methods through which transboundary water treaties are collected and examined, as well as the process through which future risks are considered, are first presented. The historic evolution of Zambezi water cooperation is then reviewed. The different types of cooperative risks are then presented for the Zambezi, followed by an examination of how existing legal frameworks may attenuate such risk. Finally, guidance for strengthening water cooperation is generated. Central to such guidance is allocating due consideration to riparians' varying motivations for cooperation given their geographical positions, developing capacity to leverage riparians' geographic position in a cooperative framework, and formulating strategies to address risk for riparians who may be reluctant to cooperate.

Methods

Taking stock: collection and review of transboundary water law

The primary data for this review are transboundary water agreements. At the time of research, the largest and most refined compilation of transboundary water law was assembled by Giordano *et al.* (2014). The compilation expanded the Transboundary Freshwater Dispute Database (TFDD) and strengthened its coding scheme by applying the 'lineage' concept. The lineage concept differentiates agreements into i) primary agreements, ii) protocols and iii) amendments. As such, 'agreement' can mean a single primary agreement, a protocol or an amendment. 'Treaty', by contrast, treats primary agreements and any related agreements as one single unit.

The compilation of transboundary water law by Giordano *et al.* (2014) contains some 688 agreements and 250 treaties, but not all of them could be utilised for analysis for the following reasons: 16 treaties had insufficient text for analysis; 17 treaties were replaced by other treaties. Given its superiority to others in existence, the database utilised by Giordano *et al.* (2014) was obtained for use in this chapter. The database is limited to active treaties concluded between states (per the definition of a 'treaty' in the Vienna Convention on the Law of Treaties) between 1820 and 2007 with sufficient text, excluding treaties that are global or regional in coverage, or that are only available in Russian or Ukrainian.

To develop an understanding of the individual agreements, the text (or synopses) of each document in the collection was examined to determine central foci and thrusts that reflect the nature of cooperation in the Zambezi. The analytical approach reflects a departure from that applied elsewhere (e.g., Lautze and Giordano 2005; Holmatov and Lautze 2016), which is focused on inclusion or exclusion of various components. This is believed to be justified by the purpose of this chapter, which is not to determine broad trends but to achieve a contextualised understanding of development of water cooperation in the Zambezi. Ultimately, our results, combined with contextual knowledge, suggested a division of transboundary water law in Africa into three periods for discussion: the imperial period (1890–1959), the transitional or development period (1960–1985) and the independent period characterised by growing economic needs and environmental concerns (1986–present).

Looking forward: understanding potential for transboundary water cooperation

Transboundary water cooperation is defined as a purposive course of action by riparian states that leads to enhanced management or development of the watercourse to their mutual satisfaction (Jägerskog and Zeitoun 2009). When it comes to explaining why riparians cooperate on transboundary waters, the standard logic is that countries work together when benefits of doing so are perceived to outweigh the costs (Qaddumi 2008; Grey *et al.* 2009). Similar motivation to realise the benefits of cooperation has alternatively been explained in the language of economic incentives (Klaphake and Scheumann 2006). Over the years, the potential to harness benefits of cooperation has been manifested in the goals contained in a voluminous body of transboundary water law. A review of the classification of agreements in the TFDD indeed reveals that the primary foci of agreements are often transboundary benefits such as flood control, hydropower development and irrigation.

Importantly, the perception of benefits to be achieved through working together is likely necessary but insufficient to realise cooperation on transboundary waters. If countries were driven only by the potential to achieve benefit, there would likely be much more cooperation on water than is evidenced today. In reality, there is a set of additional factors that affect the likelihood of reaching cooperation. Among the set of factors recognised as key to promoting water cooperation, perceived risks and opportunities feature increasingly prominently (Sadoff *et al.* 2008; Subramanian *et al.* 2012; 2014). The premise of risk discourse is that if opportunities outweigh risks, states are likely to cooperate (Qaddumi 2008). Opportunities are fairly straightforward, and can be in many ways mapped to the economic benefits outlined above. Risk has been described as follows (Sadoff *et al.* 2008):

> Perceived risks are actually a core consideration for decision-makers in a country. If a country cannot find a way to compensate for or control risk, it may choose not to enter into a cooperative agreement. Hesitation, or even resistance, observed on the part of countries regarding cooperation with other riparian countries can be better understood by evaluating perceived risks to their engagement. Perceived risks are defined as the perception that an act of cooperation will expose the country to harm, will jeopardize something of value to the country, or will threaten the political future of individual policymakers.

In perhaps the most thorough conceptualisation of states' cooperation calculus, Subramanian *et al.* (2012; 2014) developed an analytical framework for risks and opportunities in a transboundary water context. The framework focuses on perceived risks and opportunities by decision-makers in countries responding to a specific prospect of cooperation. The assumption is that countries enter into a given dialogue with at least a preliminary understanding of the potential net benefits. In other words, net cooperative benefits are a virtual 'given' – likely to have been established before negotiations to enhance cooperation have begun. As such, the more critical factor affecting the outcome of negotiations centres on states' perception of risk.

To characterise risk-to-opportunity graphically, a schematic was created (Figure 9.1; Subramanian *et al.* 2012; 2014). Countries considering cooperation will assess their positions on the *x* axis in terms of net benefits and on the *y* axis in terms of net opportunities. A country's position in the schematic presumably reflects the likelihood of cooperation in that given situation. Risk reduction and opportunity enhancement are indicated by a shift in country positions to the 'north'; increasing benefits and reducing costs will shift countries to the 'east'.

Countries impeded by risk are presumed to face one of five types of risk (Subramanian *et al.* 2012; 2014). These are: i) *Capacity and knowledge* – does the country have correct and enough information to negotiate a fair deal? And also does it have enough knowledge for basin hydrology, markets and economics in comparison to that of their partners? ii) *Accountability and voice* – does the country have a say in decision-making? iii) *Equity and access* – how fair is the

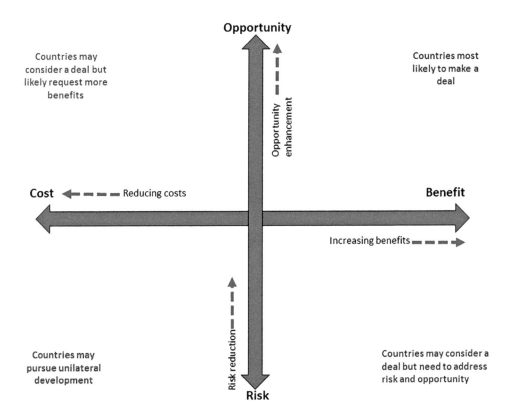

Figure 9.1 Risk to opportunity framework for cooperation
Source: Modified from Subramanian *et al.* (2012; 2014)

deal and will the country continue to have fair access to the water body? iv) *Sovereignty and autonomy* – will the country be able to make decisions independently and act in the *best* interest of the country? And v) *Stability and support* – longevity in country support of the agreement.

In their analysis, Subramanian *et al.* (2012; 2014) conclude that *equity and access* and *sovereignty and autonomy* are core risks, in that they are deep-seated and tend to resurface, even after deals were made and benefits delivered. As such, there may be less scope to mitigate such risks. *Capacity and knowledge, accountability and voice*, and *stability and support*, by contrast, are considered operational risks. These three operational risks are the key leverage points for catalysing cooperation (Table 9.1).

To capture the potential to realise cooperative solutions to the basin's challenges and opportunities, Subramanian *et al.* (2012; 2014) risk-to-opportunity framework is used as a guide to characterise cooperative potential. Literature that considered the context of water cooperation in the Zambezi was then mined to generate evidence of risks for engaging in cooperation. This literature included Nakayama (1998), Tumbare (1999), Shela (2000), Fox and Sneddon (2007),

Table 9.1 Risks that can be mitigated to foster water cooperation (adapted from Subramanian *et al.* 2012)

Risk	Explanation	Example
Capacity and knowledge	Data, knowledge and capacity may constrain a full understanding of the current and potential situation.	If the likely effects of climate variability and change have not been investigated in the context of an agreement, countries may feel that erratic or changing rainfall patterns may adversely alter de facto agreement provisions adversely.
Accountability and voice	Decision-makers may fear that co-riparians, third parties or regional institutions may not deliver the promised benefits.	A risk is that key decisions will be made without involvement of a particular riparian, or with only marginal (and outnumbered) involvement.
Stability and support	Questionable implementability of an agreement due to the presence or absence of key stakeholder support, including the likelihood of ratification	Agreeing to an unpopular agreement is perceived as a risk because it may not be ratified.

Subramanian *et al.* (2012; 2014), Jensen and Lange (2013), Söderbaum (2015) and Petersen-Perlman (2016).

Taking stock: interstate cooperation in the Zambezi River Basin

Zambezi riparians have a long history of cooperation that dates back more than a century. Initially driven by imperial European nations, early cooperative efforts were focused on navigation, power supply and infrastructure development that reflected ambitions of economic growth and prosperity. While political geography and development dynamics in the Zambezi have certainly changed between initial manifestations of cooperation in the late nineteenth century and cooperative forms in the early twenty-first century, central threads – such as viewing the basin as a vehicle for trade and regional integration, and a driver of economic growth – remain relevant (World Bank 2010). The body of transboundary water law applying to the Zambezi, which emerged out of this long history, can be broadly divided into three periods:

- First, treaties of the imperial era demarcating national boundaries and facilitating access to water that were concluded between the 1890s and 1950s between colonial governments on a bilateral basis.
- Second, the development-focused treaties between approximately 1960 and 1985, which were informed by states' specific needs and mostly bilateral.
- Third, treaties concluded after 1985, focused on growing economic needs and environmental concerns, often with the financial assistance of the international donor community.

The first international agreement concerning the Zambezi was concluded in 1891 between the United Kingdom and Portugal. The *Treaty Between Her Majesty And His Majesty The King Of Portugal, Defining Their Respective Spheres Of Influence In Africa* included the watercourses of the Limpopo, Shire and Pungwe Rivers, and was primarily focused on demarcating borders (of present-day Malawi, Mozambique, Zambia and Zimbabwe) and navigation (295ENG, TFDD).

The provisions on navigation on the Zambezi and Shire Rivers were meant to enable free access for the ships transiting through colonial territories. The agreement established a Joint Commission among signatories, with provisions for an administration system that could be implemented 'by common consent of the Riverain Powers'.

More than four decades later, in 1933, Northern Rhodesia and the Union of South Africa (on behalf of Southwest Africa – now Namibia) signed an agreement on the Caprivi Strip that granted rights to 'natives' from Northern Rhodesia to benefit from waters of the Zambezi. The *Exchange of notes between the Union of South Africa and Northern Rhodesia regarding the Eastern Boundary between the Caprivi Strip and Northern Rhodesia and the grant of privileges to Northern Rhodesia natives on the Caprivi Islands* was for livelihood issues, mainly fishing (107, TFDD). This agreement was quickly followed by the establishment of the Central African Council in 1938, a body that was created to coordinate common services among the then British colonies of Northern and Southern Rhodesia and Nyasaland. The council created the Inter-Territorial Hydro-Electric Power Commission in 1946, which began exploratory studies on potential energy sources and identified the feasibility of the Kariba and Kafue Hydroelectric Power Projects.

The 1950s saw the signing of several treaties within the basin. Following a 1949 meeting in Johannesburg, where riparians agreed to consult each other on any developments along the river, a 1950 conference resulted in the *Convention with agreements regarding use of Zambezi waters and effects of the proposed Kariba Dam* between Northern and Southern Rhodesia (151, TFDD). The treaty established interim arrangements for the collection and exchange of hydrographic information on the Zambezi River. Associated attempts to establish a Zambezi River Authority failed because of objections from Zambia.

In 1953, British and Portuguese colonial powers signed a treaty on the Shire River and Lake Nyasa/Malawi. The Exchange of notes constituting an agreement between Her Majesty's government in the United Kingdom of Great Britain and Northern Ireland and the Portuguese government providing for Portuguese participation in the Shire Valley Project was primarily not only for hydropower and flood control, but also for land reclamation and irrigation (170ENG, TFDD). According to Shela (2000), plans to develop a link from Malawi to the sea through the Shire River were developed at this stage.

Soon after, the decision to proceed with construction of the Kariba Dam was taken in 1954. Since Northern Rhodesia and Southern Rhodesia were federated states under one government at that point, the Kariba project did not initially require a treaty. Rather, a Hydro-Electric Power Act was passed in June 1954 and provided for the establishment of the Federal Hydro-Electric Board, which was charged with coordinating the generation and supply of electricity within the federation (Tumbare 2012). This Board was subsequently reconstituted as the Federal Hydro-Electric Board in May 1956 and vested with the power to construct dams and power stations, to transmit and sell electrical power, and to establish a hydrological data collection organisation in each territory.

Towards the end of 1954, an agreement between the colonial powers of Great Britain and Portugal was signed in Lisbon. The *Agreement Between the Government of the United Kingdom of Great Britain and Northern Ireland (on their own behalf and on behalf of the Government of the Federation of Rhodesia and Nyasaland) and the Government of Portugal With Regard to Certain Angolan and Northern Rhodesian Natives Living on the Kwando River* was meant to facilitate the seasonal migration of communities in the Barotse Plains, who required to temporarily settle on the side of the Kwando tributary in then-Portuguese territory during the dry season (183ENG, TFDD).

The first treaty in the second period of transboundary water law in the Zambezi (1960–1985) was a 1963 agreement on water and electricity allocation between Northern and Southern Rhodesia. With the dissolution of the federation between the two states earlier in the year, a new institutional framework was created within which the Power Board continued under the joint ownership and control of the governments of these two countries (Mutembwa 1998). The *Agreement relating to the Central African Power Corporation* (CAPCO) was reached in December 1963 to formalise this joint ownership (265ENG, TFDD).

A second treaty in this second period (1960–1985) of Zambezi's cooperative development is South Africa's agreement with Portugal on hydropower development in 1967, the *Agreement between South Africa and Portugal relating to hydropower development on the Zambezi River* (295ENG, TFDD). This agreement was focused on joint financing of the Cahora Bassa project, and was rapidly followed by *Agreement to Purchase electricity from Cahora Bassa Scheme*. This latter agreement was intended to guarantee power supply to South Africa from the Cahora Bassa project, which was completed in 1974 (HCB 2016).

A final treaty in the middle period of the Zambezi's cooperative development (1960–1985) was concluded in 1984. The now independent Mozambique, with Portugal and South Africa, signed the *Agreement between the governments of the Republic of Portugal, the People's Republic of Mozambique and the Republic of South Africa relative to the Cahora Bassa Project*, a flood and hydropower agreement that replaced the 1967 and 1969 treaties (315ENG, TFDD). Through this agreement, Mozambique acquired a stake in the Cahora Bassa project, and renegotiated the terms of power supply with South Africa (HCB 2016).

The transition to the final (and present) period of transboundary water cooperation in the Zambezi occurred with the revocation of the CAPCO Agreement by the governments of the

Figure 9.2 Cahora Bassa Dam was built through a 1967 agreement between Portugal and South Africa
Photo: Jusipbek Kazbekov

now independent states of Zambia and Zimbabwe in 1986. Through *the Agreement between the Republic of Zimbabwe and the Republic of Zambia concerning the utilization of the Zambezi River*, signed in 1987 in Harare (458ENG, TFDD), the new relationship went further than just sharing the dam for hydropower purposes, and now encompassed industrial and social development partnerships. CAPCO was dissolved and reconstituted under the Zambezi River Authority (ZRA), which was instituted through legislative acts passed simultaneously by the Parliaments of both Zambia and Zimbabwe in 1987 (ZRA 2016). CAPCO assets were distributed on the basis of the general principle that immovable assets in the territory of each state would be allocated to the national electricity authority of each state and the ZRA. The ZRA Act replaced all prior agreements between the two countries on the Kariba.

Cooperation on the Zambezi took a more expansive form with the conclusion of the *Agreement on the action plan for the environmentally sound management of the common Zambezi River System* (ZACPLAN) in 1987 (456ENG, TFDD). The treaty involved five riparians – Botswana, Mozambique, Tanzania, Zambia and Zimbabwe – and consisted of 19 projects oriented toward conservation of the Zambezi system (Nakayama, 1998). ZACPLAN provided a framework for data collection and coordinated planning, but the success of its implementation was questioned and ultimately less than 10 (of the envisioned 19 projects) were implemented when it concluded in 2008 (Fox and Sneddon 2007; Jensen and Lange 2013; Metzger and Rajapakse 2015). A possible explanation for ZACPLAN's challenges may have been its lack of a central coordinating institution or a secretariat (Shela 2000).

Soon after the *Revised Protocol on Shared Watercourse Systems in the Southern African Development Community Region* entered into force in 2003, the Zambezi riparians signed the *Agreement on the Establishment of the Zambezi Watercourse Commission* (ZAMCOM) in 2004 (624ENG, TFDD). ZAMCOM's objective is to 'promote the equitable and reasonable utilization of the water resources of the Zambezi Watercourse as well as the efficient management and sustainable development thereof' (624ENG, TFDD). The ZAMCOM Agreement provides for several institutional bodies to facilitate the cooperative process. The Council of Ministers has the overall responsibility for decision-making, supported by a technical committee of senior officials from the riparian states and a secretariat that is responsible for implementing ZAMCOM's Strategic Plan and associated activities. ZAMCOM has nine primary functions:

- Collect, evaluate and disseminate all data and information on the Zambezi watercourse as may be necessary for the implementation of this Agreement.
- Promote, support, coordinate and harmonise the management and development of the water resources of the Zambezi Watercourse.
- Advise member states on the planning, management, utilisation, development, protection and conservation of the Zambezi watercourse as well as on the role and position of the public with regard to such activities and the possible impact thereof on social and cultural heritage matters.
- Advise member states on measures necessary for the avoidance of disputes and assist in the resolution of conflicts among member states with regard to the planning and management, utilisation, development, protection and conservation of the Zambezi watercourse.
- Foster greater awareness among the inhabitants of the Zambezi watercourse of the equitable and reasonable utilisation and the efficient management and sustainable development of the resources of the Zambezi watercourse.
- Cooperate with the institutions of Southern Africa Development Community (SADC) as well as with other international and national organisations where necessary.
- Promote and assist in the harmonisation of national water policies and legislative measures.

- Carry out such other functions and responsibilities as the member states may assign from time to time.
- Promote the application and development of this Agreement according to its objective and the principles referred to under Article 12 [which contains eight principles].

In practice, implementing the ZAMCOM Agreement has taken some time. Finalisation of the agreement required ratification by six of the Zambezi's eight riparians, a process that was finally completed in 2011 (SARDC 2013). An interim secretariat was established, and an interim executive secretary appointed, at that point in Gaborone. A permanent secretariat was subsequently established, and a permanent executive secretary appointed in Harare in 2014. Staff members have been added since then and the institution is starting to take shape, with initial projects focused on the emerging Decision Support System and Strategic Plan.

Two other bilateral cooperation activities have been initiated within the Zambezi Basin. In 2003, Malawi and Mozambique signed the *Agreement on the establishment of the Joint Water Commission on the Shire River*, which was motivated by the 2001 floods in the region (IWMI 2015). In addition, cooperation between Malawi and Tanzania commenced in 2010, on the Songwe River. The Songwe River Basin Development Programme (SRBDP) is a 10-year programme aimed at food security and economic development in the basin (AfDB 2010).

Looking forward: facing risk

Clearly, cooperation in the Zambezi is extensive. More than 10 agreements have been concluded since the 1890s in the Zambezi, often on a bilateral basis, but increasingly involving more than two states. Nonetheless, ample opportunities for additional socioeconomic development remain 'on the table', opportunities that are best realised through cooperative approaches. This section attempts to depict risk in order to help explain and characterise why progress toward realising such opportunities may be slow. The section is divided into the five types of risk: i) capacity and knowledge, ii) accountability and voice, iii) equity and access, iv) sovereignty and autonomy, v) stability and support.

Capacity and knowledge

Review of key literature suggests that challenges related to capacity and knowledge may be less of an issue than they have been in the past. Shela (2000) noted limitations associated with data collection and exchange among riparians, for example, and Subramanian *et al.* (2012) explained how capacity and knowledge constraints may have hindered the conclusion of a basin-wide deal in the past. Nonetheless, there seems to be a growing trend toward knowledge expansion reflected in recent analytical activities such as the MSIOA (World Bank 2010) and the *Zambezi Environment Outlook* (SARDC 2015). Knowledge barriers, therefore, may not pose a major impediment to enhancing cooperation in the Zambezi. The degree to which human and technical capacity does or does not constrain cooperation is nonetheless less clear.

Accountability and voice

The level of voice in a cooperative framework may generate uncertainty that reduces motivation for collaboration. As noted earlier in this chapter, Petersen-Perlman (2016) stated that Zambia would like comparatively greater voice within ZAMCOM given the degree to which the country contributes to, and is dependent on, the basin. The corollary to this statement is that provision of merely equal voice – perceived to be at odds with a country's geographic position in the basin – may hinder Zambia's desire to cooperate. So, the reality is that allocating greater voice to Zambia may adversely affect motivation of other riparians to cooperate. Whatever the case, accountability and voice were not frequently identified as a constraint on cooperation in sources reviewed.

Equity and access

Equity and access issues were flagged in at least three sources. Tumbare (1999) considered international principles such as the 1997 *UN Convention on the Law of Non-navigational Uses of International Watercourses* as well as regional protocols such as the 2000 *SADC Revised Protocol on Shared Watercourses* in a Zambezi context. Subramanian *et al.* (2012) pointed out how equity concerns may constitute a barrier to Zambia's engagement in cooperative efforts. Jensen and Lange (2013: 84) noted concerns from the Zambian government on possible applications of the equitable use concept in the Zambezi. Ultimately, uncertainty related to interpretation of equitable use may comprise a risk that constrains cooperation in the Zambezi Basin.

Sovereignty and autonomy

Issues surrounding threats to sovereignty and autonomy are widely acknowledged in literature reviewed. Fox and Sneddon (2007) explain how participation in the ZAMCOM process implies that states surrender some level of autonomy, and that this may not be necessarily desired.

Figure 9.3 The Chobe–Zambezi confluence, Botswana and Zambia
Photo: Richard Beilfuss

Subramanian *et al.* (2012) noted how sovereignty and autonomy concerns affect Zambia's engagement in basin-wide cooperation. Jensen and Lange (2013) explain how a major barrier to Zambia's wholehearted participation in the ZAMCOM Agreement is the Zambian government's perceptions of the Zambezi as a national river which Zambia enjoys sovereign right to utilise. Petersen-Perlman (2016) explained how Zambia has expressed reluctance to enter into a basin-wide framework because it may compromise the country's autonomous development plans.

Stability and support

Longevity of country support did not emerge as an issue in sources reviewed. One is left to conclude that the Zambezi's countries are fairly stable, and that there is unlikely to be substantial domestic backlash faced by governments seeking to enhance cooperation with neighbours. This reality may result at least partially from the broader cooperation fostered through SADC, as well as cross-country bonds formed during struggles against minority rule in the latter half of the twentieth century.

Discussion: risk in context

The chapter has highlighted abundant cooperation in the Zambezi, reflected in more than 10 agreements concluded over the last 130 years. The chapter also highlighted how risk – in particular risk related to equity and access, and sovereignty and autonomy – may constrain cooperation. It is important to recognise that risks identified are likely to be mediated by the Zambezi's trans-boundary legal regime as well as by regional protocols and international customary law on transboundary waters.

Risks around equity and access

Risks related to equity and access appear primarily related to uncertainty in interpretation and application of the concept. Fairness to one, for example, may be perceived as favouritism to another. Article 13 of the ZAMCOM Agreement (624ENG, TFDD) refers to a set of factors that can be applied to determine equitable and reasonable utilisation of the Zambezi watercourse (Box 9.1). In principle, all factors are to be considered, though their weight is a function of their relative importance. International water law has a similar multifaceted approach to determination of equitable and reasonable use (Lautze and Giordano 2006). While both basin-specific and international law provide important guidance for equitable water sharing, they are unlikely to fully dispel ambiguity surrounding application of the concept. Relative importance of factors for determining equitable water sharing may in fact depend on perspective, for example, and application of different factors may generate different messages.

Risks around sovereignty and autonomy

Risks related to sovereignty and autonomy relate to fears that national development plans can be compromised or delayed. Article 16 of the ZAMCOM Agreement (624ENG, TFDD) outlines how member states should share data and information on planned projects that may adversely affect the watercourse or another member state, and how consultation under the ZAMCOM framework may eventually take place in the event of disagreement between states; while such consultation takes place, development plans are to remain on hold. Such provisions are aligned

---

Box 9.1: Article 13 of 2004 ZAMCOM Agreement

Equitable and Reasonable Utilisation (ERU)

The Zambezi Watercourse shall be managed and utilised in an equitable and reasonable manner.

The rules of application of ERU shall be developed by the Technical Committee as provided under Article 10 (1) (c).

In the application of ERU the Technical Committee shall take into account all the relevant factors, and circumstances including the following:

Geographic, hydrographic, hydrological, climatic, ecological and other factors of natural character.

The social, economic and environmental needs of the member states.

The population dependent on the Zambezi Watercourse in each member state.

The effects of the use or uses of the Zambezi Watercourse in one member state and other member states.

Existing and potential uses of the waters of the Zambezi Watercourse.

Conservation, protection, development and economy of the use of the water resources of the Zambezi Watercourse and the costs of measures taken to that effect.

The availability of alternatives of comparable value, to a planned or existing use of the waters of the Zambezi Watercourse.

The weight to be given to each factor is to be determined by its importance in comparison with that of other relevant factors. In determining what is an equitable and reasonable use, all relevant factors are to be considered together and a conclusion reached on the basis of the whole.

In the application of ERU, member states shall take into account the provisions of Article 14 (4).

---

with international principles and, while designed to facilitate negotiated outcomes, may no doubt trigger uneasiness related to application of an additional layer of process, which was not necessary to comply with previously. Nonetheless, there is a growing recognition of customary law on international watercourses (Dellapena 2001), which would likely require some level of negotiation among riparians sharing an international watercourse.

Bottom line

Risks are no doubt partially mitigated through basin-level, regional and customary international water law. Nonetheless, there is a lot of uncertainty related to the interpretation and application of such concepts. This uncertainty may deter engagement from certain countries such as Zambia, as well as Angola and Malawi, given their position in the basin.

Conclusions: strengthening water cooperation in the Zambezi

This chapter reviewed the evolution of transboundary water cooperation in the Zambezi Basin and identified key risks in order to help reveal entry points for strengthening water cooperation in the basin. The chapter described the evolution of transboundary water law in the basin, culminating in the 2004 ZAMCOM Agreement. The chapter also identified major risks that may constrain efforts to enhance cooperation, namely equity and access, and autonomy and sovereignty. While international legal regimes may certainly help address risk, there will be some level of risk that will no doubt go unmitigated.

Obviously, it is natural for the geography of a river basin such as the Zambezi to result in disparate risk and motivation for cooperation among riparian countries. For third parties and others such as ZAMCOM seeking to foster an intensification of cooperation, it may be wise to recognise and respond to this variation among the Zambezi's countries rather than indiscriminately seeking to enhance cooperation. Clearly, Zambia may need greatest focus to mitigate risk and increase cooperation – though dynamics in Angola and Malawi may present challenges as well.

To target or incentivise countries such as Angola, Malawi and Zambia that may be reluctant to cooperate, Subramanian *et al.* (2012: 26) have proposed outlining a clear flow of benefits, including a sequence of investments, as incentive. At least three other options exist, though not all are likely desirable.

- First, safeguards can be proposed that protect the interests of less motivated states, for example, such states could maintain a certain level of autonomy on the control and development of water resources in their states. While the ZAMCOM Agreement currently calls for notification and consultation on planned development, presumably after they are planned, one option may be to foster greater clarity on plans that can be pursued at a national level vis-à-vis those that will require transboundary cooperation. For example, elaboration of indicative flow impact thresholds below which a state can utilise the basin's water for its national interests, and above which transboundary cooperation is required, may help reduce potential risk.
- A second option may be the more immediately implementable. This option focuses on the provision of targeted training or capacity development to Angolan, Malawian and Zambian professionals on how to cooperatively leverage their power advantage for broader benefit. Such experience may help foster a transition from thinking of cooperation as a sovereign threat to regional opportunity. Small risks and sacrifices on water-related issues, for example, may be viewed in a context of bigger opportunities beyond water.
- Third, certain states could be offered a larger say in basin-wide frameworks, based on factors such as dependence on the basin and contribution to its water resources. This would increase incentives for certain countries to cooperate, but the modalities of implementation would be vague and hold potential to upset the broader balance among basin-wide riparians. Further, the authors of this chapter are unaware of an existing precedent in which variation in riparian geography in an international watercourse has been explicitly accommodated in a basin-wide institutional framework.

More broadly, the options just presented touch on issues of how ZAMCOM, as a primary body advancing basin-wide cooperation, can balance riparian interests in a way that advances cooperative approaches. While one option is for ZAMCOM to prescribe or mandate adherence to certain principles such as 'no significant harm' to downstream water uses, another option is to provide support and recommendation for how potentially national development can be undertaken in a more inclusive and cooperative fashion. Ultimately, the role that ZAMCOM has assumed – and likely will continue to assume – more closely resembles the latter option in which the basin-wide body highlights (rather than prescribes consideration for) transboundary issues. This dynamic, in turn, creates a conduit for countries to assert themselves to achieve more equitable outcomes.

The organic, rather than rigid, process for fostering basin-wide cooperation has implications for country participation in cooperative activities. Indeed, the 'relaxed' form of cooperation creates more opportunity for fit-for-purpose cooperation among relevant countries, rather than requiring participation of all countries on every issue. Developments in Zambia, for example, may only need to involve Zimbabwe and Mozambique because these are the downstream riparians potentially affected. Further, given the geographic disconnect in the Lake Nyasa/Malawi/Shire system, combined with closely linked incentives and risks of states there, largely separate development may make sense among Malawi, Mozambique and Tanzania.

It should also be noted that unlike dynamics in 'closed' basins such as the Nile, where costs (e.g., reductions in water availability) may be immediate, the 'open' nature of the Zambezi basin may imply that barriers to cooperation may relate more to future risks rather than to immediate costs. Cooperation in the context of risks, in turn, may be somewhat *grey* relative

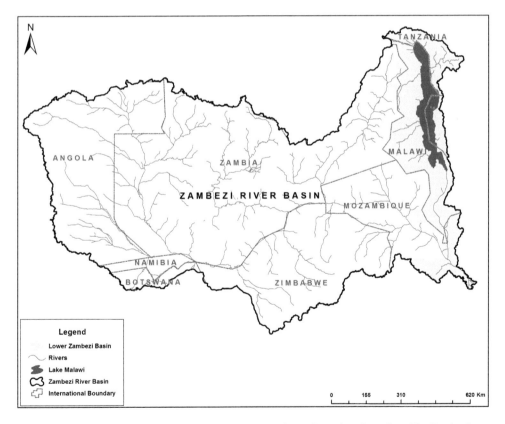

Figure 9.4 The Lake Nyasa/Malawi/Shire system is somewhat independent from the wider Zambezi Basin

Source: Luxon Nhamo/IWMI

to the *black-and-white* context of cost-based cooperation. In a closed basin, for example, countries are more likely to make transparent sacrifices in return for clear benefits. A risk-based cooperative context, by contrast, may be more focused on minimising the potential that cooperation will foreclose future development opportunities.

One point that has not been explicitly raised is the role of international actors and in particular donors. Donor support is an incentive for cooperation that cross-cuts all countries in the basin. Donors can play the important role of sponsoring projects that strengthen cooperation and foster socioeconomic development and environmental conservation. For example, the United Nations Environmental Programme (UNEP)-sponsored ZACPLAN, which facilitated the first basin-wide cooperation in the Zambezi, also funded a much-needed environmental assessment of the entire basin. Donors also subsidise the financial costs of cooperation in many African basins. Direct benefits of donor funding (e.g., jobs) as well as broader benefits (e.g., socioeconomic development) no doubt help catalyse cooperation.

Another point that has not yet been raised is that *not* cooperating brings risks. At least two manifestations of this are apparent. The first is climate change. The impacts of climate change may be more effectively addressed with cooperative rather than unilateral approaches. Leveraging the climate change message may also help catalyse cooperation (Varady *et al.* 2013). Second, opportunities for groundwater use and conjunctive management approaches may be better tapped with cooperative rather than unilateral approaches. The national management of shared groundwater resources must be implemented within a shared framework in order to realise national objectives while reducing the risks of externally driven overexploitation or pollution.

Before closing, two issues are worth pointing out. First, it must be acknowledged that risks related to equity and access, and autonomy and sovereignty, were identified by Subramanian *et al.* (2012; 2014) as deep-seated risks, and, hence less amenable to mitigation. This reality implies that cooperative risks in the Zambezi will not go away, and that ZAMCOM and other development actors may seek to develop long-term rather than, or in addition to, short-term approaches for responding to risks that may prevent countries from enhancing cooperation. In particular, it may be worthwhile to foster regular discussion around incorporating such risks into a cooperative basin-wide framework.

A second issue that should be acknowledged is that the framework applied to assess risk (Subramanian *et al.* 2012; 2014) is likely imperfect. Developed by a World Bank team, it can be considered somewhat exploratory. Nonetheless, as noted in the methods, it is the most advanced approach known to the authors for assessing risk in transboundary waters and, for better or worse, risk is likely to comprise a major barrier to enhancing cooperation on transboundary waters. Further, it is based on quite some years of practical experience of engagement in transboundary waters in Africa and elsewhere – this should carry considerable weight.

In closing, this chapter went beyond broad examination of basin cooperation to identify the major cooperative risks and ability of existing transboundary legal frameworks to mitigate those risks. Major risks that may constrain cooperation in the basin relate to equity and access, and autonomy and sovereignty; existing transboundary laws may only partially mitigate these risks. Ultimately, basin-wide cooperation in the Zambezi is still fairly nascent and basin states are still fairly young. It is hoped that the growing duration of cooperation and increasing state age, combined with an increasingly influential ZAMCOM, bring mutual trust and converging visions for the Zambezi Basin that mitigate risks and foster cooperative development paths.

Note

1   That said, it is worth noting that Zambia has now fully ratified the ZAMCOM Agreement and is participating in ZAMCOM activities in good faith.

References

AfDB (African Development Bank). 2010. *Songwe River Basin Development Programme.* Detailed Design and Investment Preparation Project. Appraisal report. February 2010. Lilongwe: Government of Malawi.

Beck, L. and Bernauer, T. 2010. *Water scenarios for the Zambezi River Basin: 2000–2050.* Center for Comparative and International Studies and Center for Environmental Decisions. Zurich: Eidgenössische Technische Hochschule Zürich (ETH Zürich).

Dellapenna, J. 2001. The customary international law of transboundary fresh waters. *International Journal of Global Environmental Issues* 1(3/4): 264–305.

Fox, C.A. and Sneddon, C. 2007. Transboundary river basin agreements in the Mekong and Zambezi basins: Enhancing environmental security or securitizing the environment? *International Environmental Agreements: Politics, Law and Economics* 7(3): 237–261.

Giordano, M., Drieschova, A., Duncan, J.A., Sayama, Y., De Stefano, L. and Wolf, A.T. 2014. A review of the evolution and state of transboundary freshwater treaties. *International Environmental Agreements: Politics, Law and Economics* 14(3): 245–264.

GIZ (Deutsche Gesellschaft für Internationale Zusammenarbeit). 2011. *Dam synchronization and flood releases in the Zambezi River Basin Project.* Gaborone: Southern Africa Development Community (SADC).

Grey, D., Sadoff, C. and Connors, G. 2009. Effective cooperation on transboundary waters: A practical perspective. *Getting transboundary water right: Theory and practice for effective cooperation, Report* 25. Washington, DC: World Bank.

Grishin, N., Bernardini, F., Enderlein, R. and Libert, B. 2006. *Transboundary water cooperation trends in the newly independent states.* Water Series No 4. New York and Geneva: United Nations.

Gwebu, T.D. 2002. Urban water scarcity management: Civic vs. state response in Bulawayo. *Habitat International* 26(3): 417–431.

Harrison, G.P. and Whittington, H.B.W. 2002. Susceptibility of the Batoka Gorge hydroelectric scheme to climate change. *Journal of Hydrology* 264(1): 230–241.

HCB (Hydro Electrica de Cahora Bassa). 2016. *This is our history.* Avavilable at www.hcb.co.mz/eng/Company/Historial (accessed on 6 December 2016).

Holmatov, B. and Lautze, J. 2016. Thinking inside the basin: scale in transboundary water management. *Natural Resources Forum* 40(3): 127–138.

IWMI (International Water Management Institute). 2015. *Thinking inside the basins: Scale in transboundary water management.* Water Policy Brief 39. Colombo, Sri Lanka.

Jägerskog, A. and Zeitoun, M. 2009. *Getting transboundary water right: Theory and practice for effective cooperation.* Report No. 25. Stockholm: Stockholm International Water Institute.

Jensen, K.M. and Lange, R.B. 2013. *Transboundary water governance in a shifting development context. New development finance, development spaces and commitment to cooperation: A comparative study of the Mekong and the Zambezi River Basin.* Copenhagen: Danish Institute for International Studies (DIIS).

Klaphake, A. and Scheumann, W. 2006. Understanding transboundary water cooperation: Evidence from Africa. Working Paper on Management in Environmental Planning. Available at www.bahnsysteme.tu-berlin.de/fileadmin/a0731/uploads/publikationen/workingpapers/WP_14_2006_Klaphake_Scheuman_Transboundary_Wat_.pdf

Lautze, J. and Giordano, M. 2005. Transboundary water law in Africa: Development, nature, and geography. *Nat. Resources Journal* 45: 1053.

Lautze, J. and Giordano, M. 2006. Does 'equity' really matter in international water law? Evidence from Africa. *Colorado Journal of International Environmental Law and Policy* 17(1): 89–122.

Metzger, J. and Rajapakse, S. 2015. Catalyzing investments in water management and development: Enabling equitable and reasonable utilization in the Mekong, Okavango and Zambezi. Paper presented at the 16th Waternet/WARFSA/GWP-SA Symposium on Integrated Water Resources Management. Mauritius, 28–30 October 2015.

Mutembwa, A. 1998. *Water and the potential for resource conflicts in southern Africa.* Cambridge: University of Cambridge, Global Security Fellows Initiative.

Nakayama, M. 1998. Politics behind Zambezi action plan. *Water Policy* 1: 397–409. Also available at http://citeseerx.ist.psu.edu/viewdoc/download?doi= 10.1.1.604.1836& rep= rep1&type=pdf

Petersen-Perlman, J.D. 2016. Projecting resilience in the Zambezi River basin through global analysis and basin realities. *Water Resources Management* 30(6): 1987–2003.

Qaddumi, H. 2008. *Practical approaches to transboundary water benefit sharing.* Working Paper 292. Results of Overseas Development Institute (ODI) research presented in preliminary form for discussion and critical comment. London: Overseas Development Institute.

Sadoff, C., Greiber, T., Smith, M. and Bergkamp, G. 2008. *Share – Managing water across boundaries*. Gland, Switzerland: International Union for the Conservation of Nature.

SARDC (Southern Africa Regional Documentation Centre) and HBS (Heinrich Böll Stiftung). 2010. *Responding to climate change impacts: Adaptation and mitigation strategies as practised in the Zambezi River Basin*. Harare: SARDC; Cape Town: HBS.

SARDC. 2013. Zambezi Watercourse Commission to be fully operational in 2014. *The Zambezi* Vol 2: July–December 2013.

SARDC. 2015. *The status report on integrated flood and drought mapping*. Harare: ZAMCOM/SADC/SARDC.

Shela, O.N. 2000. Management of shared river basins: The case of the Zambezi River. *Water Policy* 2(1): 65–81.

Söderbaum, F. 2015. Rethinking the politics of transboundary water management. *International Journal of Water Governance* 3(1): 121–132.

Spalding-Fecher, R., Yamba, F., Walimwipi, H., Kling, H., Tembo, B., Nyambe, I., Chapman, A. and Cuamba, B. 2014. Water supply and demand scenarios for the Zambezi River Basin. In: *Climate change and upstream development impacts on new hydropower projects in the Zambezi project*. Report for climate & development knowledge network. Cape Town: University of Cape Town.

Subramanian, A., Brown, B. and Wolf, A. 2012. *Reaching across the waters: Facing the risks of cooperation in international waters*. Washington, DC: World Bank Publications.

Subramanian, A., Brown, B. and Wolf, A.T. 2014. Understanding and overcoming risks to cooperation along transboundary rivers. *Water Policy* 16(5): 824–843.

Swain, A. 2012. *Understanding emerging security challenges: Threats and opportunities*. New York: Routledge.

Tillmant, A. and Kinzelbach, W. 2012. The cost of non-cooperation in international river basins. *Water Resources Research* 48(1).

Tillmant, A. and Namara, R. 2017. The economic potential of the basin. Chapter 3. In: *The Zambezi River Basin: Water and sustainable development*, (eds.), Lautze, J., Phiri, Z., Smakhtin, V. and Saruchera, D. London: Earthscan.

Tumbare, M.J. 1999. Equitable sharing of the water resources of the Zambezi River Basin. *Physics and Chemistry of the Earth, Part B: Hydrology, Oceans and Atmosphere* 24(6): 571–578.

Tumbare, M.J. 2012. *Management of river basins and dams. The Zambezi River Basin*. Lusaka: CRC Press – Book World.

Varady, R.G., Scott, C.A., Wilder, M., Morehouse, B., Pablos, N.P. and Garfin, G.M. 2013. Transboundary adaptive management to reduce climate-change vulnerability in the western US–Mexico border region. *Environmental Science & Policy* 26: 102–112.

World Bank. 2010. *The Zambezi River Basin. A multi-sector investment opportunities analysis*. June 2010. Washington, DC.

ZRA (Zambezi River Authority). 2016. Background. Available at www.zaraho.org.zm/about-us/background (accessed December 2016).

10

The potential for subbasin cooperation in the Shire

A case for bottom-up institutional development?

Charlotte de Bruyne, Jonathan Lautze
and Jusipbek Kazbekov

Key messages

- Subbasin-level cooperation may foster improvements in basin conditions and welfare of riparian states. In the Shire, cooperation can help reduce effects of floods in the downstream riparian of Mozambique. Cooperation may also help address proliferation of water hyacinth – which threatens electricity generation, as well as fish and other biodiversity – and improve navigation.
- As bargaining power and interests of the Shire's two riparians (Malawi, Mozambique) do not always align, there may be scope for mutually beneficial deals to be struck through cross-issue linkage. Malawi may provide early warning of floods and control to Mozambique, for example, in exchange for Mozambique's provision of free navigation to Malawi between the southern boundary of Malawi and the Indian Ocean.
- Given the potential benefits of subbasin cooperation and alignment of these benefits with ZAMCOM's mandate, ZAMCOM may wish to more actively promote and support subbasin cooperation in the Zambezi where it is determined to be suitable.
- Particular ways in which ZAMCOM can engage with subbasin cooperation include: i) coordination and facilitation; ii) backstopping and environmental regulation; iii) brokering and mediating to foster convergence toward agreement across issues; and iv) learning from such experiences to share lessons across subbasins and consider at a basin-level.
- More explicit recognition and emphasis on practically oriented and 'bottom-up' processes for institutional creation in African transboundary waters may dovetail with basin-level efforts for mutually beneficial results. The geography of the Zambezi presents particular opportunities for catchment or subbasin-level cooperation that are coordinated with the broader framework of ZAMCOM.

Introduction

More than 150 transboundary water treaties have emerged to cope with Africa's ubiquitous shared waters (Lautze and Giordano 2005; Kistin and Ashton 2008), and most of Africa's major watersheds now possess international river basin organisations (RBOs) (Schmeier 2012; Lautze *et al.* 2013). In West Africa, for example, notable RBOs include the Senegal River Basin Organisation (OMVS), the Volta Basin Authority (VBA), the Niger Basin Authority (NBA) and the Lake Chad Basin Commission (LCBC). In East Africa, the Nile Basin Initiative (NBI) has been evolving for more than a decade and a half. In southern Africa, notable RBOs include the Okavango River Basin Water Commission (OKACOM), the Limpopo Watercourse Commission (LIMCOM), the Orange River Basin Commission (ORASCOM) and the Zambezi Watercourse Commission (ZAMCOM). The growing volume of transboundary water law and proliferation of RBOs is widely considered to be positive, and reflects a reduced potential for conflict and an improved capacity to manage water across countries (Rangeley *et al.* 1994; Kranz *et al.* 2005; Bakker 2007; Schmeier and Schulze 2010).

Inadvertently or not, the growth of transboundary water institutions may have engendered a desire to streamline the approach to their development toward a common blueprint (RBA Centre 1999; INBO-ANBO, n.d; Bhat 2008). While institutional development according to a common blueprint may be better than no institutional development, it is worth noting that common formats are often applied to basins facing very distinct issues and conditions (Shah *et al.* 2001; Bhat 2008; Merrey 2009; Hooper 2011). Application of common approaches across basins is likely due, at least partly, to: i) limited knowledge on how to tailor RBOs to basin-specific conditions and issues; and ii) emphasis on development of RBOs at the basin-scale, a scale at which issues are more general and institutions may be able to follow a more generic format.

This chapter seeks to propose options for the shape and structure of transboundary water cooperation that are specifically tailored to issues and conditions in the Shire catchment – shared between Malawi and Mozambique. The chapter also explores how issue-responsive institutional development at a subbasin scale can be complemented and coordinated with basin-wide approaches led by ZAMCOM. The chapter first reviews water resources issues and conditions in the Shire, as well as the current state of transboundary water cooperation across the two countries. The chapter then reviews international literature and experience to identify institutional mechanisms that respond to these issues. Subsequently, three consolidated 'bundles' of mechanisms for cooperation on the Shire are proposed, and guidance for decision and negotiation points around which riparians may converge toward an agreement is provided. Lastly, the chapter discusses how ZAMCOM may support 'bottom-up' processes of institutional formation.

Background: the Shire catchment

Study area

The Shire catchment comprises one portion of the broader Zambezi Basin, and forms part of the lower Zambezi that together cover Lake Nyasa/Malawi and the Shire River system (Figure 10.1). The Shire River originates as an outlet at the southern edge of Lake Nyasa/Malawi and flows 415 km southwards where it joins the Zambezi River. As flows into Lake Nyasa/Malawi are currently unregulated and the effect of decision-making upstream of the lake outlet is estimated to be minimal, focus was placed on the Shire catchment downstream of the lake. The catchment generates a mean annual runoff of approximately 15.7 km^3 and covers a surface area of approximately 49,000 km^2; the majority of the catchment (71 per cent) and population (3.6 million) are located in Malawi, while the remaining part (29 per cent) is located in Mozambique, serving a population of approximately 0.6 million (World Bank 2010).

Shire geography

Rainfall in the Shire Basin varies between 600 mm in the lower part of the river to 2,400 mm on the Ruo tributary in the Mulanje mountains; 95 per cent of the annual precipitation occurs in the warm, wet season that stretches from November to April (Shela 2000). In the Lower Zambezi and Shire system, flows are highly variable from year to year (Beilfuss 2012). The Shire River can be divided into three sections: upper (plain), middle (steep) and lower (plain). The Upper Shire between Lake Nyasa/Malawi and the Kamuzu Barrage is mainly used for navigation and fish production. In the middle section, from south of the Kamuzu Barrage until Chikwawa, there is a 370-metre drop in elevation. The remainder of the Shire landscape is fairly flat and runs downstream from Chikwawa into Mozambique, where the river meets the Zambezi. This lower part of the Shire catchment is one of the most fertile areas in the Zambezi Basin, boasting rich deep soils with considerable irrigation potential.

Water use in the Shire

Water of the Shire catchment is mainly used for hydropower, irrigation and agriculture, and to a lesser extent navigation. The Shire also supplies water to urban areas such as Blantyre. Three hydropower stations – Nkula (124 MWt), Tedzani (90 MWt) and Kapichira (64 MWt) – generate 98 per cent of Malawi's electricity (Shela 2000; Kaunda and Mtalo 2013). Traditionally, the area south of Chikwawa is conducive to a high level of flood recession agriculture. Irrigation activities

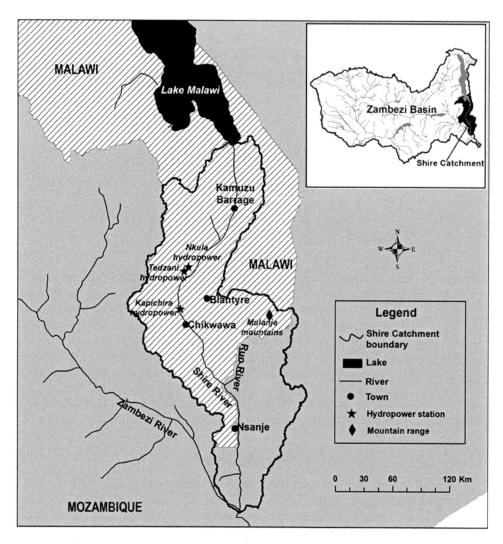

Figure 10.1 The Shire catchment
Source: IWMI

in the south of Malawi have recently increased, in part due a substantial increase of private investment and notable World Bank financing in the area of agriculture and irrigation development (Atkins 2012). In Mozambique, irrigation is likely to increase as the country forges ahead with reconstruction and development programmes, which may include rehabilitating and expanding irrigation in Mozambican portions of the Zambezi (Shela 2000).

Transboundary water issues in the Shire

As the Shire River crosses political boundaries, it gives rise to issues that are transboundary in nature. Discussions were held with personnel at relevant water authorities in Mozambique and Malawi, including the Administração Regional de Águas do Zambeze (ARA-Zambeze) in

Mozambique and the Shire River Basin Management Programme in Malawi,[1] to identify priority transboundary water issues. Results of discussions suggest four key water issues of transboundary importance: flooding, aquatic weeds (water hyacinth), navigation and future water infrastructure development.

Flooding

Flooding is a transboundary issue as water from areas in Malawi floods border areas at and south of the Ruo-Shire confluence, as well as areas uniquely in Mozambique such as the Shire-Zambezi confluence. While flooding occurred historically and in most years does not pose major problems, property-damaging and life-threatening floods occur at a frequency of approximately every five years, a rate that may be increasing.[2] Increased flood occurrence may be associated with anthropogenic climate change (Collier *et al.* 2008; Chidanti-Malunga 2011).

Aquatic weeds[3]

Water hyacinth proliferated following the construction of the Kamuzu Barrage in 1964, spreading slowly north towards Lake Nyasa/Malawi and south towards the Indian Ocean (Navarro and Phiri 2000). The invasive weed is now present in most parts of the catchment, causing problems in hydropower facilities in southern Malawi as well as in the Mozambique portions of the Shire. The proliferation of aquatic weeds appears to be affecting a recognised RAMSAR site at Marromeu, downstream from the confluence of the Shire and Zambezi Rivers in Mozambique.[4] Aquatic weed infestations at the site have already resulted in decreased fish production, displacement of natural fauna and flora, and overall loss of biodiversity (Timberlake 1998). Biological control was initiated in 1995 and attempts are currently being made to capture weeds just upstream of Kamuzu Barrage, but these have met with mixed success.

Navigation

Due to its landlocked status, Malawi has shown interest in re-establishing access to the Indian Ocean through the Shire. Investigations into the navigability of the river since 1998 have led to interest in re-establishing navigation transport activities in the mid-term future.[5] Toward this end, construction works began at the port of Nsanje, in the far south of Malawi, in 2011. Currently, an African Development Bank (AfDB 2011) study is being undertaken to assess the feasibility of implementing a former agreement reached between Malawi, Mozambique and Zambia regarding the Zambezi-Shire Waterways Project that aims to rehabilitate the navigability of the river and introduce transportation by container ships between Nsanje and the Indian Ocean.

Water infrastructure development

There is recognised potential for multipurpose infrastructure development, particularly on the Ruo tributary. On the Ruo, there is the possibility of developing infrastructure for both hydropower and flood control. Financing has nonetheless been lacking, and parameters surrounding cooperation to facilitate infrastructure development would need to be determined. It was noted that infrastructure is different in nature from the other issues as the others are *ends* in themselves, while water infrastructure is a *means* to those ends.

Figure 10.2 Nkula Hydropower Station: key existing infrastructure along the Shire River in Malawi
Photo: Jusipbek Kazbekov

Existing and potential cooperation

Zambezi-level cooperation

The level of collaboration between Malawi and Mozambique on water issues is currently limited. At a broader Zambezi level, Malawi and Mozambique cooperate within the framework of the Southern African Development Community (SADC) Water Resources Technical Committee. Some cooperation is also achieved through the ZAMCOM Agreement, which includes Angola, Botswana, Mozambique, Namibia, Tanzania, Zambia and Zimbabwe. Malawi has signed but not yet ratified this agreement, and continues to participate as an observer.

Cooperation on the Shire between Malawi and Mozambique

In the Shire specifically, an *Agreement on Establishment of the Joint Water Commission* (2003) was signed in response to the devastating floods in 2001. Despite good intentions, this agreement has not been operationalised owing to absence of technical and financial support. Informal dialogue between the riparians also exists at a ministry level between offices in Lilongwe (Malawi) and Maputo (Mozambique) in the form of exchange of letters, email and phone calls.

Cooperation on the Shire at a local level

Cooperation among subnational stakeholders within the Shire catchment appears to be minimal. There is evidence of Mozambican water managers contacting Kamuzu Barrage operators during flooding in Mozambican portions of the Shire, to request for information on water level at Lake Nyasa/Malawi.[6] Nonetheless, such interaction seems an exception to a rule in which engagement is far from routine.

Demand for cooperation between riparians in the Shire catchment

Demand for cooperation is reflected in the Shire-Zambezi Waterway Feasibility Study and the Shire-tailored transboundary treaty concluded in 2003, as well as the *ad hoc* cooperation (noted above) occurring between the Kamuzu Barrage operator and counterparts in Mozambique. Demand for cooperation was also confirmed in personal communications with different actors in the catchment (e.g., Ministry of Water Development, Malawi; ARA-Zambeze, Mozambique) as these expressed mutual concerns regarding the transboundary issues identified above. Nevertheless, the fact that the 2003 treaty has so far failed to materialise may trigger questions about impediments to operationalising cooperation on water.

Methods: transboundary water institutions

Document search

With the aim of assembling a set of transboundary institutional mechanisms that respond to the Shire's issues (i.e., flooding, aquatic weeds, navigation), three types of documents were collected and reviewed: i) academic literature; ii) project documents; and iii) transboundary water treaties. The academic literature examined included documents that discuss the transboundary relevance of flooding, aquatic weeds and navigation. Particular focus was applied to such literature that contained an African focus. Key documents in this category included Bakker (2007; 2009) and Cooley and Gleick (2011) on issues of flooding, Navarro and Phiri (2000) on water quality and aquatic weed management, and Caponera Dante (2001) on navigation.

Project documents were the second category of documents reviewed and are believed to provide important insights into on-the-ground ways to address the identified transboundary issues. Examples of important documents in this category included the *Multi-Sector Investment Opportunities Analysis* for the Zambezi (World Bank 2010), the Uganda-Egypt Aquatic Weed Control Project (1998) and the Lake Victoria Environmental Management Project for Eastern Africa (1994).

The third category of documents examined was transboundary water treaties. A content analysis of existing transboundary water treaties was conducted in order to determine if and how governance principles for flooding, navigation and aquatic weeds are adopted into shared water treaties and applied to river management. The primary data source and the largest known collection of such treaties is provided by the Transboundary Freshwater Dispute Database of Oregon State University (OSU). Treaties signed that deal with flood control, water quality and navigation were included in the analysis; further, the analysis was limited to post-1950 treaties as these were believed to provide examples most relevant to current conditions. This resulted in the selection and examination of 106 transboundary water treaties.

Identification of mechanisms for coping with transboundary issues

To identify mechanisms for responding to relevant transboundary issues, water treaties and project and academic documents were examined for text that captures ways in which countries coped with flooding, weeds and navigation. In some cases, mechanisms were mentioned explicitly and therefore their identification was straightforward; the 1961 *Treaty relating to the cooperative development of the water resources of the Columbia River Basin*, for example, explicitly establishes a joint committee to monitor water quality. In other cases, text needed to be scrutinised and interpreted to understand how it precisely addressed one of the three issues of focus.

Two additional clarifications related to the mechanism of the identification process are worth noting. First, the compilation of different instruments led to the realisation that certain instruments could be subdivided. For example, one way of dealing with floods and navigation – construction of infrastructure – can be achieved through several finance-sharing options. To account for this detail, certain instruments were presented along with sub-instruments. Second, it was apparent that descriptions of the same mechanism might have been couched in different language. For simplicity, mechanisms were distilled to common, simple language.

Organising mechanisms according to level of cooperation

Once a set of mechanisms for cooperation was identified, such mechanisms were ordered according to the level of cooperation that they embody. To generate guidance for organising mechanisms according to the level of cooperation they manifest, literature on the topic was reviewed (Sadoff and Grey 2005; Mirumachi 2007; Zeitoun and Mirumachi 2008; Leb 2013). This review yielded three frameworks that bore many similarities, yet also possessed notable differences (Table 10.1).

Sadoff and Grey (2005) divided cooperation into three stages, which are largely consistent with those outlined by Leb (2013). The first stage captures mechanisms for which implementation requires interstate *coordination* but relatively few institutional efforts. For example, jointly gathering and exchanging data and information require coordination (Sadoff and Grey 2005). The second stage captures *collaboration*, which results when national plans are adjusted either to secure gains or to mitigate harm in another riparian country (Sadoff and Grey 2005). Diverting water upstream may, for example, effectively alleviate flood risks downstream. The third stage reflects mechanisms that require effective *joint action* and riparians acting as partners in the design, investment and implementation of transboundary river development (Sadoff and Grey 2005). This level of cooperation is often formalised by a joint body with a mandate.

Mirumachi (2007) and Zeitoun and Mirumachi (2008) often speak of interactions that portray both a gradational cooperation spectrum on one axis and a conflict spectrum on the other. The cooperation spectrum advances from *ad hoc* cooperation to cooperation on technical issues, then proceeds to risk-averse cooperation to risk-taking cooperation. Their cooperative steps effectively

Table 10.1 Levels of cooperation

	From no to low cooperation		High cooperation	
Sadoff and Grey (2005)	Unilateral	Coordination	Collaboration	Joint activity
Mirumachi (2007); Zeitoun and Mirumachi (2008)	Ad hoc	Technical	Risk-averting	Risk-taking
Synthesized approach	No cooperation	Coordination and assistance; often technical	(Active) collaboration	Joint action

incorporate the element of risk, which has been identified as a key factor in state decision-making related to engagement on transboundary waters.

Ultimately, this chapter adopts a synthesis of the previous approaches. It structures cooperation into three categories: i) coordination and assistance, often technical; ii) active collaboration; and iii) joint actions. Level of risk was a more difficult topic to unambiguously assess, and hence it was not directly included in the synthesis. While this structure provides guidance for organising mechanisms according to their level of cooperation, it should be noted that (i) options for classification are not predetermined or self-evident and (ii) additional criteria would be required to measure the quality of cooperation.

Sequencing and decision points

Sequencing cooperation

In an attempt to provide practical guidance to riparians on the phase-in of water cooperation in the Shire, the way in which this cooperation is sequenced was examined. Careful consideration of sequencing allows riparians to select focal points for cooperation, to engage in a consensus-based bargaining process and to move from one equilibrium to another (Snidal 2002). Sequencing generally also facilitates the process of international cooperation as it breaks down decision-making into a series of small steps while allowing parties to update previous arrangements and expand cooperation (Young 2010: 1).

Ultimately, three 'bundles' were generated that reflect an issue-aggregated package of mechanisms in each of the three stages of cooperation. A first bundle reflects cooperation that is of mainly a coordinative nature. A second bundle reflects cooperation of a more collaborative nature. A final bundle reflects action-oriented cooperation. To develop each of these three groups, mechanisms reflecting coordination-oriented cooperation on each of the three issues were packaged, mechanisms on collaboration-based cooperation on each of the three issues were packaged, and mechanisms reflecting action-oriented cooperation on each of the three issues were packaged. When packaging mechanisms, focus was devoted to those mechanisms that received more frequent usage – as gauged by the number of examples found on each.

Decision points within issues

Packaging mechanisms according to level of cooperation reveals decision points and necessitates choices, as certain mechanisms offset or conflict with one another. In the context of each bundle, therefore, it is necessary to highlight decision points and to focus attention on specific issues for which negotiation between states could be targeted. An overview of the decision points in each issue of focus (floods, aquatic weeds and navigation) highlights the scope for negotiation within each issue.

Decision points across issues

A final point examined is the potential for cross-issue synergy that can be achieved by aggregating decision points across issues. Linkage between different policy domains is indeed a commonly applied strategy in international negotiations in order to leverage negotiation positions or to widen the range of politically desirable options (Haas 1980; Katz and Fischhendler 2011). The idea of issue linkage initially emerged to solve the problem of asymmetries among countries (Carraro *et al.* 2003). The strategy has proven particularly useful in creating leverage in the unbalanced relations between upstream and downstream countries, in which upstream riparians often have less incentive to cooperate (Wolf 1997; Dinar 2006).

To identify the potential incentive of parties to link the negotiations on different issues instead of negotiating on the issues separately and to determine opportunities that can be harnessed through such negotiation, the bargaining position of each party was assessed per issue. For floods, aquatic weeds and navigation the relative advantage was estimated per riparian, on the basis of geography and perceived country interests. It was then considered how the imbalance in bargaining power in one issue could be traded off with a (reverse) imbalance in bargaining power on another issue.

Results

Flood control mechanisms

Nine major instruments for flood control at a transboundary level were identified (Table 10.2). Six such instruments could be considered coordination-oriented. Two such instruments could be considered to manifest collaboration between countries. One measure reflected joint action between countries and contained several variants associated with the division of costs.

Coordination and assistance

Creation of a joint committee for flood control is the most frequently used mechanism for responding to floods at a transboundary level. These committees often have an inclusive

Figure 10.3 Flooding in the Lower Shire in January 2015
Photo: Geoffrey Chavula

Table 10.2 Institutional mechanisms for flood control

	Mechanisms	Number of examples
Coordination and assistance	Create a joint committee for flood control	14
	Exchange of flood-related data and information	7
	Undertake joint research on flood management and mitigation	6
	Provide mutual assistance for both emergency operations and medium-term and long-term flood control	6
	Agree to prior notification on river development that affects flow regime and influences flood risk	4
	Adopt a conflict resolution principle to mitigate disputes caused by transboundary flooding (e.g., negotiation, mediation, arbitration, adjudication)	4
Collaboration	Develop and implement early flood-warning systems and rapid response mechanisms	7
	Undertake joint monitoring of river flow (and water levels)	5
Joint action	Jointly construct, operate and maintain flood control infrastructure based on a suitable cost-sharing principle:	18
	a) Proportional division (based upon estimated or previously determined costs or arranged per jurisdiction)	8
	b) Equally divided	3
	c) Side payment and payments according to benefit	3
	d) Unforeseen costs	3

mandate to facilitate implementation of some or all of the institutional tools available for dealing with floods. In the 1952 *Convention between the government of the Union of Soviet Socialist Republics and the government of the Romanian People's Republics concerning measures to prevent floods and to regulate the water regime of the River Prut*, a committee was mandated to coordinate operation and maintenance (O&M) of infrastructural works, prepare flood protection programmes and studies, follow-up on monitoring activities and serve as a platform for data and information exchange and effective communication between the parties.

Also emerging as frequently utilised mechanisms to cope with floods were: i) exchange of flood-related data and information; ii) joint research on flood management and mitigation; and iii) provision of mutual assistance. Exchange of flood-related information and knowledge, including exchange of forecast models or precipitation and variability data, may further assist states in the prediction, prevention and control of floods. In the 1987 *Treaty on environmentally sound management of the common Zambezi River System*, Mozambique, Zambia, Tanzania, Botswana and Zimbabwe agreed to develop real-time data of the basin in terms of precipitation, streamflow, floodplains, lakes and groundwater levels. Joint research on flood management and mitigation can be widely or narrowly mandated, but generally includes the agreement to carry out joint feasibility studies for proposed infrastructure, for flood prevention and control programmes and to further develop climate, weather and forecasting models. Commitment to provide mutual assistance in case of emergencies and for medium- and long-term flood control has also been utilised.

Less notable mechanisms for coping with floods at a transboundary level included prior notification on river development and adoption of a conflict resolution mechanism. Prior notification for river development influences any unilateral development of the river, particularly those that may affect its flow or increase flood risks downstream, for example, by introducing new infrastructure or removing sediments from riverbanks. Adoption of conflict resolution to settle disputes caused by flood damage can specify the precise mechanism utilised for resolving any disagreements associated with flood damages. For example, in the case of the *1960 Indus waters treaty between the Government of India, the Government of Pakistan and the International Bank for Reconstruction and Development*, states agreed to consultation and third-party mediation if, owing to heavy floods, damage should occur to any link canals, thereby affecting irrigation capacities.

Collaboration

Collaborative mechanisms for responding to floods included joint early warning and rapid response mechanisms, and joint monitoring of river flow and water levels. Joint early warning and rapid response mechanisms may be implemented by creating extra storage capacity upstream, adopting an automatic flood warning system or forming an agreement to immediately notify the downstream party. Joint monitoring of riverflow and water levels implies that states carry out daily (manual or automatic) monitoring of precipitation and gauging sites and share these data with other parties.

Joint action

Joint action-oriented mechanisms for coping with floods included only one instrument: to jointly construct, operate and maintain flood-control infrastructure based on a suitable cost-sharing principle.[7] While infrastructure is constructed, O&M can certainly go a long way toward reducing the adverse effects of floods. Financial costs associated with such infrastructure are often difficult to mobilise in resources-constrained contexts – mobilisation of such funds is further complicated by the ways in which costs are shared across countries. Evidence exists on several cost-sharing options:

- *Proportionate division of costs* is the most common way in which flood infrastructure costs are shared. Proportionate division of costs is associated either with estimated or previously determined costs, or with each party bearing the costs of works performed in its own jurisdiction.
- *Equal cost-sharing*, for example, to equally share operation costs of hydropower or other flood-related infrastructure.
- *Cost-sharing according to benefit*, using side-payments, where one side agrees to pay the other side for the delivery of a future service. Under the 1961 Treaty relating to cooperative development of the water resources of the Columbia River Basin, the US agrees to pay Canada for the operational costs upon the commencement of flood control. In another case, according to the agreement between the People's Republic of Bulgaria and the Republic of Turkey concerning cooperation in the use of the waters of rivers flowing through the territory of both countries, states may request hydrological data from one another upon payment (including paying the other party for collecting those data).
- *Unforeseen expenditures* and circumstances can be taken into account, for example, by agreeing to share future costs upon mutual agreement or dividing them according to earlier agreed terms.

Water quality and aquatic weeds mechanisms

Eight major instruments for controlling aquatic weeds at a transboundary level were identified (Table 10.3). Four such instruments could be considered coordination-oriented. Three such instruments could be considered to manifest collaboration between countries. One measure reflected joint action between countries; this action-oriented measure contained two variants associated with the division of costs.

Coordination and assistance

Coordination and assistance mechanisms to address aquatic weeds include: (i) the creation of a joint committee; (ii) the adoption of shared water-quality standard; (iii) the conduct of joint research; and (iv) review and amendment. The most common instrument to respond to aquatic weed proliferation at a transboundary level is the creation of a joint committee for water-quality control that may include the task of conducting technical studies or delegating this to specialised subcommittees, and providing a communication platform for all relevant agencies in the field of water pollution control. The adoption of shared standards on water quality or aquatic weed control may serve to harmonise approaches to aquatic weeds, so that efforts to maintain certain standards on aquatic weeds in one country are not undermined by those of another country. Joint research based on shared data on water quality and information may assist in the development of joint water-quality control programmes and water treatment methods. Mechanisms for amendment and review allow parties to adjust a treaty and update it according to new scientific knowledge or technological innovations. Provision of water quality, for example, may be reviewed based on the effectiveness of pollution-control programmes.

Table 10.3 Mechanisms for water quality and aquatic weed control

	Mechanisms	*Number of examples*
Coordination and assistance	Form joint committee for water quality/aquatic weed control	18
	Adopt shared standards on water quality/aquatic weed control	10
	Undertake joint research based on shared water-quality data and information	6
	Review water-quality control practices and propose improvements as necessary	6
Collaboration	Undertake joint monitoring and surveillance of water quality/ aquatic weeds infestation	6
	Develop and implement joint early warning and response systems to treat water pollution/aquatic weed proliferation	6
	Implement joint targets for (proposed) water-quality control programmes	3
Joint action	Implement water quality/aquatic weed control and treatment programmes based on:	17
	(a) Cost-sharing and side payments	10
	(b) Other financial arrangements	7

Collaboration

Collaborative mechanisms for coping with aquatic weeds at a transboundary level include: i) joint monitoring and surveillance of water quality; ii) implementation of joint early warning and response systems; and iii) implementation of shared targets for water quality. Joint monitoring of water quality may serve to evaluate water-quality trends, to identify emerging problems, to develop additional water-quality controls or to adopt enforcement measures if needed. Joint early warning systems and emergency intervention procedures in the case of water pollution are already adopted in a number of basins. In the *1990 Convention of the International Commission for the protection of the Elbe*, early warning strategies have been developed according to national experiences and existing response practices. In several cases, states also agreed on the implementation of joint targets such as the achievement of water-quality objectives or the identification of programmes and measures to enhance quality control.

Joint action

Joint action to control aquatic weeds at a transboundary level consists of jointly implementing a programme to reduce or eliminate the abundance of weeds. In Lake Victoria, for example, the *Lake Victoria Environmental Management Project for Eastern Africa*, which combines biological and mechanical control strategies, has been implemented since 1994. Financing of such a programme may be achieved through cost-sharing or other financial arrangements. Cost-sharing in this field may enable the instalment of water treatment infrastructure, the costs for employing personnel necessary to carry out tasks of water-quality control and/or regulations regarding tax exemptions for these personnel. It may also support associated costs of studies and research on water pollution, the costs of implementing such studies and sharing the operation costs of a water-quality commission.

Navigation mechanisms

Seven major instruments for navigation at a transboundary level were identified (Table 10.4). Four such instruments could be considered coordination-oriented. Two such instruments could be considered to manifest collaboration between countries. One measure reflected joint action between countries.

Table 10.4 Mechanisms for navigation

	Mechanisms	Number of examples
Coordination and assistance	Adoption of freedom of navigation	7
	Adoption of uniform navigation rules and regulations	6
	Adopt conflict-resolution principle to settle disputes caused by navigation	6
	Create joint navigation committee	5
Collaboration	Jointly maintain river navigability	8
	Apply a mutual tax regime	5
Joint action	Undertake navigation works based on cost-sharing	2

Coordination and assistance

Coordination-oriented instruments related to transboundary navigation include: i) freedom of navigation; ii) uniform navigation rules; iii) joint navigation committee; and iv) conflict-resolution principle. Freedom of navigation is a long-accepted legal principle for the management of international rivers. The *International Commission for the Navigation of the River Congo*, created by the Act of Berlin in 1885, first introduced the principle to African rivers (Caponera Dante 2001). Freedom of navigation may further apply to contracting parties only or also to third states (e.g., non-signatory basin-riparians).

States should stick to uniform rules for navigation such as joint rules for pilotage, for loading and unloading and joint traffic and safety regulations. In case the treaty only governs a part of the basin, the text may prescribe coordination with previously established basin-level or commission rules. Adoption of a conflict-resolution principle can help resolve disagreements over navigation and settle judicial matters, including the persecution of vessels that committed an offence, damage claims to vessels and infrastructure or to water quality. A navigation committee is not too dissimilar from other water-related committees described above.

Collaboration

Collaborative mechanisms for coping with navigation issues at a transboundary level include: i) jointly maintaining river navigability; and ii) applying a mutual tax regime. Commitment to maintain river navigability implies the duty of each party to install and maintain navigation and kilometre marks, remove debris or blockages, restore dikes and generally improve navigability within its jurisdiction. Few treaties specifically prohibit unilateral developments that may affect navigation. Application of a mutual tax regime for river use requires more bargaining and coordination efforts from the parties involved. Treaties may either stipulate conditions for tax exemption, which apply to import of construction material and equipment, land and water vehicles or spare parts for navigation purposes. The *Convention Related to the Statute of the Senegal River* of 1964 stipulates explicitly that there may be no taxation, only retributions for services provided. Another option is to charge uniform tolls and dues for river use, calculated beforehand and/or on the basis of construction, maintenance and administration costs.

Joint action

Joint action for transboundary navigation is heavily focused on jointly undertaking navigation works, which often come at a larger cost than the mechanism described above. The costs of navigation works include dredging, deepening or widening of the riverbedding, construction of navigation canals and the removal of obstacles, which are regularly shared proportionally by dividing the expected costs beforehand and/or by dividing them per jurisdiction, for example, with each party bearing the costs of the works performed in their territory.

Sequencing cooperation

To summarise the three stages of cooperation across the three issues of focus and lay a basis for synthesising one aggregated bundle of instruments for each stage, central elements of each stage of cooperation are shown below (Figure 10.4). In what follows, a bundle of mechanisms is described that reflects a set of instruments for first-stage cooperation (coordination); a second bundle of mechanisms is then outlined that reflects a bundle of second-stage cooperation

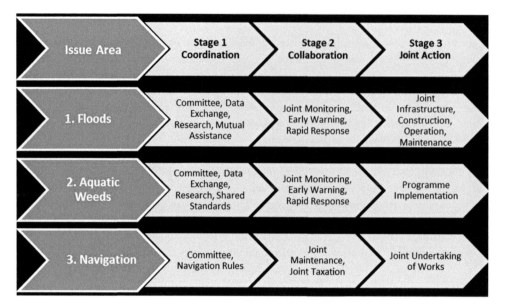

Figure 10.4 Sequencing cooperation
Source: Authors

(collaboration); and a third bundle of mechanisms captures a third stage of cooperation (joint action). Should riparians endeavour to scale up cooperation, they may wish to start with stage 1 and subsequently scale up to stages 2 and 3.

First stage cooperation: elements of transboundary water coordination in the Shire

A first stage of water cooperation in the Shire could include a joint committee dealing with data and information exchange and joint research on issues of flooding, aquatic weeds and navigation. This multipurpose body potentially results from, and coordinates, the activities of sectoral units that already exist in each issue area. In other words, the body may gather data and information from sectoral agencies that have in-house expertise on each of the issue areas in focus, such as the ministry of transport or the environmental protection department. Based on such coordination activities, the joint body could align modalities for mutual assistance in flood-related emergencies, and establish shared navigation rules and standards on aquatic weeds. Sectoral agencies at the national level may assist in the implementation of such mechanisms within their jurisdiction.

Second stage cooperation: elements of transboundary water collaboration in the Shire

A second stage of water cooperation in the Shire could include joint monitoring of river flow for floods and water quality, including weeds. It could further extend to the development of an early warning and rapid response mechanism in the event of flooding or aquatic weed infestation. As the operation of hydropower plants may be largely obstructed by the growth of weeds, riparians could consider partially financing the costs of aquatic weed response and removal through revenue from hydropower – this may in fact be cost-effective if weed reduction enables an increase in hydropower production. Related to navigation, stage 2 cooperation could include joint maintenance of the river to enable navigation if and when possible, as well as joint taxation if the riparians elect to apply taxes to vessels along the river.

Third stage cooperation: elements of joint action in the Shire

A final stage of cooperation could include the construction, O&M of joint infrastructure for flood control, joint programme implementation for aquatic weed control, and the joint undertaking of works for navigation. Infrastructure, works and programmes for these three objectives are clearly related, and it would therefore make sense to consider multipurpose transboundary infrastructure that facilitates all three objectives. It would also make sense to consider incorporating other objectives into the planning of such infrastructure – most namely, hydropower. Such a major endeavour would likely require partnership with a notable financier such as the World Bank, AfDB or China.

Decision points within issues

While the three bundles would seem to present many no-lose options for consolidation of transboundary instruments (e.g., committee creation, joint research, data exchange), some decisions would likely need to be made. Critical decision points that would be triggered by operationalising these bundles are identified as follows: i) whether navigation would be free or taxed, and, if taxed, what system would be followed; ii) the nature of cost-sharing to support any infrastructure for the control of floods or aquatic weeds (equally or proportionally divided, side payments, according to benefit and/or accounting for future costs); iii) the type of conflict -resolution principle (negotiation, mediation, arbitration, adjudication); and iv) membership and decision-making rules for joint bodies.

Of these four issues, the choice of the navigation regime and the adoption of cost-sharing principles are expected to be more contentious than conflict resolution and governance rules for joint bodies. On navigation, Mozambique may prefer the adoption of a tax regime so it can earn revenue from Malawian vessels passing through Mozambican territory, while Malawi would clearly benefit from a free navigation regime. On cost sharing for the construction, O&M of joint infrastructure or programmes for flood control or weed removal, Malawi may request compensation in the form of side payments for its efforts in alleviating flood and weed infestation risks upstream.

Operationalisation of any system of side payments requires careful thought. Considering the risks that aquatic weed infestations pose for the functioning of water treatment plants, hydropower stations, irrigation systems (and as a consequence agricultural production), Malawi has a vested interest in reducing the growth of weeds. With proposed plans to expand its irrigation potential, Mozambique finds itself in a similar position.

Decision points across issues

Interestingly, decision points may also present opportunities for synergy across issues and key pillars around which countries can negotiate (Table 10.5). It would indeed appear that – due to its upstream position – Malawi has more bargaining power on the issue of floods and aquatic weeds. Conversely, Mozambique has more bargaining power on the issue of navigation, as the country will need to endorse and accommodate the passage of Malawian vessels through its territory. As such, scope for deals to be struck could lie through trading across these specific issues.

Table 10.5 Negotiating across issues

	Floods	*Weeds*	*Navigation*
Bargaining power advantage	Malawi	Malawi	Mozambique
Possible Malawi interest	Flood control	Weed removal and control	Free uninhibited navigation
Possible Mozambique interest	Flood early warning and control	Weed removal and control	No or taxed navigation

At least two 'deals' would appear to manifest themselves through cross-issue negotiation. A first 'deal' involves flood control for navigation. Malawi could assist in reducing flood control downstream and Mozambique could, in return, safeguard river navigability and maintenance in its part of the Shire. A second 'deal' involves weed control for navigation. While the control of aquatic weeds in the Shire is in the interest of both parties, it is likely that most weeds originate in Malawi and flow down to Mozambique rather than vice versa. As such, greater control of weeds upstream will benefit Mozambique. In return, Mozambique could allow the navigation of Malawian vessels through its territory.

A final point worth focusing on is the comparative potential for progress toward cooperation on three issues. A review of riparian interests reveals greatest alignment on the issue of control of aquatic weeds. While upstream Malawi may have more bargaining power advantage on this issue, there would be a clear and common interest to reduce the proliferation of aquatic weeds in the Shire. As such, control of aquatic weeds may require the least negotiation and, therefore, hold the most potential for catalysing progress toward cooperation.

Discussion

The chapter identified transboundary water issues in the Shire catchment shared between Malawi and Mozambique, reviewed global experience to pinpoint instruments that have been used to cope with such issues in other basins, and synthesised three bundles of options that are tailored to the Shire. A first coordination-oriented form of cooperation would include the establishment of a joint committee that could serve as a platform for data exchange and research on the issues of flooding, management of aquatic weeds and rules for navigation. A second collaboration-oriented form of cooperation would focus on adopting joint flood and weed monitoring practices, and possibly agreement on a joint taxation and maintenance programme for navigation. Finally, a third action-oriented form of cooperation would centre on the construction, O&M of joint infrastructural works.

This chapter also flagged decision points within and across issues that need to be negotiated to achieve meaningful cooperation. Within issues, potentially contentious points hinge around the nature of a cost-sharing regime for navigation and the modalities of cost sharing for any infrastructure or river maintenance programmes. Across issues, key scope for progress may be achieved through finding ways for riparians to satisfy each other's interests for mutual benefit. For example, upstream Malawi could incorporate downstream Mozambique more concretely into flood planning and management activities, and in return Mozambique could offer concessions to Malawian vessels that wish to navigate from Nsanje to the Indian Ocean (and vice versa).

More broadly, by proposing a more practical and fit-for-purpose approach to transboundary water cooperation, the chapter marks a move away from models commonly rolled out in the developing world. Indeed, institutional development in transboundary basins is often undertaken in collaboration with bilateral aid agencies and development actors, who frequently draw from 'textbook' models for water organisations (Merrey 2009; Söderbaum 2015). This chapter, in contrast, proposes a 'bottom-up' process of institutional formation – tailored to the priority issues of one specific basin – in order to help complement the roll-out of more conventional 'blueprint' approaches.

The approach utilised in this chapter is believed to be somewhat out-of-the-box. While other studies (Mostert 2005; Merrey 2009; Söderbaum 2015) highlight the limitations of exporting blueprint models that are not customised to differences in hydrology, hydrogeology, demography and socioeconomics of specific basins, these rarely provide basin-specific guidance that can be utilised for implementation. For example, Mostert (2005) encouraged the donor community to increase public participation and to build upon ongoing developments in river basin management; Merrey (2009) called for focus on identifying 'African models' of transboundary water governance; Söderbaum (2015) suggested operating through regional economic communities.

As for specific constructive ways forward in the Shire, the following three recommendations are provided. First, start small. Avoid the temptation for more ambitious cooperation straight-away, and instead begin with low-intensity coordinative cooperation that can identify the best opportunity for upscaling. Second, to catalyse cooperation, exploit respective riparian advantages and interests through issue-bundling as appropriate. Third, and more broadly, complement and coordinate adaptive and bottom-up cooperation with basin-wide water cooperation.

Ultimately, the set of issues identified through consultation in this chapter, and set of instruments used to respond to such issues, diverge noticeably from conventional approaches often employed. More effective and sustainable institutions are likely to be those built in response to contextual realities rather than in response to global norms, and contextual realities may be at scales other than the basin.

In conclusion, it would seem that the proliferation of cooperation at a full-basin scale in recent decades can be associated with an increase in softer, more politicised, and arguably more precarious cooperation – reflected in the number of RBOs struggling to secure riparian funding. It would nonetheless appear that meaningful and practical water cooperation occurs at more local scales. To the extent possible, one wonders about the potential for meaningful local water cooperation to trickle up to the basin scale. While ultimately good water management is likely to require harmonisation of basin and local developments, it seems the potential to harness and build on momentum at the local level may not be receiving the attention it deserves. The bottom line here is that there is no generic best approach to balancing scales in transboundary river basin management; recommendations provided immediately above indeed call for adapting to context. The evidence in this chapter thus highlights a potential role and management modalities for transboundary tributary-level water cooperation in the Shire. Contextualised in basin frameworks, local issue-responsive water cooperation may resonate elsewhere if modalities are examined there as well.

Conclusion: role for ZAMCOM

This chapter has highlighted options for strengthening subbasin cooperation to address challenges faced by two Zambezi riparians. Importantly, addressing challenges at a subbasin level comprises one way to foster equitable and reasonable use of Zambezi's waters and improve sustainable development in the basin – points which are central to ZAMCOM's mandate. As such, while not conventionally considered part of a basin-wide RBO's mandate, ZAMCOM may seek to identify opportunities for, and support, subbasin cooperation where it is appropriate. Notably, subbasin cooperation is also emerging on another Zambezi subbasin: the Songwe. Additional opportunities for subbasin cooperation may be identified. Such opportunities reflect avenues to improve conditions in the basin that should not be overlooked.

Related to the first point, ZAMCOM may seek to *coordinate and facilitate* subbasin cooperation. Coordination could take various forms, but could cover areas such as hosting an annual workshop focused on particular subbasins; such an effort could foster horizontal experience-sharing among organisations seeking to improve conditions in subbasins, as well as vertical exchange of experiences between ZAMCOM and subbasin RBOs. Facilitation could likewise take various forms but could include assessment of capacity needs and provision of in-demand training to actors in particular subbasins. Greater interaction with such subbasin actors could indeed lead to mutual benefits, as ZAMCOM may grow more grounded in more localised transboundary issues and ways to address them.

ZAMCOM may also seek to *backstop and regulate* subbasin cooperation through data provision and environmental regulation. Backstopping may take the form of provision of data and analyses relevant to decision-making at a subbasin scale; given the decision support system (DSS) project that is about to take effect, thought may indeed be given to undertaking modelling efforts at nested scales that correspond to subbasins. Regulation may take the form of environmental assessments to ensure that potential developments in subbasins will not inflict undue harm on the environment.

A fourth way in which ZAMCOM can support cooperation on subbasins is to *mediate and broker* compromise solutions where such opportunities present themselves. In the Shire, Mozambique possesses a geographic advantage on navigation while Malawi has a geographic advantage on flood control. While riparians may find ways to reach a mutually beneficial agreement on their own, in which Malawi provides early warning – and potentially increased water storage – to reduce floods in Mozambique and Mozambique allows free navigation of Malawian vessels, it may equally be that an external push is required through an outside actor perceived as an honest broker. ZAMCOM may play the role of honest broker.

A final way in which ZAMCOM may wish to engage with budding cooperation in the basin is to *learn from it*. Compilation of cooperative experiences in the basin may indeed create a powerful set of evidence that can filter up and potentially provide guidance to basin-level approaches for strengthening cooperation. Mining actual cooperative experiences in specific geographies in the basin may generate guidance and lessons that may complement the nature of those obtained from international best practice on transboundary water management.

Notes

1   Input was also sought from other notable actors such as the World Bank, the African Development Bank and the European Commission.
2   Major floods indeed occurred in 2001, 2007, 2012 and again in 2015.
3   Although the chapter often refers interchangeably to 'aquatic weeds' and 'water hyacinth', there is specific concern regarding the invasive species of water hyacinth.
4   A recognised RAMSAR site is a 'wetland of international importance'.
5   Evidence suggests that the Lower Shire was used for navigational purposes prior to 1970 (Shela 2000).
6   Personal communication from Cpt. Gerald Mbiro (Operator of Kamuzu Barrage), 17 May 2014.
7   Infrastructure for transboundary flood control is usually constructed upon mutual consent (which forms the basis of the treaty) and as a consequence is maintained and operated jointly.

References

AfDB (African Development Bank). 2011. Feasibility study for the Shire-Zambezi Waterways Development Project: Appraisal Report. Available at www.africanwaterfacility.org/fileadmin/uploads/awf/Projects/AWF-Project-appraisal-report-MULTIN-SHIREZAMBEZI.pdf

Atkins. 2012. Shire Integrated Flood Risk Management Project. Volume I – Final Report. Bristol, England: Atkins Limited.

Bakker, M. 2007. Transboundary river floods: Vulnerability of continents, international river basins and countries. PhD dissertation. Oregon State University.

Bakker, M. 2009. Transboundary river floods: Examining countries, international river basins and continents. *Water Policy* 11(3): 269–288.

Beilfuss, R. 2012. *A risky climate for southern African Hydro*. Berkeley: International Rivers.

Bhat, A. 2008. The politics of model maintenance: The Murray Darling and Brantas river basins compared. *Water Alternatives* 1(2): 201.

Caponera Dante, A. 2001. Patterns of cooperation in international law: Principles and institutions. *Natural Resources Journal* 25: 536–587.

Carraro, C., Marchiori, C. and Oreffice, S. 2003. Endogenous minimum participation in international environmental treaties. Available at www.feem.it/userfiles/attach/Publication/NDL2003/NDL2003-113.pdf

Chidanti-Malunga, J. 2011. Adaptive strategies to climate change in southern Malawi. *Physics and Chemistry of the Earth, Parts A/B/C* 36(14): 1043–1046.

Collier, P., Conway, G. and Venables, T. 2008. Climate change and Africa. *Oxford Review of Economic Policy* 24(2): 337–353.

Cooley, H. and Gleick, P.H. 2011. Climate-proofing transboundary water agreements. *Hydrological Sciences Journal* 56(4): 711–718.

Dinar, S. 2006. Assessing side-payment and cost-sharing patterns in international water agreements: The geographic and economic connection. *Political Geography* 25(4): 412–437.

GEF (Global Environmental Fund). 2005. Lake Victoria Environmental Management Project. *Lake Victoria Environmental Management Project*. Available at www.thegef.org

Giordano, M.A. 2003. Managing the quality of international rivers: Global principles and basin practice. *Nat. Resources J.* 43: 111.

Haas, E.B. 1980. Why collaborate? Issue-linkage and international regimes. *World Politics* 32(3): 357–405.

Hooper, B.P. 2011. Integrated water resources management and river basin governance. *Journal of Contemporary Water Research and Education* 126(1): 3.

INBO-ANBO Project. No date. *Development of IWRM performance indicators for African transboundary basins management*. International Network of Basin Organizations, African Network of Basin Organizations, supported by International Office of Water, Ecologic.

Katz, D. and Fischhendler, I. 2011. Spatial and temporal dynamics of linkage strategies in Arab–Israeli water negotiations. *Political Geography* 30(1): 13–24.

Kaunda, C.S. and Mtalo, F. 2013. Impacts of environmental degradation and climate change on electricity generation in Malawi. *International Journal of Energy and Environment* 4(1): 481–496.

Kistin, E.J. and Ashton, P.J. 2008. Adapting to change in transboundary rivers: An analysis of treaty flexibility on the Orange-Senqu River Basin. *Water Resources Development* 24(3): 385–400.

Kranz, N., Vorwerk, A. and Interwies, E. 2005. Transboundary river basin management regimes: The Amu Darya basin case study. Report of the NeWater project. Berlin: Ecologic.

Lautze, J. and Giordano, M. 2005. Transboundary water law in Africa: Development, nature, and geography. *Natural Resources Journal* 45(4): 1053–1087.

Lautze, J., Wegerich, K., Kazbekov, J. and Yakubov, M. 2013. International river basin organizations: Variation, options and insights. *Water International* 38(1): 30–42.

Leb, C. 2013. *Cooperation in the law of transboundary water resources*. Cambridge: Cambridge University Press.

Merrey, D.J. 2009. African models for transnational river basin organisations in Africa: An unexplored dimension. *Water Alternatives* 2(2): 183.

Mirumachi, N. 2007. Introducing transboundary waters interaction nexus (TWINS): Model of interaction dynamics in transboundary waters. In: *Third International Workshop on Hydro-Hegemony*, pp. 12–13.

Mostert, E. 2005. *How can international donors promote transboundary water management?* Bonn: Deutsches Institut für Entwicklungspolitik.

Navarro, L.A. and Phiri, G. (eds.) 2000. *Water hyacinth in Africa and the Middle East: A survey of problems and solutions*. IDRC.

Oregon State University. Transboundary Freshwater Dispute Database. Department of Geosciences. Available at www.transboundarywaters.orst.edu

Peel, M.C., Pegram, G.G. and McMahon, T.A. 2004. Global analysis of runs of annual precipitation and runoff equal to or below the median: Run length. *International Journal of Climatology* 24(7): 807–822.

Rangeley, R., Thiam, B.M., Andersen, R.A. and Lyle, C. 1994. International river basin organizations in sub-Saharan Africa. *World Bank Technical Paper* 250.

RBA Centre (Centre on River Basin Administration, Analysis and Management). 1999. *Recommendations and guidelines on sustainable river basin management.* Workshop Report on the International Workshop on River Basin Management, The Hague, 27–29 October. Delft: RBA Centre, Delft University of Technology.

Sadoff, C.W. and Grey, D. 2005. Cooperation on international rivers: A continuum for securing and sharing benefits. *Water International* 30(4): 420–427.

Schmeier, S. and Schulze, S. 2010. Governing environmental change in international river basins: The role of river basin organizations. *Berlin Conference on the Human Dimensions of Global Environmental Change.* Vol. 8.

Schmeier, S. 2012. *Governing international watercourses: River basin organizations and the sustainable governance of internationally shared rivers and lakes.* Oxford: Routledge.

Shah, T., Makin, I. and Sakthivadivel, R. 2001. Limits to leapfrogging: Issues in transposing successful river basin management institutions in the developing world. In: *Intersectoral management of river basins,* (ed.) Abernethy, C., pp. 89–114.

Shela, N.O. 2000. Naturalisation of Lake Malawi levels and Shire River flows. 1st WARFSA/WaterNet Symposium, Sustainable Use of Water Resources, Maputo, 1–2 November. Available at www.waternet online.ihe.nl/downloads/uploads/symposium/mozambique-2000/SHELA.PDF,

Snidal, D. 2002. Rational choice and international relations. *Handbook of International Relations* 73: 74–76.

Söderbaum, F. 2015. Rethinking the politics of transboundary water management. *International Journal of Water Governance* 3(1): 121–132.

Timberlake, J. 1998. *Biodiversity of the Zambezi Basin wetlands. Phase 1: Review and preliminary assessment of available information. Volume 1: Main report.* Consultancy report for IUCN-Regional Office for Southern Africa. Harare, Zimbabwe.

Wolf, A.T. 1997. International water conflict resolution lesson learned from cooperative analysis. *International Journal of Water Resources Management* 13(3): 333–365.

World Bank. 2010. *The Zambesi River Basin: A multi-sector investment opportunities analysis.* Volume 1, Summary report.

Young, O.R. 2010. *Institutional dynamics: Emergent patterns in international environmental governance.* Cambridge, MA: MIT Press.

Zeitoun, M. and Mirumachi, N. 2008. Transboundary water interaction I: Reconsidering conflict and cooperation. *International Environmental Agreements: Politics, Law and Economics* 8(4): 297–316.

11

Water security

*Davison Saruchera, Jonathan Lautze, Luxon Nhamo
and Bunyod Holmatov*

Key messages

- Defining water security is important in order to guide its practice. In this chapter, water security is assessed within a framework that encompasses five key dimensions: environment, basic human needs, vulnerability, agriculture and energy. This framework uses relevant and measurable indicators to assess the basin's current water security, and identifies sectors that require urgent interventions.

- With the exception of the environment, the Zambezi Basin faces severe challenges to water security. Vulnerability (i.e., susceptibility to droughts and floods) and agricultural water security are the basin's major challenges; provision of basic water supply and sanitation is also a major challenge in several countries, notably Angola, Tanzania and Mozambique.
- Achieving water security will require investment to reduce vulnerability (e.g., construction of water storage infrastructure) and improvements in agricultural water use. Applied research focused on alternative water management options, in partnership with regional institutions like the International Water Management Institute (IWMI), the Development Bank of Southern Africa and the Southern Africa Development Community (SADC), can enhance the implementation of such investments.
- The Zambezi Watercourse Commission (ZAMCOM) can play a role in improving water security through promotion of green growth paths that foster infrastructure development (e.g., dams and hydropower plants) while enhancing the basin's environmental services. ZAMCOM can also help attract investment through the creation of a context of cooperation in which large, multipurpose investments that transcend borders can be realised.

Introduction

While alternative interpretations exist, the concept of water security is typically focused on reducing risk and vulnerability to assure water availability for a variety of essential and productive uses. Grey and Sadoff (2007) describe water security as the reliability of water supply for domestic use and livelihood production, and safety from risk of water-related hazards. Bakker (2012) defines water security as an 'acceptable level of water-related risks to humans and ecosystems, availability of water for livelihoods support, national security, human health, and ecosystem services'. Grey *et al.* (2013) describe water security as a 'tolerable level of water-related risk to society'.

Water security has achieved prominence in global, regional and basin-specific discussions. Globally, water security has influenced conceptualisations of water in the United Nations Sustainable Development Goal (SDG) process (UN-Water 2016). Regionally, the African Ministerial Council on Water (AMCOW) identified water security as one of its key priorities on the continent (AMCOW *et al.* 2012), and the Southern Africa Development Community (SADC) refers to the importance of water security and recommends steps towards achieving it (SADC 2005). In the Zambezi Basin, biophysical and socioeconomic risks have been postulated to create political stress (Wolf *et al.* 2003). Further, economic growth and rising population have been described as threats to long-term water security (Beck and Bernauer 2011).

Systematic assessment of water security in Africa remains scant, and little effort has been made to assess the concept at a basin level. In Asia and the Pacific, Lautze and Manthrithilake (2012) assessed water security at a national level using a five-component framework. The Asian Development Bank (ADB), in its Asian Water Development Outlook, also developed a national-level water security framework with five dimensions (ADB 2013; 2016). At a global scale, national-level water security has been assessed by Fischer *et al.* (2015) using a framework with four components in 160 countries, while Sadoff *et al.* (2015) developed a framework with four headline risks to determine water security in river basins and major cities. Only very recently has a national-level analytical framework been applied to southern Africa (Holmatov *et al.* 2017). However, to date, no attempt to measure water security at a basin level has been made in southern Africa.

This chapter assesses water security in the Zambezi Basin. It draws on previous work to build a framework that contains five dimensions – environment, basic human needs, vulnerability, agriculture and energy. Numeric indicators were applied to measure water security in each riparian in the Zambezi Basin, and the aggregation of results of indicator application provides a basin-level approximation of the state of water security. Structurally, we first review water security frameworks in the literature. We next discuss the rationale and methodology for the framework used in this chapter. Results from the assessment are then presented, discussed and mined to generate guidance for ZAMCOM. The last section recapitulates the chapter's main messages.

Water security frameworks

At least seven frameworks for assessing water security have been developed. Zeitoun (2011) developed a framework with six elements of water security – human, national, water resources, food, energy and climate. Lautze and Manthrithilake (2012) developed a framework with five components of water security – basic needs, food production, environmental needs, management of risk and independence, for the Asian Pacific region. Water Aid (2012) also built a water security framework for assessing community-level access to water, based on four dimensions – reliable access, water quantity, water quality and the risk of water-related disasters. ADB (2013) applied a framework that covers five dimensions of water security – household, economic, urban, environment and disaster resilience – to assess the Asia Pacific region. The UN Water's *A Post-2015 Global Goal for Water*, produced via global stakeholder consultations, describes water security as a composite of six pillars – drinking water, sanitation and hygiene, water quality and wastewater reuse, water resources management, water use efficiency and protection of ecosystems (UN-Water 2016).

More recently, two additional approaches were developed. Sadoff *et al.* (2015) proposed a water security framework comprising four 'headline' risks – drought and water scarcity, floods, water supply and sanitation, and ecosystem degradation and pollution. The framework was applied to several regions, river basins, groundwater aquifers and major cities, including three river basins in east and west Africa and a city in southern Africa. Fischer *et al.* (2015) also produced a framework with four indicators – per capita total renewable water resources, intensity of water use (ratio of total water withdrawals to renewable water resources), coefficient of variation of monthly runoff, and the dependency on total renewable water resources generated externally. This framework was applied in 160 countries using quantitative indicators.

Only Holmatov *et al.* (2017) applied an approach to assess economic water security in southern Africa. Their work applied a dimension of the ADB's updated framework. This dimension contained four components – economic (broad), agricultural, energy and industrial water security. This framework was applied to the SADC region, measuring economic water security at national level.

Measuring water security in the Zambezi Basin

Assessment framework

A review of existing frameworks reveals five common denominators, namely: water for environmental needs, availability of water for basic human needs, vulnerability to water-related disasters, the role of water in food production and water in energy production. The ecological dimension of water security is contained in four frameworks. Access to domestic water (a basic human need) is explicitly mentioned in six frameworks. Vulnerability to climate-induced water risks, such as drought and floods, appears in six frameworks. Water for agriculture is explicitly stated in three frameworks. Energy, specifically the role of hydropower in the context of economic development, is mentioned in two frameworks.

Drawing from such previous work, this chapter adopts a basin-level water security framework built on five dimensions to assess water security in the Zambezi Basin (Table 11.1): i) environment, ii) basic human needs, iii) vulnerability, iv) agriculture and v) energy. While the assessment sought to measure water security in each dimension at basin country unit (BCU) level, not all data were available at this scale. When data were not available at a BCU level, country-level data were utilised. Of the nine indicators used in the study, five were populated with BCU-level data and four with national-level data.

Environment

The first dimension in the framework is focused on the environment. Specifically, this dimension concentrates on the degree to which flow satisfies environmental needs. For a river to maintain its ecological functions sustainably, a level of flow that serves to preserve the natural system of the river course must be maintained (Zehnder *et al.* 2003). The environmental water requirements are determined by adding the estimated environmental low-flow requirements (LFR-minimum flow needed for breeding of aquatic species) to the estimated environmental high-flow requirements (HFR-minimum flow needed for channel maintenance processes, e.g., wetland flooding) (Smakhtin *et al.* 2004). Ultimately, environmental water security is a function of satisfaction of the environmental flow in each riparian. The more water available in excess of that needed to satisfy environmental flow requirements, the more environmentally water secure a riparian is presumed to be.

Satisfaction of environmental flows was assessed by comparing i) renewable water resources less withdrawal and ii) environmental flow requirements. Environmental flows for the Zambezi Basin are estimated as 30 per cent of river discharge, being the low-flow level of the sum of LFR and HFR (IWMI 2014). Total renewable water resources data were obtained from the Transboundary Freshwater Spatial Database (TFSD) (TFDD 2011), and water withdrawal data were obtained from the World Bank (2010). The total river discharge remaining after total withdrawal was compared with the environmental flow requirements, to determine surplus flow. To determine the percentage of water that is withdrawn, water withdrawal was divided by total discharge and multiplied by 100.

Basic human needs

Water security for basic human needs is a function of access to potable water and access to sanitation. Data on access to potable water and access to sanitation were obtained from the World Health Organization (WHO) and the United Nations Children's Emergency Fund (UNICEF) joint monitoring programme's Water and Sanitation Information Database (WHO-UNICEF 2016). The database measures access by using population percentages. The data, updated in 2015, are given only at national level. Due to a lack of basin-level data, the national-level figures in each country were accepted as being representative of the BCU.

Vulnerability

This dimension focuses on a population's exposure to climate-induced water risks. To measure this exposure, three indicators were applied: biophysical vulnerability, drought risk and socioeconomic drought vulnerability. Data were obtained from the WaterData Portal (IWMI

Table 11.1 Assessment framework

Water security dimension	Indicator	Indicator logic	Metric	Scale of measurement	Data source and year
Environment	Satisfaction of environmental flows	Riparians' observance of the ecological river flow threshold	Percentage of surplus water in the river	BCU	TFDD (2011) and IWMI (2014)
Basic human needs	Access to a potable water source	A measure of the household access to a reliable potable water source, within a minimum distance	Percentage of the population	Country	WHO/UNICEF (2016)
	Access to sanitation	A measure of the household access to adequate sanitation	Percentage of the population	Country	WHO/UNICEF (2016)
Vulnerability	Biophysical vulnerability index	Extent to which a system is vulnerable to climate change	Index (0–10)	BCU	IWMI (2014)
	Drought risk index	Exposure to climatic drought	Index (0–10)	BCU	IWMI (2014)
	Socioeconomic drought vulnerability index	Vulnerability of individual countries to socio-economic drought	Index (0–100)	Country	IWMI (2014)
Agriculture	Agricultural water productivity	A measure of the agriculture output per volume of water used	M$/km^3	BCU	World Bank (2016)
	Self-sufficiency of agriculture production	The ratio of agricultural goods consumption to agricultural goods production (agricultural net virtual water imports)	Ratio	Country	Hoekstra and Mekonnen (2012) World Bank (2016)

continued . . .

Table 11.1 Continued

Water security dimension	Indicator	Indicator logic	Metric	Scale of measurement	Data source and year
Energy	Risk of failing to optimally generate hydropower due to hydrologic variability	Water security for energy is higher when flow is available for optimal energy generation from hydropower	Percentage of years of energy generation below historical generation levels	BCU	Spalding-Fecher *et al.* (2016)

2014). For the first two indicators, the data are provided in global raster format, and spatial calculations in GIS were used to determine vulnerability in each BCU. For the third indicator, the data are presented in shapefile format providing only national-level information. The national-level data were therefore presumed to represent the BCU.

The biophysical vulnerability index measures the sensitivity of agriculture to drought (Eriyagama *et al.* 2009). It assesses exposure of a system to climatic incidences of meteorological drought using depth of soil cover, soil degradation, surface runoff and groundwater recharge. A 0–10 scale is used for the index, with 10 indicating maximum vulnerability.

The drought risk index measures the probability of drought occurring in a given year. The index is based on the reliability of both precipitation and river discharge, and it is measured on a 0–10 scale, where a higher value denotes higher risk.

The socioeconomic drought vulnerability index expresses exposure to socioeconomic drought and is measured by the contribution of agriculture to the national GDP and crop diversity. The lower the agricultural contribution, the lesser the vulnerability of the riparian. Similarly, the higher the crop diversity, the lesser the vulnerability of the riparian. The logic is that a riparian that is less dependent on agriculture, and/or with a wider mix of crops, is less exposed to the effects of meteorological drought. The index scale ranges from 0–100, with 100 reflecting maximum vulnerability.

Agriculture

Agricultural water security is assessed using two indicators: water productivity and self-sufficiency of agricultural production. For water productivity, the value of agricultural production per unit volume of water is assessed – the greater the agricultural production per unit volume of water, the more secure the riparian. Productive water use frees up water for other uses and increases a riparian's capacity to cope with scarcity. Self-sufficiency in agriculture is focused on a riparian's reliance on internal water sources to meet its consumption of agricultural goods. The higher the reliance on external water sources for agricultural production, the more insecure the riparian because virtual water imports expose a riparian to global market fluctuations.

Water productivity in agriculture measures the production of crops per unit volume of water depleted or evapotranspired (ET). Data were collected from two sources. To identify the cultivated area in the basin, the irrigated area map of Africa from the Global Agro-Ecological Zones (GAEZ 2016) was used. Additionally, to determine total evapotranspiration from the

Figure 11.1 Mangroves near Quelimane, Mozambique; environmental water security preserves
　　　　　ecological functions of the river system
Photo: Richard Beilfuss

Figure 11.2 A boy fetches water from a village standpipe for his basic needs in Malawi
Photo: Leonard John Abrams

identified cropland for 2014 for each BCU, data from the satellite-based MODIS Global Evapotranspiration Project, MOD16, was used (NASA 2016). To determine the monetary value of agricultural production, agricultural GDP in 2014 was obtained from the World Bank. GDP figures from the World Bank are provided only at national level, so they were extrapolated to BCU scale based on the area of the BCU relative to the area of the entire country. Agricultural GDP at a BCU level was then divided by the evapotranspiration in the BCU.

Self-sufficiency of agricultural production was measured as the annual water footprint of agricultural goods consumption divided by the annual water footprint of agricultural goods production. Data on the annual water footprint of agricultural goods consumption and production were obtained from Hoekstra and Mekonnen (2012). Since the dataset was last updated in 2005, the authors employed secondary indicators to extrapolate the data to 2014. The water footprint of agricultural goods consumption was deduced using population change, and for agricultural goods production, 2005 data were multiplied by the ratio of a country's agricultural GDP change between 2005 and 2014. The 2014 country-level population data and agricultural GDP were obtained from the World Bank (2016).

Energy

Sustainable supply of energy will not only enable economic development in the basin, but also contribute to the general social and economic security of the basin population. To measure the degree to which energy derived from hydropower production is sustainable, the percentage of years in which future energy production is likely to fall below historic production was considered. Using data from Spalding-Fecher *et al.* (2016), data on the percentage that future energy production is predicted to fall below historic energy production in dry and wet years were averaged. Data were only available on three dams: Kariba, Cahora Bassa and Upper Kafue. These were used to gauge water security for energy in the three BCUs in which they are located.

Scoring system and aggregation

Water security was assessed in four steps. First, the indicators were populated with raw data. Second, indicator results were transferred to a 1–5 scale, with 5 representing the greatest water security and 1 representing the least (Table 11.2). Third, as most dimensions comprised multiple indicators, results from the application of particular indicators were averaged so that results for each dimension fall on a 1–5 scale. Fourth, the basin's overall water security was assessed by adding the scores in the respective dimensions for each riparian. Importantly, because the energy dimension was only covered in three of the eight basin country units, it was not included in the aggregate water security score.

The 1–5 scoring system is consistent with the approach employed by ADB (2013, 2016) and Lautze and Manthrithilake (2012). The scale 'bands' applied to translate initial results of indicator application from raw values into a 1–5 classification were largely drawn from existing work. Information on potable water and sanitation, used in basic needs, was taken from GWP (2012). Bands applied to indicator results from vulnerability were adapted from Eriyagama *et al.* (2009). Bands applied to indicator results from agriculture were the same as those used by ADB (2016).

Since the maximum possible score in each of the four numerically assessed dimensions is 5, the maximum water security score is 20. Importantly, since the minimum possible score in each dimension is 1, the lowest score is 4 out of 20. The overall score range is therefore 4 to 20, with 12 being the median score.

Table 11.2 Scale bands

Score	Environment	Basic Human Needs		Vulnerability			Agriculture		Energy
	Satisfaction of environmental flows (% of surplus water in the basin)	Access to a potable water source (% of the population)	Access to sanitation (% of the population)	Biophysical vulnerability index	Drought risk index	Socioeconomic drought vulnerability index	Water productivity in agriculture (million USD/km^3)	Self-sufficiency of agricultural production (index)	Percentage of years of energy generation below historical generation levels
1	Less than 30 per cent of water un–withdrawn	0–60%	0–60%	8.1–10	8.1–10	81–100	0–100	Greater than 3	Greater than 50%
2	Just over 30 per cent of water un–withdrawn (30–45 per cent)	61–70%	61–70%	6.1–8.0	6.1–8.0	61–80	100–200	1.5–3	31–50%
3	Environmental flows satisfied with room to spare: 45–60 per cent of water un–withdrawn	71–80%	71–80%	4.1–6.0	4.1–6.0	41–60	200–350	1–1.5	16–30%
4	Environmental flows satisfied with substantial room to spare: 60–75 per cent of water un–withdrawn	81–90%	81–90%	2.1–4.0	2.1–4.0	21–40	350–1,000	0.5–1	5–15%
5	Greater than 75 per cent of water un–withdrawn	91–100%	91–100%	0–2.0	0–2.0	0–20	Greater than 1,000	Less than 0.5	Less than 5%

As the most recent year that most numerical data were available for was 2014, efforts were made to harmonise data from other years to reflect conditions in 2014.[1] Harmonisation to 2014 was achieved for all indicators except those in the environment and basic human needs dimensions. For the environment dimension, water discharge data were available only for 2011 and environmental water requirements were estimated in 2004. Nevertheless, this is unlikely to affect results since environmental water requirements were presumed to be fairly constant. The basic human needs data are computed for five years, and the current 2010–2015 dataset therefore encompasses 2014 values.

Results

The basin's water security appears below average to average, as riparians score between 10 and 12 (Figure 11.3). Security in most of the basin is buoyed by the reality that environmental water requirements are met due to low water use. Nonetheless, security levels in basic human needs and agriculture are variable, and vulnerability presents a widespread challenge. The most water secure riparian is Botswana, which scored just above 12, and the least water secure country is Tanzania, which scored 10. Importantly, these results do not imply an abundance of water supply – Zambezi Basin portions of Botswana, for example, may not be particularly water-abundant. These results do suggest that Botswana's set of water-related risks across the outlined dimensions (environment, human needs, vulnerability and agriculture) are moderately lower than other portions of the Zambezi.

Environmental flow requirements are satisfied in the basin as all riparians score between 4 and 5 (Figure 11.4). This suggests very low water use, and sufficient freshwater to meet the ecological requirements of the basin. As a result, water for environmental goods, for example, wetlands, should generally exist. The basin is therefore environmentally water-secure. Comparison of these results with other basins suggests that the Zambezi is among the best

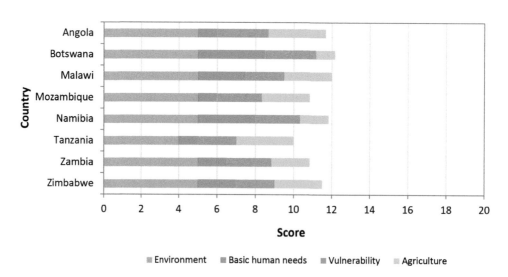

Figure 11.3 Overall water security (20-point scale)
Source: Authors

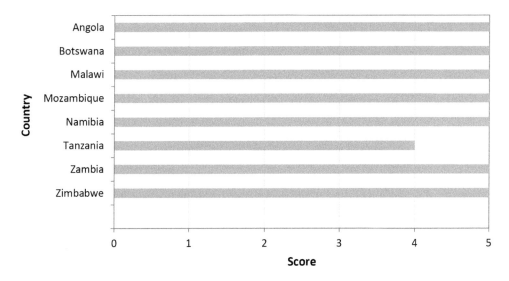

Figure 11.4 Satisfaction of environmental water requirements (5-point scale)
Source: Authors

preserved in the world, not far removed from the Amazon and the Congo. Environmental water security is indeed often much lower in major transboundary basins, such as in the Aral Sea, Ganges and Orange-Senqu (IWMI 2014).

The degree to which water is secure for basic human needs varies across the basin (Figure 11.5). Most riparians show low security levels, with only three riparians scoring 2.5 or above. The least secure are Angola, Mozambique and Tanzania, while Botswana is the most secure.

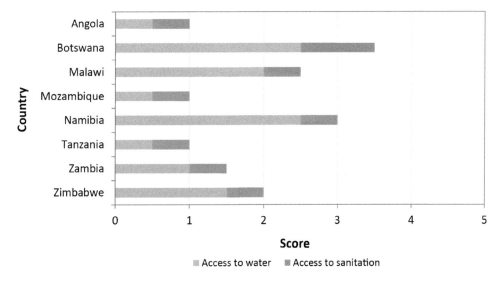

Figure 11.5 Basic human needs (5-point scale)
Source: Authors

Riparians' access to water is much higher than their access to sanitation. Most riparians face challenges in providing adequate sanitation – none of them achieves even a median score. The security level for this dimension, although variable, is mostly low. Contextualisation of these water and sanitation access conditions suggests that levels in the Zambezi riparians are among the lowest in the world, on a par with those in the Mekong Basin.

Vulnerability is a major issue across the basin (Figure 11.6). Angola and Botswana are the least vulnerable, but none of the riparians achieved a score greater than 3. Zambezi riparians face the greatest challenges in biophysical vulnerability, with Botswana, Namibia and Zimbabwe carrying the highest risk. Drought risk is also a major threat, with all riparians facing similar levels of risk. Relatively high water security is achieved on the socioeconomic vulnerability index, according to which Botswana and Angola manifest lesser vulnerability. In summary, all riparians appear vulnerable to water-related risks. While the level of vulnerability is very high in the Zambezi, equal or greater vulnerability levels exist in basins like the Aral Sea, Nile and Okavango.

Levels of agricultural water security vary largely among Zambezi riparians (Figure 11.7). Botswana is the least secure, while Angola is the most secure. While riparians are moderately self-sufficient in agricultural production, Botswana and, to a lesser extent, Namibia rely on virtual water imports. Riparians face bigger challenges in agricultural water productivity, where production relative to water use is consistently low. The relative paucity of irrigation in the Zambezi Basin may contribute the low productivity that is evidenced. The basin is, on average, reasonably insecure on water security for agriculture.

Among the three countries with large hydropower dams in the basin (Figure 11.8), Zimbabwe faces the greatest risk as current and future flow variability may jeopardise the reliability of supplies into and through the Kariba Dam. Zambia's energy security is somewhat stronger than Zimbabwe's, given its use of Upper Kafue as well as Kariba – risk is nonetheless still reasonable in Zambia. Mozambique, which generates energy through the Cahora Bassa Dam, has the lowest risk.

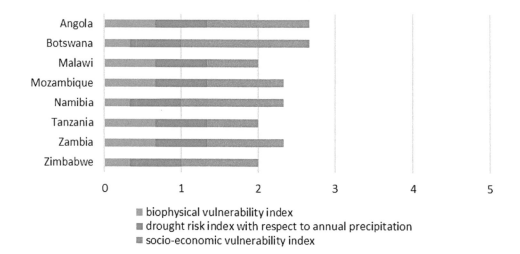

Figure 11.6 Vulnerability (5-point scale)
Source: Authors

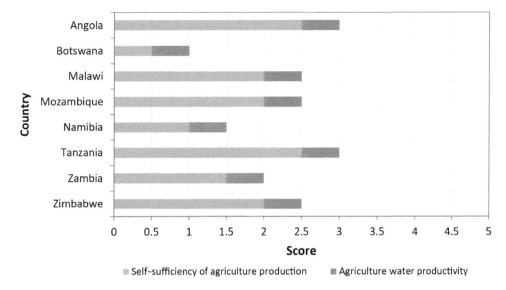

Figure 11.7 Agriculture (5-point scale)
Source: Authors

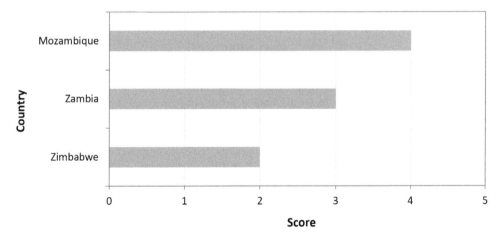

Figure 11.8 Climate risk to hydropower (5-point scale)
Source: Authors

Discussion

This chapter developed a five-dimension framework to assess water security in the Zambezi Basin, consisting of environment, basic human needs, vulnerability, agriculture and energy. It is the first of its kind to specifically measure the level of water security in a major basin. Given the widespread calls for achieving water security in Africa (SADC 2005; NASAC 2014; AMCOW 2016), acknowledged at the outset of this chapter, it is believed the approach that has been applied can play a critical role in fostering progress toward key developmental targets in the region. Regional institutions like SADC and ZAMCOM may indeed wish to draw on the chapter's results to i) situate the basin's water conditions in an explicitly water-security context and ii) strengthen the formulation of strategic action plans and water-related development targets.

Overarching findings

The application of a water security framework to the Zambezi generated at least three clear findings. First, water security in the basin is fairly mediocre at present, with high vulnerability. While overall water security is high for no country in the basin, the most secure riparian in the basin is Botswana, closely followed by Malawi, Angola and Namibia. Second, agricultural water security is low. Only two countries, Angola and Tanzania, show a moderate level of agricultural water security. Third, environmental water security is very high in the basin and water requirements for environmental needs should be easily satisfied.

Vulnerability

Vulnerability is a challenge across the basin. The threat of drought is frequent in the whole of southern Africa, increasing both biophysical and socioeconomic vulnerability in an area whose economy is largely agrarian-based (World Bank 2010). While no previous study was specifically focused on vulnerability in the basin, high drought vulnerability can be substantiated by the findings of Vorosmarty and Moore (1991) and Mavhura *et al.* (2015). Both studies found that climate-induced droughts are frequent in the basin, and coping capacities are not equipped to withstand the effects of droughts.

Agriculture

Agricultural water security is low, mainly because of the poor security of agricultural water productivity. The reasons are not immediately clear, but low productivity is most likely related to farming methods, choice of crops and limited irrigation (Fanadzo *et al.* 2009). The finding on low agricultural water productivity is consistent with evidence presented in Cai *et al.* (2011) and Holmatov *et al.* (2017), who also concluded that agricultural water productivity is very low in the region. Low agricultural productivity in general, linked to cropping choices and farming methods in southern Africa, was also confirmed by Ehui and Pender (2005).

Environment

Consistent with the more rigorous evaluation of ecosystem services in McCartney and Nyambe (Chapter 7), this chapter found water provision for the environment to be a strength. Nonetheless, water withdrawals may rise significantly due to the construction of hydraulic infrastructure. Already, plans to build several large dams have been finalised, and irrigation is also set to more than double in the next few decades (World Bank 2010). This will considerably increase withdrawal levels and test the basin's capacity to preserve environmental flows.

Results in context

Direct comparison of results in this chapter with other work proved difficult since methods are not identical. However, the work of Lautze and Manthrithilake (2012) and ADB (2013) in the Asia-Pacific can be used to generate approximate comparisons. Comparison of water security in Zambezi riparians with water security levels in Asia-Pacific countries outlined in ADB (2013) suggests that water security levels of Asia-Pacific countries are substantially greater than those of Zambezi riparians. For example, nearly 60 per cent of countries scored greater than 3 in the Asia-Pacific, whereas only 30 per cent of countries scored greater than 3 in the Zambezi. Examination by Lautze and Manthrithilake (2012) generates a similar finding; in their analysis, over 70 per cent of Asia Pacific countries scored 3 or greater. Nonetheless, Zambezi riparians manifest superior water security levels in the environmental dimension.

Water security and energy: conceptual issues

The framework applied in this chapter used the degree of climate risks to hydropower to reflect the water security of energy supplies. This approach differed from others (e.g., Zeitoun 2011; ADB 2013; Holmatov *et al.* 2017). None of the measures applied – in this chapter or elsewhere – are without flaws. Such flaws may result from the nature of linkages between water and energy on the one hand, and water and the other dimensions typically included in water security analyses on the other. Unlike agriculture, the environmental and domestic needs for which water is an essential input, water is not required for energy production as economies can conceivably generate all of their electricity through sources that do not utilise water. Further, even if hydropower is a major source of energy, it can easily be transmitted across basins as manifested in the Southern Africa Power Pool. The bottom line is that these realities have potentially confounded the framework and scale in which water security assessment is undertaken – rendering assessment of water-energy security more elusive.

Conclusions

General recommendations

The results confirm the utility of basin-level assessments of water security and the disaggregation of basin water security into that of particular riparians. The results highlight that while vulnerability is a basin-wide challenge, sanitation is a more pressing concern for Angola and Mozambique, and self-sufficiency in agriculture production is a key concern in Botswana and Namibia. Conventional options for responding to these challenges are as follows:

- Vulnerability – to mitigate drought, water supply can be better assured through expansion of storage facilities. Large and small dams can reduce drought risk, and at the same time create other opportunities that lessen socioeconomic vulnerability – for example, hydro-power production and aqua-tourism can reduce dependency on agriculture, encouraging economic diversity.
- Agriculture – expansion of irrigation can improve self-sufficient production while drought-resilient crop choices, improved farming methods and irrigation improvement can improve agricultural water productivity. The cultivation of low-value crops can be improved by changing crop varieties, but irrigation water management will require more comprehensive solutions (Mutiro and Lautze 2015).
- Water supply and sanitation – the pathway to expanding water supply is reasonably well known. Sanitation expansion presents options from low to high tech. In either case, a key issue is the mobilisation and channelling of finance to enable the expansion of small infrastructure.
- Interventions to foster improvements in one area should avoid or minimise costs in another. In particular, ways in which environmental conservation – currently a strength in the basin – can be maintained and enhanced while fostering developments in other water-related sectors should be identified. Consideration of environmental flows, wetland protection and ecologically conscious dam construction designs should be promoted.

Role for ZAMCOM

The chapter's main finding is that basin water security is mediocre, explained by high vulnerability, low agricultural water security and challenges in achieving basic human needs. The provision of water for environmental requirements is nonetheless very high. Major recommendations based on this are: i) augment water storage infrastructure; ii) increase water productivity through a range of measures including irrigation improvement and expansion; iii) in certain riparians, expand domestic water supply and sanitation programs; and iv) identify and implement options for sustainable compromises that foster development while preserving water for the environment.

Against this backdrop, at least five entry points for ZAMCOM exist in improving water security in the basin. First, ZAMCOM could facilitate convergence toward definition of relevant water resources management and water security indicators and subsequently, based on results of their application, production of 'state of the basin' assessments at a regular frequency.

Second, ZAMCOM can play a central role in maintaining environmental water security. While this intervention does not seem urgent now, one of the RBO's core mandates is to protect and conserve the watercourse. As such, investment that manifests green and sustainable development should be encouraged. In view of the expected infrastructure development in the basin, ZAMCOM can set guidelines for smart construction and identify and promote options for water storage that are less environmentally intrusive.

Figure 11.9 The Liwonde Barrage, which controls water levels in Lake Nyasa/Malawi, is being rehabilitated under the Shire River Basin Management Programme. ZAMCOM may facilitate a context that attracts investment such as this and encourages the undertaking of maintenance and upgrading in a cooperative fashion.

Photo: Jusipbek Kazbekov

Third, improving water productivity may require a range of solutions (see Chapter 6), many of which are likely to fall outside ZAMCOM's mandate. Nevertheless, ZAMCOM can play a knowledge broker's role through identifying irrigation options and assessing their institutional and environmental sustainability, scalability, profitability and suitability in different contexts. There is room for partnering with regional institutions to support applied research that evaluates ways to increase water productivity according to a suite of parameters.

Fourth, ZAMCOM can also help raise awareness on sanitation provision. This is conventionally a national government responsibility, but the RBO can influence the process by bringing attention to the cost of pollution due to poor sanitation, and raise awareness both in national governments and basin populations. Presently, poor sanitation, mainly from rapid urbanisation, is affecting water quality and creating other social costs (see Chapter 8).

Fifth, ZAMCOM can help to attract much-needed investment through the creation of a context of cooperation in which large, multipurpose investments that transcend borders can be realised. Investments can focus on new infrastructure and maintenance and upgrading of existing infrastructure.

Ultimately, optimal and sustainable development is achieved through a cooperative framework. ZAMCOM can therefore play a critical role through catalysing a meaningful and substantive cooperative foundation that fosters coordinated approaches and incentivises development financiers.

Summing up

This chapter found that, with the exception of the environment, the Zambezi Basin faces severe challenges to water security. Vulnerability (i.e., risk associated with droughts and floods) and agricultural water security are the basin's major concerns; provision of basic water supply and sanitation is also a major challenge in several countries, notably Angola, Tanzania and Mozambique. With the recent formation of ZAMCOM and a potentially increasing role for the RBO in the basin, the time is ripe to realise cooperative solutions that improve water security.

We acknowledge two caveats in this chapter. First, the use of national-level data in some indicators may have slightly distorted some of the results. However, given the absence of certain data at a BCU scale, this was unavoidable. Second, limitations in application of the energy dimension may have compromised the comprehensiveness of the framework utilised in this chapter. Nonetheless, challenges associated with incorporating energy into water security frameworks have been noted elsewhere (e.g., Lautze and Manthrithilake 2012).

In summing up, achieving water security will require investment to reduce vulnerability, for example, construction of water storage infrastructure, and improved agricultural water use. Applied research that is focused on the efficacy of alternative water management interventions, in partnership with regional institutions, can enhance the implementation of such investments. ZAMCOM can play a role in improving water security through promotion of green growth paths that foster infrastructure development while conserving the basin's environmental services. ZAMCOM can also help attract investment through the creation of a context of cooperation in which large, multipurpose investments that transcend borders can be realised.

Note

1   In the agricultural dimensions, the 2005 water footprint data were successfully extrapolated to 2014. The qualitative information used to assess the energy dimensions was also not adjusted because it remains valid for 2014. The information was obtained from 2015 reports, which were assumed to essentially reflect the operations of the previous year.

References

ADB (Asian Development Bank). 2013. Asian water development outlook 2013. Available at www.adb.org/sites/default/files/publication/30190/asian-water-development-outlook-2013.pdf

ADB. 2016. Asian water development outlook 2016. Available at www.adb.org/sites/default/files/publication/189411/awdo-2016.pdf

AMCOW (The African Ministerial Council on Water). 2016. World Water Day: Africa supports post 2015 goal on water security. AMCOW. Available at www.amcow-online.org/index.php?option=com_content&view= article&id=307&Itemid=169&lang=en (accessed 5 April 2016).

AMCOW, CDKN and GWP. 2012. Water security and climate resilient development: Technical background document. Available at www.wcdrr.org/wcdrr-data/uploads/867/Water %20security%20and%20climate%20resilient%20development_Tech%20background%20doc%20(AMCOW%20and%20GWP%202012)%20English.pdf

Bakker, K. 2012. Water security: Research challenges and opportunities. *Science* 337(6097): 914–915.

Beck, L. and Bernauer, T. 2011. How will combined changes in water demand and climate affect water availability in the Zambezi river basin? *Global Environmental Change* 21(3): 1061–1072.

Cai, X., Molden, D., Mainuddin, M., Sharmad, B., Ahmad, M. and Karimib, P. 2011. Producing more food with less water in a changing world: Assessment of water productivity in 10 major river basins. *Water International* 36(1): 42–62.

Ehui, S. and Pender, J. 2005. Resource degradation, low agricultural productivity, and poverty in sub-Saharan Africa: Pathways out of the spiral. *Agricultural Economics* 32(s1): 225–242.

Eriyagama, N., Smakhtin, V. and Gamage, N. 2009. *Mapping drought patterns and impacts: A global perspective.* IWMI Research Report 133. Colombo, Sri Lanka: International Water Management Institute. 31p.

Fanadzo, M., Chiduza, C. and Mnkeni, P.N.S. 2009. Investigation of agronomic factors constraining productivity of grain maize (Zea mays L.) at Zanyokwe irrigation scheme, Eastern Cape, South Africa. *Journal of Applied Biosciences* 17: 948–958.

Fischer, G., Hizsnyik, E., Tramberend, S. and Wiberg, D. 2015. *Towards indicators for water security – A global hydro-economic classification of water challenges.* International Institute for Applied Systems Analysis: Interim Report IR-15–013. Available at www.iiasa.ac.at/publication/more_IR-15-013.php

GAEZ (Global Agro-Ecological Zones). Data portal. Available at www.gaez.iiasa.ac.at (accessed on 15 April 2016).

Grey, D., Garrick, D., Blackmore, D., Kelman, J., Muller, M. and Sadoff, C. 2013. Water security in one blue planet: Twenty-first century policy challenges for science. *Philosophical Transactions of the Royal Society A 371*: 20120406.

Grey, D. and Sadoff, C.W. 2007. Sink or swim? Water security for growth and development. *Water Policy* 9: 545–571.

GWP (Global Water Partnership). 2012. *Proceedings from the GWP workshop: Assessing water security with appropriate indicators.* GWP Technical Committee. November 2012. Stockholm.

Hoekstra, A.Y. and Mekonnen, M.M. 2012. The water footprint of humanity. *Proceedings of the National Academy of Sciences* 109(9): 3232–3237. See also http://waterfootprint.org/en/resources/water-footprint-statistics/#CP2

Holmatov, B., Lautze, J., Manthrithilake, H. and Makin I. (2017). Water security for productive economies: Applying an assessment framework in southern Africa. *Physics and Chemistry of the Earth.* Parts A/B/C online.

IWMI (International Water Management Institute). 2014. Water data portal. Integrated portal for IMWI's research data. Available at http://waterdata.iwmi.org.

Lautze, J. and Manthrithilake, H. 2012. Water security: Old concepts, new package, what value? *Natural Resources Forum* 36: 76–87.

Mavhura, E., Manatsa, D. and Mushore, T. 2015. Adaptation to drought in arid and semi-arid environments: Case of the Zambezi Valley, Zimbabwe. *Journal of Disaster Risk Studies* 7(1).

Mutiro, J. and Lautze, J. 2015. Irrigation in southern Africa: Success or failure? *Irrigation and Drainage.* Published online in Wiley Online Library (wileyonlinelibrary.com). doi: 10.1002/ird.1892.

NASA (National Aeronautics and Space Administration). 2016. MODIS. Available at http://modis.gsfc.nasa.gov/data/dataprod/dataproducts.php?MOD_NUMBER=16 (accessed on 10 June 2016).

NASAC (Network of African Science Academies). 2014. *The grand challenge of water security in Africa: Recommendations to policymakers.* Policymakers' Booklet on the State of the Water Sector in Africa. Nairobi: NASAC.

SADC (Southern African Development Community). 2005. Regional water policy. Available at www.sadc.int/files/1913/5292/8376/regional_water_policy.pdf/

Sadoff, C.W., Hall, J.W., Grey, D., Aerts, J.C.J.H., Ait-Kadi, M., Brown, C., Cox, A., Dadson, S., Garrick, D., Kelman, J., McCornick, P., Ringler, C., Rosegrant, M., Whittington, D. and Wiberg, D. 2015. *Securing water, sustaining growth: Report of the GWP/OECD Task Force on water security and sustainable growth*. UK: University of Oxford, 180p.

Smakhtin, V.U., Revenga, C. and Döll, P. 2004. *Taking into account environmental water requirements in global-scale water resources assessments*. Comprehensive Assessment of Water Management in Agriculture Research Report 2. Colombo, Sri Lanka: International Water Management Institute.

Spalding-Fecher, R., Chapman, A., Yamba, F., Walimwimpi, H., Kling, H., Tembo, B., Nyambe, I. and Cuamba, B. 2016. The vulnerability of hydropower production in the Zambezi River Basin to the impacts of climate change and irrigation development. *Mitigation and Adaptation Strategies for Global Change* 21(5): 721–742.

TFDD (Transboundary Freshwater Dispute Database). 2011. *Oregon State University*. Available at http://gis.nacse.org/tfdd/map/result.php?bcode=ZAMB&bccode=ZAMB_ZMB&maptype=Population (accessed on 20 March 2016).

UN-Water. 2016. Sustainable development goals. 17 ways to change our world. Available at www.un.org/sustainabledevelopment/water-and-sanitation/ (accessed on 13 June 2016).

Vorosmarty, C.J. and Moore, B. 1991. Modelling basin-scale hydrology in support of physical climate and global biogeochemical studies: An example using the Zambezi River. *Surveys in Geophysics* 12: 271–311.

Water Aid. 2012. *Water security framework*. London: WaterAid.

WHO/UNICEF. 2016. *Joint monitoring programme for water supply and sanitation*. Available at www.wssinfo.org/documents/?tx_displaycontroller[type]=country_files (accessed on 25 March 2016).

Wolf, A.T., Yoffe, S.B. and Giordano, M. 2003. International waters: Identifying basins at risk. *Water Policy* 5(1): 29–60.

World Bank. 2010. *The Zambezi River Basin. A multi-sector investment opportunities analysis*. June 2010. Washington, DC.

World Bank. 2016. Data indicators. Available at http://data.worldbank.org/indicator Data (accessed on 25 October 2016).

Zehnder, A.J.B., Yang, H. and Schertenleib, R. 2003. Water issues, the need for action at different levels. *Aquatic Science* 65: 1–20.

Zeitoun, M. 2011. The global web of national water security. *Global Policy* 11(1): 1–11.

12

Achieving Sustainable Development Goal 6 in the Zambezi River Basin

Lisa Guppy, Manzoor Qadir and Jonathan Lautze

Key messages

- While progress to date in different countries varies, a rapid scale-up in effort and resources will be needed for all countries in the Zambezi River Basin to achieve Sustainable Development Goal (SDG) 6.

- To report on progress accurately, water-related monitoring and evaluation will need to be redesigned and scaled up, perhaps most extensively for SDG targets 6.3, 6.4 and 6.6.
- To move beyond simply 'ticking off' indicators, Zambezi riparians must consider: impacts on vulnerable groups, including women and girls; interdependencies between targets under SDG 6; and interlinkages between SDG 6 and other Sustainable Development Goals.
- ZAMCOM could play an important role in the SDG era by accelerating progress in at least three ways: i) provide leadership and expertise in swiftly aligning basin and national policies and strategies to SDGs; ii) be an 'honest broker' and assess the potential synergies and trade-offs between national strategies for different, and sometimes competing, SDG targets; and iii) adapt international monitoring guidelines and metadata for SDG 6 to a Zambezi context, and promote and support their adoption for improved basin-wide reporting, planning and decision-making.

Introduction

The outcome of a global multi-year process, the Sustainable Development Goals (SDGs) provide a powerful frame for responding to development challenges across the world. Adopted in late 2015 with a time horizon of 2030, the SDGs have established new, more expansive goalposts for improving the world's conditions. Consisting of 17 goals, 169 targets and 230 indicators in total, the SDGs have a dedicated water goal – Goal 6 – that seeks to 'ensure availability and sustainable management of water and sanitation for all'.

Water is key to sustainable development, as the achievement of SDG 6 can support the realisation of other SDGs. For example, clean and adequate water supplies are needed to ensure human health; water resources underpin agriculture and industry, including energy production; and without adequate treatment, wastewater degrades terrestrial and marine ecosystems. Ultimately, to harness the contribution of water to the SDGs, the High Level Panel on Water writes that 'the world needs to transform the way it manages its water resources, as well as improve water and sanitation related services for billions of people' (HLPW 2016, p.3).

The SDGs have driven a large and increasing body of literature. Reports and publications that examine issues related to the formulation of Goal 6 alone is voluminous. The African Ministers' Council on Water (AMCOW), United Nations Global Compact (UNGC), the United Nations Open Working Group on Sustainable Development Goals, the United Nations University (UNU) and UN-Water, for example, produced documents on how the water SDG should be formulated (AMCOW 2013; UNGC 2013; UNU and UNOSD 2013; UN 2014; UN-Water 2014). Others such as Hajer *et al.* (2015), UN-Water (2015a), Bhaduri *et al.* (2016) and Boas *et al.* (2016) have begun to examine how to foster the most efficient implementation of SDGs.

Despite this important work, no effort to-date has examined how improving basin management in one of the world's large shared watercourses can contribute to achieving the SDGs. This chapter therefore takes the case of the Zambezi and seeks to identify changes that can catalyse progress toward realising SDG 6. The chapter begins by presenting the SDG process and describes the targets and indicators associated with SDG 6. The chapter next places current conditions in the Zambezi in the framework of these targets and indicators. Last, the chapter proposes ways in which improved basin management can accelerate achievement of the SDGs in the Zambezi.

Sustainable Development Goal 6

The 2030 Agenda for Sustainable Development is the UN-led global development framework that builds on the Millennium Development Goals (MDGs), which expired in 2015. Under the 2030 Agenda, the SDGs are comprised of 169 international development targets agreed to by UN member states, generally for the 2016–2030 period. International processes for implementation of the SDGs are now gathering momentum, and a plethora of SDG mechanisms and bodies have been formed both within and outside UN structures.

The United Nations High Level Political Forum (HLPF) on Sustainable Development first met in 2014; it is the main forum for sustainable development issues within the UN framework, and is the peak body overseeing global implementation and review. The HLPF oversees the annual SDG Progress Report and the Global Sustainable Development Report, which is a meta assessment of specific SDG issues or nexuses of issues. Every year, the HLPF will focus on certain countries: 2016 was the first year of the review, but no basin countries were included. In 2017, Botswana and Zimbabwe will be reviewed in the report.

Another body that is particularly important for SDG 6 is the High Level Panel on Water (HLPW). The HLPW is a leading political forum that was co-convened by the Secretary General of the United Nations and the President of the World Bank Group, and is made up primarily of ruling heads of state from 11 countries, including the co-chairs – the Presidents of Mexico and Mauritius. The HLPW Action Plan was released in 2016 and promises to be a 'living document' for global leadership.

At a monitoring level, the Inter-Agency and Expert Group on Sustainable Development Goal Indicators (IAEG-SDGs) and the High Level Group for Partnership, Coordination and Capacity-Building for Statistics for the 2030 Agenda for Sustainable Development (HLG-PCCB) are active. The key tasks for these bodies are to ensure that the indicators are measurable, and to define how and when they will be measured and reported on. Governments in the basin will be interacting with these bodies directly until 2030. There are also multiple international initiatives that aim to support the monitoring and reporting of SDG 6 indicators particularly. These can be viewed together under the UN-Water banner as the integrated monitoring initiative (see UN Water, 2016a).

These international bodies must lead an ambitious and challenging agenda, not least because the HLPF – and the 2030 Agenda itself– emphasise the principle of 'Ensuring no-one is left behind'. In this sense, the Zambezi riparians not only have an internationally recognised responsibility to achieve the SDGs, they have a clear responsibility to achieve them for all peoples in the basin, including the disadvantaged.

The SDGs treat water more holistically than did the MDGs. Whereas the MDGs focused narrowly on water and sanitation, SDG 6 applies a more comprehensive interpretation of water-related issues in six core targets and two additional implementing targets, which are listed with their indicators in Table 12.1.

Considering the state of the Zambezi in an SDG framework

Zambezi Basin countries have begun to prepare and plan for the Sustainable Development Goals. With 230 indicators to progress against, the SDGs will require significant effort to achieve by 2030 for most countries, with likely more effort being required from low- and middle-income countries (LMICs). Therefore, it is important that in the Zambezi basin, political priorities, resources and investments are well targeted, efficient and effective. Analysing and prioritising gaps while building on strengths will be important for all governments in the basin. This section outlines current conditions in the Zambezi, and reflects on basin-level challenges and opportunities at the level of SDG 6 targets and indicators. As there is a recognised paucity of water-related data and information across the basin, this section includes reflection on monitoring for each target, and the capacity of basin riparians to monitor and report against SDG 6 targets.

Table 12.1 SDG 6 targets and indicators (UN 2016; UNSD 2016)

Target	Indicator
6.1 By 2030, achieve universal and equitable access to safe and affordable drinking water for all	*6.1.1 Proportion of population using safely managed drinking water services* Definition: Population using a basic drinking water source ('improved' sources of drinking water used for MDG monitoring, i.e., piped water into dwelling, yard or plot; public taps or standpipes; boreholes or tubewells; protected dug wells; protected springs and rainwater) which is located on premises and available when needed and free of faecal and priority chemical contamination.
6.2 By 2030, achieve access to adequate and equitable sanitation and hygiene for all and end open defecation, paying special attention to the needs of women and girls and those in vulnerable situations	*6.2.1 Proportion of population using safely managed sanitation services, including a handwashing facility with soap and water* Definition: Population using a basic sanitation facility at the household level ('improved' sanitation facilities used for MDG monitoring, i.e., flush or pour flush toilets to sewer systems, septic tanks or pit latrines, ventilated improved pit latrines, pit latrines with a slab, and composting toilets, the same categories as improved sources of drinking water used for MDG monitoring) which is not shared with other households and where excreta is safely disposed in situ or treated off-site. Definition: Population with a handwashing facility (a device to contain, transport or regulate the flow of water to facilitate handwashing) with soap and water at home.
6.3 By 2030, improve water quality by reducing pollution, eliminating dumping and minimising release of hazardous chemicals and materials, halving the proportion of untreated wastewater and substantially increasing recycling and safe reuse globally	*6.3.1 Proportion of wastewater safely treated* Definition: Proportion of wastewater generated both by households (sewage and faecal sludge), as well as economic activities (based on System of Environmental and Economic Accounting for Water, SEEA categories) safely treated compared to total wastewater generated both through households and economic activities. While the definition conceptually includes wastewater generated from all economic activities, monitoring will focus on wastewater generated from the release of hazardous chemicals and materials, halving the proportion of untreated wastewater and at least doubling recycling and safe reuse globally *6.3.2 Proportion of bodies of water with good ambient water quality* Definition: Proportion of water bodies (area) in a country with good ambient water quality compared to all water bodies in the country. 'Good' indicates an ambient water quality that does not damage ecosystem function and human health according to core ambient water quality indicators.
6.4 By 2030, substantially increase water-use efficiency across all sectors and ensure sustainable withdrawals and supply of freshwater to address water scarcity and substantially reduce the number of people suffering from water scarcity	*6.4.1 Change in water use efficiency over time* Definition: This indicator is defined as the output over time of a given major sector per volume of (net) water withdrawn (showing the trend in water use efficiency). Following ISIC 4 coding, sectors are defined as agriculture, forestry and fishing (ISIC 4A); manufacturing, constructions, mining and quarrying (ISIC 4-B, 4-C and 4-F); electricity industry (ISIC 4-D); and the municipal sector (ISIC 4-E). *6.4.2 Level of water stress: freshwater withdrawal as a proportion of available freshwater resources* Definition: Ratio between total freshwater withdrawn by all major sectors (as defined by ISIC standards) and total renewable freshwater

continued . . .

Table 12.1 Continued

Target	Indicator
	resources, taking into account environmental water requirements. The indicator builds on MDG indicator 7.5 and also accounts for environmental water requirements.
6.5 By 2030, implement integrated water resources management at all levels, including through transboundary cooperation as appropriate	*6.5.1 Degree of integrated water resources management implementation* This indicator reflects the extent to which integrated water resources management (IWRM) is implemented, structured in four components: policies, institutions, management tools and financing. It takes into account the various users and uses of water with the aim of promoting positive social, economic and environmental impacts on all levels, including transboundary, where appropriate. *6.5.2 Proportion of transboundary basin area with an operational arrangement for water cooperation* Definition: Proportion of surface area of transboundary basins that have an operational agreement/arrangement and/or institution for transboundary water cooperation. Regular meetings of the riparian countries to discuss IWRM and exchange information are required for an arrangement to be defined as 'operational'.
6.6 By 2020, protect and restore water-related ecosystems, including mountains, forests, wetlands, rivers, aquifers and lakes	*6.6.1 Change in the extent of water-related ecosystems over time* Definition: Percentage of change in water-related ecosystems over time (% change/year). The indicator would track changes over time in the extent of wetlands, forests and drylands, and in the minimum flows of rivers, volumes of freshwater in lakes and dams, and the groundwater table. The Ramsar Convention broad definition of 'wetland' is used, which includes rivers and lakes, enabling three of the biome types mentioned in the target to be assessed – wetlands, rivers, lakes – plus other wetland types.
6.a By 2030, expand international cooperation and capacity-building support to developing countries in water- and sanitation-related activities and programmes, including water harvesting, desalination, water efficiency, wastewater treatment, recycling and reuse technologies	*6.a.1 Amount of water- and sanitation-related official development assistance that is part of a government-coordinated spending plan* Definition: Official Development Assistance (ODA) is defined as flows of official financing administered with the promotion of the economic development and welfare of developing countries as the main objective, and which are concessional in character with a grant element of at least 25 per cent. A government-coordinated spending plan is defined as a financing plan/budget for the water and sanitation sector, clearly assessing the available sources of finance and strategies for financing future needs. The indicator is computed as the proportion between the amount of water- and sanitation-related Official Development Assistance that a government receives, and the total amount budgeted for water and sanitation in a government-coordinated spending plan, which allows for a better understanding of how much countries depend/rely on ODA and highlighting countries' total water and sanitation budgets over time.
6.b Support and strengthen the participation of local communities in improving water and sanitation management	*6.b.1 Proportion of local administrative units with established and operational policies and procedures for participation of local communities in water and sanitation management* Definition: Indicator tracks the presence, at the national level, of clearly defined procedures in laws or policies for participation by service users (for aspects related to WASH), and the presence of formal stakeholder structures established at sub-catchment level (for aspects related to the management of water, wastewater and ecosystem resources).

Target 6.1: Achieving universal and equitable access to safe and affordable drinking water

During the MDG era, target 7.C was to *halve, by 2015, the proportion of people without sustainable access to safe drinking water and basic sanitation*. However, controversially, it was not 'safe' water that was monitored; instead, indicator 7.8 required the monitoring of *improved drinking water sources*, which are described in Table 12.1. Under SDG target 6.1, indicator 6.1.1 also monitors improved drinking water sources, but new components have been added to emphasise the 'safe management' of water. Improved water supply sources must now also be located on premises, be available when needed and be free of fecal and priority chemical contamination.

Despite these differences, MDG reporting tracked most basin countries from 1990 to 2015, and that reporting can bring context to domestic water in the SDG era. Zimbabwe was one of the few countries that were reported to experience worsening water supply services; in 1990, Zimbabwe reported that 79 per cent of its total population was covered by improved water supply, and in 2015 that proportion had dropped to 77 per cent (WHO/UNICEF 2015). Tanzania and Angola were reported to have made 'limited or no progress'. Mozambique and Zambia made 'moderate progress', although Mozambique started from a low baseline in 1990 – 35 per cent – to reach only 51 per cent in 2015 (WHO/UNICEF 2015). Namibia and Malawi met their MDG targets with 90 per cent and 91 per cent of their total populations covered by improved water sources respectively. In the best position, Botswana reported that 96 per cent of its total population was covered, with significant growth in water piped to premises (WHO/UNICEF 2015).

This target will require significant investments in monitoring. Basin countries must decide how they will measure water availability, which may be particularly challenging in rural areas and in urban slums. Water utilities and authorities now also have to prove that the water supply is continuously free from priority contaminants, which will, in most countries in the basin, put an additional burden on monitoring systems. A related challenge is that the shift from improved water to safely managed water has 'lifted the bar', and it may therefore be difficult for countries to show early progress against indicator 6.1.1 because, if accurately measured, the proportion of people covered will only drop in the early years of the SDGs.

Looking forward, whether Zambezi Basin countries will make real progress in domestic water supply improvements depends on a wide range of issues, not all of which are captured by the indicator set to measure target 6.1. For example, as shown in Table 12.1, target 6.1 sets the aim of having affordable water but indicator 6.1.1 does not require any measurement of affordability. In a similar vein, the target calls for equitable access to water, which is also essentially missing in the indicator. Finally, there have been many calls by international actors to monitor indicator 6.1.1 beyond households and include health facilities, schools, workplaces and similar settings. With some notable exceptions, the safety and availability of water at these kinds of institutions is poorly monitored and understood, particularly in rural areas within the Zambezi River Basin.

To meet this target, basin countries will contend with constraints common to water supply in LMICs including: limited funds; financial losses due to low levels of accountability and transparency in the sector; limited data to support better planning and policy; and a shortage of skilled human capacity. Progress against target 6.1 will require considerable and sustained increases in technical, human and financial resources to the water supply sector, particularly in Zimbabwe, Tanzania, Angola and Mozambique. Additionally, water quality concerns will be especially relevant for urban areas in the basin, and it may be that basin-wide cooperation can play a critical role in coordinating water quality efforts in order to achieve this target.

Target 6.2: Achieving access to adequate and equitable sanitation and hygiene

The MDG indicator for sanitation measured *the proportion of population using an improved sanitation facility*. In the SDG era, governments must additionally report if these facilities are shared with other households, and if excreta are safely disposed in situ or treated off-site. Despite these differences, reporting from the MDG era can highlight sanitation trends to 2015. Once more, Zimbabwe experienced worsening coverage; in 1990, Zimbabwe reported 40 per cent of its total population were covered by improved sanitation, and in 2015 that proportion had dropped to 37 per cent (WHO/UNICEF 2015). Mozambique, Namibia, Tanzania and Zambia made 'limited or no progress', with Tanzania in the worst position, reporting that only 16 per cent of its total population was covered by improved sanitation by 2015. Malawi made 'moderate progress', and Botswana and Angola made 'good progress', increasing sanitation coverage by 20 per cent and 30 per cent respectively, with Botswana reaching a coverage of 63 per cent by 2015 and Angola reaching 52 per cent (WHO/UNICEF 2015).

Consistent with evidence from the MDGs, findings in Chapter 11 note how most riparians face challenges in providing adequate sanitation – none of them achieves even a median score and the security level for sanitation, although variable, is mostly low. Contextualisation of these water and sanitation access conditions suggests that levels in the Zambezi riparians are among the lowest in the world, on a par with those in the Mekong Basin.

For many countries in the basin, the first challenge will be how to interpret and measure indicator 6.2.2. For example, national governments may define the 'safe disposal' of excreta differently. The choice of safety standards that are used will in turn be key to how progress is captured and reported. Additionally, in arguments mirroring those made for SDG target 6.1, indicator 6.2.1 does not capture all aspects of target 6.2. Target 6.2 refers explicitly to vulnerable women and girls, and to the needs of vulnerable groups, but this is not reflected in the indicator. Because of this, a critical component of equity in sanitation will go unmeasured and, in some parts of the Zambezi Basin, even the scope or magnitude of gender-defined hardship related to inadequate sanitation will remain poorly understood.

The bottom line is that the scale of past and current problems and gaps associated with safely managed sanitation and hygiene in Zambezi riparians means that most will find it challenging to achieve universal coverage by 2030. It can be argued that only transformative changes in the way sanitation and hygiene are perceived and managed will lead to SDG 6.2 success.

Target 6.3: Improving water quality by reducing pollution, and substantially increasing recycling and safe reuse globally

As noted in Chapter 8, pollution of surface and groundwater resources is a major environmental problem for the Zambezi River Basin. Settlements produce sewage effluent, industries produce industrial wastes and wastewater, and the agricultural sector uses fertilisers, insecticides and pesticides; all contribute to the pollution of the surface and groundwater resources. Such pollution negatively affects ecosystems through, for example, water quality deterioration and eutrophication of lakes and reservoirs, impaired fish reproduction and growth, and increasing costs for improving water quality for domestic, industrial or agricultural uses.

Overall, basin countries are producing 1,530 million m^3 of wastewater annually, which is expected to reach 2,796 million m^3 by the end of the SDG timeframe in 2030; which is approximately an 83 per cent increase, mainly due to expected rapid urbanisation and population growth. As noted in Chapter 8, while the basin's larger cities and towns have sewage treatment works, the amount of solid waste generated in the Zambezi Basin's towns and cities far exceeds their capacity for collection, treatment and disposal (ZAMCOM *et al.* 2015). For instance, wastewater treatment plants (WWTPs) in Lilongwe only connect 15 per cent of the population (Table 8.2). As a result, major cities including Lusaka, Kafue, Livingstone, Harare, Blantyre and smaller towns still depend on on-site systems, like septic tanks, or discharge their collected but only partially treated or untreated sewage into the tributaries of the Zambezi River system. Most urban areas are still using crude dumping methods for solid waste, as the emphasis is not on safe disposal. For example, the city of Lusaka produces about 1,400 tons of waste daily, yet only 10 per cent of this amount is collected by the municipality and 16 per cent by private companies (Table 8.4).

Framing the issue in an SDG context through application of indicators 6.3.1 – *the proportion of wastewater safely treated* – and 6.3.2 – *the proportion of bodies of water with good ambient water quality* – will be challenging for basin governments, as it will require the building of new monitoring systems, infrastructure, capacity and technology. This will be limited by the availability of information on wastewater treatment, which is crucially important not only for reporting against indicators, but for policy-makers, researchers and practitioners, as well as public institutions, to develop national and local action plans aiming at safe, productive and fit-for-purpose use of wastewater and/or its safe disposal. In addition, wastewater reuse and recycling, both of which receive specific reference in this target, are not fully captured by the two agreed indicators.

Unless stakeholders create a new level of commitment and ambition to extend the monitoring of SDG 6.3 outside of 6.3.1 and 6.3.2, it will be difficult to measure real achievement against target 6.3. With progress on wastewater treatment and its fit-for-purpose use remaining very slow in Zambezi Basin countries, it will need radical change for this target to be met.

Target 6.4: Increase water-use efficiency across all sectors and ensure sustainable withdrawals and supply of freshwater to address water scarcity

As noted in Chapter 2, the Zambezi River Basin is generally endowed with rich water resources comprising both surface water and groundwater. The aggregate proportion of the basin's water that is used – mostly from surface sources – stands at about 20 per cent. While extraction of groundwater by volume is much lower than that of surface water, groundwater is a vital resource for social, economic and environmental sustainability across the eight riparian states of the basin.

Nonetheless, low and somewhat outdated water infrastructure development is a major constraint for access to water. Further, scarcity is an issue in parts of the basin such as Botswana and western Zimbabwe.

Additionally, as noted in Chapter 11, Zambezi riparians face challenges in agricultural water productivity, where production relative to water use is consistently low. The reasons for this are tied to farming methods, choice of crops and limited irrigation. Indeed, Chapter 6 highlighted how small-scale agricultural water management technologies relevant to the basin have met with mixed success. While evidence of success in terms of increased yields and income clearly exists, numerous challenges – often related to management and governance that foster maintenance and sustainability – are also present.

Achieving the two indicators for target 6.4 – a *change in water use efficiency over time* and *levels of water stress* – may present challenges particularly as reporting on indicator 6.4.2 necessitates the estimation and monitoring of environmental water requirements, termed 'environmental flows' (EF). However, current guidance for SDG 6.4.2 from UN-Water merely states that EF can be calculated using a variety of methods, which leaves room for much debate and confusion for countries in the Zambezi and other large basins (GEMI 2016), where exposure to EF has been limited to date.

To improve on this situation, Zambezi riparians can draw on global estimates of EF from the International Water Management Institute data portal (http://waterdata.iwmi.org/Applica tions/Global_Assessment_Environmental_Water_Requirements_Scarcity/). Countries can make use of these data for initial EF assessments for the Zambezi River Basin, and can build on the data to improve national estimates.

In terms of achieving improved water use efficiency over time, costs associated with increasing efficiency can be high, particularly for agriculture. Further, the basin's relative water abundance may drive questions about the need for efficiency improvements – at least at current levels of withdrawal. However, it could be argued that now is an appropriate time to assess and plan for the increasing pressures on water resources, which have been touched on already in this chapter; and that improving water use efficiency may be a proactive strategy to maintain water abundance to 2030.

For indicator 6.4.2, reaching real commitment around environmental flows may be slow to achieve at national and basin levels, due in part to the transboundary nature of such an endeavour. EF rely significantly on external sources in many of the riparian countries, and ensuring EF in a downstream country will depend on whether or not EF are safeguarded in an upstream country. Success will be best achieved when there is coordination and cooperation between countries and as such, planning, resourcing and establishing monitoring systems for EF will take time.

Target 6.5: Implement integrated water resources management at all levels, including through transboundary cooperation as appropriate

As noted in Chapter 10, the Zambezi has a long history of cooperation that has recently evolved into a more inclusive and integrated framework manifested in the creation of ZAMCOM. Indeed, soon after the *Revised Protocol on Shared Watercourse Systems in the Southern African Development Community Region* entered into force in 2003, the Zambezi riparians signed the *Agreement on the Establishment of the Zambezi Watercourse Commission* (ZAMCOM) in 2004. ZAMCOM's objective is to 'promote the equitable and reasonable utilization of the water resources of the Zambezi Watercourse as well as the efficient management and sustainable development thereof' (624ENG, TFDD). The ZAMCOM Agreement enables several institutional bodies to facilitate the cooperative process. The Council of Ministers has the overall responsibility for decision-making, supported by a technical committee of senior officials from the riparian states and a secretariat that is responsible for implementing ZAMCOM's Strategic Plan and associated activities. ZAMCOM has nine primary functions (Chapter 10). At a transboundary level, IWRM can be assessed as good.

In terms of monitoring, internationally defined methodologies will require some additional reporting mechanisms to report on indicators 6.5.1 and 6.5.2. However, governments within the Zambezi River Basin are, on the whole, in a strong position to monitor and report on this target.

Similarly, under the guidance of ZAMCOM, it could be expected that Zambezi Basin governments have a strong foundation to achieve target 6.5 by 2030.

Target 6.6: Protect and restore water-related ecosystems, including mountains, forests, wetlands, rivers, aquifers and lakes

As outlined in Chapter 7, a high proportion (approximately 80 per cent) of the Zambezi Basin is covered in near-natural ecosystems. Wetlands are a major feature of the basin (Table 7.3), covering an area that is reported to be 63,266 km² (4.7 per cent) but is certainly larger in reality because smaller wetlands, called dambos, are widespread but typically unmapped. Some twenty million people (ca. 50 per cent of the population) of the basin are estimated to be concentrated around wetlands (ZAMCOM *et al.* 2015), largely because of the wide range of ecosystem services they provide, including provision of water and fertile soils for agriculture. The basin also contains a mosaic of miombo woodland, grassland, savannah and agricultural land (Table 7.2).

As noted in Chapter 7, the social and economic value of ecosystem services in the Zambezi River Basin is vast, directly and indirectly supporting the livelihoods of millions of people and making significant contributions to the economies of all eight riparian countries. Despite their value, pressures on ecosystems are accumulating, ecosystem services are increasingly under threat and the gap between supply and demand is closing. Multiple factors are driving these changes; in addition to significant environmental pressures, prevailing high levels of poverty and food insecurity, reflected in relatively low values of HDI in all riparian countries, suggest that current economic growth is not sufficiently inclusive or equitable, and is unlikely to be sustainable in the long term. Ultimately, the future of the river basin and the people who live in it will depend in large measure on the stewardship of its ecosystems and the benefits that they provide.

The indicator for target 6.6 – *change in the extent of water-related ecosystems over time* – focuses on these issues. Arguably, however, target 6.6 will be the most complex to address; for example, as noted by Hemson (2016, p. 31), 'the protection and restoration of water-related ecosystems will require extensive interdepartmental co-operation and co-ordination across multiple tiers of government'. Complexity compounds the problem that, uniquely, target 6.6 has a deadline of 2020. This date was chosen in order to align with the Aichi Biodiversity Targets, which run from 2010 to 2020, as described under the Convention on Biological Diversity. All eight countries that share the Zambezi River Basin have defined national targets under this convention.

Indicator 6.6.1 calls for the monitoring of the extent of several kinds of ecosystems as well as quantities of water, including the minimum flows of rivers and streams, and estimates of groundwater volume. Implementation of this monitoring will be technically and financially challenging, particularly for the low-income countries in the basin. Even if remote sensing is scaled up as a first step towards monitoring across the basin, the resources required to interpret, verify and contextualise earth observations and accurately report on 6.6.1 will be significant.

In seeking to achieve SDG 6.6, it is certainly positive that overall demands on ecosystem services do not yet exceed supply. Nevertheless, as pressures on ecosystems in the basin grow rapidly, multiple factors, not least economic development, climate change, population increase and demographic change, are driving changes in the state of ecosystems. Degradation (such as deforestation, soil erosion and deteriorating water quality) is increasing and ecosystem services are increasingly under threat, with potentially serious implications particularly for the livelihoods of the poor. It is important that basin governments look to enhance short- and long-term planning to prepare for and resource critical ecosystem changes in order to ensure that SDG 6.6 is achieved.

Target 6.a: By 2030, expand international cooperation and capacity-building support to developing countries in water- and sanitation-related activities and programmes, including water harvesting, desalination, water efficiency, wastewater treatment, recycling and reuse technologies

Lessons learned from the MDG era suggest that effective planning, policy and preparation in the early years of the 2030 Agenda for Sustainable Development will be critical to final water-related SDG success. In 2016, the Overseas Development Institute (ODI) made clear that 'the longer governments take to act, the harder it will be to deliver on their promises by 2030', and that overall, every three years of inaction will mean that the amount of effort needed to succeed will increase exponentially (Stuart *et al.* 2016, p. 4). As well as earlier action, more intense action is needed; ODI reported that in order to achieve target 6.2 on universal sanitation, global progress will need to exceed current trends by almost four times (Nicolai *et al.* 2015). Finally, innovative policy and planning will be needed to allocate resources to achieving SDG 6, particularly in low-resource settings; a World Bank report (Hutton and Varughese 2016) found that capital investments must increase by approximately three times to achieve the water supply, sanitation and hygiene SDG targets 6.1 and 6.2 globally.

Target 6.a is critical for the Zambezi River Basin because in order to achieve SDG 6, the governments of the basin will have to rapidly and significantly scale up efforts, particularly in terms of water governance, and of capacity and resourcing to multiple sectors across basin, national and sub-national levels.

As implied by the wording of target 6.a, increased efforts may also be required from bodies and agencies operating outside the basin. In 2015, UN-Water noted that: 'While the design and implementation of sustainable development policies will be at the national level, achieving sustainable development will require international support and cooperation' (UN-Water 2015b, p. 7). A component of that support will be a perspective on global processes, including climatic and environmental, social and economic processes. Other components will be the creation of tools, platforms and hubs that national stakeholders can draw from, and the funding and capacity-building opportunities that are already being packaged for SDG 6 progress.

Target 6.b: Support and strengthen the participation of local communities in improving water and sanitation management

The impetus behind this target can be argued to be a core value of the 2030 Agenda – ensuring no one is left behind. Essentially, UN-Water included this target to promote the participation of local communities as well as 'relevant stakeholders' in water and sanitation planning and management (UN-Water 2016b, p. 23). It is, from one perspective, combating 'the illusion that top-down steering by governments and intergovernmental organizations alone can address global problems' (Hajer *et al.* 2015), and promoting interaction with multiple stakeholders for SDG 6 processes from community to basin levels.

Issues around monitoring may be more complex for this target. In a working draft produced in September 2016, the Global Partnership for Effective Development Cooperation wrote that monitoring should not be done only for its own sake or for the sake of reporting target success, but that it should feed directly into processes and initiatives at all levels that impact institutional and behavioural change. They continue by stating that the usefulness of data and evidence output from SDG monitoring is 'creating incentives for change and dialogue on core issues of development cooperation'.

In this vein, disaggregated data may be an important part of monitoring and reporting on this target; and as this is an 'implementation' target, this importance can be reflected in all other SDG 6 targets and indicators.

Disaggregated data are those that are able to report on results for specific groups. Commonly, data are disaggregated by sex, age and certain components of vulnerability, which can include ethnicity, levels of poverty and disability.

For reporting on this target as well as most of the other SDG 6 targets and indicators, it is critical that the position of different groups of peoples, including vulnerable groups, can be scrutinised, shared and understood. From a larger perspective, if a wider vision of water-related success is envisioned for the basin, analysis and discussion of disaggregated data must influence governance, policy, legal, environmental and other critical frameworks and processes in order to ensure that the needs and values of many peoples are being met, and that no one is left behind.

Interlinkages between SDG 6 targets

As is implied by the discussions above, it would be a mistake to view any target of SDG 6 only in isolation. There are interlinkages and interdependencies between the targets that must be considered across sectors and riparians throughout the basin.

There are obvious and explicit links between targets: for example, between 6.2 (the provision of adequate sanitation and hygiene) and 6.3 (the proportion of wastewater safely treated). Similarly, improving water-use efficiency (6.4) could mean more water is available for drinking (6.1) and safe hygiene (6.2). There are also implicit, potential trade-offs – for example, extracting water for drinking (6.1) should not impact negatively on the conservation of water-related ecosystems (6.6).

UN-Water has suggested that integrated water resources management (IWRM), as described in target 6.5, can be a framework with which to address many of these interdependencies by encouraging the balancing of the needs of different sectors and stakeholders (2016b). However, whether national- and sub-national-level IWRM is advanced enough in many of the Zambezi riparians to enable this balancing act may be a difficult question to answer at this time.

Interlinkages between Sustainable Development Goals

There is a growing body of literature pointing to interlinkages – both positive and negative – between Sustainable Development Goals. This is a critical area to clarify; Nilsson *et al.* (2016a) write: 'if countries ignore the overlaps and simply start trying to tick off targets one by one, they risk perverse outcomes'. Building on inter-goal synergies and avoiding negative trade-offs will also, in many cases, lead to a better use of resources and time.

There are many international initiatives that governments in the basin could use to understand SDG linkages, which could in turn enhance science, policy and political decisions for sustainable development. For example, Boas *et al.* (2016) write that the adoption of the SDGs has given impetus to nexus thinking in policy and science, which should be afforded new focus. The nexus approach is being increasingly adopted in high-level reports – for example, the Global Sustainable Development Report (GSDR) 2016 – and in international fora, such as the 2016 Dresden Nexus Conference on Water, Soil and Waste.

Further, the International Institute for Sustainable Development SDG Knowledge Hub lists several tools on their website that allow governments to analyse linkages between Sustainable Development Goals from different perspectives. For example, the International Council for Science (ICSU) have drafted a framework to characterise interactions among SDGs and their targets using a scoring system within a country context (Nilsson *et al.* 2016a; Nilsson *et al.* 2016b); and the Organisation for Economic Co-operation and Development (OECD) has revised its Framework for Policy Coherence for Sustainable Development (PCSD) for the SDG era.

However, most SDG-focused tools have only been developed in the last year, and real results from their use in different countries is still to be reported. How national and regional bodies in the Zambezi can practically use such tools or develop their own may influence how successful SDGs are as a whole to 2030.

Summary: basin management and the SDGs

This chapter emphasised that the enormous task of achieving all the SDGs will require sustainable development efforts across the Zambezi River Basin that are well targeted, efficient and effective. It will be important to build on strengths, create synergies and minimise negative trade-offs in order to make significant progress.

When focusing on SDG 6, one obvious strength that basin countries might leverage is the significant progress already made with basin cooperation. ZAMCOM may be able to advance the SDG progress of individual Zambezi countries in at least three ways.

First, ZAMCOM could clearly assess how the Integrated Water Resources Management Strategy for the Zambezi River Basin and other basin-level documents are aligned with the 2030 Agenda for Sustainable Development and the SDGs, and then describe how that alignment will be strengthened in revisions to basin policies and strategies in the near future. The realignment of national policy and strategy will be a critical task for most countries now at the onset of the SDG era, and this work by ZAMCOM could offer a template for basin countries to follow. This may be particularly welcomed by basin governments if the template can embody a nexus approach which, if adapted to key policies and strategies in each basin country, could explicitly leverage cross-border as well as cross-sector cooperation.

This approach may also bring to the fore issues such as environmental flow protection, the benefits of which may become clearer when discussed in the contexts of, for example, ecosystems services and their role in poverty alleviation; and the role of EF during droughts and other hydrometereological disasters that may increasingly impact the basin in the near future.

Second, ZAMCOM could also play a role as an 'honest broker', seeking to ensure that the SDG efforts of one riparian do not impact negatively on another, and continuously analysing how progress in one may benefit others. If ZAMCOM could be empowered with funding, skills and capacity to dynamically assess target and goal interactions and interdependencies that emerge in policy and strategy as governments begin to address SDG 6, it could be of significant benefit to decision-makers in each basin country.

Monitoring is a third area that may benefit from a basin-level perspective. It is generally accepted that there is insufficient water-related data being collected and analysed in the basin, which can limit evidence-based decision- and policy-making. The nine indicators described in this chapter can provide a standard for the minimum monitoring required over the SDG era. If ZAMCOM can take current data guidelines and metadata for the SDGs, adapt them to Zambezi conditions and promote and support their adoption, monitoring for IWRM in the future can only improve. Ultimately, as has been discussed for individual targets, Zambezi riparians must move beyond indicators to achieve the whole of SDG 6, and there will certainly be a similar role for more ambitious basin-wide collaboration around monitoring in the future.

In closing, water is undoubtedly central to sustainable development, and successful water management will serve as a foundation for the achievement of many of the 17 SDGs. Although achieving SDG 6 in the Zambezi River Basin will require significant scale-up of effort from all riparian countries, governments, communities and stakeholders in the basin now have an opportunity to collaborate to achieve them in the coming years.

Basin management, and leadership from ZAMCOM in particular, can play a crucial role in facilitating and promoting this collaboration. If basin management can accelerate the current level of progress toward achievement of SDG 6, it could prove to be the impetus for sustainable and sustained progress in the Zambezi River Basin.

References

AMCOW. 2013. Outcome Document for the Water Sector Post-2015. African Ministers' Council on Water: Thematic consultations. March 2013. Tunis.

Bhaduri, A., Bogardi, J., Siddiqi, A., Voigt, H., Vörösmarty, C., Pahl-Wostl, C., Bunn, S., Shrivastava, P., Lawford, R., Foster, S., Kremer, H., Renaud, F., Bruns, A. and Osuna, V. 2016. Achieving sustainable development goals from a water perspective. *Frontiers in Environmental Science* 4(October). Available at http://journal.frontiersin.org/article/10.3389/fenvs.2016.00064/full

Boas, I., Biermann, F. and Kanie, N. 2016. Cross-sectoral strategies in global sustainability governance: Towards a nexus approach. *International Environmental Agreements: Politics, Law and Economics* 16(3): 449–464.

GEMI. 2016. Step by step monitoring methodology for indicator 6.4.2. GEMI – Integrated Monitoring of Water and Sanitation Related SDG Targets. Available at www.unwater.org/publications/publications-detail/ar/c/428727/

Global Partnership for Effective Development Co-operation. 2016. Parameters for a strengthened and refined monitoring framework, working draft. 30 September 2016. Available at http://effectivecoopera tion.org/wp-content/uploads/2016/11/Parametersforrefinedmonitoringframework-workingdraft.docx.pdf

Hajer, M., Nilsson, M., Raworth, K., Bakker, P., Berkhout, F., de Boer, Y., Rockström, J., Ludwig, K. and Kok, M. 2015. Beyond cockpit-ism: Four insights to enhance the transformative potential of the sustainable development goals. *Sustainability* 7(2): 1651–1660.

Hemson, D. 2016. Water, sanitation and health: South African remaining and existing issues. *Sahr* 2016(1): 1–34.

Hutton, G. and Varughese, M. 2016. The costs of meeting the 2030 sustainable development goal targets on drinking water, sanitation, and hygiene – summary report. Available at www.worldbank.org/en/topic/ water/publication/the-costs-of-meeting-the-2030-sustainable-development-goal-targets-on-drinking-water-sanitation-and-hygiene?CID=WAT_TT_Water_EN_EXT

HLPW (High Level Panel on Water). 2016. Available at https://sustainabledevelopment.un.org/content/ documents/11280HLPW_Action_Plan_DEF_11-1.pdf

Nicolai, S., Hoy, C., Berliner, T. and Aedy, T. 2015. Projecting progress: Reaching the SDGs by 2030. Flagship report (September), p. 48. Available at www.odi.org/sites/odi.org.uk/files/odi-assets/publica tions-opinion-files/9839.pdf.

Nilsson, M., Griggs, D., Visback, M. and Ringler, C. 2016a. A draft framework for understanding SDG interactions, ICSU – International Council for Science. Available at www.icsu.org/publications/reports-and-reviews/working-paper-framework-for-understanding-sdg-interactions-2016/SDG-interactions-working-paper.pdf

Nilsson, M., Griggs, D. and Visback, M. 2016b. Map the interactions between sustainable development goals. *Nature* 534(15): 320–322. Available at http://dx.doi.org/10.1787/

Stuart, E., Bird, E., Bhatkal, T., Greenhill, R., Lally, S., Rabinowitz, G., Samman, E. and Binat Sarwar, M. 2016. Leaving no one behind: A critical path for the first 1,000 days of the Sustainable Development Goals. Available at www.odi.org/sites/odi.org.uk/files/resource-documents/10691.pdf

UN. 2014. Outcome document – open working group proposal on sustainable development goals. Sustainable Development Knowledge Platform. United Nations. Avaialble at http://sustainabledevelopment.un.org/ focussdgs.html

UN. 2016. Report of the inter-agency and expert group on sustainable development goal indicators (E/CN.3/2016/2/Rev.1), Annex IV. United Nations Statistical Commission.

UNGC. 2013. Architects of a better world: Building the post-2015 business engagement architecture. United Nations Global Compact. Available at www.unglobalcompact.org/docs/about_the_gc/Architecture.pdf

UNSD. 2016. SDG indicators metadata repository: Metadata for Goal 6. United Nations Statistical Division. Available at http://unstats.un.org/sdgs/metadata/ (as at January 2017).

UNU and UNOSD. 2013. Catalyzing water for sustainable development and growth: Framing water within the post-2015 development agenda. United Nations University Institute for Water, Environment and Health, UN Office of Sustainable Development and Stockholm Environment Institute. Hamilton. 2013.

UN-Water. 2014. A post-2015 global goal for water: Synthesis of key findings and recommendations from UN-Water. Available at www.un.org/waterforlifedecade/pdf/27_01_2014_un-water_paper_on_a_post 2015_global_goal_for_water.pdf

UN-Water. 2015a. Means of implementation: A focus on Sustainable Development Goals 6 and 17. Available at www.unwater.org/publications/publications-detail/en/c/284949/

UN-Water. 2015b. *Water and sustainable development: From vision to action.* New York.

UN-Water. 2016a. Water and sanitation interlinkages across the 2030 Agenda for Sustainable Development. Available at www.unwater.org/publications/publications-detail/ar/c/429651/

UN-Water. 2016b. *Integrated monitoring guide for SDG 6: Targets and global indicators*. New York.

WHO/UNICEF. 2015. 2015 update and MDG assessment. Joint Monitoring Programme for Water Supply and Sanitation. Available at http://files.unicef.org/publications/files/Progress_on_Sanitation_and_Drinking_Water_2015_Update_.pdf

ZAMCOM (Zambezi Watercourse Commission), SADC (Southern African Development Community) and SARDC (Southern African Research Documentation Centre). 2015. *Zambezi Environmental Outlook 2015*. Harae, Gaborone.

INDEX

Taylor & Francis eBooks

Helping you to choose the right eBooks for your Library

Add Routledge titles to your library's digital collection today. Taylor and Francis ebooks contains over 50,000 titles in the Humanities, Social Sciences, Behavioural Sciences, Built Environment and Law.

Choose from a range of subject packages or create your own!

Benefits for you

» Free MARC records
» COUNTER-compliant usage statistics
» Flexible purchase and pricing options
» All titles DRM-free.

Benefits for your user

» Off-site, anytime access via Athens or referring URL
» Print or copy pages or chapters
» Full content search
» Bookmark, highlight and annotate text
» Access to thousands of pages of quality research at the click of a button.

REQUEST YOUR **FREE** INSTITUTIONAL TRIAL TODAY

Free Trials Available
We offer free trials to qualifying academic, corporate and government customers.

eCollections – Choose from over 30 subject eCollections, including:

Archaeology	Language Learning
Architecture	Law
Asian Studies	Literature
Business & Management	Media & Communication
Classical Studies	Middle East Studies
Construction	Music
Creative & Media Arts	Philosophy
Criminology & Criminal Justice	Planning
Economics	Politics
Education	Psychology & Mental Health
Energy	Religion
Engineering	Security
English Language & Linguistics	Social Work
Environment & Sustainability	Sociology
Geography	Sport
Health Studies	Theatre & Performance
History	Tourism, Hospitality & Events

For more information, pricing enquiries or to order a free trial, please contact your local sales team:
www.tandfebooks.com/page/sales

 Routledge
Taylor & Francis Group

The home of
Routledge books

www.tandfebooks.com

*For Product Safety Concerns and Information please contact
our EU representative GPSR@taylorandfrancis.com Taylor & Francis
Verlag GmbH, Kaufingerstraße 24, 80331 München, Germany*

T - #0273 - 160425 - C280 - 246/174/12 - PB - 9780367736040 - Gloss Lamination